Legal Frameworks for Transparency in Water Utilities Regulation

Transparency in the regulation of water utilities is essential in order to ensure quality and fairness. This book explores and compares different regulatory arrangements in the water utilities sectors in three jurisdictions to determine which regulatory and ownership model is most transparent and why. The three jurisdictions considered are England (UK), Victoria (Australia) and Jakarta (Indonesia).

Following an introduction to the importance of transparency in water utilities regulation, the book provides an overview of the three chosen jurisdictions and their legal and institutional frameworks. Through a comparison of these the author explores the contested and difficult terrain of 'privatisation', as (often) opposed to public ownership, in which it is shown that the relationships between transparency and ownership models are not as clear-cut as might be assumed.

Chapters consider various aspects and outcomes of the regulatory process and the role of transparency, including topics such as regulators' internal governance mechanisms, utilities corporate governance, licensing and information flow, freedom of information and transparency in tariffs and pricing, as well as customer service. The book concludes with a summary of lessons learned to inform the refinement of transparency in utilities regulation.

Mohamad Mova Al'Afghani is Director of the Center for Regulation, Policy and Governance (CRPG) and Lecturer in the Faculty of Law at the Universitas Ibn Khaldun Bogor, Indonesia.

Earthscan Studies in Water Resource Management

Water, Power and Identity
The cultural politics of water in the Andes
Rutgerd Boelens

Water and Cities in Latin America
Challenges for sustainable development
Edited by Ismael Aguilar-Barajas, Jürgen Mahlknecht, Jonathan Kaledin and Marianne Kjellén

Catchment and River Basin Management
Integrating science and governance
Edited by Laurence Smith, Keith Porter, Kevin M. Hiscock, Mary Jane Porter and David Benson

Transboundary Water Management and the Climate Change Debate
Anton Earle, Ana Elisa Cascão, Stina Hansson, Anders Jägerskog, Ashok Swain and Joakim Öjendal

Rules, Norms and NGO Advocacy Strategies
Hydropower development on the Mekong River
Yumiko Yasuda

The Mekong: A Socio-legal Approach to River Basin Development
Ben Boer, Philip Hirsch, Fleur Johns, Ben Saul and Natalia Scurrah

Trans-jurisdictional Water Law and Governance
Edited by Janice Gray, Cameron Holley and Rosemary Rayfuse

Water and Rural Communities
Local politics, meaning and place
Lia Bryant with Jodie George

Land and Hydropolitics in the Nile River Basin
Challenges and new investments
Edited by Emil Sandström, Anders Jägerskog and Terje Oestigaard

Legal Frameworks for Transparency in Water Utilities Regulation
A comparative perspective
Mohamad Mova Al'Afghani

Water Regimes
Beyond the public and private sector debate
Edited by Dominique Lorrain and Franck Poupeau

For more information and to view forthcoming titles in this series, please visit the Routledge website: www.routledge.com/books/series/ECWRM/

Legal Frameworks for Transparency in Water Utilities Regulation

A comparative perspective

Mohamad Mova Al'Afghani

First published 2016
by Routledge
2 Park Square, Milton Park, Abingdon, Oxon OX14 4RN
and by Routledge
711 Third Avenue, New York, NY 10017

Routledge is an imprint of the Taylor & Francis Group, an informa business

© 2016 Mohamad Mova Al'Afghani

The right of Mohamad Mova Al'Afghani to be identified as author of this work has been asserted by him in accordance with sections 77 and 78 of the Copyright, Designs and Patents Act 1988.

All rights reserved. No part of this book may be reprinted or reproduced or utilised in any form or by any electronic, mechanical, or other means, now known or hereafter invented, including photocopying and recording, or in any information storage or retrieval system, without permission in writing from the publishers.

Trademark notice: Product or corporate names may be trademarks or registered trademarks, and are used only for identification and explanation without intent to infringe.

British Library Cataloguing-in-Publication Data
A catalogue record for this book is available from the British Library

Library of Congress Cataloging in Publication Data
Names: Al'Afghani, Mohamad Mova, author.
Title: Legal frameworks for transparency in water utilities regulation : a comparative perspective / Mohamad Mova Al'Afghani.
Description: New York : Routledge, 2016. | Includes bibliographical references and index.
Identifiers: LCCN 2016011103| ISBN 9781138930810 (hbk) | ISBN 9781315680170 (ebk)
Subjects: LCSH: Water utilities—Law and legislation—Great Britain. | Water utilities—Law and legislation—Australia—Victoria. | Water utilities—Law and legislation—Indonesia—Jakarta. | Water-supply—Government policy. | Privatization—Law and legislation.
Classification: LCC K3984 .A93 2015 | DDC 343.09/24—dc23
LC record available at http://lccn.loc.gov/2016011103

ISBN: 978-1-138-93081-0 (hbk)
ISBN: 978-1-315-68017-0 (ebk)

Typeset in Bembo
by Swales & Willis Ltd, Exeter, Devon, UK

Contents

List of illustrations	vi
Foreword	vii
Acknowledgements	ix
Summary	xi
Acronyms and abbreviations	xii
1 Introduction	1
2 Policy in involving the private sector	53
3 The regulator, licences and information flow	67
4 Regulatory functions	93
5 Transparency in utilities' corporate governance	122
6 The role of the Freedom of Information Law	144
7 Conclusion	179
Appendix	205
Bibliography	208
Index	227

Illustrations

Tables

1.1	Regulated water businesses in Victoria	23
1.2	Recapitulation of primary regulatory institutions overseeing Victorian water businesses	28
1.3	Water companies in England and Wales	31
1.4	Recapitulation of sectoral rules and regulatory institutions	37
1.5	Recapitulation of laws and regulations establishing Jakarta's water business	42
1.6	Jakarta's water concession, actors and their interest	46
6.1	Actors involved in water services in Victoria	145
6.2	Application of FoI/EIR to water regulators	147
6.3	Applicability of the FoI Law to institutions involved in water utilities regulation	158

Figures

1.1	Aetra's ownership structure	47

Foreword

It is my pleasure to write a foreword to this book, which has emerged from the PhD study of Mohamad Mova Al'Afghani here at the Centre for Water Law, Policy and Science (under the auspices of UNESCO) at the University of Dundee.

Governance has become a pervasive concept, not just in water. Its origins in political science point to its usefulness in supplementing formal government mechanisms and opening the latter up to a wider range of participants and groups, and recognising the limitations of governments in pluralist global structures. In the water world, it is highly relevant to both resource management and service delivery. For the former, we think of river basin planning and integrated water resource management frameworks, and within that, to the engagement of a wide range of stakeholders, institutions and civil society, especially where difficult decisions have to be taken as to allocation of an increasingly scarce resource. In service delivery, we are also concerned with stakeholder engagement at different levels and for different purposes – the operators, the regulators, the policy makers, and of course the users and potential users of the service. The latter groups suffer most from asymmetries of information; even where data are provided, they may be complex and technical.

Governance and transparency are closely linked, and many analyses of governance, especially by lawyers, focus on transparency and participation broadly – access to information flows, participation in decision-making and access to justice. Lawyers writing on the regulation of services, not just water, consider these different aspects of governance as part of a broader analysis of 'regulation' than purely an economic perspective. For many utilities, and certainly for water, economic regulation – price setting, at its narrowest – must also take cognisance of the need to meet environmental requirements and social policy goals. Lawyers are also well placed to analyse any effects arising from ownership structures that might impact on governance and facilitate (or not) better regulation of the service. Hence this book assesses the regulatory and governance structures for the water services in three jurisdictions – Indonesia, England and Victoria, Australia. Each of these have very different ownership structures and very different legal frameworks, but each of them has to address the perennial linked questions of who should receive the service, what standards should apply and what price should be paid.

This valuable contribution seeks to unpick our understanding of transparency in the regulation and governance of water services by analysing each of these jurisdictions against an analytical framework which initially came from the literature, and then iteratively developed as the legal research progressed. Importantly, the author also looks at the internal corporate governance of the service providers themselves, noting correctly that this is often overlooked in focusing either on the roles of the regulators or policymakers, or on how to engage consumers.

As demand for water increases, pressure on the resource intensifies and the need for services is still imperative, this book is timely. The UN has agreed a Sustainable Development Goal for water, and unsurprisingly it focuses on service delivery. I expect that both the analytical framework, and the detailed analysis, will be of interest to many working in this field in the next critical decade.

Dr Sarah Hendry, Lecturer in Law, Centre for Water Law, Policy and Science (under the auspices of UNESCO), University of Dundee

Acknowledgements

This book is based on the author's PhD at the IHP-HELP UNESCO Centre for Water Law, Policy and Science at the University of Dundee, funded by a scholarship programme from the Scottish government.

I would like to thank my supervisors Professor Patricia Wouters for her leadership and inspiration and Dr Sarah Hendry for her guidance and supervision throughout my PhD process and for their encouragement to publish my work. My gratitude goes to Dr Alistair Rieu-Clarke for his facilitation in the publication of this monograph.

Some parts of this book have been published in journals, namely the *Journal of Water Law* 20.129 and *IDS Bulletin* 43.2. Many of the ideas, concepts and inspiration in the book come from several conferences and seminars I attended during my PhD study. This includes an expert meeting in 2010 organised by the UN Special Rapporteur on The Right to Water in Geneva; 2011 STEPS Conference organised by IDS in Sussex; the 2010 World Water Week organised by Waterlex and BothEnds in Stockholm; and the PhD seminars at the University of Dundee.

I am indebted to Michael Hantke-Domas, Riant Nugroho, Monica Garcia-Quesada, Wilma Woudenberg, Vishnu K. Rao, Muhammad Reza, Hamong Santono, Gerard Payen, Jack Moss, Phillipe Pedrini, Nila Ardhianie, Meyritha Maryanie, Inga Winkler, Frederic Boehm, Adriaan Bedner, Bart Teeuwen, Dyah Paramita and D Eko Prayitno for the discussion and exchanges as well as the Tifa Foundation for supporting my field research in Jakarta. My gratitude goes to Ashley Wright for her guidance during the writing of this book. I would also like to thank the *Civitas Academica* of Universitas Ibn Khaldun Bogor for their institutional support.

To my fellow PhD colleagues, Dr Hugo Tremblay, Dr Jing Lee, Dr Bjoern-Oliver Magsis, Dr Dinara Ziganshina, Dr Yumiko Yasuda, Dr Musa Abseno, Dr Ana-Maria Daza, Dr Tran Tran, thank you for your company and for the good times we had in Dundee.

To my mum and dad in Bogor and Jakarta and my siblings: Jibriel, Aftaf and Nishrin, thank you for all your prayers and support.

To my beloved children, Besha and Bulent: your laughter always makes my day. Here, I speak about the disclosure of things. The mysterious truth lies in the self-disclosure of nothing.

Finally, to my beloved wife Mulia, who is in the process of writing her own PhD, thank you for your patience, love and extraordinary perseverance.

Mohamad Mova Al'Afghani, Bogor, 12 December 2015

Summary

This book evaluates transparency in the context of water utilities regulation by comparing regulatory frameworks in three jurisdictions: Victoria (Australia), England (United Kingdom) and Jakarta (Indonesia). Each of these jurisdictions is selected because of its particular ownership and regulatory model. This book develops a framework and applies it to those jurisdictions to assess whether a specific ownership or regulatory model will have implications for transparency.

The framework used to analyse whether water utilities regulation is transparent is as follows: (i) the policy in involving the private sector in water provision, (ii) the regulator's internal governance including appointment and dismissal, (iii) licence governance which includes the criteria for approving licences, licence conditions and the legal obligation to publish licences, (iv) means for acquiring information, (v) means for disclosing information, (vi) investment and price determination, (vii) service levels and customer service, (viii) utilities' non-compliance and enforcement mechanisms, (ix) redress mechanism, (x) utilities' corporate boards and their accountability, (xi) related-party transactions and regulatory accounts, (xii) applicability of access to information rules to water services institutions and (xiii) exemption of access to information rules.

Acronyms and abbreviations

AASB	Australian Accounting Standards Board
Bapepam LK	Badan Pengawas Pasar Modal dan Lembaga Keuangan (Indonesia). *Capital Market and Financial Institution Supervisory Agency*
BP Migas	Badan Pelaksana Kegiatan Usaha Hulu Minyak dan Gas Bumi. *Regulatory Task Force for Upstream Oil and Gas Business*
BPP-SPAM	Badan Pendukung Pengembangan Sistem Penyediaan Air Minum (Indonesia). *Drinking Water Provision System Developing Agency*
CA 2006	Companies Act 2006 (UK)
CC Water	Consumer Council for Water (UK)
CoI	conflict of interest
CPS	Contract Publishing System (Victoria)
DEFRA	Department for Environment, Food and Rural Affairs (England)
DELWP	Department of Environment, Land, Water and Planning (Victoria)
DSE	Department of Sustainability and the Environment (Victoria)
DWI	Drinking Water Inspectorate (England)
EA	Environmental Agency (England)
EIR	Environmental Information Regulation (England)
ESC	Essential Services Commission (Victoria)
EWOV	Energy and Water Ombudsman Victoria
FoI	Freedom of Information
FRD12A	Financial Reporting Directive 12 A (Victoria)
GMS	General Meeting of Shareholders
GR-16	Indonesia's Peraturan Pemerintah 16 Tahun 2005 (*Government Regulation 16 Year 2005*)
IC	Information Commission
KIP	Komisi Informasi Pusat (Indonesia's Central Information Commission)
MALE	maximum access, limited exemption
NRA	National Rivers Authority (England, now defunct and merged into EA)
Ofwat	Water Services Regulatory Authority (England)

PPP	public–private partnership
PSAK	Pernyataan Standar Akuntansi Keuangan (*Indonesia's Accounting Standards*)
PSC	Production Sharing Contract
PSP	private sector participation
RAC	Regulatory Accounting Code (Victoria)
RAG	Regulatory Accounting Guideline (England)
SKK Migas	Satuan Kerja Khusus Pelaksana Kegiatan Usaha Hulu Minyak dan Gas Bumi. *Special Task Force for Upstream Oil and Gas Business Activities*
SOE	state-owned enterprise
VCAT	Victoria Civil and Administrative Tribunal
VGPB	Victoria Government Procurement Board
WA 2014	Water Act 2014 (England)
WIA 1991	Water Industry Act 1991 (England)
WIA 1994	Water Industry Act 1994 (Victoria)
WSL	Water Supply Licence
WSSL	Water Supply and Sewerage Licensing

1 Introduction

1.1 Governance failure in the water sector

The Global Water Partnership stated in 2000 that the water crisis is mainly a crisis of governance.[1] The Camdessus Report acknowledged that the root of the problem in water services is due to the lack of governance.[2] Transparency, as well as participation and accountability, have been identified as the keys to good governance.[3] The 2008 Global Corruption Report, which focuses on the water sector, attributed the lack of transparency as the driver of corruption.[4]

One of the principles for effective water governance is that it should be open and transparent, in that language should be accessible and understandable and all policy decisions, particularly with regard to financial transactions, should be transparent.[5] Transparency has been defined as 'a process by which information about existing conditions, decisions and actions is made accessible, visible and understandable'.[6] According to Allan and Rogers, transparency and accountability 'are built on the free flow of Information'.[7] The Preamble of the Aarhus Convention states transparency as one of its purposes and this is established by enabling 'access to information'.[8]

---

1 Global Water Partnership, *Towards water security: a framework for action* (Global Water Partnership; World Water Forum 2000)
2 J Winpenny and M Camdessus, *Financing water for all: Report of the world panel on financing water infrastructure* (Global Water Partnership, World Water Council, World Water Forum 2003)
3 Madhav Godbole, *Public accountability and transparency: the imperatives of good governance* (Orient Longman 2003)
4 D Zinnbauer and R Dobson (eds), *Global Corruption Report 2008: Corruption in the Water Sector* (Cambridge University Press; Transparency International 2008)
5 P Rogers and A Hall, *Effective water governance (TEC background papers no. 7)* (Global Water Partnership, Stockholm 2003)
6 International Monetary Fund, 'International Monetary Fund Reports on the International Financial Architecture by the G22 Working Group on Transparency and Accountability, Working Group on Strengthening Financial Systems and Working Group on International Financial Crises (Group of 22)' <www.imf.org/external/np/g22/index.htm> accessed May 28, 2009
7 Rogers and Hall, *Effective water governance (TEC background papers no. 7)* (Global Water Partnership, Stockholm 2003)
8 See the Preamble of Aarhus Convention. Convention on Access to Information, Public Participation in Decision Making and Access to Justice in Environmental Matters, 25 June 1998 (Aarhus Convention) 38 International Legal Materials (ILM) (1999) 515

2 *Introduction*

Lack of transparency is a concern for water services around the world: Budapest,[9] Johannesburg,[10] Jakarta,[11] Malaysia,[12] China[13] and the Czech Republic.[14] In the UK, even with its advanced regulatory system, the House of Commons Select Committee on Environmental Audit still deemed that Ofwat is still unable 'to strike the right balance between commercial confidentiality and operational transparency'.[15] Research by the Interfaith Center on Corporate Responsibility (ICCR) which represents over 100 billion USD in invested capital concludes that disclosure by water utilities on environmental, social and governance information is 'murky'.[16] It warned investors to be cautious and, in the absence of a mandatory disclosure requirement, to take extra care to compel the companies to disclose more.[17]

Private sector participation (PSP) is often associated with the decrease of transparency. According to Swyngendouw this is caused by the commodification of information that was formerly in the public domain.[18] In turn, this limits access to data and information required by social groups. However, commodification might not be the only reason why information is held. In some cases, confidentiality is also used as a pretext by governmental agencies as a shield against political embarrassment.[19] The (supposed) lack of transparency in PSP is often used to demonstrate the advantages of state ownership by its proponents: 'The potential for transparency is an essential advantage of public utilities over privatised water delivery', because in privatised water delivery 'key information is defined as out of reach due to reasons of commercial confidentiality'.[20] Whether or not publicly owned utilities are free from confidentiality claims and whether secrecy is prevalent in privatised utilities will be tested in this book.

In line with the criticism that PSP reduces transparency, Mulgan considered that companies often abused their right to secrecy using contracts they entered into with government. He thus suggested that private companies

---

9 E Lobina, 'Problems with private water concessions: a review of experiences and analysis of dynamics', in A K Biswas and C Tortajada (eds), *Water pricing and public-private partnership* (Routledge 2005)

10 D McKinley, 'Water is life: the anti-privatisation forum and the struggle against water privatisation' (Public Citizen 2003)

11 Interview with Dr Riant Nugroho at the Jakarta Water Regulatory Body, 20 April 2009

12 'Watchdog: Why is water deal under OSA?' Malaysiakini <www.malaysiakini.com/news/62323> accessed 2 November 2009

13 Y Ge, 'Rethinking China's Urban Water Privatization' (Water Justice 2008) <www.waterjustice.org/?mi=1&res_id=245> accessed 13 May 2016

14 H Skapová, *Water industry privatisation in the Czech Republic: money down the drain?* (Transparency International – Czech Republic 2009)

15 'House of Commons – Environmental Audit – Seventh Report' <http://goo.gl/7DHxt3> accessed 22 May 2016

16 L H Lowe, P Jones and R Brown, *Liquid assets: responsible investment in water services* (ICCR 2009)

17 ibid

18 E Swyngedouw, 'Dispossessing H$_2$O: the contested terrain of water privatization', 16 Capitalism Nature Socialism 81

19 S Zifcak, 'Contractualism, democracy and ethics' 60 Australian Journal of Public Administration 86

20 B Brennan and others, *Reclaiming Public Water! Participatory alternatives to privatization* (Transnational institute (TNI) 2004) p.270

engaged in public services should expect more intrusion compared to those in normal dealings.[21]

Lobina and Hall explained that one of the failures of public–private partnership (PPP) in the water sector is the failure of knowledge transfer from the multinational corporations to the local partner. The multinationals will only be keen to transfer a limited degree of technical knowledge which does not endanger their superior position with their local partner. According to them 'commercial operations invariably prefer confidentiality and secrecy, as it protects their ability to manage financial affairs to maximise the benefit to their owners'.[22] They added that it is 'the private operator [which has] control over who can access the text of the concession agreement and tariff formulae'.

Still within the PSP spectrum, there are criticisms with regard to the 'regulation by contract' model. According to Eberhard:

> Transparency is also often compromised in regulatory contracts, such as concession agreements or power purchase agreements. Few of these contracts are open to public scrutiny. Government officials and private operators often justify such secrecy on the grounds of 'commercial necessity or competition'. But it is unclear why the secrecy is needed if the operator has been granted a de facto or de jure monopoly that eliminates any possibility of competition, at least for a significant number of years.[23]

Rouse also criticised 'regulation by contract':

> What it [regulation by contract] doesn't do is provide any means of regulating the contract owner, nor does it provide for transparency and public participation. On the contrary, it tends to reduce transparency and assumes that governments can look after the consumers' interests. Also, this lack of transparency risks providing the conditions for corruption.[24]

Meanwhile, Prosser[25] had warned against viewing regulatory relationships as 'essentially contractual': 'the concept of an overall regulatory contract fits badly with the openness to changing democratic goals and principles.'

One must bear in mind that the claims that 'privatisation' decreases transparency are not without contenders. Proponents of PSP such as Payen *et al.*[26] and

---

21 R Mulgan, 'Contracting Out and Accountability' 56 Australian Journal of Public Administration 106
22 E Lobina and D Hall, 'The comparative advantage of the public sector in the development of urban water supply' 8 Progress in Development Studies 85
23 A Eberhard, 'Infrastructure regulation in developing countries: an exploration of hybrid and transitional models' (African Forum of Utility Regulators, 3rd Annual Conference, 15–16 March 2006, Windhoek, Namibia)
24 M Rouse, *Institutional governance and regulation of water services*, vol. 2 (2007) pp.26–27
25 T Prosser, 'Regulatory contracts and stakeholder regulation' 76 Annals of Public and Cooperative Economics 35
26 G Payen, J Moss and T Van Waeyenberge, *Private water operators contribute to making the Right to Water & Sanitation real, AquaFed's submission, Part 3 Avoiding misconceptions on private water operators in*

Marin[27] oppose the idea that 'privatisations' are not transparent. Payen *et al.*[28] and Marin[29] contend that licences or PPP contracts always spell out in great detail the private sector's performance targets and also contain some form of mandatory reporting to their public counterpart. Often such a mechanism provides for better transparency than an unregulated public sector. Can it be that both the proponents and opponents of PSPs are correct and the problem is merely of their definition and idea of transparency? Transparency can have various meanings and dimensions. Hendry, for example, associates 'transparency' in the context of water utilities regulation with the revelation of not only cost structure or finances[30] but also access to information.[31] Thus, there can be situations where the cost structure is well defined but the public has no access to information.

A large body of literature on the topic of transparency and privatisation comes from Australia. Mulgan, for example, came to the conclusion that public sector accountability is generally more stringent, despite the fact that the power of the private sector is growing to match that of the state.[32] He stated that the degree of disclosure and the level of scrutiny in the private sector is less than is required of ministers in parliaments.[33] Freiberg, focusing on accountability issues on the contracting out of prisons, argues that contractual arrangements between government and correctional agencies must be open, as it is a matter of 'public interest'.[34] Meanwhile, Sands opined that a commercial confidentiality clause in PPP contracts 'effectively limits citizen access to publicly owned information, thereby jeopardizing the chance of informed public debate and healthy public accountability outcome.'[35]

---

relation to the Right to Water and Sanitation (AquaFed 2010); also G Payen, *UN Human Rights Council Public hearing by the Independent Expert on the Right to Water, Introductory remarks by Gerard Payen* (AquaFed 2010)

27 P Marin, *Public-private partnerships for urban water utilities: a review of experiences in developing countries* (World Bank Publications 2009)

28 Payen, Moss and Waeyenberge, *Private water operators contribute to making the Right to Water & Sanitation real, AquaFed's submission, Part 3 Avoiding misconceptions on private water operators in relation to the Right to Water and Sanitation* (AquaFed 2010) see para 6.2; also Payen, *UN Human Rights Council Public hearing by the Independent Expert on the Right to Water, Introductory remarks by Gerard Payen* (AquaFed 2010) para 2

29 Marin, *Public-private partnerships for urban water utilities: a review of experiences in developing countries* (World Bank Publications 2009) p.131

30 S M Hendry, 'An Analytical Framework for Reform of National Water Law' (PhD thesis, University of Dundee 2008). Transparency is associated with billing (p.345), cost recovery (p.352), accounting (p.387), comparative information or benchmarking (p.410), tarriffs (p.292)

31 ibid p.430

32 R Mulgan, 'Comparing accountability in the public and private sectors' 59 Australian Journal of Public Administration 87

33 ibid

34 A Freiberg, 'Commercial confidentiality, criminal justice and the public interest' 9 Current Issues in Criminal Justice 125; for similar concern in England, see S Shaw, 'Prisons: who gains from commercial confidentiality?' [Routledge] 13 Public Money & Management 7

35 V Sands, 'The right to know and obligation to provide: public private partnerships, public knowledge, public accountability, public disenfranchisement and prisons cases' 29 University of New South Wales Law Journal 334

1.2 Transparency and economic regulation

The natural monopolistic character of the water supply sector makes it not feasible for direct competition to work. Regulation came to supplant the absence of competition with the hope of correcting market failure.[36] Transparency is one of the tools to enable economic regulation.

In economic terms, the relationship between regulators and utilities is often conceptualised in a 'principal–agent relation',[37] in which a problem occurs when a party *hires* another party to perform some activities in their interest. In a water utilities context, the principal–agent problem can be found in several parts, between the regulator and utilities (regulator as principal and utilities as agent) and between the regulator and legislator/public in general (regulator as agent and legislator/public as principal). In each situation, there is a problem of information asymmetry where the agent has more information about the job they are doing than the principal. The utilities always have more knowledge of their actual cost structure than the regulators. Meanwhile, the regulators always have more knowledge of the regulated utilities compared to the legislators. As an agent always has more informational advantage than the principal, it always has the incentive to cheat in order to maximise its own welfare. What needs to be done in this case is to make information available to the principal(s),[38] in this case the regulators and the public.

There are some ways to reduce information asymmetry between regulators and utilities, namely, by facilitating competition, applying incentive regulation and conducting information gathering.[39] Even if the last two options are feasible, there is no way to avoid information asymmetry as, irrespective of any method used, the regulator may always be required to audit the company. Hence, information gathering will always be a substantial part of the regulation process.[40]

Information gathering is costly, it requires a certain amount of regulatory capacity to decipher the information and the decision resulting from this process is susceptible to capture. One way of avoiding potential capture is by providing the result of information gathering to the public. The public, in spite of

---

36 A Jouravlev and United Nations, *Water utility regulation: issues and options for Latin America and the Caribbean* (Economic Commission for Latin America and the Caribbean 2000). See also M P Hantke-Domas, 'Economic Regulation of Public Utilites with Natural Monopoly Features. A Study of Limitations Imposed by Property Rights from a Legal & Economic Approach' (Dissertation, University East Anglia 2005) and Hendry, 'An Analytical Framework for Reform of National Water Law' (PhD thesis, University of Dundee 2008)

37 On the innacuracy and possible danger of using the principal agent analogy to regulation, see Prosser, 'Regulatory contracts and stakeholder regulation' 76 Annals of Public and Cooperative Economics 35

38 The idea of multiple principle-agent relationships is discussed by Laffont and Tirole, J J Laffont and J Tirole, *A theory of incentives in procurement and regulation* (MIT Press 1993)

39 P Burns and A Estache, 'Infrastructure concessions, information flows, and regulatory risk' 203 Public Policy for the Private Sector

40 R Green and M R Pardina, *Resetting price controls for privatized utilities: a manual for regulators* (World Bank Publications 1999)

their diverse interest and lower per capita gain in intervening in the regulatory process, can potentially consist of a pool of different parties, from academics, practitioners, industry (including competitors or potential entrants), potential investors (shareholders or creditors) to customers; each having an interest in information regarding the utility. The public can form alliances (for example, between consumer organisations and competitors) and combine their knowledge to scrutinise the information and the regulatory process. Disclosure would bring these benefits: (i) aiding the regulator in deciphering information derived from the utility, (ii) proposing alternative policy based on the information, (iii) creating incentive for the firm to improve accounting quality, (iv) preventing collusion and corruption between the regulator and the utility and (v) developing the industry by sharing best practices and know-how and, therefore, lowering the barrier to entry.[41] Not all information submitted by utilities to the regulator is available for public disclosure as it might be restricted by sectoral regulation or an obligation of confidence not to disclose it to the public.

It is important to note that the 'public lawyer' approaches have different motivation and values to promote than the 'economic regulation' school and this could influence how transparency should be implemented in practice, especially if there is no direct justification of economic benefit. Aronson argued that the public lawyer concept of 'public interest' is wider than only correcting market failure or granting cross subsidy.[42] For them, public interest involves other values such as fairness, consistency, rationality, participation, legality, accountability and accessibility of judicial and administrative grievance procedures. Aronson further rejected the trade-off between transparency and commercial confidentiality and argued for the expansion (rather than contraction) of the governmental notion of transparency when it involves privatisation and contracting with private actors.[43]

The debates over regulation had incorporated more political rationales of regulatory objectives which would go along with Aronson's arguments above. Prosser argued that the objectives of regulation are not constrained into the maximisation of economic efficiency – although this remains important – but also have more rights-based and egalitarian justifications.[44] Such a position has been widely acknowledged in recent regulatory debates as reflected in the

---

41 See F Boehm, *Anti-corruption strategies as safeguard for public service sector reforms* (Internet Centre for Corruption Research (ICGG) Working Paper No. 22, 2007); F Boehm, *Regulatory Capture Revisited–Lessons from Economics of Corruption* (Internet Centre for Corruption Research (ICGG) Working Paper No. 22, 2007); F Boehm, 'Regulatory capture revisited: is there an anti-corruption agenda in regulation?' (Internet Centre for Corruption Research (ICGG) Working Paper No. 22, 2007); F Boehm and J Olaya, 'Corruption in public contracting auctions: the role of transparency in bidding processes' 77 Annals of Public and Cooperative Economics 431
42 M Aronson, 'A public lawyer's response to privatization and outsourcing' in M Taggart (ed.), *The province of administrative law* (Oxford, UK: Hart Publishing 1997)
43 ibid
44 T Prosser, *Law and the regulators* (Oxford University Press, USA 1997) p.31

works of Majone,[45] Graham[46] or Lodge and Stirton,[47] for example. This shift toward non-economic arguments means that transparency in utility regulation should be fostered not only because of the economic rationale, but also because there are underlying equity and democratic justifications. Nevertheless, when there is a conflict between efficiency values versus 'public law' values, the resolution is not always clear-cut.

Another strain of the debate focuses on the issue of natural monopoly and confidentiality. Authors such as Palast, Oppenheim and MacGregor[48] considered that commercial secrecy is an oxymoron, especially in cases where firms do not have competitors, such as in some segments of the electricity industry.[49] A similar position is advocated by Simpson[50] who argues that 'in a natural monopoly there is no justification for commercial confidentiality during the life of a contract'. Eberhard also considers that a de facto or de jure monopoly granted to operators should render it difficult for them to justify secrecy.[51] Meanwhile, while not rejecting confidentiality in its entirety, the UK's Department of Trade and Industry suggests that information provided by monopoly businesses to the regulator should 'generally be disclosable' whereas for markets emerging into competition, the extent of disclosure required is related to the degree of the company's market power.[52]

We can sum up the discussion in sections 1.1. and 1.2 into several hypotheses. The hypotheses are: (a) that confidentiality in a natural monopoly context is oxymoronic or unjustified, (b) that privatisation (or the delegation of) some or all of the parts of the water services cycle diminishes transparency, and (c) that regulation by contract has specific transparency problems. Whether these hypotheses are correct will be tested in this book.

1.3 Appeals to disclosures

Various reports appeal to legal frameworks on disclosure, such as the Freedom of Information law, in order to ensure transparency in water services. Transparency International, in its 2008 Global Corruption Report (GCR 2008), stresses that 'strong' Freedom of Information laws 'provide the foundation for transparency

---

[45] G Majone, 'The regulatory state and its legitimacy problems' 22 West European Politics 1
[46] C Graham, *Regulating public utilities: a constitutional approach* (Hart 2000)
[47] M Lodge and L Stirton, 'Regulating in the interest of the citizen: towards a single model of regulatory transparency' 50 Social and Economic Studies 103
[48] G Palast, J Oppenheim and T MacGregor, *Democracy and regulation: how the public can govern essential services* (Pluto Press 2003)
[49] ibid
[50] R Simpson, 'Down and dirty: providing water for the world' 14 Consumer Policy Review 146
[51] Eberhard, 'Infrastructure regulation in developing countries: an exploration of hybrid and transitional models' (African Forum of Utility Regulators, 3rd Annual Conference, 15–16 March 2006, Windhoek, Namibia)
[52] Department of Trade and Industry, *A Fair Deal for Consumers: Modernising the Framework for Utility Regulation* (CM 3898, London, The Stationery Office 1998) Proposal 7.6

8 *Introduction*

in the water sector'.[53] The GCR 2008 also recommends that states 'adopt and implement transparency and participation as guiding principles for all water governance'.[54]

Supporters of PSP also rely on transparency. The *Padco Report*, facilitated by USAID to attract private investment, depends on the Freedom of Information (FoI) law, sunshine rules and capital market regulation, primarily citing the US experience.[55] Authors such as Graham and Prosser contrasted the US condition with the UK, where not even a minimal sunshine rule was discussed.[56] Many other commentators acclaimed the US model of regulation with its sunshine laws[57] and rules on *ex parte* contacts.[58] A survey of 39 regulators worldwide conducted by NERA Economic Consulting for the World Bank recommends that governments legislate a legal framework for regulatory transparency, either at a national or regional level.[59] These appeals for disclosure or transparency frameworks have a basis in economic regulation theories, which suggest that publication of accounts will give an incentive to regulators to improve their accounting capacity and encourages the firm to establish credibility.[60] Disclosure is regarded as an anti-capture,[61] anti-corruption strategy and a prerequisite for participation.[62]

1.4 The framework for transparency

1.4.1 *Policy in involving the private sector*

Procurement and the preceding decision to delegate services is an important stage. When Jakarta's Regional-Owned Water Utility was in financial trouble,

---

53 Zinnbauer and Dobson (eds), *Global Corruption Report 2008: corruption in the water sector* (Cambridge University Press; Transparency International 2008) p.117 (conclusion)
54 ibid see 'Recommendation 4', p.xxviii
55 PadCo, 'A Review of Reports by Private-Sector-Participation Skeptics', prepared for Municipal Infrastructure Investment Unit (MIIU), South Africa and The United States Agency for International Development (USAID), Contract No. 674-0312-C-00-8023-0' (February 2002) <www.ircwash.org/sites/default/files/PADCO-2002-Review.pdf> accessed 16 May 2016. See also D Hall, 'Secret reports and public concerns. a reply to the USAID Paper on water privatisation "Skeptics"' (London: Public Services International Research Unit (PSIRU))
56 C Graham and T Prosser, *Privatizing public enterprises: constitutions, the state, and regulation in comparative perspective* (Clarendon Press, Oxford 1991)
57 Palast, Oppenheim and MacGregor, *Democracy and regulation: how the public can govern essential services* (Pluto Press 2003)
58 W P Olson, 'Secrecy and utility regulation' 18 The Electricity Journal 48
59 R Hern and others, *Regulatory transparency: international assessment and emerging lessons: a Final Report for the World Bank* (NERA Economic Consulting 2005)
60 J J Laffont, *Regulation and development* (Cambridge University Press 2005)
61 F Boehm, *Anti-corruption strategies as safeguard for public service sector reforms* (Internet Centre for Corruption Research (ICGG) Working Paper No. 22, 2007)
62 B Page and K Bakker, 'Water governance and water users in a privatised water industry: participation in policy-making and in water services provision: a case study of England and Wales' 3 International Journal of Water 38

the World Bank got involved and persuaded the Indonesian government to privatise its water utilities.[63] The decision to privatise water in 1997 never involved the public. There was no public discussion or debate.

From the above experience, it is then imperative for the analytical framework to address the question of delegation to the private sector, unless the delegation question is determined at the legislative process, in which this book assumes that there is transparency. Noting that there are power asymmetries between states and multinationals and the characteristics of water as a political good, the Human Right to Water agenda explores the appropriate procedures for transparency and public participation in the decision-making process in instances where governments seek to involve the private sector in water services.[64] The General Comment 15 on the Human Right to Water asks states to guarantee the right to participate in any decision-making process, which includes also the 'full and equal access of information' concerning water held by states or third parties.[65] The decision to delegate should be democratic, participatory and transparent.[66]

Some Human Right to Water advocates went as far as suggesting a referendum for the model for decision making if privatisation is to be adopted, whereas the private sector tends to consider that discretion exercised by a democratically elected government is sufficient.[67]

Nevertheless, before discussing the issue of delegation to the private sector and its procurement, central to the analytical framework is how the question of ownership is resolved in the legal framework. Prior to ascertaining this, it would be required to provide an overview of the legal and institutional frameworks in each case study as well as an analysis of each jurisdiction's mode of ownership and regulation. Only when there is clarity on the question of ownership in the legal framework, would be selection of private providers through bidding and contract negotiation follow.

Discussion on procurement might not be applicable to England where its utilities are fully divested but it is certainly relevant in Victoria and Jakarta. Again, in procurement, the question of transparency is relevant.[68] The situation

---

63 A Harsono, 'When water and political power intersect' Nieman Reports <www.nieman.harvard.edu/reportsitem.aspx?id=101044>

64 C de-Albuquerque, *Report of the independent expert on the issue of human rights obligations related to access to safe drinking water and sanitation*, A/HRC/15/31 (2010) See recommendation (e):

65 United Nations, *Substantive issues arising in the implementation of the International Covenant on Economic, Social and Cultural Rights, General Comment No. 15 (2002) The right to water (arts. 11 and 12 of the International Covenant on Economic, Social and Cultural Rights)* E/C.12/2002/11, 20 January 2003 (2003) para 48

66 de-Albuquerque, *Report of the independent expert on the issue of human rights obligations related to access to safe drinking water and sanitation*, A/HRC/15/31 (2010) para 34

67 P Turri, 'Private sector participation in water services provision' <www.fes-globalization.org/geneva/documents/Private%20Sector%20Participation%20in%20Water%20Services%20Provision_Turri.pdf>.

68 Boehm and Olaya, 'Corruption in public contracting auctions: the role of transparency in bidding processes' 77 Annals of Public and Cooperative Economics 431

where the private sector bribes officials to win a water contract is not specific to developing countries. Miloon Kothari, the United Nations Special Rapporteur on Adequate Housing (2000–2008), and Hall pointed out the lack of transparency in the French water concession system, and referred to the case where Suez-Lyonnaise and Vivendi were convicted by a French court for paying bribes to obtain water concessions and received prison sentences.[69]

One part of the procurement chain is the publication of the final contract. This is of relevance due to the experiences of several countries in which the terms of the final contract is kept secret.[70] The Independent Expert on the Right to Water, in her report, outlined that the:

> subsequent process of tendering, bidding and contract negotiation also must be transparent. The terms of reference and the final contract should be made available for public scrutiny and commenting. Commercial confidentiality must not jeopardize the transparency requirements provided for under the human rights framework.[71]

1.4.2 Regulators' internal governance

Not least important in discussing regulatory institutions is the debate on regulatory independence.[72] To ensure independence, the process of selecting regulatory personnel must be transparent. However, it is a commonplace that in developing countries regulators are faced with limited capacity, limited commitment, limited accountability and limited fiscal efficiency.[73] There have

---

69 M Kothari, 'Privatising human rights: the impact of globalisation on adequate housing, water and sanitation' Social Watch Report. On the case of Grenoble, Angoulême and St-Denis see Hall, D., 'Water in Public Hands' <http://unpan1.un.org/intradoc/groups/public/documents/APCITY/UNPAN010131.pdf> accessed 16 May 2016

70 For Indonesia see A Daryanto, *Jawaban Surat KRuHA (Letter No. 581/DIV.T&P/XI/2011 dated 8 November 2011 on PAM JAYA's response to FoI Request by KRuHA)* (PAM Jaya 2011); M M Al'Afghani and others, *Transparansi Lembaga-lembaga Regulator Penyediaan Air Minum Di DKI Jakarta* (ECOTAS/KRuHA/TIFA, 2011); disclosure of final contracts is also denied in Slovakia. See R Havlicek, 'Learning from privatisation of water services in Trencin, Slovakia' in B Brennan and others (eds), *Reclaiming public water: achievements, struggles and visions from around the world* (Transnational Institute and Corporate Europe Observatory 2005); also in Gdansk and Hungary see D Hall, 'Introduction' in B Brennan and others (eds), *Reclaiming public water: achievements, struggles and visions from around the world* (Transnational Institute and Corporate Europe Observatory 2005)

71 de-Albuquerque, *Report of the independent expert on the issue of human rights obligations related to access to safe drinking water and sanitation, A/HRC/15/31* (2010) recommendation (e)

72 See, for example, Majone, 'The regulatory state and its legitimacy problems' 22 West European Politics 1; M Scholten, 'Independence vs. Accountability: Dilemma or Misperception?' (The Netherlands Institute of Government Annual Work Conference, Maastricht, 26 November 2010); W Smith, 'Utility regulators: the independence debate' 127 Public Policy for the Private Sector

73 For discussion on regulation in developing countries see Laffont, *Regulation and development* (Cambridge University Press 2005); also A Estache and L Wren-Lewis, 'Towards a theory of regulation for developing countries: insights from Jean-Jacques Laffont's last book' 47 Journal of Economic Literature 729 drawing on Laffont's latest work

been cases where positions in the regulatory body are filled with incompetent persons or people having a conflict of interest with the regulated companies. It is, therefore, important to ensure that the criteria and eligibility for regulators' appointments are made transparent, the capability of the prospective candidates is communicated to the public and that existing or potential conflicts of interest are disclosed.

1.4.3 Licensing and information flow

In many cases, one of the tasks of the regulators is to issue licences. As natural monopolies, water utilities licences are often exclusive to a particular area and provide the licence holders with a legal monopoly to operate in that area. Licences normally come with conditions.[74] The conditions need to be clear and transparent and the granting of such licences must also be transparent. The transparency of licences is correlated with some other aspects: service levels and violations of service levels. These service levels could be imposed within licence conditions. Licences could be revoked by government or regulators when service levels are violated. The transparency of licensing provides justifications for governmental actions if the company breaches the requirement imposed in their licences. The transparency of licensing thus depends on three conditions: the criteria for approval, the conditions of licences and whether there are obligations to publish licences.

Information is the prerequisite of regulation.[75] Without any power to acquire information from utilities or other parties, it would be impossible for regulators to carry out their duties. It is thus necessary to analyse the 'means' for acquiring information. At the same time, the breadth and depth of information available in the public domain will depend on the aforementioned power to acquire information and whether there are disclosure policies that would enable regulators to disclose regulatory information.[76] In this respect, the means for disclosing information warrants some analysis.

1.4.4 Regulatory functions

As Hendry[77] and Graham[78] both note, one of the regulatory tasks is to ensure that providers maintain service levels. Service levels, in addition to tariffs and protection of vulnerable groups, are essentially at the heart of regulation.

---

74 For the importance of licences in English utility regulation, see Graham, *Regulating public utilities: a constitutional approach* (Hart 2000) p.33

75 In general see Laffont and Tirole, *A theory of incentives in procurement and regulation* (MIT Press 1993) also Burns and Estache, 'Infrastructure concessions, information flows, and regulatory risk' 203 Public Policy for the Private Sector

76 Graham, *Regulating public utilities: a constitutional approach* (Hart 2000) pp.31–38

77 Hendry, 'An Analytical Framework for Reform of National Water Law' (PhD thesis, University of Dundee 2008) Chapter 5

78 Graham, *Regulating public utilities: a constitutional approach* (Hart 2000) pp.39–40

It is – in addition to determining prices or rate of return – one of the primary reasons why a water company is regulated and a manifestation of the price that consumers are paying. Therefore, it is logical that consumers are informed about what the service levels are since it is what they can legally expect to get from the water company. Transparency of service levels requires not only that the standards of supply, customer service, compliance review and consumer grievances are made transparent but also that non-compliance with service levels and the consequences for companies in breach be disclosed.

Service levels could be elaborated on in the form of legislation or, alternatively, embodied in a contract. There could be a problem with transparency if the service levels are set through contractual terms – which are not published – rather than if they were set through legislation, which by default is always promulgated.

Closely related to service level is the utilities' investment policy. Regulation can serve many values: environment, equity or higher water quality. This could trigger trade-offs in the 'regulatory quadrangle': prices, network expansion, water quality and the environment. If utilities invest in expanding the network to provide more coverage, then less money is spent on investing in other priorities. What is it that the consumer really wants? Better water quality, more extension to the poorer consumers or higher environmental standards? Consumers need to be informed of the utilities' investment plans so that they can give proper feedback. Hence, utilities' investment planning should be made transparent and participatory.

At the same time, network expansion or other forms of investment as discussed above could also mean higher prices. To some who cannot afford a price hike, such burdens are unacceptable. In developing countries especially, utilities' prices are politically sensitive. There have been cases in the past where a riot has occurred because of price increases.[79] In big cities where the gap between the rich and the poor is wide, prices could be related to supply security. There have been cases in Jakarta where mains water pipes are being tapped into illegally by the citizens to provide for their daily consumption as they cannot afford to pay the price.[80] More investment might require a tariff increase, but a tariff increase can provoke unrest.[81]

The private sector tends to take the position that a tariff increase is the only solution as they believe that the poor actually pay more with the status quo.[82] However, previous research by Bakker indicates that the discussion on willingness to pay is too simplistic as it does not take into account disincentives embedded within the current system, such as high transaction costs and high

---

79 D Wood, 'Bridging the governance gap: civil society, democratization and electricity sector reform' (Arusha Conference, 'New Frontiers of Social Policy', 12–15 December 2005)
80 'Water Worries: Special Issue' *The Jakarta Globe* (25 July 2009) <www.slideshare.net/ArteronWater/water-worries-from-the-jakarta-globe> accessed 16 May 2016
81 ibid
82 ibid

connection fees.[83] In order to mitigate such adverse effects, cross subsidisation might be required. Furthermore, to a certain extent, even the lower part of the tariff band might need to get a tariff increase on the condition that more flexibility is given to the poor. In order to be legitimate, cross subsidisation and the increasing of the tariff rate need to be effectively communicated to the poor. This requires transparency of the tariff-setting methodology for the consumption of intermediary organisations such as civil society, and a simplified explanation of a tariff increase combined with ease of payment mechanisms for the poor.

When a utility fails to submit the required information, or if it is in breach of its service level, investment or customer service obligation, then typically the regulator will provide sanctions. How sanctions are imposed and their underlying rationale is, therefore, an important part of the analytical framework. Transparent and accountable sanctioning will provide legitimacy. On the other hand, reckless sanctioning depicts partiality or incompetencies in regulating.

Next, the framework focuses on *redress*.[84] Redress is an important feature of legal accountability and is relevant to all parties: utilities, consumers and other stakeholders. Transparency brings legitimacy and credibility into the redress system. In normal circumstances, the courts are the primary institutions referred to for redress. However, water services disputes are of a kind that require quick settlement and the specific expertise of the industry. There are different ways in which redress can be provided. In some jurisdictions such as Victoria, Australia, the disputes between consumer and the water companies are referred to the industrial ombudsman. In England, a specific consumers' representative body is given the authority to investigate consumer claims under the legislation.

1.4.5 Transparency in utilities' corporate governance

One of the most important actors in a water project is the utility itself. It is thus not adequate to pay attention only to regulatory institutions and their decision-making process. Utilities are typically subjected to some form of corporate rules depending on the form of the entity. These rules may contain important transparency elements.

When the utility is state-owned or a statutory corporation (Victoria), then it is likely to be regulated under a state enterprise law, a specific charter prescribed for the utility or a legislation. In full divestiture, such as England, the

---

83 See K Bakker, 'Trickle down? Private sector participation and the pro-poor water supply debate in Jakarta, Indonesia' 38 Geoforum 855
84 See Graham, *Regulating public utilities: a constitutional approach* (Hart 2000) pp.40–41 and M G Quesada, *Water and sanitation services in Europe: do legal frameworks provide for 'good governance'?* (UNESCO Centre for Water Law Policy and Science at the University of Dundee 2010) which includes 'access to justice' as one component of good governance. See also Hendry, 'An Analytical Framework for Reform of National Water Law' (PhD thesis, University of Dundee 2008) Annex A.2. 'Access to Justice and Dispute Resolution', comparing UK, Queensland and South Africa water sectors.

utility may be regulated under normal company law but with some element of its governance contained in its licence conditions. In concessions between a state-owned utility and a private company, such as Jakarta, then one company is regulated by a region-owned enterprise law and the other falls under normal (private) company law.

The lack of governance in water utilities is illustrated by Tortajada.[85] In the majority of Asian water utilities staff, including senior managers, are often selected because of their political connections, instead of their management abilities or technical skills. Managers often do not have any autonomy to make decisions, and when they do have it is often the case that they lack managerial capability. Water utilities are overstaffed and the positions are often filled due to nepotism or political connections. This poor governance may be reflected in the huge burden of the utilities in paying inefficient employees and lower employee wages compared to normal market rates in the other industries. Eventually this will result in poor water services and higher costs. Aguas Argentina provides another example of lack of corporate governance.[86]

Aguas Argentina, the project company, had a low standard of corporate governance. There was a lack of disclosure on internal control mechanisms toward Aguas Argentina under the guise of proprietary and 'commercially sensitive' information. It is alleged that the company maintained this for the purpose of safeguarding its position in case renegotiation occurred.[87] This lack of transparency made the project unpopular with civil societies, prompting the government to nationalise the company. Hence, unless developing countries embrace corporate governance, PSP will not be likely to deliver improved performance with accountability.[88]

Porporato and Robbins[89] opined that government intervention in water services is justified not only because of the naturally monopolistic character of the industry, but also because of the externalities present. Hence, to them, the question of government involvement in the water services sector exists irrespective of the natural monopoly problem. Should the natural monopoly be reduced and competition introduced, they argued, government would still be involved in regulating the water sector. Both the natural monopoly feature and the presence of negative externalities will shape the feature of corporate governance in water utilities.

---

85 C Tortajada, 'Water management in Singapore' 22 International Journal of Water Resources Development 227

86 M Porporato and P T Robbins, 'Privatisation and corporate governance in emerging economies: what went wrong with Aguas Argentinas SA?' 2 International Journal of Economics and Business Research 187

87 The company won the bid due to lower price. Later, renegotiation did occur, asking the government to increase tariffs in order to speed up collection rate. ibid

88 A Dyck, 'Privatization and corporate governance: principles, evidence, and future challenges' 16 The World Bank Research Observer 59

89 Porporato and Robbins, 'Privatisation and corporate governance in emerging economies: what went wrong with Aguas Argentinas SA?' 2 International Journal of Economics and Business Research 187

The role of transparency in corporate governance in general has been widely acknowledged. The earliest corporate governance guidelines, such as the Cadbury Report, had pointed out the need for transparency. In the words of the Cadbury Report: 'The lifeblood of markets is information.' The Cadbury Report considers that barriers to the flow of information are representative of market imperfections and that transparency will contribute to the efficient working of the market economy, prompt boards to take action and allow stakeholders to scrutinise the company.[90]

Other corporate governance guidelines such as the Greenbury Report (1995), Hampel Report (1998), Turnbull Report (1999) and the Paul Myners report (DTI, 1996; HMT, 2001) also highlight the importance of transparency.[91] International organisations have also issued important documents and guidelines such as the OECD series on 'Principles on Corporate Governance' and the UNCTAD (2006) guidance on corporate governance disclosure which stresses the importance of transparency.[92] These frameworks are designed to apply to corporations in general and not specifically to address a regulated natural monopoly.

The UNCTAD guidance defines 'board' as 'the highest governing and monitoring body or bodies of an enterprise on which executive and non-executive or supervisory board members sit'.[93] Most corporate governance documents recognise the need to disclose the names and composition of the board. Another key point is the disclosure of the board's role, functions and accountability mechanisms. Such disclosure is necessary for accountability purposes where the board members may be held responsible to the extent of their role and responsibility. When there is clarity on roles and responsibilities, the accountability mechanism will be much clearer as the accountee will know where and of whom accountability should be asked.

Utilities might need to purchase goods or contract out services from third parties. Unless regulated, utilities may purchase goods and services at a price higher than the market price from an affiliated company. The profit from such purchase then flows down to the utility's shareholders through the parent company. In the end, the investor receives profit at the expense of the utility's consumer. Thus, transparency is required. In theory, transparency of utilities' accounts will provide incentives for consumers and potential providers to track

---

90 See A Cadbury, *Report of the committee on the financial aspects of corporate governance* (Gee Publishing, London 1992)

91 R Greenbury, *Directors' remuneration: report of a study group chaired by Sir Richard Greenbury* (Gee Publishing 1995); R Hampel, *Committee on Corporate Governance: final report* (Gee 1998); Institute of Chartered Accountants in England and Wales, *Internal control: guidance for directors on the combined code (Turnbull Report)* (Institute of Chartered Accountants in England & Wales 1999); P Myners, *Developing a winning partnership: how companies and institutional investors are working together* (Department of Trade and Industry 1996) P Myners, *Report on institutional investment* (HM Treasury, London, 2001)

92 OECD, *OECD principles of corporate governance* (2004); UNCTAD, *Guidance on good practices in corporate governance disclosure* (2006)

93 UNCTAD, *Guidance on good practices in corporate governance disclosure* (2006) p.12

16 *Introduction*

down the possibilities of transfer pricing and any other anticompetitive behaviour.[94] For regulated monopolies, reporting to regulators must often be based on specific regulatory accounts.[95] Regulatory accounts normally require more specific and industry-focused information by economic regulators for benchmarking, determining prices or allowable rate of return. On the other hand, statutory accounts require more general corporate information.

The UNCTAD guidelines recommend that at least the nature, type and elements of the related-party transactions and the decision-making process for approving such related-party transactions are disclosed.[96] Normally, procurement between a regulated company and a third party is covered by the regulatory account. There could be a requirement to disclose to the regulator (but not necessarily the public) if the utility's trading partners are, in fact, a related party. Usually, there is no prohibition to transact with a related party as long as the procedure to assess that the transaction is entered into at a fair market value is fulfilled. The framework will not discuss the content of the regulatory account in detail. It will analyse the legal mechanisms used in applying and enforcing regulatory accounts and in making financial reports available to the public.

UNCTAD Guidance on Corporate Governance Disclosure considers information on beneficiary ownership structure as vital for informed investment decisions, especially with respect to the equity of shareholders.[97] Disclosure on the top shareholding position is regarded as part of the effort to protect minority shareholders. Specific shareholder's rights which have implications toward company control, such as those related to voting or the appointment of directors should be disclosed. In cases where control of the company is performed through different entities, the UNCTAD guidance promotes the disclosure of the ultimate controller. Echoing the OECD principles, the UNCTAD Guidance also favours the disclosure of ultimate ownership, in addition to disclosure on record ownership. Related to the question of ownership above is 'corporate restructuring' (the change of a company's structure through merger, acquisition, sale of assets or other means for the purpose of improving economic performance). Through restructuring, the liability that carries with the ownership of a company could shift from one party to another. Ownership changes may also impact on the reliability of the investor's commitment to continually invest in water services and to fill the new managerial positions with people having expertise in the field. The nationality of ultimate ownership may also have an implication on how friendly the investor state would be with respect to human rights and corruption issues. There may also be problems related to

---

94 R Baldwin and M Cave, *Understanding regulation: theory, strategy, and practice* (Oxford University Press 1999) p.308

95 Inter-Regulatory Working Group, *The role of regulatory accounts in regulated industries: a joint consultation paper by the Directors General of Oftel, Ofgem, Ofwat, Electricity & Gas Supply (Northern Ireland), Rail Regulator and Civil Aviation Authority* (2001)

96 UNCTAD, *Guidance on good practices in corporate governance disclosure* (2006) p.6

97 ibid p.8

unemployment and soaring prices as a response of water utility restructuring. The problem of corporate restructuring will become interesting in a regulated environment because the regulator's jurisdiction will only cover the regulated company and not its parent companies.

1.4.6 *The role of freedom of information laws*

Last but not least is the role of FoI laws which set 'passive disclosure rules' for institutions in water services. The rest of the framework above will analyse how legal frameworks obligate 'active disclosure' in institutions involved in water utilities regulation. This is still incomplete because a comprehensively transparent system requires also a set of passive disclosure rules.

A passive disclosure rule sets requirements upon public bodies to provide information if requested by any person. Any information is subjected to the rule, unless it falls under the exemption clause. A passive disclosure rule is normally provided by access to information legislation. The existence of a FoI law alone, however, is not sufficient in guaranteeing transparency as such a regime needs further evaluation. Two crucial elements of a passive disclosure rule that will be used to evaluate the access to information regime are (i) its applicability to institutions in water services and (ii) the exemption clauses, which in turn comprise of Law Enforcement and Investigation; Decision Making and Policy Formulation; Obligation of Confidence; and Commercial Information.[98]

1.4.7 *Case study: Victoria, England, Jakarta*

Why compare Victoria, England and Jakarta? There are at least five reasons why comparing the three jurisdictions above is desirable: (1) experience with FoI Law in England and Victoria; (2) recent implementation of FoI Law in Indonesia; (3) advanced water services regulation in England; (4) experience with public ownership and contracting out in Victoria; (5) and hybrid British-French model of 'privatisation' with independent regulator in Jakarta, Indonesia. These factors capture a wide variety of institutional governance in water services.

Due to different form of governments and autonomy arrangements, in many parts the comparison will refer directly to the national or federal entity. Thus, since Victoria is also regulated by federal legislations, the comparison will refer directly to Australia. Likewise, since Indonesia is a unitary state, most regulations in Jakarta are national regulations in which the comparison will be compelled to refer directly to Indonesia.

Both England and Victoria have considerable experience with FoI Law. The United Kingdom enacted the FoI Act in 2000[99] and the Environmental

---

98 See M Fitch and C Graham, 'The draft Freedom of Information Bill – implications for utilities' 10 Utilities Law Review 257
99 Freedom of Information Act 2000, 2000 c.36

Information Regulations in 2004. The number of requests made under English FoI per year is around 120,000. The FoI costs in 2005 were 35.5m GBP.[100]

Being a country well known for 'privatising' its essential services, the UK experience is important in understanding how the FoI regimes can adapt and respond to such challenges. It is intriguing to explore whether access to information laws are applicable to the privatised water utilities and, if they are, how the exemption clauses will operate.[101]

Victoria has the oldest FoI Law compared to England and Indonesia, valid since 1982.[102] The interpretation and development of the Victorian FoI experience has also been influenced by FoI reforms at Commonwealth level as well as in other Australian jurisdictions. The Victorian FoI Act has been revised several times to reflect the demands of its age, including the advent of outsourcing.[103]

While the UK FoI is interesting from the point of view of how access to information regimes adapt to the problem of divestiture, the Victorian FoI is interesting in terms of its adaptation to contracting out. Contracting out of government services has been criticised for reducing accountability and transparency. As mentioned, Australian public law experts such as Aronson rejected the trade-off between transparency and commercial confidentiality and argued for the expansion (rather than contraction) of the governmental notion of transparency when it involves privatisation and contracting with private actors.[104]

Due to limitations in finances and expertise, outsourcing is often inevitable for the public sector to engage with the private sector. In this circumstance, the expectation for transparency lies with the FoI regime. It is thus relevant to investigate how FoI regimes have been reformed and applied to such conditions.

Meanwhile, Indonesia enacted the FoI Law in 2008[105] and it took effect in 2010. The FoI institution has just been set up and made operational and still lacks experience in dealing with FoI disputes. Compared to the UK FoIs, the number of exemptions on Indonesia's FoI is lower and the exemption clauses are more narrowly construed.

In terms of applicability, unlike the UK FoIs, the Indonesian FoI provides a definition of public authorities. This covers state-owned companies. However, since some water utilities are 'privatised' (by way of concession) there is a low chance that the FoI can be applied directly to them.

The Indonesian FoI provides some minimum duty of publication to public authorities and this covers regulators. However, the duty to publish only covers a limited extent of the public authorities' finances and performance.

---

100 'Freedom of information: Every expense spared | The Economist' (19 December 2006) <www.economist.com/node/8459574> accessed 16 May 2016
101 The term 'privatisation' is ambiguous, nevertheless, it is used widely in the literature The book will use 'Private Sector Participation' in order to describe a privatisation in terms of ownership models
102 Freedom of Information Act 1982 No. 9859 of 1982
103 R Snell, 'Freedom of information: the experience of the Australian states – an epiphany?' 29 Federal Law Review 343
104 Aronson, 'A Public Lawyer's Response to Privatization and Outsourcing' in Taggart (ed.), *The Province of Administrative Law* (Oxford, UK: Hart Publishing 1997)
105 Undang Undang No. 14 Tahun 2008 Tentang Keterbukaan Informasi Publik

The Public Service Law mandates public authorities to publish key terms of contracts with private parties and also some performance aspects of the contract.[106]

In England, water services have been undergoing reforms ever since they were 'privatised'. The Water Industry Act 1991[107] has been amended several times.[108] The most interesting feature of the English water services law is the creation of an independent body of an economic regulator, Ofwat. Ofwat is given a lengthy mandate under the Acts mentioned above, and this covers the power of enforcement and adjudication.

The initial intent for 'privatising' the water sector – with the RPI-K formula – is to provide ease of regulation. The yardstick competition was expected to provide light touch regulation. However, what followed afterwards was a tremendous restructuring of the water industry accompanied by the creation of complex institutions. Competition appeared to be difficult to implement and, as such, regulation seemed to be perpetual, not a matter of 'holding the fort' until competitive forces arrived. Furthermore, the light touch of regulation in the water services sector has not been proven as Ofwat was still required to rigorously collect information from the utilities. This is changing under the risk-based approach, but the merits remain to be seen in coming years. Such information-gathering exercises contribute significantly to the cost of regulation. In 2003–2004, Ofwat's annual budget was around 12.5 million GBP which represents around 50 pence on each water bill.[109]

Considerable price increases followed the divestiture, with the gains transferred to companies and shareholders.[110] Meanwhile, there was a growing risk of social disparity given the companies' power to disconnect those who could not afford to pay. When the WIA 1991 was amended, the law prohibited disconnection to private dwellings for the reason of non-payment.[111] This marks the acknowledgement that regulation of water services cannot be constrained to a purely economic agenda as there are social issues as well.

The UK experience shows that the privatisation of water utilities is not an easy task, as it can only be materialised through adequate regulatory capacity which includes expertise and supply of budget and it must also be supported by a good system of governance.

In contrast to England, Victoria's water utilities are state-owned monopolies (statutory corporations). Comparing different ownership models is relevant for the study, because lack of transparency is often perceived as the result of privatisation.[112] But, are state-owned utilities transparent?

---

106 Undang Undang No. 25 Tahun 2009 Tentang Pelayanan Publik
107 Water Industry Act 1991 c.56
108 The latest amendment at the time of writing is the Water Act 2014
109 T Ballance and A Taylor, *Competition and economic regulation in water: the future of the European water industry* (IWA Publishing 2005)
110 K Bakker, 'Paying for water: water charging and equity in England and Wales' 26 Transactions of the Institute of British Geographers 143
111 Water Industry Act 1991 c.56 Schedule 4A
112 For example, D Hall and E Lobina, 'Private to public: international lessons of water remunicipalisation in Grenoble, France' (American Water Resources Association, Dundee, 6–8

20 *Introduction*

The regulatory structure in Victoria is arguably simpler than England's, as is the role of the institutions. The Essential Services Commission (ESC) is a multi utility regulator tasked with regulating not only water, but also energy and ports, among others. The Victorian water sector is segregated into several different companies on the bulk water supply and retail side, all of which are publicly owned and economically regulated by the ESC.

Furthermore, even when utilities are state owned, there is usually a part of the service which is delivered through PSP. In Victoria, this occurs at the bulk water supply side where the state-owned bulk water supply company Melbourne Water entered into a concession contract with AquaSure, a private company. Jakarta's water utilities (both the bulk water supply and the retail companies) are also publicly owned. PSP is also found in the Jakarta case study, but this is conducted at treatment and distribution level. Notwithstanding these differences, the book will compare the transparency of the contractual arrangements between Victoria and Jakarta.

The rise of contracting out of government services in Australia in general has sparked interest from public lawyers on its impact on transparency and accountability. Victorian experiences in dealing with contracting out may therefore contribute to the similar situation in Indonesia.

The full divestiture model, such as that found in England, is not possible in Indonesia. The Indonesian Constitution mandated that 'branches of production which are vital for the State and which affect the life of most people are controlled by the State' and this has been interpreted to extend into water utilities.[113] However, in practice, shares in state-owned water utilities have been partially sold to investors and concession contracts between water utilities and private parties have been taking place.

The most recent Constitutional Court Decision in Indonesia discouraged exploitation of water resources by the private sector and encouraged public ownership.[114] There is still no clarity as to the Indonesian 'model' of water services. The Victorian model where public ownership prevails with some economic regulation, therefore, becomes interesting.

The condition of the Indonesian water utilities is already bleak. Around 220 water utilities hold more than 400 outstanding loans to the central government and 63 per cent of these are in default, with the total amount of debt

---

August 2001); M Minow, 'Public and private partnerships: accounting for the new religion' Harvard Law Review 1229; Psiru, 'Undermining Democracy and the Environment, PSI Briefing, The Hague World Water Forum' <www.psiru.org/reports/2000-03-W-Htrans.doc > accessed 25 December 2011; Swyngedouw, 'Dispossessing H$_2$O: the contested terrain of water privatization' 16 Capitalism Nature Socialism 81

113 Judicial Review of the Law No. 7 of 2004 on Water Resources, Constitutional Court of the Republic of Indonesia, Judgment of 13 July 2005, No. 058-059-060-063/PUUII/2004.

114 *Putusan Mahkamah Konstitusi Nomor 85/PUU-XI/2013 Tentang Pengujuan Undang Undang Nomor 7 Tahun 2004 Tentang Sumber Daya Air*.

amounting to 500 million USD.[115] The provision for water supply financing is estimated (optimistically) to be at 50 million USD per year.[116]

The concession model that applies in Jakarta follows the 'French model' of water privatisation but the French system does not have any independent body tasked with the economic regulation of water services. Instead, some part of the regulatory function is dealt with by the French Administrative Court with the Conseil d'État at the top.[117]

The Indonesian (Jakarta) version of concession also depends on contracts that were signed between the municipal government, the regional (state-owned) utilities and the private entities. The Jakarta concession mandates for the creation of an independent regulator tasked with supervising the private concessionaires, adjudicating disputes among the private concessionaire and the state-owned water utility, and advising the governor on charges. The governor reinforces this mandate in a gubernatorial decision. Similar to its counterparts in England and Victoria, the Jakarta regulator requires information from the utility and has the obligation to disclose some information for transparency purposes.

The author is aware that there are other jurisdictions that would make interesting case studies to be compared with one another. The French model of water services provision is said to be the origin of the expanding trend toward regulation by contract in the water sector.[118] Why not compare France? France is unique due to the position of its administrative court as a quasi-super regulator in managing contracts. This is a particular feature that makes the so-called 'French model' work in its country of origin. Such a feature is not enjoyed by many other countries, such as Indonesia. Most countries utilise an independent regulatory body to manage the relationship between the government and the private sector and these have also been implemented to supervise government-owned utilities.

The Dutch water sector is also particularly interesting because it implements 'sunshine rules' for its water utilities.[119] However, PSP is prohibited by law, and as such it would be impossible to assess the loss of transparency due to the delegation to the private sector.

---

115 ibid
116 *Alternative Financing For Water Utilities in Indonesia: A Review of Lessons and Challanges* (Report by Development Alternatives, Inc for review by the United States Agency for International Development under Contract No 497-M-00-05-00005-00, 2008)
117 For a complete account on the French system see C T Shugart, 'Regulation-by-Contract and Municipal Services: The Problem of Contractual Incompleteness' (PhD Thesis, Harvard University 1998) especially p.35
118 See M Finger and J Allouche, *Water privatisation: trans-national corporations and the re-regulation of the water industry* (Taylor & Francis 2002)
119 K DeWitte, 'On Analyzing Drinking Water Monopolies by Robust Non-Parametric Efficiency Estimations' (PhD thesis, University of Leuven 2009); D Saal and K De Witte, 'Is a little sunshine all we need? On the impact of sunshine regulation on profits, productivity and prices in the Dutch drinking water sector' 20 Journal of Regulatory Economics 61

22 Introduction

Furthermore, one of the aspects that this book attempts to explain is transparency of the decision-making process in independent regulatory bodies. With the absence of such bodies in the French and Dutch water sectors, it would be impossible to draw comparison.

1.5 Victoria

1.5.1 Federal regulation and the National Water Initiative

The Australian Constitution at Article 100[120] prohibits the Federal government from limiting the powers of the states toward the 'reasonable use' of the waters of rivers for conservation or irrigation. Historically, the Constitution does not give the Federal government the powers over environmental matters. However, the Federal government generally has jurisdiction to prescribe legislation over interstate and international trade, corporations, taxations and matters of foreign affairs.[121]

As a result, water services in Victoria are a combination of complex regulatory arrangements between the Federal and the Victorian (state) government. Major parts of the regulatory framework are enacted by the state under policy guidelines from the Federal government while the rest is federal legislation.

Federal policy guidelines in the water sector came mainly from the Council of Australian Government (CoAG), in the form of the National Water Initiative (NWI).[122] The NWI contains principles of reform of state water laws. The Victorian government, as a signatory party to the 1994 CoAG reform initiative and the 2004 CoAG NWI Intergovernmental Agreement, has enacted the Victorian NWI implementation plan.[123]

The Victorian NWI implementation plan contains measures which are relevant to water utilities' reforms, among others, reforms in urban water governance in the form of upper bound pricing, development of pricing policies for recycled water/storm water, and for rural and regional water services in the form of review and development of pricing policies for trade wastes.[124] Benchmarking efforts are also carried out under the Victorian NWI implementation plan, also including new investment, refurbishment of infrastructure and the setting up of independent pricing bodies for water storage and delivery. Some of these plans are under way and some have already been completed.

---

120 An Act to constitute the Commonwealth of Australia (taking into account alterations up to Act No. 84 of 1977) Article 100

121 An Act to constitute the Commonwealth of Australia s.51

122 The Commonwealth of Australia and others, *Intergovernmental Agreement on a National Water Initiative* (2004)

123 The Commonwealth of Australia and others, *The Council of Australian Governments' Water Reform Framework* (1994); The Commonwealth of Australia and others, *Intergovernmental Agreement on a National Water Initiative* (2004); Government of Victoria, *Victoria's NWI Implementation Plan* (2006)

124 Government of Victoria, *Victoria's NWI Implementation Plan* (2006)

1.5.2 Victorian water businesses

Victoria's water industry comprises of: (1) Melbourne Water Corporation responsible for the collection, storage and supply of bulk water; (2) three retail water services companies supplying the metropolitan Melbourne area: City West Water, South East Water, Yarra Valley Water ('The Three Retailers'); (3) 15 regional-urban water authorities (RUWA); and (4) five rural water authorities responsible for approving water trade and transfer of water shares.

Table 1.1 lists regulated water businesses in Victoria.

Water corporations are established through the Water Act 1989.[125] The three retailers were set up under the (Commonwealth) Corporations Act 2001[126] in

Table 1.1 Regulated water businesses in Victoria

Corporation	Function/area	Legal basis of incorporation
Melbourne Water (also serves as RWA)	Bulkwater and bulk sewerage service in Melbourne as well as the management of rivers, creeks and major drainage system in Port Philip and Westernport.	Water Act 1989 (Vic) and Water (Governance) Act of 2006 (Vic)
Gippsland and Southern Rural Water (RWA)	Domestic, irrigation and stock and bulkwater supply in regional Victoria	
Goulburn Murray Rural Water (RWA)		
Grampians Wimmera Mallee Water (RWA)	Water, sewerage, irrigation and domestic and stock services	
Lower Murray Urban and Rural Water (RWA)		
Barwon Water	Water and sewerage services in regional Victoria	
Central Highlands Water		
Coliban Water (RWA)		
East Gippsland Water		
Gippsland Water		
Goulburn Valley Water		
North East Water		
South Gippsland Water		
Western Water,		
Westernport Water		
Wannon Region Water Authority		
City West Water	Retail water supply and sewerage services in Melbourne metropolitan area	Water Act 1989 (Vic)
South East Water		
Yarra Valley Water		

---

125 Water Act 1989 No. 80 of 1989
126 Corporations Act 2001

24 *Introduction*

conjunction with the State Owned Enterprise Act 1992 (SOE Act).[127] This has produced some complexities, for example they can be subjected to non-commercial activities by the Victorian government but these are subject to mutual agreement between each of the companies and the government, which then allows the government to reimburse its non-commercial activities.[128] In 2012, the Three Retailers, City West Water, South East Water and Yarra Valley Water, were transformed into statutory corporations under Water Act 1989. Thus, all water entities in Victoria are now statutory corporations.

The analytical framework in this book will be applicable to highly networked water utilities which are separate legal entities from the state. As such, only the governance systems of The Three Retailers and Melbourne Water are evaluated and the other regional-urban water utilities which supply water to towns and rural areas are excluded.

The book will also assess the governance framework for PSP between the Victorian government, Melbourne Water and a private entity called AquaSure, a consortium comprising of Thiess, Degremont (a subsidiary of Suez) and Macquarie Capital to build a water desalination plant in Wonthaggi. The 30-year 3.5 billion USD build-operate-transfer desalination contract is financed both through debt and equity.[129] There were controversies surrounding the project as to the actual sum of money paid each year to AquaSure, irrespective of water sold,[130] and the confidentiality of the contract provisions.[131]

1.5.3 Sectoral rules and regulatory institutions applicable to Victorian water businesses

The legislative framework for the metropolitan water sector is comprised of a number of Acts. The most significant Victorian Acts are the Water Act 1989[132] and the Water Industry Act 1994 (WIA).[133]

Water services in Victoria are regulated primarily by six main institutions explained below. In some instances, the regulating powers of these institutions overlap.

---

127 State Owned Enterprises Act 1992 (Victoria), No. 90 of 1992, Version No. 036
128 ibidibid s.72 also Financial Management Act 1994 No. 18 of 1994 (Victoria), Version No. 061 Part 2
129 'Public Private Partnership' (*Government of Victoria*) <http://web.archive.org/web/20110225003309/http://www.ourwater.vic.gov.au/programs/desalination/about-us/ppp> accessed 16 May 2016, p.2
130 B Schneiders and R Millar, 'Brumby's giant money pit' <www.theage.com.au/victoria/brumbys-giant-money-pit-20100827-13w2n.html> accessed 24 November 2010
131 AAP, 'Govt's desal figure misleading: Brumby' (24 November 2010) <http://news.smh.com.au/breaking-news-national/govts-desal-figure-misleading-brumby-20100917-15ewb.html> accessed 5 August 2011
132 Water Act 1989 No. 80 of 1989, Version 102
133 Water Industry Act 1994 No. 121 of 1994, Version No. 063

1.5.3.1 Minister for Water

For the regional-urban water businesses, rural water businesses and Melbourne Water, the Minister for Water requests reports and information, creates policy, issues directions and sets standards and obligations and appoints board members. The Minister for Water is also tasked by the WIA with issuing Statements of Obligation to The Three Retailers.[134]

The Three Retailers must comply with a 'Statement of Obligation' (SOO). The Minister of Water has the power to make, issue, amend, vary or revoke a SOO, after consulting with the ESC and the Treasurer.[135] The WIA 1994 does not limit the scope of regulation through the SOO, thus, the minister can virtually regulate anything[136] as long as it is not in contravention of higher laws. At the time of writing the minister has issued two types of SOO applicable to water businesses. The 2012 SOO obligates the retailers to prepare and deliver a *Water Plan* for the ESC to determine prices; clarify governance and risk management, board performance, customer and community engagement, consultation with other authorities, response to incidents and assets management; planning and service delivery, environmental management, payment schemes and contributions.[137] In 2009, the Minister of Water issued an additional SOO (System Management) to The Three Retailers to regulate bulkwater entitlements from Melbourne Water to The Three Retailers.[138]

1.5.3.2 Essential Services Commission

The Essential Services Commission (ESC) regulates performance assessment (through benchmarking) and pricing. ESC is a multi utility regulator enacted through the Essential Services Commission Act of 2004 ('ESC Act').[139] The ESC is considered an 'independent pricing body' as required by the Victorian NWI implementation plan.[140] The ESC is tasked with determining prices,[141] standards and conditions of service,[142] and issuing regulatory codes[143]. It also has the power to require the regulated industries to submit information for regulatory purposes.[144]

---

134 ibid s.4I
135 ibid s.4I
136 ibid s.4I (2) and (3)
137 See 'Statement of Obligations (General) 2012'.
138 See Water Industry Act 1994, Statement of Obligation, City West Water Limited (Systems Management)
139 Essential Services Commission Act 2001 No. 62 of 2001
140 Government of Victoria, *Victoria's NWI Implementation Plan* (2006)
141 Essential Services Commission Act 2001 No. 62 of 2001, s.33
142 Water Industry Act 1994 No. 121 of 1994, Version No. 063 s.4.e
143 ibid, s.4.f
144 ibid, s.4.g

26 *Introduction*

Another instrument which prescribes the power of the ESC is the Water Industry Regulatory Order (WIRO).[145] The WIRO is an Order issued by the governor by virtue of the WIA and the ESC Act. The WIRO itself is a single document (which is amended from time to time) and governs all business entities regulated by the ESC.

The WIRO and the WIA also empower the ESC to enact Codes.[146] In practice, these Codes contain important details of the ESC operation. Regulatory accounts and customer service have a legal basis under these Codes. The ESC has issued several regulatory accounting codes, customer services codes and two guidelines, one on new network connections and the other for approving, conducting and reporting audits.

1.5.3.3 *Energy and Water Ombudsman*

Disputes between water businesses and consumers are referred to the Energy and Water Ombudsman (EWOV). The EWOV is a company limited by guarantee (and not having share capital) set up under the 2001 Corporations Act.[147] Water businesses are obliged to enter into an agreement with EWOV to settle their disputes with customers. According to the EWOV Charter,[148] its jurisdiction does not extend to complaints relating to tariff setting or determination of price structures, presumably because this has been reserved for the ESC.[149] Government policies are also excluded from EWOV's jurisdiction as well as those cases that are being referred to tribunals or the courts and any matters that are specifically stipulated by legislation. The same applies for 'events beyond reasonable control of the participants'[150] as the remedies for such a *force majeure* are set out in legislation and its enforcement is subjected to judiciary bodies.

Finally, the jurisdiction of EWOV does not cover actions undertaken by the utilities in ensuring the security of water supply by virtue of administrative or regulatory power.[151] This exclusion is typical in the redress mechanism in water utilities as the question of policy and economic regulation is reserved by the executive (Minister of Water) and the economic regulator (ESC). EWOV is intended to deal only with the day-to-day operation of a regulated business and not with large-scale cases affecting the sustainability of a water supply system such as those related to a *force majeure*.

1.5.3.4 *Other departments*

Water businesses in Victoria are regulated by several other departments. The Treasurer of the Department of Treasury and Finance regulates financial

---

145 Water Industry Regulatory Order (WIRO) 2012.
146 Water Industry Act 1994 No. 121 of 1994, Version No. 063 s.4F also ibid ss.15–17
147 Energy and Water Ombudsman Victoria, *Constitution of Energy and Water Ombudsman (Victoria) Limited* (2010)
148 Energy and Water Ombudsman Victoria, *Energy and Water Ombudsman Charter 30 May 2006* (2006)
149 ibid para 4 (Jurisdiction)
150 ibid para 4.1(g)
151 ibid para 4.2(h)

management of the water businesses while drinking water standards are regulated by the Secretary to the Department of Health. Activities related to waste water discharges and other environmental protection issues are carried out by the Environment Protection Authority (EPA).

1.5.3.5 General administrative, corporate and economic rules applicable to Victorian water businesses

Water businesses in Victoria are also covered by general administrative and corporate rules in addition to the sectoral rules as discussed above. The Three Retailers were companies fully owned by the Victorian Government under The Corporations Act 2001 but were then reconstituted as statutory water corporations under the 1989 Water Act.[152]

The Audit Act 1994[153] establishes the power of the Victorian Auditor General to commence audit against government departments or government-owned corporations, at their request and expense. The Public Administration Act 2004[154] is also applicable to the water companies, by virtue of the Water Governance Act 2006.[155] The Australian Competition and Consumer Commission (ACCC) has enforcement jurisdiction over Water Market Rules 2009 and the Water Charge (Termination Fees) Rules 2009 by virtue of the Water Act 2007 (Cth).[156] The jurisdiction of the ACCC under the Water Act 2007 does not extend into Victorian urban water supplies. However, the ACCC has jurisdiction over the competitive parts of Victorian water businesses under the Trade Practices Act 1974 (Cth).[157] Victoria also has the FoI Law 1982 which is applicable to certain government-owned corporations and regulatory institutions.[158]

1.6 England

The United Kingdom of Great Britain and Northern Ireland is a unitary state between four countries comprising England, Wales, Scotland and Northern Ireland. Each of these countries has a different legal system. Northern Ireland, Wales and Scotland have their own legislatures but with different degrees of devolved powers. England has no sub-national parliament of its own and falls directly under Westminster's legislative authority. Each of these countries has its own model for the governance of water services. This book only focuses on England.

---

152 Corporations Act 2001; Water Amendment (Governance and Other Reforms) Act 2012 No. 17 of 2012
153 Audit Act 1994, No. 2 of 1994 (Victoria), Version No. 051
154 Public Administration Act (Victoria) 2004 No. 108 of 2004 Version No. 024
155 Water (Governance) Act 2006 Act No. 85/2006
156 Water Act 2007, Act No. 137 of 2007 also Water Charge (Termination Fees) Rules 2009 – F2009L02425 Water Market Rules 2009 – F2009L02424
157 Trade Practices Act 1974, Act No. 51 of 1974 as amended
158 Freedom of Information Act 1982 No. 9859 of 1982

Table 1.2 Recapitulation of primary regulatory institutions overseeing Victorian water businesses

Area	Institutions	Primary legal basis	Regulatory outputs
General policy/ direction and licensing	Minister of Water; Department of Sustainability and Environment (now Department of Environment, Land, Water and Planning)	Water Industry Act 1994 (Vic)	Appointments, SOO, Directions
Financial management	Treasurer at the Department of Treasury	Financial Management Act 1994 (Vic)	Financial reporting guidelines
Drinking Water	Secretary at the Department of Health	Safe Drinking Water Act 2003 (Vic)	Drinking Water Standard
Pricing and monitoring of performance	Essential Services Commission	Essential Services Commission Act 2001 (Vic), Water Industry Act 1994 (Vic)	Price determinations (S. 33 of ESC Act). Standards and conditions of service (S.4E of WIA). Codes (in relation to its functions and powers (S.4F of the WIA)). Information requirement from regulated businesses (S 4G of the WIA). Water Industry Regulatory Order (WIRO)
Environmental protection, waste water discharges	Environment Protection Authority	Environment Protection Act 1970 (Vic)	Waste water licence
Consumer dispute	Energy and Water Ombudsman	Direct (not applicable to The Three Retailers): Water Act 1989 (Vic) Through licences (for The Three Retailers): Water Industry Act 1994 (Vic), Essential Services Commission Act 2001 (Vic)	Binding decision

Freedom of Information	Victorian Ombudsman, Victorian Civil & Administrative Tribunal (VCAT)	Freedom of Information Act 1982 (Vic)	Recommendation (from Ombudsman) Decision (from VCAT)
Competition (Federal Jurisdiction)	Australian Competition and Consumer Commission	Trade Practices Act 1974, Water Act 2007 (Cth)	Decision

Water services in England have undergone several institutional changes throughout history. During the period 1750–1870, water services were provided mostly by the private sector following the *laissez-faire* principle where state intervention has to be minimised.[159] Realising that this was not successful, the government enacted an Act to control the private companies.[160] By 1875, local authorities were required to ensure adequate water supplies in their areas, if necessary, by acquiring privately owned networks, which led to the remunicipalisation movement until 1945.[161] In 1973 the government consolidated and then regionalised all municipal water services into 10 Regional Water Authorities (RWA) which took over the responsibility of 157 water undertakings, 29 river authorities and 1,393 sanitary authorities, along with the principles of Integrated Water Resources Management.[162] However, the regionalisation process was perceived as a failure and the RWAs were deemed not able to protect environmental and potable water quality. By this time, the EC had begun enacting various legislations on water quality, notably the bathing and drinking water directives,[163] as well as enforcing them against the UK.[164] The politicisation of the environment, serious enforcement effort by the EC, the perceived failure of the RWAs and a conservative approach to market liberalism all provided a background to water privatisation.[165] A discussion

---

159   K J Bakker, *An uncooperative commodity: privatizing water in England and Wales* (Oxford University Press, USA 2003) pp.46–49

160   ibid p.48. See also J Hassan, *A history of water in modern England and Wales* (Manchester University Press: distributed in the USA by St Martin's Press 1998) p.17

161   Hassan, *A history of water in modern England and Wales* (Manchester University Press: distributed in the USA by St Martin's Press 1998) p.18

162   ibid p.126

163   Council Directive 76/160/EEC of 8 December 1975 concerning the quality of bathing water, Official Journal L 031, 05/02/1976 P. 0001–0007 and Council Directive 80/778/EEC of 15 July 1980 relating to the quality of water intended for human consumption, Official Journal L 229, 30/08/1980 P. 0011–0029

164   See Case C-56/90, *Commission of the European Communities v United Kingdom of Great Britain and Northern Ireland* – Directive 76/160/EEC – Bathing water, European Court reports 1993 Page I-04109

165   See generally Hassan, *A history of water in modern England and Wales* (Manchester University Press: distributed in the USA by St Martin's Press 1998) and Bakker, *An uncooperative commodity: Privatizing water in England and Wales* (Oxford University Press, USA 2003)

paper was issued in 1986 paving the way for the privatisation and, in 1987, the Conservative government who had previously privatised other utilities (British Gas in 1986 and British Telecom in 1984) returned to power and proceeded with its previous plan to privatise the water industry.[166]

Full divestiture of the 10 RWAs (with minimal enterprise or managerial reorganisation) – rather than a long-term contract model such as concession – was opted for as the method of privatisation. The 1989 Water Act was the privatising legislation which also sets the foundation for post-'privatisation' regulatory architecture. The RWAs are converted into water services companies and their former river basin management duties and consumer protection duties are transferred, respectively, to the newly established National River Authorities and the Office of Water Services (Ofwat).[167] Other than statutes and secondary laws, licences are used as the main regulatory instrument. The post-divestiture regulatory architecture is thus far much more complicated than the previous publicly owned arrangements. The government's desire to remove water infrastructure financing from the public budget led to the inevitable creation of powerful monopolies. If the regulatory arrangements were to malfunction the political and economic cost would be dire and, as a consequence, a complex regulatory system would be required to safeguard the public interest.[168]

It is generally agreed that there are at least three key regulatory actors in the English water industry: the drinking water quality regulator, the environmental regulator and the economic regulator.[169] Drinking water quality is regulated by the Drinking Water Inspectorate (DWI) while the NRA and Ofwat are, respectively, the economic and environmental regulators. This structure was changed in 1995 where the NRA was incorporated into the Environmental Agency.

There are 10 Water and Sewerage Companies (WaSC) and 13 Water Only Companies (WOC) in England and Wales. There is a variation of form of legal entities among the water businesses. At the time of writing, of all the 10 WaSCs, two (United Utilities and Seven Trent) are a Public Limited Companies (plc), one (Welsh Water) is a company limited by guarantee, while the rest are privately held companies (Ltd). Meanwhile, the WOCs are either plcs or Ltds.

---

166 Ofwat and Defra, 'The development of water industry in England and Wales' <www.ofwat.gov.uk/wp-content/uploads/2015/11/rpt_com_devwatindust270106.pdf> accessed 16 May 2016
167 Hassan, *A history of water in modern England and Wales* (Manchester University Press: distributed in the USA by St Martin's Press 1998) p.170. The transfer of river basin management and environmental duties to the NRA was a result of long parliamentary scrutiny.
168 ibid p.170
169 Hendry, 'An Analytical Framework for Reform of National Water Law' (PhD thesis, University of Dundee 2008); also Quesada, *Water and sanitation services in Europe: do legal frameworks provide for 'good governance'?* (UNESCO Centre for Water Law Policy and Science at the University of Dundee 2010); Hassan, *A history of water in modern England and Wales* (Manchester University Press: distributed in the USA by St Martin's Press 1998) p.180

Table 1.3 Water companies in England and Wales

Water and sewerage companies	Water only companies
Anglian Water Services Ltd	Bristol Water plc
Northumbrian Water Ltd	Bournemouth & West Hampshire Water plc
Severn Trent Water plc	Cambridge Water plc
South West Water Services Ltd	Dee Valley Water plc
Southern Water Services Ltd	Cholderton & District Water Co. Ltd
Thames Water Utilities Ltd	Portsmouth Water plc
United Utilities Water plc	Albion Water
Dwr Cymru Cyfyngedig Welsh Water	South Staffordshire Water plc
Wessex Water Services Ltd	Sutton & East Surrey Water plc
Yorkshire Water Services Ltd	Affinity Water
	Peel Water Networks
	Veolia Water Projects
	Hartlepool Water

1.6.1 Sectoral rules and regulatory institutions overseeing England's water businesses

1.6.1.1 The Water Services Regulation Authority (Ofwat)

The Water Services Regulation Authority (now the statutory name of Ofwat) is a non-ministerial government department established in 1989. The Water Act 1989 which was also the privatising legislation for water services in England and Wales sets the duties, rights and responsibilities of the Director General of Water Services[170] and authorises the Director to arrange and appoint staff and delegate responsibilities to his staff.[171] The Water Act 2003 abolished the office of Director General of Water Services[172] and replaced[173] the role of the single director of Ofwat with a board,[174] bearing the name 'Water Services Regulation Authority'. The replacement of the Director General with a regulatory board is consistent with the UK's best practice on regulation[175] and has been conducted

---

170 Water Act 1989 c.15 for example, Sections 5 and 7
171 ibid Schedule 3 of the Original version, s.5 paras 1–4
172 Water Act 2003 c.37 s.34(3) s.34(3)
173 ibid c.56 with s.1A
174 ibid schedule 1, s.1(1) 'The Authority shall consist of a chairman, and at least two other members, appointed by the Secretary of State'
175 See Hendry, 'An Analytical Framework for Reform of National Water Law' (PhD thesis, University of Dundee 2008) p.304

in other utilities. Since the 2003 amendments, the Water Services Regulation Authority continues to use the name Ofwat.

The primary duties of Ofwat (and the Secretary of State) under the original WIA 1991 were to ensure that the undertakers are able to perform their functions and that they are able to secure reasonable return on their capital,[176] and its secondary duties are to protect consumers' interests, promote efficiency and facilitate competition.[177] With the ascent of the Labour government to power, these were later amended (in force in 2005) by the 2003 Water Act, making the furtherance of the consumer objective a first duty, followed by the duties to ensure that undertakers are able to carry out their functions properly, duties to ensure reasonable returns on capital and duties to enforce licence conditions.[178] However, the duty to further the consumer objective should be achieved 'wherever appropriate by promoting effective competition'.[179] The 2014 Water Act added another primary duty: 'to further the resilience objective', which is meant to ensure long-term service security in the face of environmental pressures, population growth and changes in consumer behaviour by way of long-term planning, investment and efficient water resources management.[180]

Ofwat regulates water companies through licences. As discussed above, it has the duty to ensure that licence conditions are met by the companies. In performing this task, Ofwat is equipped with the power to impose sanctions on water companies.

Ofwat uses the price cap as the instrument of economic regulation. By capping prices (and not dividends) water companies are expected to be able to boost performance by increasing efficiency. The cost-efficiency savings as a result of the company's performance can then be credited back to the company while at the same time used as a factor in price reduction.[181] The price cap[182] is embedded in each water company's Licence Condition 'B' (regarding Charges)[183] and is reviewed once every five years (initially it was planned for a 10 year review). Until 2011, utilities were required to produce their annual 'June Return' data. This has now changed and utilities are required to submit an 'annual performance report' (see section 3.3.1). Through this (and their

---

176 Water Industry Act 1991 c.56 s.2(2)
177 ibid s.2 (3)
178 Water Act 2003 c.37 ss.39(3), 105(3); S.I. 2005/968, Article 2(f)
179 Ofwat and Defra, 'The Development of Water Industry in England and Wales' <www.ofwat.gov.uk/wp-content/uploads/2015/11/rpt_com_devwatindust270106.pdf> p.98 accessed 16 May 2016. M Cave, *Independent review of competition and innovation in water markets: final report* (Defra 2009)
180 Water Act 2014; 2014 c.21 (England) s.22
181 S King, 'Principles of price cap regulation' in M Arblaster and M Jamison (eds), *Infrastructure regulation and market reform: principles and practice* (ACCC and PURC 1998)
182 See R Green, 'Has price cap regulation of UK utilities been a success?' 132 Public Policy for the Private Sector; A Booker, 'Incentive regulation in water – case study' (Utility Regulation Training Program 1997)
183 The Licence Conditions are imposed by OFWAT under the authority provided by the Water Industry Act 1991 c.56 s.11

business plan), Ofwat compares water companies' cost information and then uses it to determine the K factor in its price cap formula ('yardstick competition'). The allowed price cap is thus determined using the industry's average unit cost.[184] Yardstick competition and the combination of the authority to impose sanctions and award a favourable K factor that would allow the company to recoup its profit, serve as the carrot-and-stick of the English regulatory system.

The 2003 Water Act also inserted new principles of emerging regulatory practice, by requiring that Ofwat 'shall have regard to the principles of best regulatory practice (including the principles under which regulatory activities should be transparent, accountable, proportionate, consistent and targeted only at cases in which action is needed)'.[185] Since there is no other provision in the WIA 1991, which elaborates the elements of 'best regulatory practice' in more detail, the provision above entails no direct practical legal consequences to Ofwat. Having said that, the principles of 'better regulation' are practised by Ofwat and its elements are well reflected in its policies.

1.6.1.2 Environment Agency

The Environment Agency (EA) is a result of consolidation[186] of several regulatory bodies: the NRA, Her Majesty's Inspectorate of Pollution (HMIP) and the Waste Regulation Authorities. The purpose of the consolidation was to provide an integrated approach to environmental protection by combining the regulatory authorities on land, air and water in a single body.[187]

The EA is one of the most important actors in the regulation of the English water industry since it is tasked with the control of pollution[188] and the management and conservation of water resources,[189] both of which are factors influencing water charges imposed on consumers and the company's investment decisions. The Environment Act 1995 specifically clarified that the EA's function of protection against pollution shall include the protection of any waters – surface or underground – from which any water undertaker is authorised to take water.[190]

184　J L Bernstein, 'Price cap regulation and productivity growth' 1 International Productivity Monitor 23
185　Water Industry Act 1991 c.56 s.2(4) as amended by Water Act 2003 c.37 ss.39(4). On 'Better Regulation' and its evolution see R Baldwin, 'Regulation lite: the rise of emissions trading' 2 Regulation & Governance 193; Better Regulation Executive, 'Better regulation' (Department for Business Innovation and Skills 2008) <http://webarchive.nationalarchives.gov.uk/+/http://www.berr.gov.uk/whatwedo/bre/index.html/index.html> accessed 21 May 2012; Better Regulation Task Force, *Regulation – less is more. Reducing burdens, improving outcomes* (London: Cabinet Office 2005)
186　Environment Act 1995 c.25 s.2
187　Ofwat and Defra, 'The Development of Water Industry in England and Wales' <www.ofwat.gov.uk/wp-content/uploads/2015/11/rpt_com_devwatindust270106.pdf> p.9 accessed 16 May 2016
188　Environment Act 1995 c.25 s.5
189　ibid s.6
190　ibid s.10

34 *Introduction*

The EA issues abstraction licences and discharges permits to the water companies. The Water Resources Act (WRA) 1991 specifies the types, form and content of licences, the mechanism for applying them, the rights and obligations attached to the licence, the right to appeal against licensing decisions and matters pertaining to modification of licences.[191] Abstractions are charged on a cost-recovery basis. The EA has the power to prosecute water companies who are in breach of their licence condition or cause pollution.[192]

Discharge exemptions and permits[193] are regulated by the Environmental Permitting Regulations which also stipulate that the EA may impose consent conditions.[194] If water companies are in breach of consent conditions, the EA will send an enforcement notice to the companies specifying the contravention or potential contravention. If the enforcement notice is not complied with, a criminal and/or financial penalty follows.[195] Companies must submit a 25-year water resources plan which the EA will review.

1.6.1.3 *Drinking Water Inspectorate*

The Drinking Water Inspectorate (DWI) monitors and supervises tap water quality distributed by water companies in England and Wales. The DWI was set up in 1990 through the 1989 Water Act.[196] The organisation conducts technical audits of water companies, assesses their sampling programmes and investigates consumer complaints and water quality incidents.[197] The DWI also liaises with Ofwat for its periodic reviews.[198]

The WIA 1991 and WA 2003 amend and add more authority to the DWI in conducting its tasks.[199] The DWI's Chief Inspector of Drinking Water is appointed by the Secretary of State for Environment, Food and Rural Affairs but operates independently from DEFRA.

European legislation sets the basic standards for English drinking water quality regulation and this is empowered by the WIA 1991, WA 2003 and implemented in several statutory instruments.[200] The WIA empowers the Secretary of State to require the water companies to publish information about the quality

---

191 Water Resources Act 1991 c.57 s.36A, s.46, ss.34–38, s.40, ss.43–45, ss.51–59
192 Ofwat and Defra, 'The Development of Water Industry in England and Wales' <www.ofwat.gov.uk/wp-content/uploads/2015/11/rpt_com_devwatindust270106.pdf> p.50 accessed 16 May 2016
193 Water Resources Act 1991 c.57 ss.88–90
194 The Environmental Permitting (England and Wales) Regulations 2010; 2010 No. 675.
195 Ibid. S 36
196 Water Industry Act 1991 c.56 s.86
197 DWI, 'About Us' (Drinking Water Inspectorate UK) <http://dwi.defra.gov.uk/about/index.htm> accessed 20 April 2010
198 ibid
199 Water Industry Act 1991 c.56 s.86. Water Act 2003 repealed the term and directly referred to the 'Chief Inspector of Drinking Water'
200 Directive 98/83/EC of 3 November 1998 on the quality of water intended for human consumption, O.J. 330 pp.32–54

of the water supplied by them.[201] The DWI has the power to investigate[202] the possible contravention of water companies' duties[203] with respect to drinking water quality and, on the other hand, the water companies have legal obligations to assist the inspector and provide him with all information that may be required to perform investigation.[204]

1.6.1.4 Consumer Council for Water

The Consumer Council for Water is a statutory body whose task is to represent consumers' interests in the English water industry, primarily by taking complaints and investigating them against the water industry. The body originated from the regional 'Customer Services Committee' (CSC) created at the beginning of the privatisation through the 1989 Water Act and further reinforced by the 1991 Water Industry Act.[205] Originally, the CSCs were established in every water company and were structurally a part of Ofwat.[206] This changed when the 2003 Water Act abolished the CSCs and established the 'Consumer Council for Water' (CC Water) with a separate structure from Ofwat.

The Water Act 2003 provides CC Water with wide authority and responsibilities. The authority includes the power to require Ofwat or water companies to supply it with information[207] and to investigate complaints.[208]

1.6.1.5 Competition and Markets Authority

The Competition and Markets Authority (CMA) is a result of a merger between the Office of Fair Trading (OFT) and the Competition Commission. The WIA 1991 tasked the OFT with referring water companies' mergers to the Commission,[209] except under certain circumstances.[210] This task is now carried out by the CMA. The CMA and Ofwat have concurrent[211] jurisdiction with respect to investigation and enforcement agreements between undertakings,

---

201 Water Industry Act 1991 c.56 s.6 (5) and (6) (as amended)
202 ibid s.86(1B)(a)
203 ibid The duties of the water undertakers with respect to water quality are laid down under ss.68, 69 and 79
204 ibid s.86(3) (as amended)
205 Water Act 1989 c.15 s.6 and Water Industry Act 1991 c.56 ss.28–29
206 The preamble of the 1989 Water Act states: 'An [A.D. 1989.] Act to ... provide for the appointment and functions of a Director General of Water Services and of customer service committees; ...'
207 Water Industry Act 1991 c.56 s.27h as amended by WA 2003 s.44
208 ibid s.29A
209 ibid s.32. See also Hendry, 'An Analytical Framework for Reform of National Water Law' (PhD thesis, University of Dundee 2008) p.359
210 Water Act 2014; 2014 c.21 (England) (n 156) s.14
211 Water Industry Act 1991 c.56 s.31 as amended by Competition Act 1998 c.41 s.5(6). S.31 of the Water Industry Act 1991 c.56 also empowers OFWAT, concurrently with the OFT, to investigate directly violation of EC Treaty Articles 81(1) and 82. The concurrent jurisdiction is also enabled by the Enterprise Act 2002, 2002 c.40

decisions or concerted practices which may affect trade or with the objectives or effect in preventing, restricting or distorting competition[212] or constitute an 'abuse of dominant position'.[213]

1.6.1.6 DEFRA

The Department for Environment, Food and Rural Affairs (DEFRA) – chaired by the Secretary for the Environment, Food and Rural Affairs – has wide powers in creating policies for the water industry and the environment.

DEFRA is involved in standard setting, drafting legislation, policy making and in the appointment of Ofwat officers.[214] Although Ofwat is independent in performing its tasks and is directly accountable to parliament, DEFRA continues to supervise Ofwat's work.

In 2010, DEFRA announced an Ofwat review, with the purpose of examining 'how the industry regulator works, whether it offers good value for money and if it is delivering what the Government and customers expect'.[215] DEFRA had carried out an online survey which fed in to its 'Water White Paper'.[216] As far as water services are involved, The Water White Paper incorporates recommendations from the Cave, Walker and Gray reports.[217] Some of these suggestions were later incorporated into the 2014 Water Act. The next section will elaborate the implication of the re-regulation strategy of the English water industry.

1.6.2 Further re-regulation of the English water industry

DEFRA commissioned several reviews of the English water industry. An independent review was carried out by Martin Cave on competition and innovation in the water industry.[218] Another review on charging for household water and sewerage services was led by OFRAIL's chair Anna Walker.[219] DEFRA also conducted a review of Ofwat and CC Water, led by David Gray.[220] Finally,

---

212 Competition Act 1998 c.41 s2.1 and Water Industry Act 1991 c.56 s.31(3)(a) also Enterprise and Regulatory Reform Act 2013; 2013 c.24 s.55
213 Competition Act 1998 c.41 s.18 and Water Industry Act 1991 c.56 s.31(3)(b)
214 'The Authority shall consist of a chairman, and at least two other members, appointed by the Secretary of State'. Water Industry Act 1991 c.56 Schedule 1A, para 1 (1)
215 'Ofwat review will consider future challenges facing industry' (Defra) <www.defra.gov.uk/news/2010/08/26/ofwat-review/> accessed 25 April 2011
216 Department for Environment Food and Rural Affairs, 'Water White Paper' (Defra) <www.officialdocuments.gov.uk/document/cm82/8230/8230.pdf> accessed 16 February 2011
217 Cave, *Independent review of competition and innovation in water markets: final report* (Defra 2009); D Gray, *Review of Ofwat and consumer representation in the water sector* (Defra and the Welsh Government, 2011); A Walker, *The independent review of charging for household water and sewerage services: final report* (Defra 2009)
218 Cave, *Independent review of competition and innovation in water markets: final report* (Defra 2009)
219 Walker, *The independent review of charging for household water and sewerage services: final report* (Defra 2009)
220 Gray, *Review of Ofwat and consumer representation in the water sector* (Defra and the Welsh Government 2011)

Table 1.4 Recapitulation of sectoral rules and regulatory institutions

Institution	Function	Enabling rules
Ofwat	Regulation of the water industry in general: price setting, consumer protection, competition	Water Act 1989 Water Industry Act 1991 Licence Condition
Environment Agency	Pollution control, management and conservation of water resources, issuance of abstraction licence and discharge permits	Water Resources Act 1991 Environment Act 1995
Drinking Water Inspectorate	Water quality regulator, technical audit on water companies, investigating consumer complaints and water quality incidents	Water Industry Act 1991
Consumer Council for Water	Representing consumers' interests, taking complaints, investigating water industry on consumer complaints	Water Act 1989 Water Industry Act 1991 Water Act 2003
Competition Commission	Accepting referrals on merger issues, adjudicating breaches of competition law concurrently with Ofwat	Water Industry Act 1991 Competition Act 1998 Enterprise Act 2002
Department of Environment, Food and Rural Affairs	Standard setting, drafting of legislations and policies, appointment of regulators, industry restructuring	Water Act 1989 Water Resources Act 1991 Water Industry Act 1991 Environment Act 1995 Water Act 2003

in December 2011, DEFRA published the water white paper.[221] The water bill was introduced in 2013 and the Water Act received Royal Assent in 2014.

Part of the coalition government's programme was to 'examine the conclusions of the Cave and Walker Reviews, and reform the water industry to ensure more efficient use of water and the protection of poorer households'.[222] Gray's Ofwat review, meanwhile, confirms that there will be no significant changes to the structure of the water industry and, therefore, both Ofwat and CC Water are to be retained.[223] The most important part of the Gray review is probably its call to reduce the regulatory burden and to induce 'positive' incentives. Gray was of the opinion that at the moment Ofwat is focusing too much on negative incentives in the form of penalties and compliance mechanisms. At the same time, he felt

---

221 Department for Environment, Food and Rural Affairs, *Water for Life (White Paper)* (Stationery Office 2011)
222 D Cameron and N Clegg, *The Coalition: our programme for government* (2010) p.17
223 Gray, *Review of Ofwat and consumer representation in the water sector* (Defra and the Welsh Government 2011)

that the regulatory burden is too excessive.[224] Gray's review appears to go along with a previous report from Harris, which also calls for the reduction of regulatory burdens and incentivisation of companies with good track records of reporting and complying.[225] The Harris report calls for a reduction in the information requirement and to focus information gathering on material issues related to prices and service levels.[226] The English water industry is thus moving toward utilities' self-regulation and 'risk-based' approach to compliance mechanisms. This pressure toward loosening the regulatory grip is well reflected in Ofwat's consultation which outlines that the practical implication of this is that Ofwat will reduce its information requirement, such as the June Return.[227] This move could have significant implications for the quantity of information available in the public domain.

In many aspects, the Cave review calls for more transparency in the water sector. Cave calls for the publication of trade prices[228] which is required for the trading of abstraction licences and discharge consents in order to reduce the barriers to trading.[229] However, this is probably more of an issue for water resources dealt with by the EA, rather than Ofwat. Cave also calls for more transparency in the merger system. In his view, the current merger system lacks ex-ante transparency with respect to Ofwat's methodology in assessing the impact of potential mergers to the loss of comparators,[230] whereas mergers could actually benefit consumers and the environment. This will need to be reformed in the future, by requiring Ofwat to publish its methodology.[231] Cave recommends that indicative long-run marginal prices for the wholesale supply of water and waste water services at a water resource zone level and transport costs should be based on a common methodology and published.[232]

The Water Act 2014 accommodates *some* of the recommendations in the above reviews, particularly with respect to further liberalisation of the English water industry.

1.7 Jakarta

1.7.1 Central and local regulations

Water services in Indonesia are regulated by a combination of rules enacted at central and local levels. The primary legislation for water in Indonesia is currently the Law 11 Year 1974 on Irrigation.

---

224 ibid
225 K Harris, *Improving regulatory reporting and compliance* (Report for Ofwat, 2010)
226 ibid
227 Ofwat, *Regulatory compliance – a proportionate and targeted approach, A consultation* (2011)
228 See p.34 in Cave, *Independent review of competition and innovation in water markets: final report* (Defra 2009)
229 One of the barriers to liberalisation on the upstream (bulkwater supply) level is information asymmetry between incumbent utilities and entrants. Entrants have – in Cave's terms – *'little information on which to decide whether, where and how to enter'* (ibid p.46)
230 ibid p.95
231 ibid p.89. He explained: 'The benefits of a transparent assessment methodology are in giving merging parties much greater regulatory certainty about the criteria, weightings and methodology that OFWAT would use in the evidence that it submits to the Competition Commission', p.91
232 ibid p.54

Previously, Indonesia had a modern and comprehensive water resources management law, Law 7 Year 2004.[233] Although out of 100 articles in Law 7/2004, only one article, article 80, is specifically dedicated to water services, the law provides a legal umbrella for further regulation of water services through implementing regulations. One of the key regulations was Peraturan Pemerintah No. 16 Year 2005 on the Development of Water Supply System (GR-16).[234] However, these regulations are no longer valid since the Water Law 7 Year 2004 was invalidated by the Constitutional Court in 2015. The effect of such validation is that all implementing regulation on the water law also becomes invalid, and that includes GR-16.

Due to regional autonomy, water services become the responsibility of regional governments. Article 16.h of Law 7/2004 confirmed this by requiring municipalities and regencies to be responsible for fulfilling the minimum daily basic need for water of its population.[235] The article does not detail whether this covers water for both sanitation and hygiene or whether it also encompasses sewerage services, neither does it contain any minimum quantity of drinking water that a regional government must guarantee.

As the central government regulates water services only in general terms, there is more space for detailed regulation on a local level. This is performed for the most part through regional by-laws which are enacted by local parliaments. Regulation by regional by-laws must adhere to the principles laid down by higher forms of enactments and central government rules, such as the defunct Law 7/2004 and GR-16. However, in practice, conflict is often found between regulation and policies at central level and local level; especially common is conflict between guidelines issued by ministries at central level and regional by-laws. When in contradiction with higher rules such as a law (enacted by the House of Representatives at the central level) or a Government Regulation (a form of delegated legislation by the executive), regional by-laws and the other types of local rules can be annulled or revoked through a judicial review. Perusahaan Daerah Air Minum or PDAM (regional-owned waterwork companies – see below for more explanation) are established through regional by-laws. In addition to enacting PDAM's statutes, some regions also use regional by-laws to regulate water supply standards and customer service.[236] The capital of Indonesia, Jakarta, a city with a population of 10 million, regulates its regional-owned waterwork utility PAM Jaya through two regional by-laws.[237]

---

233 Undang Undang No. 7 Tahun 2004 Tentang Sumber Daya Air
234 Peraturan Pemerintah No. 16 Tahun 2005 Tentang Pengembangan Sistem Penyediaan Air Minum
235 Undang Undang No. 7 Tahun 2004 Tentang Sumber Daya Air
236 Peraturan Daerah Kota Bogor No. 4 Tahun 2004 Tentang Perusahaan Daerah Air Minum Tirta Pakuan Kota Bogor; Peraturan Daerah Kota Bogor Nomor 5 Tahun 2006 Tentang Pelayanan Air Minum Perusahaan Daerah Air Minum Tirta Pakuan Kota Bogor
237 Peraturan Daerah Khusus Ibukota Jakarta No. 13 Tahun 1992 Tentang Perusahaan Daerah Air Minum Daerah Khusus Ibukota Jakarta (PAM Jaya); and Peraturan Daerah Khusus Ibukota Jakarta No. 11 Tahun 1993 Tentang Pelayanan Air Minum di Wilayah Daerah Khusus Ibukota Jakarta

1.7.2 Jakarta's water businesses

Jakarta's water businesses are comprised of a bulkwater supplier, a regional-owned water utility company and two retail water companies, operating in the eastern and western parts of Jakarta, divided by the Ciliwung river.

1.7.2.1 Government-owned entities

1.7.2.1.1 PERUM JASA TIRTA II

The bulk water supplier, PT Jasa Tirta II (PJT II), is a government-owned company with assets and liabilities separate from the state budget. The company was originally established in 1967 through a Governmental Regulation (GR) with the mandate to manage the Jatiluhur reservoir, dam and hydropower.[238] The statute has been amended several times through various GRs, its latest being Government Regulation No. 7 Year 2010 (GR 7/2010) which also determines the PJT II's accountability line to ministers.[239] The PJT II serves the bulk water needs of several regions including Jakarta. However, not all of Jakarta's bulk water needs are sourced from PJT II. Some are also derived from rivers and transfer from other provinces.

The purpose of PJT II according to GR 7/2010 is the provision of bulk water supply for drinking water, electricity, farming, industry, ports and other needs requiring utilisation of water resources.[240] The company is also in charge of managing a hydropower facility, the Juanda hydropower located at the Jatiluhur dam, and other small hydropower facilities on its river basins.[241] The company is allowed to conduct other business activities such as tourism, consulting and land use services.[242]

1.7.2.1.2 PAM JAYA

PAM Jaya is a regional SOE owned by the Jakarta Regional Government, established under Jakarta Regional by-law 13 Year 1992 (by-law 13/1992).[243] According to by-law 13 Article 5, its purpose is to 'fulfil the population's need of drinking water in an effort to increase social welfare, to increase the income of the regional government and to be involved in developing the regional economy'. Article 6 specifies PAM Jaya's 'main' purpose, which is 'to conduct all efforts directly related to the provision and distribution of drinking water, which fulfils the prerequisite of good health and to provide good services to

---

238 PT Jasa Tirta II, 'Latar Belakang Pembentukan PT Jasa Tirta II' <www.jasatirta2.co.id/pjt.php?x=org&y=15ce99f2079b95cf251cb78b9d4a27df> accessed 16 May 2016
239 Peraturan Pemerintah No.7 Tahun 2010 Tentang Perusahaan Umum (Perum) Jasa Tirta II
240 ibid Article 4
241 Article 2
242 Ibid. The list of river basins managed by Perum Jasa Tirta II is on Article 3
243 Peraturan Daerah Khusus Ibukota Jakarta No. 13 Tahun 1992 Tentang Perusahaan Daerah Air Minum Daerah Khusus Ibukota Jakarta (PAM Jaya)

Introduction   41

the community by adhering to the company's economic principles'.[244] Article 7 further enumerates that in order to carry out its purpose under the previous article, the company has the obligation to, among others, put effort into providing drinking water in accordance with the programme outlined by the regional government; develop, manage and maintain water treatment plants, bulk water sources, water storage facilities; develop and maintain public hydrants, water terminals and water tanks, install water mains and distribution pipes, conduct survey and data collection for the purpose of setting water tariffs, provide services for water connections from and for the society, companies, housing, hotels and others; document water meters, conduct billing and collect receivables in accordance with prevailing laws and regulations; enforce action against illegal users; provide drinking water for municipal facilities, assist the governor in regulating, licensing and controlling drinking water facilities conducted by third parties; provide licences and monitor installations in Jakarta territory; and develop its human resources and employees' welfare in order to increase public service.[245]

By-law 13/1992 also determines the capital of PAM Jaya, which is separated from the Jakarta government's budget and assets.[246] The company may increase its capital in accordance with prevailing regulations.[247] The company's capital may be derived from the accrual of internal funds (presumably through interest rates or other gains); capital injection from regional government funds; government and third party aid; and loans, including offshore loans.[248]

The corporate governance structure of PAM Jaya is stipulated under by-law 13/1992. The company organ consists of directors, a supervisory body and an internal supervisory body.[249] There are rules on the appointment and dismissal of the utility's directors and the supervisory bodies.[250] The utility is barred from conducting certain activities, such as entering into cooperation with third parties for more than one year, without the approval of Jakarta's regional governor. PAM Jaya's statute requires that a cooperation agreement with the length of more than one year shall require the governor's written approval. Nevertheless, it is silent as to the regulation of scope and types of cooperation. A concession agreement, for example, has a considerable length and scope. By-law 13 does not regulate specifically on this type of cooperation.[251]

---

244 ibid Article 6. It is not clear what the article means by 'the company's economic principles'.
245 ibid Article 7. The article does not stipulate what sorts of permits/licences PAM Jaya issues and the mechanism for obtaining them.
246 ibid Article 8
247 ibid
248 ibid Article 10
249 ibid Articles 11, 20 and 28
250 ibid Articles 17 and 26
251 ibid Article 15. Other types of activities requiring written consent from the governor are encumberance of assets, obtaining offshore and onshore loans and acquisition of shares in other companies

42 Introduction

Table 1.5 Recapitulation of laws and regulations establishing Jakarta's water business

Corporation	Function/area	Legal basis of incorporation
Perum Jasa Tirta II	Government-owned bulk water supplier, not only for Jakarta province but also for other provinces on the western part of the Java Island	SOE Law 19/2003, GR 74/2010 (Statute of PT Jasa Tirta II)
Perusahaan Daerah Air Minum Jakarta (PAM Jaya)	Regional government; regional government-owned retail water service for the whole Jakarta region	Regional SOE Law No. 5/1962; regional by-law 13/1992 (Statute of PAM Jaya); by-law 11/1993
PT PAM Lyonnaise Jaya (Palyja)	Concessionaire of PAM Jaya, responsible for retail water supply in the eastern part of Jakarta	Corporation Law 40/2007, Company's Deed of Establishment
PT Aetra (formerly PT Thames PAM Jaya)	Concessionaire of PAM Jaya, responsible for retail water supply in the western part of Jakarta	Corporation Law 40/2007, Company's Deed of Establishment

1.7.2.2 The Cooperation Agreement

The other institutions involved in providing Jakarta's drinking water are PT Aetra (formerly TPJ) and PT PAM Lyonnaise Jaya (Palyja). Both of them are private companies established under the Corporation Law. Before embarking on the legal and regulatory environment in which these institutions operates, it is important to explain the historical setting which led to the involvement of the private sector in Jakarta's water supply.

There is a vast literature addressing the problems of the Jakarta water concession, among others Bakker,[252] Kooy,[253] Iwanami,[254] Argo,[255] Jensen,[256] Ardhianie,[257] Nugroho,[258] Braadbaart[259] and Lanti,[260] including investigative reports from

---

252 K Bakker, 'Conflicts over water supply in Jakarta, Indonesia' in B Barraqué and E Vlachos (eds), *Urban water conflicts, an analysis on the origins and nature of water-related unrest and conflicts in the urban context* (UNESCO Working series SC-2006/WS/19. 2006); Bakker, 'Trickle down? Private sector participation and the pro-poor water supply debate in Jakarta, Indonesia' 38 Geoforum 855

253 M É Kooy, 'Relations of power, networks of water: governing urban waters, spaces, and populations in (post) colonial Jakarta' (University of British Columbia 2008)

254 M Iwanami and A Nickson, 'Assessing the regulatory model for water supply in Jakarta' 28 Public Administration and Development 291

255 T A Argo, 'Thirsty downstream: the provision of clean water in Jakarta, Indonesia' (University of British Columbia 2001)

256 O Jensen, 'Troubled partnerships: problems and coping strategies in Jakarta's water concessions' (4th Conference on Applied Infrastructure Research, Berlin)

257 W Hadipuro and N Ardhianie, *Amandemen Kontrak Konsesi Air Jakarta* (2008)

258 R Nugroho, *Dilemma of Jakarta Water Service Post Public Private Partnership (PPP)* (2009); R Nugroho, *Reasons not to privatize water undertaking* (2010)

259 O Braadbaart, 'Privatizing water. The Jakarta concession and the limits of contract' in P Boomgaard (ed.), *A World of Water: Rain, Rivers and Seas in Southeast Asian Histories* (KITLV Press 2007) p.297

260 A Lanti, 'A regulatory approach to the Jakarta water supply concession contracts' 22 International Journal of Water Resources Development 255

Harsono.[261] All of this literature provides negative accounts of Jakarta's water privatisation, both from the point of view of its governance process and the concession's overall performance. Except for Lanti's paper, however, none of them pays specific attention to possible legal and regulatory solutions.

In late 1991, the World Bank and a foreign aid organisation from Japan provided a loan to PAM Jaya, in order to repair and expand its infrastructure.[262] Soon after the loan was provided, the World Bank approached the Indonesian government to allow PSP in Jakarta's water system. In 1995, the coverage of PAM Jaya was only 45 per cent, 30 per cent of which received intermittent supply.[263] In 1996 the percentage of unaccounted for water was more than 55 per cent. Due to these problems, more investment was needed in order to expand its coverage.[264] The government at that time thought that inviting the private sector in would result in lower tariffs and bring investment to repair leaked networks, and so put an end to the city's ailing water infrastructure.[265]

Thames acted first[266] by forming an alliance with Sigit Harjojudanto who was the son of the ruling President Soeharto[267] in exchange for a 20 per cent ownership of the project company. This move was later followed by Suez in forming an alliance with the Salim group, also an associate of the former President Soeharto.[268]

Soeharto's regime was a centralised regime. The central government decided what was considered best for the regions, including Jakarta. Neither the local Jakarta parliament nor the Governor at that time dared to challenge Soeharto's order. Without any public tender and to the disappointment of the World Bank,[269] Soeharto finally agreed to privatise Jakarta's water supply in 1995 and

---

261 A Harsono, 'Water and politics in the fall of Suharto', The Center for Public Integrity <www.publicintegrity.org/2003/02/10/5725/water-and-politics-fall-suharto> accessed 16 May 2016; Harsono, 'When water and political power intersect', Nieman Reports <www.nieman.harvard.edu/reportsitem.aspx?id=101044>

262 See Harsono, 'Water and politics in the fall of Suharto' The Center for Public Integrity <www.publicintegrity.org/2003/02/10/5725/water-and-politics-fall-suharto> accessed 16 May 2016; Harsono, 'When water and political power intersect' Nieman Reports <www.nieman.harvard.edu/reportsitem.aspx?id=101044>

263 See Jensen, 'Troubled partnerships: problems and coping strategies in Jakarta's water concessions' (4th Conference on Applied Infrastructure Research Berlin)

264 Lanti, 'A regulatory approach to the Jakarta water supply concession contracts' 22 International Journal of Water Resources Development 255

265 O Braadbaart, 'Privatizing water. The Jakarta concession and the limits of contract' in P Boomgaard (ed.), *A World of Water: Rain, Rivers and Seas in Southeast Asian Histories* (KITLV Press 2007) p.297

266 Harsono, 'Water and politics in the fall of Suharto', The Center for Public Integrity <www.publicintegrity.org/2003/02/10/5725/water-and-politics-fall-suharto> accessed 16 May 2016; Harsono, 'When water and political power intersect' Nieman Reports <www.nieman.harvard.edu/reportsitem.aspx?id=101044>

267 Harsono, 'When water and political power intersect' Nieman Reports <www.nieman.harvard.edu/reportsitem.aspx?id=101044>

268 '"Access to politics is essential. The water business is always political," Bernard Lafrogne, a Suez representative in Jakarta, told me' (Harsono, 'When water and political power intersect' Nieman Reports <www.nieman.harvard.edu/reportsitem.aspx?id=101044>)

269 See Braadbaart, 'Privatizing water. The Jakarta concession and the limits of contract' in P Boomgaard (ed.), *A World of Water: Rain, Rivers and Seas in Southeast Asian Histories* (KITLV Press 2007) p.297

subsequently ordered the Ministry of Public Work at that time to divide Jakarta into two service regions bordering the Ciliwung river.[270] One part was to be given to Soeharto's son Harjojudanto and Thames, and the other half to the Salim group and Suez. The negotiation process took two years.

However, PAM Jaya and its employees had a direct interest in the privatisation plan and so initially resisted the concession contract.[271] PAM Jaya has a strategic position as the owner of water infrastructure assets and has been the operator of the services since its inception and will be the institution that receives the assets back from the concessionaires after the contract periods end. Only after pressure from the central government did PAM Jaya finally accept the plan.[272]

As Braadbaart notes, the contract was signed with the most important contractual risks borne by PAM Jaya: (1) currency risk, (2) gradual tariff increase and projected sales and (3) bulk water supplies. One of the most fatal blows to the contractual design is linking the security of these risks to the private sector's performance. In the event that PAM Jaya failed to secure the risks, the private sector would not be obligated to materialise its commitments.[273]

PAM Jaya's strategic bargaining position at that time is reflected in the 1998 contract and the 2001 contract restatement: PAM Jaya is both a party to the contracts with the concessionaires and a 'regulator' at the same time, responsible for monitoring and supervising the contractual provisions.[274] Its consent, jointly with the concessionaire,[275] is also required to withdraw revenue from tariff collection from the escrow account.

In 1998, following the Asian monetary crisis, riots broke out. The executives and expatriates of these concessionaires fled to Singapore to seek refuge, while Palyja (the Suez subsidiary) left only one person in charge of its management.[276] Fearful of poisoning and contamination, the director of PAM Jaya demanded that the concessionaires relinquish control of their operations and

---

270 Braadbaart suggests that it was Sigit who persuaded his father, President Soeharto, to privatise Jakarta's water. ibid
271 Jensen, 'Troubled partnerships: problems and coping strategies in Jakarta's water concessions' (4th Conference on Applied Infrastructure Research Berlin); O Jensen and F Blanc-Brude, 'The handshake: why do governments and firms sign Private Sector Participation deals? Evidence from the Water and Sanitation Sector in developing countries', SSRN eLibrary. With PAM Jaya still objecting to a number of issues, the contract was signed. Braadbaart, 'Privatizing water. The Jakarta concession and the limits of contract' A World of Water Rain, Rivers and Seas in Southeast Asian Histories 297
272 Braadbaart, 'Privatizing water. The Jakarta concession and the limits of contract' in P Boomgaard (ed.), *A World of Water: Rain, Rivers and Seas in Southeast Asian Histories* (KITLV Press 2007) p.297
273 Personal communication, *Field Interview with Stakeholders, Jakarta, 11 January 2011*
274 See Smith, 'Utility regulators: the independence debate' 127 Public Policy for the Private Sector.
275 Cooperation Agreement Between PAM Jaya and The Concessionaire, 2001
276 See Harsono, 'Water and politics in the fall of Suharto' The Center for Public Integrity <www.publicintegrity.org/2003/02/10/5725/water-and-politics-fall-suharto> accessed 16 May 2016; Harsono, 'When water and political power intersect' Nieman Reports <www.nieman.harvard.edu/reportsitem.aspx?id=101044>

pressed them to hand the company back to the public.[277] The concessionaire agreed that the company's operation would be transferred but was furious with the pressure to end the concession contract. Finally, the executives fled back to Jakarta and threatened to bring the case to international arbitration.[278]

In May 1998, Soeharto stepped down and was replaced by the Habibie government. Due to the UK's and France's diplomatic lobbies and fearing that further conflict with multinationals would drive away foreign investment, the Habibie government agreed to keep the concession contracts and, in turn, both Suez and Thames agreed to renegotiate the terms of the contracts.[279] In the aftermath of Soeharto's downfall, his cronies were hunted down for corruption charges and were becoming the target of public resentment. Both the Salim group (who partnered with Thames) and Harjojudanto (partnered with Suez) then became a liability rather than an asset. The concessionaires finally decided to terminate their ties with the former President Soeharto's cronies, each having to pay dearly the price to repurchase the shares and other severance fees.

Although both TPJ and Palyja lost income for two consecutive years following the financial crisis,[280] neither company decided to terminate its contract although the contracts do provide for the concessionaire to be repaid for the investment made during the lifetime of the contract – the so called 'termination fee'. Jensen theorises that the concessionaires thought that this would be unlikely due to the government's financial situation following the 1998 monetary crisis. Had the concessionaires decided to exit during that period, they might have left the country without anything other than a substantial loss. Another factor could be the multinationals' own corporate strategy in the region.[281] With 300 or more water utilities operating and around 230 million residents, Indonesia is a potential market and thus it is probably not a good idea to end a dispute with arbitration. The other signatories to the concession, the Jakarta Governor and PAM Jaya, also have an interest in preserving the concession, as depicted in Table 1.6.

---

277 Harsono, 'Water and politics in the fall of Suharto' The Center for Public Integrity <www.publicintegrity.org/2003/02/10/5725/water-and-politics-fall-suharto> accessed 16 May 2016; Harsono, 'When water and political power intersect' Nieman Reports <www.nieman.harvard.edu/reportsitem.aspx?id=101044>

278 Harsono, 'Water and politics in the fall of Suharto' The Center for Public Integrity <www.publicintegrity.org/2003/02/10/5725/water-and-politics-fall-suharto> accessed 16 May 2016; Harsono, 'When water and political power intersect' Nieman Reports <www.nieman.harvard.edu/reportsitem.aspx?id=101044>

279 Harsono, 'Water and politics in the fall of Suharto' The Center for Public Integrity <www.publicintegrity.org/2003/02/10/5725/water-and-politics-fall-suharto> accessed 16 May 2016; Harsono, 'When water and political power intersect' Nieman Reports <www.nieman.harvard.edu/reportsitem.aspx?id=101044>

280 Jensen, 'Troubled partnerships: problems and coping strategies in Jakarta's water concessions' (4th Conference on Applied Infrastructure Research, Berlin)

281 ibid

46 Introduction

Table 1.6 Jakarta's water concession, actors and their interest (Jensen, 2005)[282]

Actor	Interest
PAM Jaya	Maximise status/employment/budget/scope of responsibility
	Reduce financial indebtedness
	Minimise chances of intervention by local or central government
Governor	Maximise domestic political support
	Minimise chances of central government intervention
	Maintain international reputation
Palyja/Aetra (formerly TPJ)	Maximise returns over the life of the contract
	Comply with firm's international strategy
	Minimise current losses
	Minimise financial risk

In 2001, the concessionaires, PAM Jaya and the Jakarta government, amended the terms of the contracts. Two identical Cooperation Agreements were prepared, one between PAM Jaya and TPJ (now Aetra) and the other between Palyja and PAM Jaya. Both contracts contain the signature of Jakarta's Governor at that time, Sutiyoso. The 2001 restatement contract then captured and preserved the power structure of the 1998 contract, with the exception that another player was added on to the regulatory system, albeit with a vague mandate and responsibility: the Jakarta Water Sector Regulatory Body (JWSRB).

Five years later, in 2006, the companies sold a substantial portion of their shares. Suez sold 49 per cent of its shares to Astratel and Citigroup and Thames completely withdrew from its Indonesian business, selling 95 per cent of its shares in TPJ to a Singaporean consortium, Aquatico and the other 5 per cent to Alberta Utilities. TPJ later changed its name to 'Aetra'.

In 2011, a coalition of NGOs filed a Citizen Law Suit to the Central Jakarta District Court demanding the invalidation of the Cooperation Contract and thus, the termination of Jakarta Water 'Privatisation' (Jakarta Water CLS). In February 2015, the Central Jakarta District Court granted the plaintiff's demand, declaring that the defendant (Jakarta Governor and PAM Jaya) had conducted a tortious act to the detriment of the people of Jakarta and declared that the Cooperation Contract, along with its amendments and addenda were annulled and declared not enforceable.[283]

This was a bold move by the court and created precedent where infrastructure contracts can be declared invalid through the Citizen Law Suit mechanism. Anti-privatisation activists rejoiced and the media was of the opinion that the Jakarta privatisation had ended with the Court's verdict.[284] This assumption was incorrect. The case is currently under a pending appeal to the High Court.

---

282 ibid
283 *Putusan Nomor 527/PDTG/2012/P.NJKTPST* (Central Jakarta District Court)
284 'Jakarta court cancels world's biggest water privatisation after 18 year failure' (*Transnational Institute*) <www.tni.org/en/pressrelease/jakarta-court-cancels-worlds-biggest-water-privatisation-after-18-year-failure> accessed 13 November 2015; C Elyda, 'Court decision ends privatization of water in Jakarta.' <www.thejakartapost.com/news/2015/03/24/court-decision-ends-privatization-water-jakarta.html>

Introduction 47

After the High Court, there will still be several other legal channels that both applicant and defendant can take. There is also the possibility that the case will be dragged into an international investment arbitration. At the moment, Jakarta water services are still operated under Palyja and Aetra.

1.7.2.3 Aetra

Aetra (formerly TPJ) was a subsidiary of Thames but later Thames withdrew and sold all of its shares to a Singaporean consortium, Aquatico.[285] The ultimate owner of Aetra through Aquatico is said to be Recapital Advisors (80%) and Glendale Partners (20%). Both companies own Aquatico through layers of Special Purpose Vehicles (SPV): Arrosez (Recapital) and Praeo (Glendale), both of which are British Virgin Island SPVs.[286]

Due to the use of SPVs, PAM Jaya, and the Jakarta Regional Government who awarded the Cooperation Agreement to TPJ (later Aetra) were unable to find the link between TPJ and its ultimate owners. Only after the Jakarta Regional Government threatened to block the transfer of shares, was legal opinion from the buyer's lawyers presented, certifying the link of ownership from Aquatico to TPJ. It is not known if the Jakarta Regional Government was able to obtain all true and certified copies of the company's deeds, including the two British Virgin Island SPVs, Arrosez and Praeo, in addition to legal opinion. Aetra's 2009 annual report does not contain any reference to the two British Virgin Island SPVs above.[287]

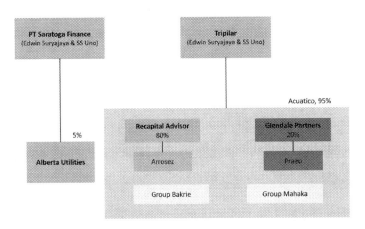

Figure 1.1 Aetra's ownership structure (Ardhianie, 2006)[288]

---

285 PT Aetra, <www.aetra.co.id/index.php/id_id/profilPerusahaan/page?id=pemegang-saham> accessed 16 May 2016
286 AS Sawitri, 'Committee questions Acuatico's suitability as tap water operator', *The Jakarta Post* (Jakarta, 20 November 2006) <http://x.crpg.info/1YpdVwj> accessed 13 May 2016; AS Sawitri, 'Regulatory body casts doubt on takeover bid', *The Jakarta Post* (Jakarta, 14 December 2006)
287 PT Aetra Air Jakarta, *Laporan Tahunan PT Aetra Air Jakarta Tahun 2009* (2009)
288 N Ardhianie, *Kontroversi Penjualan PT Thames Pam Jaya (TPJ)* (Amrta Institute for Water Literacy, 2006)

48 *Introduction*

TPJ later changed its name to Aetra and issued several types of bonds in the capital market, to be matured, respectively, in 2011, 2013 and 2015.[289] Due to this bond issue, Aetra is bound to comply with Indonesian capital market regulations. The participation of Aetra in the capital market is supposed to be able to transform its corporate governance structure and enables more transparency compared to other utilities which are not bound by capital market rules.

1.7.2.4 Palyja

Palyja is incorporated under the Corporation Law. Fifty-one per cent of Palyja's share is owned by Suez Environnement. Another 30 per cent is owned by Astratel Nusantara, an arm of the Indonesian-based Astra group which concentrates on infrastructure business, while the other 19 per cent is owned by Citigroup financial.[290] During an interview, the author was informed that Palyja does not use any intermediaries in its shareholdings with Suez Environnement.[291]

1.7.3 Is the Jakarta Water Cooperation Agreement a concession (konsesi)?

The framework for the Jakarta Cooperation Agreement is different from the national framework. The agreement was entered into in 1998 during the 'New Order' regime and persists until now. In 2015 a local Jakarta court granted a class action lawsuit to annul the Cooperation Contract.[292]

However, this does not automatically invalidate the contract, since a final decision must go through several stages of appeals, cassation and *peninjauan kembali* (review by the Supreme Court) and, possibly, international arbitration. This may take years to complete and, in the meantime, the contract remains valid. It is thus relevant to discuss whether the Cooperation Agreement can be considered as some form of concession – or in other words, an administrative licence.

For some authors, a *concession* [the italicised word is to denote the term in its legal[293] sense] is a combination of licences, permits and dispensations followed

---

289 PT Aetra, 'Obligasi' (2008) <www.aetra.co.id/index.php/id_id/hubunganInvestor/page?id=penjualan-obligasi> accessed 13 May 2016

290 PT PAM Lyonnaise Jaya, *2009 Annual Report* (2009)

291 Personal communication, *Field Interview with Palyja, Jakarta, 10 January 2011*

292 C Elyda, 'Court decision ends privatization of water in Jakarta' <www.thejakartapost.com/news/2015/03/24/court-decision-ends-privatization-water-jakarta.html> accessed 15 July 2015

293 Concession, the World Bank said, 'gives a private operator responsibility not only for the operation and maintenance of assets but also for financing and managing investment. Asset ownership typically rests with the government from a legal perspective, however, and rights to all the assets, including those created by the operator, typically revert to the government when the arrangement ends – often after 25 or 30 years.' See Public-Private Infrastructure Advisory Facility, *Approaches to private participation in water services: a toolkit* (International Bank for Reconstruction and Development and the World Bank 2006) p.10

by a set limited 'governmental authority' to the concessionaire.[294] Earlier Indonesian administrative law writers such as Prajudi had already warned that *concession* is vulnerable to legal abuse.[295] Prajudi gave examples where concessionaires could be given governmental authority, which might even enable them to relocate villages [presumably depending on the terms of the *concession*], including, to operate an airstrip, form an internal security unit and develop networked infrastructure such as roads, electricity and telephone lines.[296] This, Prajudi said, could eventually cause socio-political problems. As such, *concession* contracts require a thorough due diligence and investigation toward the company's bona fides, not only in terms of its financial, but also political and moral reputation.[297]

Syarifudin[298] considers that the undertaking delegated to the private sector in *concession* contracts is essentially a governmental duty. One of the consequences of a *concession* contract is, therefore, that the concessionaire could be considered as a public official acting on governmental duties.[299] However, contemporary author Simatupang is of the opinion that the Jakarta Cooperation Agreement is not a 'decision' reviewable by the Administrative Court.[300]

There is another type of contract entered into by the government with the private sector which is not considered to be a form of *concession*, as it is not perceived to be exercising a governmental function. These are the ordinary types of contracts entered into by authorities in the course of their daily functions. Hadjon[301] et al. stated that governmental authority as a legal person may enter into agreements with other legal persons or natural persons, be that in the form of sale and purchase, lease agreement, work services or it can even bequeath its property. These types of contracts are not subject to public law, although the mechanism in which they are entered into may be constrained by public law regulating the use of state budget or assets.[302] Although such contracts can be preceded by administrative decision, the Law on Administrative Courts stipulates that such an agreement (and the initial decision to contract-out) does not fall under its jurisdiction.[303]

Meanwhile, Simatupang is of the opinion that despite the delegation of powers from the government to the private sector in Jakarta (for example,

---

294 P Atmosudirdjo, *Hukum administrasi negara* (Ghalia Indonesia 1981) pp.98–99. See also Y S Pudyatmoko, *Perizinan: Problem dan Upaya Pembenahan* (Grasindo 2009) quoting Prajudi, p.10
295 Atmosudirdjo, *Hukum administrasi negara* (Ghalia Indonesia 1981) pp.98–99
296 ibid pp.98–99
297 ibid p.98
298 Syafrudin, 'Perizinan Untuk Berbagai Kegiatan', unpublished paper, as quoted by Pudyatmoko in Pudyatmoko, *Perizinan: Problem dan Upaya Pembenahan* (Grasindo 2009)
299 S F Marbun, *Peradilan administrasi negara dan upaya administratif di Indonesia* (UII Press 2003) p.60
300 D P Simatupang, *Jawaban Tentang Konsesi* (email correspondence 2011)
301 P M Hadjon and others, *Pengantar Hukum Administrasi Indonesia (Introduction to Indonesian Administrative Law)* (Gadjah Mada University Press 1993) pp.166–167
302 Iibid pp.166–167
303 Undang Undang No. 5 Tahun 1986 Tentang Peradilan Tata Usaha Negara Article 2.b. This article precludes 'civil acts' but the elucidation refers to ordinary sale and purchase agreements containing no delegation of public services

50 *Introduction*

the power to disconnect from the network), the contract remains an ordinary private contract not reviewable by the Administrative Court and the decision made by the concessionaire remains a private decision.[304]

The categorisation of types of contracts will have implications for transparency. If a contract is considered a *concession* (in the 'legal' sense of the term), doctrinally, the contract is then a form of licence and the concessionaire is in exercise of a public function and can even be considered as a public official whose decision – by way of delegation from the government – is regarded as an administrative decision. By implication, such a contract will be considered a public document and should, therefore, be disclosed to the public. If, on the other hand, the contract is regarded as an ordinary contract entered into by the government in the course of its daily function, it falls entirely under private law and not under the competence of the Administrative Court. The rules on public procurement carry no effect as to the form of the contract. Both concession contracts and ordinary contracts can be generated through public procurement.

Is the Jakarta water cooperation agreement between PAM Jaya and Palyja and between PAM Jaya and Aetra a *concession* contract or an ordinary private contract? Although the agreement has been referred to in the literature[305] and the media as the 'Jakarta Concession', the official title of the agreement between PAM Jaya and Palyja/Aetra is actually the 'Cooperation Agreement' (*Perjanjian Kerja Sama*). This is because the term used in the PAM Jaya statute[306] which regulates and grants capacity to its directors to engage with third parties is through the mechanism of a 'Cooperation Agreement'.

The content of the 'Cooperation Agreement', however, enabled Palyja and Aetra to enter into legal relationships with the customer 'acting both in its own right and for and on behalf of [PAM Jaya]',[307] and required that such customer contracts be adjusted in accordance with the Cooperation Agreement and allowed the disconnection of the flow of water to customers on behalf of PAM Jaya,[308] including acting in emergency situations[309] which may entail

---

304 Simatupang, *Jawaban Tentang Konsesi* (email correspondence 2011). However, in several cases involving fines imposed by the State Electricity Company to its customers, the Supreme Court ruled that despite the fact that the contracts signed between the company and its customers are standard private contracts, the imposition of fines is subject to the court's jurisdiction as the power to impose fines has its source in Government Regulations. See A Bedner, *Administrative courts in Indonesia: a socio-legal study* (Martinus Nijhoff Publishers 2001) p.69

305 For example, in Braadbaart, 'Privatizing water. The Jakarta concession and the limits of contract' in P Boomgaard (ed.), *A World of Water: Rain, Rivers and Seas in Southeast Asian Histories* (KITLV Press 2007) p.297; also O Jensen, 'Troubled partnerships: problems and coping strategies in Jakarta's water concessions' (4th Conference on Applied Infrastructure Research), even in the regulator's whitebook: A Lanti and others, *The first ten years of implementation of the Jakarta Water Supply 25-Year Concession Agreement (1998–2008)* (Jakarta Water Supply Regulatory Body (JWSRB) 2009); also Lanti, 'A regulatory approach to the Jakarta Water Supply concession contracts' 22 International Journal of Water Resources Development 255

306 Peraturan Daerah Khusus Ibukota Jakarta No. 13 Tahun 1992 Tentang Perusahaan Daerah Air Minum Daerah Khusus Ibukota Jakarta (PAM Jaya) Article 45

307 Cooperation Agreement Between PAM Jaya and The Concessionaire, 2001 Clause 19.8

308 ibid Clause 28.5.c

309 ibid Clause 36.2

disruption of water services. Given such powers provided to the private providers, the argument that the contracts between PAM Jaya and Palyja and Aetra are a *concession* by nature is appealing.[310]

Success of a *concession* depends on institutional capacity, especially a well-developed body of jurisprudence on *concession* problems and the role of the administrative court in performing legal evaluation to the concession project[311] and in protecting and defending the public interest. What is absent in Indonesia is a well-developed jurisprudence on *concession* (and on other administrative law contracts!) and the limited role of the administrative court which, unlike the French Conseil d'État, cannot function as 'quasi-regulator' or 'super-regulator'.[312] The Conseil d'État can perform regulatory functions such as resolving consumer contracts or even modifying contractual terms[313] but Indonesian Administrative Courts are constrained from doing so.[314] If a claim is proven, the judgment can only contain one of the following obligations: 'rescission of the litigated administrative decision, the issuance of an administrative decision in case of a constructive refusal, or the rescission of the litigated decision and the issuance of a new decision.'[315] Even the original administrative decision will never be 'quashed' by the Indonesian Court.[316] What the Court does is simply obligate the public official to revoke, renew, adjust or issue a new administrative decision.

Unlike the ideal *concessions*,[317] the delegation of public service functions in the Jakarta Water Supply Cooperation Agreement contract is not enabled

---

310 Management of public services under French Law can be carried out through rentals (*l'affermage*), public management contracts (*la gérance*), direct state control (*la régie*), or *concession*. D Hurstel and M A Pecquet-Carpenter, 'Public interest and private management: incompatible partners?' in S Cotter and D Campbell (eds), *Comparative law yearbook of international business 1995* (Kluwer Law Intl. 1995). According to Llorens, concession under French law contains five elements: the purpose of the public service covered under the contract; the delegation of the public service to a co-contracting party; the means of remuneration of the concession holder; the responsibility of initial investment costs; and the duration of the contract. See Francois Llorens, *The current definition of Public Service Concession in internal law*, Strasbourg Law School, as quoted by Hurstel and Pecquet-Carpenter above
311 ibid
312 J Stern, 'The relationship between regulation and contracts in infrastructure industries', CCRP Working Paper No: 1 <www.city.ac.uk/__data/assets/pdf_file/0014/81032/stern_relationship_between_regulation_and_contract.pdf> accessed 13 May 2016
313 ibid
314 A case can either be rejected, proven, dismissed or declared as lapsed. See Undang Undang No. 5 Tahun 1986 Tentang Peradilan Tata Usaha Negara Article 97.7 and Bedner, *Administrative courts in Indonesia: a socio-legal study* (Martinus Nijhoff Publishers 2001) p.128
315 Bedner, *Administrative courts in Indonesia: a socio-legal study* (Martinus Nijhoff Publishers 2001) section 19, p.128. This is based on Undang Undang No. 5 Tahun 1986 Tentang Peradilan Tata Usaha Negara Article 97.9
316 Bedner, *Administrative courts in Indonesia: a socio-legal study* (Martinus Nijhoff Publishers 2001) p.128
317 See report by Cour des Comptes, 1997, 'La gestion des services publics locaux d'eau et d'assainissement', *Paris, Les Editions du Journal Officiel*, January, as cited by J C Elnaboulsi, 'Organization, management and delegation in the French water industry' 72 Annals of Public and Cooperative Economics 507. Elnabousi continued: 'The lack of transparency is identified as a major problem by the report. The move to delegation was rarely properly evaluated. Contracts are ambiguous. Sub-contracting goes to sister companies in the same group without competition, and procedures are exempted from procurement rules. As a result, says the report, "The lack of supervision and control of delegated public services, aggravated by the lack of transparency of this form of management, has led to abuses"'.

through strong oversight by the Administrative Court. In fact, the Cooperation Agreement contains a clause which refers any dispute between PAM Jaya and the concessionaires to international arbitration. This dispute settlement clause – ideally – cannot prevent an ordinary citizen from filing a suit before the Administrative Court against any decision made by the concessionaires or PAM Jaya but, to a certain extent, does limit the state's control and oversight of the delegation of its public service.[318] Finally, the use of confidentiality provisions on the Cooperation Agreement which covers both the contractual documents itself and any regulatory information generated therefrom, appears to contradict the original concept of a concession, which is to advance public interest by the use of 'private' hands.

Hence, although the Jakarta Cooperation Agreement contains the element of public service delegation from PAM Jaya to the concessionaires, the contract design departs from the original idea and intention of a *concession*. Instead of overarching state control, public interest oversight is limited by the use of confidentiality provisions and referral to international arbitration bodies. The drafters of the contract also fail to calculate Indonesia's Administrative Court's lack of institutional capacity in adjudicating such contracts.

---

318 In order to succeed, concessions and other modes of delegation of public service to the private sector require strong state presence, enabled by the legal and contractual framework. See Elnabousi, ibid. International arbitration clause on Jakarta's Water Supply Cooperation Contract effectively renders Jakarta's regional government toothless. With them being unable to make worthy threats, ex post opportunism may flourish.

2 Policy in involving the private sector

Since England fully divested its water utilities through a parliamentary Act, the process by which the public sector is initially divested is not relevant for this book and has been discussed elsewhere. With full 'privatisation' such as in England, any further involvement of the private sector becomes a business-to-business arrangement, between a private water utility and another private provider, subject only to some arm's length rules from the regulator, which will be discussed later.

Conversely, in Indonesia and Victoria – and many other countries – a range of public–private involvement is taking place. In these instances the question of procurement and contracting between business and government and the extent of PSP becomes relevant.

The Independent Expert on the Human Right to Water and Sanitation, in her 2010 report, highlighted the need to have a 'democratic, participatory and transparent process' in the decision to delegate water services.[1] She added that one of the main prerequisites of genuine participation would be the 'disclosure of adequate and sufficient information and actual access to information, referring in particular to the instruments that delegate service provision'.[2] This chapter will compare Victoria and Indonesia in terms of the transparency in involving the private sector.

2.1 The decision to delegate

In Victoria, the questions of ownership and the regulatory model for water utility in Commonwealth Australia are reserved for the state.[3] The status of Victorian water services as 'publicly owned' is entrenched in Victoria's State Constitution since an amendment was introduced in 2003.[4] Article 97 of the Victoria Constitution states: 'If at any time on or after the commencement of

---

1 de-Albuquerque, *Report of the independent expert on the issue of human rights obligations related to access to safe drinking water and sanitation, A/HRC/15/31* (2010)
2 ibid
3 An Act to constitute the Commonwealth of Australia, Article 100
4 Constitution (Water Authorities) Act 2003 Act No. 37 of 2003

section 5 of the Constitution (Water Authorities) Act 2003 a public authority has responsibility for ensuring the delivery of a water service, that or another public authority must continue to have that responsibility' and that it must 'be accountable to a responsible Minister of the Crown for ensuring the delivery of that service'.[5] This provision can only be modified when the special majority requirement is fulfilled which requires the approval of approximately three-fifths of parliament members.[6]

The Act clarifies that a 'Public Authority' can mean a statutory authority, a council, a company whose shares are held by or on behalf of the state or an agency head.[7] The utilities can thus be in the form of a statutory corporation or an ordinary company established under the Corporations Act.

Within the public ownership spectrum, there are still debates as to the most efficient form of entities, as each form entails its own costs and benefits.[8] If utilities are in the form of a statutory corporation, the Parliament can have more influence on the corporate governance including, for example, in determining the composition of the Board of Directors and how they should be appointed. This is not the case with respect to publicly owned companies established under the Corporations Act.

A second disadvantage of the Corporations Act is the executive's relative lack of influence in providing direction to the company. The executive has the power to issue direction to utilities but this process is perceived to be less transparent compared to what happens in a statutory corporation.[9]

The other disadvantage lies in the difficulties of reconciling commercial with non-commercial objectives.[10] In Victoria, this is currently balanced through the SOO and the WIRO, but both instruments have been perceived as inadequate as far as protecting vulnerable groups and the environment are concerned because the duties are imposed on regulators and not directly upon utilities.[11]

In 2012, the Water Amendment Act transformed the Three Retailers from State Owned Enterprise under the Corporations Act into Statutory Corporations under the Water Act 1989.[12]

Having said that public ownership is entrenched, the Constitution never prohibits PSP. The Constitution does not prohibit arrangements with another body, including an independent contractor, for the provision of water services

---

5 Constitution Act 1975, No. 8750 of 1975, Version No. 196 s.97(1)(2)
6 ibid s.18(2)(h)
7 ibid s.96(a)–(d)
8 Victorian Competition and Efficiency Commission, *Water Ways: Inquiry into Reform of the Metropolitan Retail Water Sector, Final Report February 2008* (2008) p.163
9 ibid
10 Some jurisdictions, such as England, provide a non profit company limited by guarantee model of corporation. This has been used for Yorkshire Water. However, such a model requires full divestiture which is not compatible with the current constitution.
11 Victorian Competition and Efficiency Commission, *Water Ways: Inquiry into Reform of the Metropolitan Retail Water Sector, Final Report February 2008* (2008) p.164
12 Water Amendment (Governance and Other Reforms) Act 2012 No. 17 of 2012 (n 128)

so long as the public authority retains the responsibility and remains accountable to the Minister.[13] Meanwhile, restructuring of water services is allowed as long as they remain accountable to the Minister.[14]

The Victorian Constitution provides no clarity as to the degree of PSP allowed by it under section 97 (3).[15] In cases of affermage or concession, for example, public authorities retain ownership of the assets and remain accountable to ministers, however, as is the case with Jakarta, the private sector will have a considerable degree of control over the services whereas, on the other hand, the state's powers in regulating the sector diminishes due to the contractual nature of the relationship.

In the Australian Commonwealth, the source of power to contract government services can come directly from executive's prerogative, statutory authority or through the common law.[16] The power to contract government services through the executive's prerogative is deemed to be vested in the Commonwealth's Constitution.[17] Alternatively, a statute can also confer to the executive that it has the power to enter into a contract with private parties. When this is the case, the statute may provide limitation to government on the subject on which they can contract with the private sector. Finally, the power to contract can come from the common law. In this case, the government is perceived as an embodiment of the Crown. The Crown, like an ordinary legal person, is deemed to have the ability to enter into a contract with another party.[18]

According to Seddon, for the Commonwealth government, its power to contract is limited by constitutional provisions and several legislations. However, that is not the case for states such as Victoria. In Victoria and the other states, the source of power to contract stems mainly from the prerogative rights.[19] Therefore, as Seddon concludes, for state governments, there is nothing that prevents them from entering into contracts with private parties.[20] It also follows that they can contract out any kind of services they deem appropriate.

In Indonesia, when the Cooperation Agreement was entered into in 1997, Indonesia was a centralistic state and all strategic decisions pertaining to regional matters – that includes water services in Jakarta and elsewhere – were determined by the central government. After Soeharto's downfall, the decentralisation programme started. The central government was only left responsible for dealing with matters including: defence, monetary policies, diplomacy, the judiciary and matters concerning the recognition of religion.[21] Water services regulation is included as a part of governmental function

---

13 Constitution Act 1975, No. 8750 of 1975, Version No. 196 s.97(4). See para (3)
14 ibid s.97(4)
15 ibid s.97(3)
16 N Seddon, *Government contracts: federal, state and local* (4th edn, Federation Press 2009) pp.55–86
17 ibid
18 ibid
19 ibid p.77
20 ibid
21 Indonesia, 'Undang Undang No.32 Tahun 2004 Tentang Pemerintahan Daerah'

decentralised to the regions. The regions then have full control in deciding the question of ownership and the regulatory models they wish to apply, subject to constraints provided by national legislation.

That said, central government's policies and regulations still influence (or to some extent even constrain) the regional governments' powers in determining ownership and regulatory models for water utilities. Except for regional by-laws, most legal products applicable for water utilities are regulations enacted by the central government. It is a commonplace that inconsistencies between central and local regulations are found.

The decisions of the Indonesian Constitutional Court also shape policy making in this area. Indonesia had a comprehensive Water Resources Legislation, Law No.7 Year 2004, and was judicially reviewed several times, the first in 2005 in which the court declared the law 'conditionally constitutional'[22] and finally in 2015, in which the law was finally invalidated in its entirety by the court. Irrigation Law 11 Year 1974 was reinstated by the court in order to fill the 'legal vacuum'. However, since the irrigation law consists of only 17 Articles and none of the provisions regulate anything to do with drinking water or sanitation, the problem with the legal vacuum remains unresolved.

With respect to the private sector's involvement in the water sector, the court in its 2015 decision, prescribed the so-called '6 principles' in water resources management[23]:

- The water commercialization shall not impede, override, and/or abolish the right of the people to the land, water and the natural riches contained therein. They shall be controlled by the State and exploited to the greatest benefit of the people;
- The state shall fulfill the people's right to water since the access to water is a human right. Article 28 I (4) Constitution 1945 stipulates that 'Protecting, advancing, upholding and fulfilling the human rights are the responsibility of the state, especially the government';
- Environmental sustainability is a part of human rights; therefore, Article 28H (1) Constitution 1945 states 'Every person shall have the right to live in physical and spiritual prosperity, to have a home and to enjoy a good and healthy environment, and shall have the right to obtain medical care';
- Based on Article 33 (3) Constitution 1945, water, which is an important sector of production that affects the lives of the people shall be under the powers of the State, and shall be used to the greatest benefit of the people. Therefore, the supervision and the control by the state regarding water is absolute;

---

22 See *Judicial Review of Law Number 7 Year 2004 regarding Water Resources, Judgment of 13 July 2005, No. 058-059-060-063/PUUII/2004* (Constitutional Court of the Republic of Indonesia)
23 *Putusan Mahkamah Konstitusi Nomor 85/PUU-XI/2013 Tentang Pengujuan Undang Undang Nomor 7 Tahun 2004 Tentang Sumber Daya Air* (n 91)

- Another form of control by the state due to the importance of water that affects the lives of the people, is prioritizing permits for water commercialization to the State Owned Enterprise (BUMN) or Region-Owned Enterprise (BUMD);
- In the event all the restrictions above have been fulfilled and there is an availability of water, the Government may grant permits to private enterprises to commercialize water based on strict requirements.

These prescriptions do not in any way provide clarity as to how the private sector can participate in the water sector, or even, more specifically, in the drinking and sewerage sectors. The court made no mention of private sector projects that have been taking place and are ongoing. What can be concluded from the above prescription is simply that state-owned enterprises are given the priority to manage water resources and that PSP is only possible after the requirements above are met. How the requirements themselves can be enumerated is the subject of an ongoing debate, the court provides no clue on how to implement its prescription.

A draft government regulation[24] (a secondary legislation) is currently being debated among stakeholders, but with no solid legal basis on the provisions of a primary legislation which specifically mandate water supply and sanitation, it is difficult to suggest that this effort will be fruitful. Given the circumstances, it might be a long time before a new water law containing a model for Indonesian water resources (and services) governance can be developed and enacted.

What about contracting in water services? The court makes no mention about contracting. However, state control is actually at the core of the debate and it is possible that state control can be diminished by contract. The draft government regulations which are in circulation suggest that the private sector's involvement be confined only to the investment and production unit, distribution unit (with a build-operate-transfer scheme) and investment and operation of technology (through performance-based contracts). This leaves only the services unit, which deals with direct connections to customers, which cannot be 'privatised' under the draft regulation.

2.2 Procurements

When the Cooperation Agreement was signed in 1997 in Jakarta, it was not subjected to any procurement rule. A simple procurement rule did exist at that time as a part of regulation implementing the state budget,[25] but was circumvented. The decision to procure in Jakarta's water services was made

---

24 Rancangan Peraturan Pemerintah Tentang Sistem Penyediaan Air Minum (versi 29 April).
25 Keputusan Presiden Nomor 11 Tahun 1973 tentang Pedoman pelaksanaan Anggaran Pendapatan dan Belanja Negara tahun 1973/1974 (Presidential Decree No. 11 Year 1973 on the Guidelines of Implementation of the 1973/1974 State Budget). This rule is not specifically dedicated to procurement but merely contains guidelines on how to spend state budget.

58 *Policy in involving the private sector*

unilaterally by the government through lobbies made by multinationals toward Soeharto's son and cronies. The first rule dedicated to public procurement was enacted in 2000 through a Presidential Decree[26] and has, ever since, been amended and reformed, through the help of international financial institutions.

2.2.1 Procurement committees

In Victoria, nothing in the Australian Constitution and prevailing laws can prevent the government from entering into a contract for the provision of water services with third parties, public scrutiny in Victoria relies mostly on ordinary procurement rules.[27] There are some conflict of interest (CoI)[28] disclosure rules under the Victoria Government Purchasing Board Guideline[29] and the Victorian Public Service Code of Conduct but they are made internally to the superiors of the public officials. CoI disclosure on these guidelines is not directed to the public or tender participants.[30]

In Indonesia, CoI is regulated under PR-54 and encompasses both CoI among the members of the procurement unit and the official appointing them[31] and CoI which arises due to the position of a supplier as a planner and supervisor on the same project.[32] As regards CoI between procurement unit and suppliers, PR-54 stipulates that parties involved in procurement shall not hold a double role (for example, on the one hand, being a director at the supplying company and, on the other hand, acting as a member of the procurement committee) or 'affiliation', which may arise out of marriage or familial relation, or be in control of or managing (directly or indirectly) the supplier company or hold a controlling number of shares (defined as more than 50%).[33] There are no provisions on the disclosure of CoI.

2.2.2 Tender processes and expression of interest

Many authorities consider the announcement of tender from the authorities to be the pinnacle of transparency in procurement. For example, the Independent

---

26 Keputusan Presiden No. 18 Tahun 2000 tentang Pengadaan Barang/Jasa Instansi Pemerintah
27 Infrastructure Australia Act 2008 No. 17, 2008. Australian states may issue specific guidelines based on this national guideline Department of Treasury & Finance (Victoria), *National PPP Guidelines, Partnerships Victoria Requirements* (2010)
28 Public Administration Act (Victoria) 2004 No. 108 of 2004 Version No. 024 s.7(1)
29 Government of Victoria (Strategy and Policy Government Services Group Department of Treasury and Finance), *Good practice guidelines, conduct of commercial engagements* (July 2011) Annex A
30 Australian Government, *National Public Private Partnership guidelines, volume 2: practitioners' guide* (2011) Appendix C (Conflict of Interest on Public Officials); Office of Public Employment, *Code of Conduct for the Victorian public sector* (Government of Victoria 1995) sections 34–42
31 Peraturan Presiden No. 54 Tahun 2010 Tentang Pengadaan Barang/Jasa Pemerintah Article 17
32 ibid Article 19(4)
33 ibid Elucidation of PR-54/2010, Article 6(e). A person who becomes a director and/or commissioner, and companies which are involved in the same procurement, are also considered to lead a 'double role'. See para B

Expert on the Human Rights to Water concludes that 'the subsequent process of tendering, bidding and contract negotiation also must be transparent'.[34] Some argued that transparency will trigger competition[35] and that the EC Public Works Directive requires the publication of contract notices in order to guarantee competition.[36]

The Australian National PPP guidelines emphasise transparency in every stage of the project cycle. 'Full disclosure should be the default position of a PPP contract with the private sector.'[37] The national guidelines require probity within the government, and in the relationship between the government and 'any other government stakeholders'.[38] There is no emphasis in managing good relations with end users of the PPP project, who are the public themselves, however, this is much better than the Indonesian procurement framework. Public interest must be assessed at every stage which also covers accountability and transparency, affected individuals and communities, consumer rights, public access, security and privacy.[39] The PPP guidelines recognise government's accountability 'risk' in PPPs and prescribe that the assessment factors should cover the scrutiny by the auditor-general, ministerial accountability to parliament and the availability of administrative law remedies.[40]

In Victoria, according to the National PPP Guidelines, in order to ensure transparency, release of EoI should be advertised publicly or made through a procurement website.[41] This is done through the Tenders Victoria website.[42]

In Indonesia, under PR-54, announcement of procurement through the procuring institution's website, official announcement board and the national procurement portal is obligatory for all modes of procurements: tender, simple tender, direct appointment, public selection and simple selection, the purpose of which is to allow those with corresponding qualifications to apply.[43] Announcements through daily newspapers are allowed for limited tender, but such newspapers must have a wide circulation.

---

34 de-Albuquerque, *Report of the independent expert on the issue of human rights obligations related to access to safe drinking water and sanitation*, A/HRC/15/31 (2010)
35 C Bovis, *EC public procurement: case law and regulation* (Oxford University Press 2006) at p.153
36 Directive 2004/18/EC of the European Parliament and of the Council of 31 March 2004 on the coordination of procedures for the award of public works contracts, public supply contracts and public service contracts O. J. L. 134, 30.4.2004, pp.114–240, in particular see Preamble, para 36
37 Australian Government, *National Public Private Partnership guidelines, volume 2: practitioners' guide* (2011) para 6.5.3 *General Disclosure Principle*
38 ibid para H.7.5 p.133
39 Department of Treasury & Finance (Victoria), *Partnerships Victoria Requirements, Annexure 7, Public Interest* (2009)
40 Australian Government, *National Public Private Partnership guidelines, volume 2: practitioners' guide* (2011) appendix H.7.5, pp.133–134
41 ibid para 4.3
42 Department of Treasury & Finance (Victoria), *National PPP Guidelines, Partnerships Victoria Requirements* (2010) para 13 'Tenders Vic, Victorian Government Tenders System' (*Government of Victoria* 2012) <www.tenders.vic.gov.au> accessed 3 January 2012
43 Peraturan Presiden No. 54 Tahun 2010 Tentang Pengadaan Barang/Jasa Pemerintah Articles 36.3; 37.3; 42.2; 43; 73.1 and 2

2.2.3 Execution of the contract

In Victoria, the guidelines stipulate:[44] 'As a general principle, this requirement for visibility and accountability means that *full disclosure should be the default position for a PPP contract with the private sector*, except for consideration of voluntary disclosure of the following: trade secrets; genuinely confidential business information; and material which, if disclosed, would seriously harm the public interest' (emphasis by author).

From the above paragraph, it would appear that disclosure is intended only after the final stage of the procurement process – after the execution of contract and closing is achieved. The guidelines stress that 'Confidentiality is particularly important during the bid stage where bidders supply confidential and sensitive commercial information'[45] and that the disclosure of cost structures would compromise the competitive bidding process while at the same time acknowledging that transparency 'of the bid process is paramount to give bidders certainty and to meet public procurement probity requirements'.[46]

An innovative approach by the guidelines is the requirement for government to ensure that information on project performance[47] is available for release after the contract is executed. Private parties should acknowledge that disclosure by government by operation of the FoI Act will not amount to a breach of confidentiality.[48]

This requirement must be incorporated in the contract during the drafting period. The guideline contains no clue as to how this is applied in practice. Presumably, this could be made operational through insertion of a waiver clause side-by-side with the standard confidentiality clause, which will apply when disclosure under FoI is made. However, a confidentiality obligation does not only arise from a contract, it can also arise from general common law, in which event the waiver clause would not be able to derogate.

The Wonthaggi Desalination Contract[49] contains a general confidentiality clause which binds all the companies and individuals (the contractor, guarantor, reviewer and auditor, including Melbourne Water but not the state) from

---

44　Government of Victoria, 'National Public Private Partnership guidelines volume 2: practitioners' guide' (2008), p.32

45　ibid 'While government is committed to a policy of openness and transparency, *a strong measure* of confidentiality may be required during the procurement process', Australian Government, *National Public Private Partnership guidelines, volume 2: practitioners' guide* (2011) para 13.4 p.66

46　ibid

47　Accountability for performance is only a part of other sets of accountability features in a democratic government. The other types of accountability are accountability for finances and accountability for fairness. See R D Behn, *Rethinking democratic accountability* (Brookings Institution Press 2001)

48　Australian Government, *National Public Private Partnership guidelines, volume 2: practitioners' guide* (2011) para 6.5.3

49　Article 14.1 of the D&C Direct Deed: 'D&C Contractor, the D&C Guarantor and the Independent Reviewer & Environmental Auditor must keep the contents of this deed and all documents and information made available to it under, or in connection with, or in the course of the performance of, this deed or any other Project Document, confidential and must not disclose the same to any other person without the prior written consent of the other party.' The Minister for Water of the State of Victoria and others, *Victorian Desalination Project D&C Direct Deed* (2009)

Policy in involving the private sector   61

disclosing the contract and any document and information resulting from its activity. Through these general terms, the contract bars the parties from disclosing any of the project information to anyone, including to the government or regulator. However, this general confidentiality clause is limited by several exceptions, which include public disclosure by the state, its ministries or agencies under the Freedom of Information Act 1982 (Vic), the Ombudsman Act 1973 (Vic) or to satisfy the requirements of the Victorian Auditor General or the government policy concerning Partnerships Victoria, for the purpose of parliamentary accountability.[50] However, the D&C contract also bars some of the parties – but not the state –from voluntary disclosure.[51]

No such standard 'FoI Waiver Clause' is available in Indonesia.

2.3 Publication of contracts

In Victoria, on October 2000, the Bracks Labour government issued a transparency policy which includes the requirement to disclose Victorian government contracts to the public domain.[52] Any contract worth more than 100,000 USD in value must disclose its full title and contracts over 10 million USD should be published on the internet in a full and readily accessible format.[53] This internet publication scheme is administered by the Victoria Government Procurement Board (VGPB).

In 2005, the Victorian Department of Treasury and Finance issued directive FRD 12A[54] 'Disclosure of Major Contracts'. The directive refers to Bracks' policy statement[55] and the implementation guidelines.[56] Disclosure requirements are applicable to all 'departments' as defined by section 3 of the Financial Management Act 1994.[57]

---

50 14.2 Exceptions to confidentiality. Clause 14.1 will not apply in the following circumstances: (a) any disclosure required by Law or legally binding Approval. See ibid

51 Article 14.4.c.1 of the D&C Direct Deed: 'Each of Project Co, the D&C Contractor, the D&C Guarantor and the Independent Reviewer & Environmental Auditor must not, and must ensure that its Associates do not, make any public disclosures, announcements or statements in relation to the Project or the State's or the State's Associates' involvement in the Project without the State's prior consent and, if such disclosure, announcement or statement is required under clause 14.2, such consent will not be unreasonably withheld'; ibid

52 S Bracks, *Ensuring Openness and Probity in Victorian Government Contracts, A Policy Statement* (Victorian Government 2010) In the Australian Capital Territory, disclosure of contract is not only a matter of policy but also stipulated in the legislation. See Government Procurement Act 2001 (ACT) Part 3 <www.legislation.act.gov.au/a/2001-28/current/pdf/2001-28.pdf>. See also Freedom of Information Act 1981 (Nsw) s.15A (Disclosure of government contracts with the private sector) <www.legislation.nsw.gov.au/fullhtml/inforce/act+5+1989+cd+0+N#pt.2-sec.15a>

53 Some of the contracts are available on the Victoria Government Contract Publishing System website <www.tenders.vic.gov.au/tenders/contract/view.do?id=9265&returnUrl=%252Fcontract%252Flist.do%253F%2524%257Brequest.queryString%257D> accessed 13 May 2016

54 Department of Treasury & Finance (Victoria), *FRD 12A Disclosure of Major Contracts* (2005)

55 Bracks, *Ensuring Openness and Probity in Victorian Government Contracts, A Policy Statement* (Victorian Government 2010)

56 S Bracks, *Ensuring Openness and Probity in Victorian Government Contracts, Implementation Guidelines* (2010)

57 Financial Management Act 1994 No. 18 of 1994 (Victoria), Version No. 061

Premier Bracks' policy permits limited excision of contractual terms from disclosure, subject to the principles laid down under the Victorian FoI Act and the VCAT's decisions. The policy statement further requires that the scope and grounds of such excision must be provided.[58] There are three reasons for exemptions or excision from disclosure under the policy statement: (1) trade secrets, (2) genuinely confidential business information and (3) material which if disclosed would seriously harm the public interest. Confidential business information is defined as information which is 'likely to expose [a private sector contractor] unreasonably to disadvantage'.[59] When confidentiality is granted, the policy requires that it is time limited up to six months and should be disclosed afterwards.[60]

In a June 2010 report[61] by the Victorian Auditor General it was revealed that government departments appear to be reluctant to disclose the full text of contracts (which is required for contracts worth more than 10 million USD). The audit finds that in three selected departments, only on 12 occasions were contracts worth more than 100,000 USD disclosed. Forty-three of the 144 contracts valued over 10 million USD had not been disclosed and logged on to the Contract Publishing System (CPS) website as required by the policy statement. The Auditor General concluded that the level of non-compliance of publishing contracts worth more than 10 million USD is higher, and that it does 'reflect systemic breakdowns in disclosure and reporting controls that diminish transparency'.[62]

The differential treatment on disclosure based on the value of contracts (those which cost more than 100,000 USD need to be given a title and those worth more than 10 million USD need to be fully disclosed and logged into VGPB's Contract Publishing System) may have triggered 'creative compliance'. On one occasion the Auditor General implied that several contracts on water quantity and quality monitoring by the Department of Environment and Sustainability, jointly worth 11.9 million USD, were split into several parts, presumably in order to avoid the disclosure requirement. DSE subsequently denied the possibility of tender splitting and stated that each of the contracts was awarded through separate tender processes. The Auditor General replied: 'the fact that these contracts were entered into on the same day, for a similar time period and to provide identical services by the same supplier indicates poor procurement practice and results in avoiding the intended level of disclosure'.[63]

---

58 Bracks, *Ensuring Openness and Probity in Victorian Government Contracts, A Policy Statement* (Victorian Government 2010) 41 para 26
59 ibid
60 ibid para 23
61 D D R Pearson, *Managing the requirements for disclosing private sector contracts* (Auditor General of Victoria 2010)
62 ibid p.vii
63 ibid p.xi

Contracts between AquaSure and the Victorian Government for the establishment of Victoria's desalination plant also fall under the scope of this policy. One of the points of controversy with the Desal contract is the obligation to pay for water produced irrespective of whether it is used ('Water Security Payment') and the overall actual cost (per litre) of desalinated water.[64] The figures are important because, according to one author, the actual cost of desalination will increase up to 4.8 billion USD in the 30th year or even more since the pressurisation of water transmission to regions with higher altitude may cause mains to burst.[65] This could eventually add to the cost that consumers have to pay in the coming years.[66]

The contracts were finally published – in bulk – on the VGPB's Contract Publishing System website under the category of 'Building and Construction Machinery and Accessories' but with some items being excised.[67] Forty-five items were excised from the Wonthaggi Desal Contracts;[68] these included calculation of early termination payments for the supply of electricity, annual minimum quantity of electronic tradable renewal energy certificates, details of annual supply of water volume and compensation for relevant intervening events. The detail of the water security payment is blacked out in the version published in CPS[69] and was not revealed in a parliamentary inquiry.[70]

The Victorian Auditor General acknowledged that excisions on the Wonthaggi Desal Contracts were made after consultation with the Secretary of the DSE (now the Department of Environment, Land, Water and Planning

---

64 M Fyfe, 'Voters out of loop in ALP's Victoria: a state of secrecy' *The Age* <www.theage.com.au/national/voters-out-of-loop-in-alps-victoria-a-state-of-secrecy-20101009-16d3b.html> accessed 15 November 2010

65 K Davidson, 'Water plans drift behind a veil of secrecy' <www.smh.com.au/opinion/politics/water-plans-drift-behind-a-veil-of-secrecy-20100411-s0os.html> accessed 14 November 2010

66 'He concluded that each year, on average, every Melbourne water ratepayer would pay $345. "John Brumby has in effect signed up every household and business in Melbourne to a debt which averages about $9560".' R Millar and B Schneiders, 'Desal plant a $570m-a-year drain', *The Age* <www.theage.com.au/victoria/desal-plant-a-570mayear-drain-20100916-15enu.html> accessed 20 September 2011

67 DTF, 'Victorian Desalination Project' (Contract Publishing System, Department of Treasury and Finance, Victoria) <www.old.tenders.vic.gov.au/domino/Web_Notes/eTenders/etdrPublishing.nsf/ContractsByCategory/6CC923E330DE8F5CCA25767A00109C1E?OpenDocument#Downloads> accessed November 10, 2010

68 Pearson, *Managing the Requirements for Disclosing Private Sector Contracts* (2010)

69 The Minister for Water of the State of Victoria and others, *Project Deed Schedule 1* (2009)

70 Standing Committee on Finance and Public Administration, *Inquiry into the business case for water infrastructure ('Transcript), Hearing with Chloe Munro, Chairman of AquaSure Pty Ltd, 17 June 2010* (Victoria Parliament 2010). The dialogue runs as follows: 'The CHAIR – I guess to put the question directly: will the water usage payment essentially be the same dollar value, irrespective of the actual volume of water ordered? Ms MUNRO – I understand the question; however, I am not at liberty to answer that. Mr BARBER – Have a look at that table down the bottom, Chair. The CHAIR – The table down the bottom, Mr Barber, would be much more helpful if it had numbers on it'. Chloe Munro is AquaSure's Pty Ltd's chairman and is bound by the confidentiality provision. The State Government, however, is not bound by such provision.

64 *Policy in involving the private sector*

or 'DELWP') and approved by the Minister of Water.[71] Out of 65 excision proposals, 45 were approved. However, the parts that are excised are not summarised on the VGPB's Contract Publishing System website and the reason for excision is also absent.

DSE's failure to provide reasons for excision appeared to be in contravention of Bracks' policy, which requires that excisions are made on a case-by-case basis, in accordance with the principles of the 1982 Freedom of Information Act and are enforced with a time limit. DSE has no protocol to provide for the future release of information.[72] Responding to the Auditor General's query on why excisions are not supplemented by explanations, DSE argued that it had followed all disclosure requirements on Partnership Victoria and that no such requirements exist on FRD12A.[73] It also stated that it would provide additional explanation for such excision – 'as required'[74] – in its upcoming (2010) annual report. However, in its 2010 annual report, the DSE still did not provide justifications for excisions.[75] It said only that it would disclose the items excised 'if and when the circumstances giving rise to the exemption are no longer present'.[76] When and how these circumstances arise was not explained and, as such, there was no exact date given as to when the excised items would be published.

Arguably DSE's argument could be technically correct since FRD12A – although it refers to Bracks' Policy Statement which requires excisions to be justified[77] – does not explicitly mandate that government departments need to provide reasons for excision. Nevertheless, it defeats the spirit of Bracks' Policy Statement. This likely occurs due to the reliance of the contract publication requirement on a set of policies, instead of legislations.

In Indonesia, none of the articles in PR-54 regulate the publication of contracts. The law on Public Service[78] and the Law on Freedom of Information,[79]

---

71 Pearson, *Managing the Requirements for Disclosing Private Sector Contracts* (2010), p.14 'The process to excise information also included consultation with the Minister for Water, the Victorian Civil and Administrative Tribunal and the Privacy Commissioner. DSE also sought independent legal advice. The secretary endorsed and the Minister for Water approved 45 excisions deemed commercially sensitive.'
72 ibid p.15
73 See para 5 of DSE letter to Victorian Auditor General, ibid
74 ibid
75 It only provides several paragraphs with the heading 'Disclosure of major contracts note for the Victorian desalination plant' explaining that it 'carried out a comprehensive assessment of the proposed excisions against the above criteria, and obtained all required approvals before releasing the documents publicly in November 2009'. Government of Victoria (Department of Sustainability and Environment), *Annual Report 2010* (2010), p.228
76 ibid Furthermore it states that 'The 45 excisions from disclosure on the basis of current state exemption requirements are to be disclosed in accordance with the state's requirements, if and when the circumstances giving rise to the exemption are no longer present, or those circumstances no longer give a basis for exemption under the Freedom of Information Act 1982 and/ or relevant state guidelines or requirements.'
77 Department of Treasury & Finance (Victoria), *FRD 12A Disclosure of Major Contracts* (2005)
78 Undang Undang No. 25 Tahun 2009 Tentang Pelayanan Publik Article 13(1)(b), (d) and (e)
79 Undang Undang No.14 Tahun 2008 Tentang Keterbukaan Informasi Publik, Article 11.1(e)

which are higher forms of rule than the PR-54, both require that contracts are published by government agencies. However, PR-54 does not refer to the requirement of contract publication under both laws, although it was enacted after both laws were approved by the House of Representatives. The only law that was referred to by PR-54 is the law on state budget 1/2004.

The Independent Expert in its report noted that it is crucial that 'The terms of reference and the final contract should be made available for public scrutiny and commenting. Commercial confidentiality must not jeopardize the transparency requirements provided for under the human rights framework'.[80] It is a serious omission that PR-54 did not refer to the Freedom of Information and Public Service Law, especially with respect to the requirement to publish contracts. Procurement should serve the public service value of transparency and not simply be a method by which the government may obtain value-for-money in its purchasings. In fact, the national model of procurement documents which were developed with the help of the Asian Development Bank imposes confidentiality requirements on the providers.

According to the standard model procurement contract, Clause 3.2:[81]

> The Contractor, Subcontractor (if any) and Personnel without prior written approval from the CO, shall be forbidden during the Contract Period and for a certain period of time afterward as determined in the SCC, to:(a) use the Contract Document or any other document/information produced by the contractor work for purposes other than for the execution of this Contract; (b) disclose the above said documents/information to any third party.

In the above standard clause, disclosure by the provider would be prohibited unless approved by the commitment-making official (CO), who is the principal or owner/user of the project.[82]

Under the national model of procurement, the provider's employees and personnel are also required to exercise confidentiality. Clause 4.4 reads: 'With reference to Clause 3.2 GCC, all personnel are required to maintain confidentiality regarding their work. If required by the CO, the personnel may at any time be required to take an oath of confidentiality.'[83]

The national model of procurement does not impose corresponding obligations of confidentiality on the authorities.[84] This provides latitude of discretion

---

80 de-Albuquerque, *Report of the independent expert on the issue of human rights obligations related to access to safe drinking water and sanitation, A/HRC/15/31* (2010)
81 Center for Public Procurement Policy Development, *Model National Procurement Document* (2007) Procurement of Works with Prequalification, General Conditions of Contract, clause 3.2. Similar terms apply to other types of procurement: services, consultancies and goods. This confidentiality may be extended after the contract period has ended. See 'Special Conditions of Contract' on each model
82 ibid Procurement of Works with Prequalification, General Conditions of Contract, clause 1.22
83 ibid Procurement of Works with Prequalification, General Conditions of Contract, clause 4.4
84 ibid

for the authorities to disclose information. However, other contracting parties are bound to the confidentiality provision. In several instances, it is the public authority and not the provider who objects to the disclosure of contracts and other information.

Confidentiality at the prequalification stage and during the bidding process and evaluation has a purpose to stimulate competition among the tenderers. After the winner has been determined, however, there is no compelling justification to prevent information about the winning bid, including its contractual arrangements, from being disclosed.

Finally, the existence of a confidentiality clause in the contract shall not prevent the operation of other laws, such as the freedom of information and public service laws, which mandate the disclosure of contracts between a public body and a third party. The Victorian procurement policy allows confidentiality clauses to be used, but requires such clauses to be complemented with another clause that will exempt the applicability of the confidentiality provision in the event of a Freedom of Information request. The purpose of this design is to avoid the authority being held liable in disclosing information supplied by the provider.

Indeed, the obligation of confidentiality on the existing Model of National Procurement Document in Indonesia is directed solely toward the provider and not the authorities. This is something of an improvement when compared to previous contracts which put the confidence obligation equally between providers and the authorities, such as Jakarta's Cooperation Agreement. But there can be occasions where such providers are also a public body under the Indonesian Freedom of Information Law which subjects them to some transparency rules, including disclosure of contracts and responding to an FoI request, as they are entities entrusted with governmental functions. Without an exemption clause on their contract, they are bound to a duty of confidentiality toward the authorities and can be held liable for any breach.

3 The regulator, licences and information flow

This chapter will discuss three important topics in regulatory governance: (1) the regulator and check and balances mechanism that applies to them; (2) the governance of licences; and (3) information flow between regulated entities, the regulator and the public.

3.1 The regulator's internal governance

3.1.1 Selection and removal of economic regulators

In Victoria, the Essential Services Commission consists of a Chairperson and several full-time and part-time additional Commissioners, the number of which is determined by the Minister.[1] Additional members may be appointed on a full-time or part-time basis or only for a specific period, or a specific inquiry or determination. The Chairperson[2] and additional members[3] of the Commission are appointed by the Governor in council. Requirement for and qualifications of the members of the Commission are regulated in the ESC Act. Both Chairperson and additional members of the Commission should have qualifications – either because of their knowledge or experiences – in one or more of these fields: industry, commerce, economics, law or public administration.[4]

The Governor may suspend the Commissioners from office, at which event the Minister must provide a full statement elaborating the grounds of such suspension to the House.[5] Suspensions may only escalate into removal if the House in Parliament approves the removal through a resolution. Pursuant to such resolution, the Governor must remove the Commissioner. However, if within 42 days after the Minister has provided such a statement to the House, the House fails to produce a resolution, the Governor must reinstate the Commissioner to office.[6]

---

1 Essential Services Commission Act 2001 No. 62 of 2001, s.17
2 ibid s.18(1)
3 ibid s.21(1)
4 ibid s.18, s.21
5 ibid s.19(4), s.22(5)
6 ibid

68 Regulator, licences and information flow

In England, the regulation of Ofwat's internal governance in the WIA is minimal, presumably in order to allow the regulatory body to be independent, with the focus on the Secretary of State's powers to appoint and remove Ofwat's members and Chairman. The WIA prescribes that Ofwat shall consist of at least a chairman and two other members,[7] appointed by the Secretary of State for a five-year term.[8] The Secretary of State also holds the power to remove the chairman or Ofwat members from their offices on the grounds of 'incapacity' or 'misbehaviour'.[9] In practice, Ofwat's structure consists of a Chairman, a chief executive and a number of executive and non-executive directors.[10]

In the wake of the Nolan Report,[11] all public appointments in the UK are subject to standards[12] imposed by The Commissioner for Public Appointments[13] requiring transparency in appointments, including the setting up of a recruitment website.[14] Ofwat and DEFRA also set up a recruitment website and indicate that candidates may be required to appear before a Parliamentary Select Committee.[15]

Other than the question of appointment and removal of Ofwat members or chairman, Ofwat is free to arrange its own household.[16] The WIA enables Ofwat to appoint staff, subject to the approval of the Minister of Civil Service and applicable rules on civil servants.[17] One of the most significant discretions granted to Ofwat by the WIA in managing its household is its power to regulate its own procedure and to enact a code of practice.[18] These two instruments contain lengthy and detailed regulations with significant implications for Ofwat's internal governance.

Ofwat is accountable to parliament and is statutorily required to present two kinds of reports annually: the first is the 'forward work programme' containing its expenditure plans as well as non-routine projects and the second is the annual report.[19] The WIA also prescribes the minimum content of the

---

7   Water Industry Act 1991 c.56 Schedule 1A para 1(1)
8   ibid Schedule 1A para 3(1)
9   ibid Schedule 1A para 3(2)(a)
10 Ofwat, *Rules of procedure for the Water Services Regulation Authority* (2010)
11 Great Britain Committee on Standards in Public Life, *Standards in public life, First Report of the Committee of Standards in Public Life (Nolan Report)* (1995)
12 The Commissioner for Public Appointment, *Code of Practice for Ministerial Appointments to Public Bodies* (2009)
13 Public Appointments Order in Council 2002, Notice: 1006 (Issue: 56648), 30 July 2002 (as amended)
14 The Commissioner for Public Appointment, *Code of Practice for Ministerial Appointments to Public Bodies* (2009) paras 5.33–5.36 'Publishing Vacancies'
15 ofwatrecruitmentboard.com, 'Background to the appointments' <www.ofwatboardrecruitment.com/sections/about_the_org/background_to_the_appointments> accessed 12 November 2011
16 Consider also, OFWAT's supplementary power to 'do anything which is calculated to facilitate, or is conducive or incidental to, the performance of its functions', including forming advisory bodies. See Water Industry Act 1991 c.56 Schedule 1A para 12
17 ibid Schedule 1A para 5
18 ibid Schedule 1A paras 8 and 9. This should be done by consultation with the Secretary of State, the Welsh Assembly, The Environment Agency, the Consumer Council, undertakers, licensed water suppliers and any other parties which OFWAT 'considers appropriate'. See para 9(3)
19 These are obligatory under ss.192A and 192B. See ibid

annual report.[20] In addition, Ofwat is required by other legislation to create and report its resource account to the Comptroller/Auditor General to the House of Commons.[21] The Secretary of State is required by law to arrange the publication of such reports and in practice such reports, including the Comptroller's certificate, are published by Ofwat on its website.[22]

In Jakarta, the governance structure of Jakarta's water services following the Cooperation Agreement becomes complicated. The JWSRB has no sufficient mandate to regulate and does not have the power to issue penalties or fines to the concessionaire. Its role is limited only to mediating disputes, organising coordination with bureaucratic offices and advising the Jakarta Governor on tariff issues. Final prices are determined by the Jakarta Governor and monitoring and supervision of contracts is done by PAM Jaya. Nevertheless, the Cooperation Agreement suggests that in the future JWSRB should be reinforced through a regional by-law.[23] This move opens up opportunities for JWSRB to gain more regulatory authority.

The organisation of JWSRB is arranged simultaneously by two instruments which often overlap: the Jakarta Governor's Regulation[24] and the Cooperation Agreement of 2001.[25] The provision on selection and removal of economic regulators is contained in Pergub-118. Members are appointed by the Governor and can be removed from their position.[26] The prerequisites of becoming a member of the regulatory body are: an Indonesian national 35–65 years of age, passed the fit and proper test, never been convicted of crime, declared bankrupt or under guardianship, has not been working for the concessionaire within the two years prior to its membership in the regulatory body and who will provide an undertaking that they will not be working for the concessionaires two years after their appointment, and finally, it is preferable that they have specific experience in drinking water provision, either from the technical, legal, financial or customer relations' perspectives, and is known among the professionals.[27] The provision concerning this undertaking is an improvement from the earlier version of the rule which does not regulate the 'revolving door' situation properly.[28] Nevertheless, it is not clear on what would be the result if the 'undertaking' is violated.

---

20 ibid s.192B (2)
21 Government Resources and Accounts Act 2000, 2000 c.20
22 Water Industry Act 1991 c.56 s.192B (5) See OFWAT publication of its annual report and resource account *Annual report and accounts 2010–11 For the period 1 April 2010 to 31 March 2011* (Water Services Regulation Authority (Ofwat), 2011)
23 Cooperation Agreement Between PAM Jaya and The Concessionaire, 2001
24 Peraturan Gubernur DKI Jakarta No. 118 Tahun 2011 Tentang Badan Regulator Pelayanan Air Minum
25 Cooperation Agreement Between PAM Jaya and The Concessionaire, 2001
26 Peraturan Gubernur DKI Jakarta No. 118 Tahun 2011 Tentang Badan Regulator Pelayanan Air Minum Article 12
27 ibid Article 11
28 ibid See Article 9 which puts the prerequisite of 'will not be working for the concessionaire' as conditions of appointment. See also the previous rule Peraturan Gubernur No. 54 Tahun 2005 Tentang Badan Regulator Pelayanan Air Minum

70 *Regulator, licences and information flow*

Pergub-118 stipulates that the selection process will be conducted by the Jakarta investment authority, which may impose additional prerequisites (presumably, as long as it does not contradict what has been stipulated in the Pergub 118).[29] An announcement must be made to the public explaining that a selection is to be commenced together with the details of the task, responsibility, prerequisites of appointment, authority and their rights as a member of the JWSRB.[30] A professional consultant – presumably under contract with the Jakarta investment authority – should be hired to assess the candidates.[31] The Pergub-118 does not stipulate the format and timing of an announcement except that it requires that it should be made before the appointment.

Membership of the regulatory body ceases when a member resigns, is mentally or physically ill for more than three consecutive months, is deceased, his term of office has ended or he violates the laws and regulations.[32] Pergub-118 stipulates that a member of the regulatory body who violates laws and regulations can be temporarily suspended by the Governor[33] for a period of a maximum of six months. Membership of the regulatory body can be reinstated by the Governor if the alleged violation is unproven.[34]

Almost similar to Ofwat, who must present its resource account to the comptroller, the JWSRB is also obligated by Pergub-118 to propose its expenditure plan to the Governor, through PAM Jaya.[35] Interestingly, although the Governor is the party who approves the regulator's expenditure plan, the regulator is accountable and must deliver its expenditure accountability report to PAM Jaya, which actually is also a regulated entity.[36] Futhermore, it is PAM Jaya that is tasked with evaluating the regulator's expenditure report.[37] The role of the Governor is constrained to legalising and providing *acquit de charge* to the report, *after* and based on the evaluation report made by PAM Jaya.[38] This overlap signifies the power game between actors of the concession. Thus, although JWSRB's finance is secured through direct allocation from the escrow account, its budgetary planning is not independent since the 'regulator' is accountable to, and supervised by, the regulatee.

3.1.2 Conflict of interest

In Victoria, there is not much on regulation of CoI, presumably because it involves only state-owned enterprises. As a rule, the Chairperson of ESC

---

29 Peraturan Gubernur DKI Jakarta No. 118 Tahun 2011 Tentang Badan Regulator Pelayanan Air Minum, Article 12
30 ibid Article 13
31 ibid Article 13
32 ibid Article 14
33 ibid Article 14
34 ibid Article 15
35 ibid Article 20(4)
36 ibid Article 22(3)
37 ibid Article 22(3)
38 ibid Article 22(3)

cannot directly or indirectly engage in any other paid employment unless approved by the Governor.[39] This rule, however, is not applicable to the other members of the Commission.

There is an obligation – applicable to all members of the Commission – to disclose existing or foreseeable pecuniary interest[40] to the Minister as soon as a member becomes aware of it. Following such declaration, the Commissioner is barred[41] from taking any part in any matters related to the decision, unless otherwise agreed by the Minister. Failure to comply with the obligation to declare pecuniary interest to the Minister does not affect the validity of any decision taken by the Commission.

In England, rules on CoI are embodied in Ofwat's procedure[42] which is enabled through the WIA.[43] This is quite different from Victoria, above, where the regulator's CoI rules are prescribed through legislation.

Ofwat's rules of Procedure require the disclosure of any CoI.[44] No clear distinction is made between 'existing' or 'foreseeable' CoI.[45] When in doubt if a matter amounts to a CoI, an Ofwat member has the obligation to disclose,[46] in which event the person may either choose to absent himself from any discussion and decision or ask the Chairman how to proceed.[47] The Procedure provides Ofwat's Chairman with the discretion of how to proceed in such circumstances, by deciding that the member should absent himself from any discussion or decision related to his interest, or to allow him to be present but without the right to participate, or to allow him to be present and participate in discussions and decisions but only with respect to statements of facts.[48] If parties affected by a CoI have been consulted and do not raise any objection, the matter may cease to be treated as a CoI.[49]

Definition of a CoI in Ofwat's Procedure encompasses both pecuniary and non-pecuniary interest[50] similar to Victoria's ESC CoI rule.[51] 'Interest' may consist of equity or any other financial interest and any employment, consultancy, directorship or other remunerative agreement with companies and its affiliates which are currently regulated (or may in the future be regulated) by

---

39 Essential Services Commission Act 2001 No. 62 of 2001, s.18
40 Pecuniary interest as a result of supply of goods and services available to members of the public under similar terms and conditions are excluded from this rule, ibid s.27
41 ibid s.27(3)
42 Ofwat, *Rules of procedure for the Water Services Regulation Authority* (2010)
43 Water Industry Act 1991, c.56 Schedule 1A para 7
44 Ofwat, *Rules of Procedure for the Water Services Regulation Authority* (2010) para 19
45 Compare this with the obligation to disclose 'existing or foreseeable pecuniary interest' in Victoria
46 Ofwat, *Rules of Procedure for the Water Services Regulation Authority* (2010) para 20
47 ibid para 22
48 ibid para 24
49 ibid Annex A para 1.5
50 ibid Annex A para 1.4: 'any interest or duty that is held by a Board Member – whether or not financial in nature – that a fair-minded and informed observer, having considered all of the relevant facts, would conclude gave rise to a real possibility of bias in relation to a matter which that Board Member is required to consider or decide'
51 Essential Services Commission Act 2001 No. 62 of 2001, s.27

72 *Regulator, licences and information flow*

Ofwat.[52] When spouses, partners or children of an Ofwat member possess such 'Interest'[53] as defined above, there is an obligation to notify the Chairman[54] who will then prescribe a course of action.

One of Ofwat's good practices on CoI is the maintenance of a Register of Board Members' Disclosable Interests[55] (Register), which is a public document and must be amended from time to time to ensure its accuracy.[56] As the Procedure outlines, the purpose of such Register is to 'ensure transparency in relation to any interests of Board Members – or of their spouses, partners and dependent children – that have or might be perceived as having the potential, to give rise to a conflict of interest'.[57] As such, the information contained in the Register also encompasses existing or past relationships between dependants of Ofwat Members with Ofwat regulated companies.[58]

In regulating a possible 'revolving door', the Procedure requires Board Members to obtain approval from Ofwat's Chairman and DEFRA if – within the period of two years subsequent to their retirement from Ofwat – they wish to accept an appointment from (or those which in the future may be) an Ofwat regulated company, its affiliates or major supplier or contractors.[59]

One of the incentives for the Board Members to comply with the Procedure is the possibility of litigation directed against them personally (and not to Ofwat as an institution) from parties aggrieved by their misconduct. The Procedure hinted that personal criminal and civil liability may be incurred by Ofwat's Chairman or other members, in cases involving fraudulent or negligent statement, breach of confidence or insider trading.[60]

In order to function, such a mechanism may require water companies to be listed in the capital market and for sufficient competition ('for' or 'in' the market or through 'yardstick') to exist. When some degree of competition exists, regulated companies will have adequate interest to pursue litigation against members of the regulatory body for their impartiality. If the companies are not listed in the capital market (such as is the case in Victoria) or if competition is limited or absent (such as is the case in Jakarta, where only two companies are regulated), there may not be adequate economic interest for the regulated

---

52 Ofwat, *Rules of Procedure for the Water Services Regulation Authority* (2010)
53 ibid para 4.3
54 ibid para 4.6
55 This is also practised by other regulatory boards in the UK, see Ofcom's 'Register of disclosable interests – Ofcom Board' (*Ofcom*, 2011) <www.ofcom.org.uk/about/how-ofcom-is-run/ofcom-board-2/members/register-of-disclosable-interests/> accessed 11 May 2011
56 Ofwat, *Rules of Procedure for the Water Services Regulation Authority* (2010) paras 4.7 and 4.8, Annex A
57 ibid para 4.9
58 This could be in the form of company directorship to employment, consultancy activities, equities or financial interest, as well as other remunerative agreements. ibid para 4.12
59 ibid Annex A para. 6. The purpose of this, other than to avoid the suspicion of a revolving door (see para 6.2.a) is also to protect competitors from unjustified exploitation of trade secrets or confidential information to which the said OFWAT Members have had access during the course of their work (see para 6.2.b).
60 ibid Annex G (Code of Conduct) para 13

companies to commence civil or criminal litigation against the members of the regulatory body for their impartiality or negligence.

In Jakarta, CoI is regulated in a Governor's Regulation (Pergub-118). Except for Article 11 which provides that one of the prerequisites for appointment is that the person 'has not been working for the concessionaire within two years prior to their appointment in the regulatory body' and Article 14.1.d forbidding members of the regulatory body to be formally employed by another institution, there are no other provisions in Pergub-118 on CoI. The prohibition on holding other formal employment might be difficult to enforce and at the same time be ineffective in preventing CoI. As outside appointments might or might not cause CoI, the best mechanism to prevent and avoid it is through disclosure rules, as practised in England. Earlier, this book discussed that Victoria's ESC members are allowed to hold other positions. Since the members of the regulatory body are not government employees, no other public law rules are applicable to them.

3.2 Licence governance

3.2.1 Licence types

In Victoria, Melbourne Water does not have any licences since most of the governance system is provided through legislation and the company is, itself, acting under delegated responsibility from the government in issuing licences for water diversion. Meanwhile, The Three Retailers: City West Water, South East Water and Yarra Valley Water, *had* their own separate business licences. There are five types of licences: (1) a water licence; (2) a water and sewerage licence; (3) a drainage licence; (4) a sewage treatment licence; and (5) a water headworks licence.[61]

In England, following divestiture, the ten water and sewerage companies are provided with licences by the Secretary of State and Ofwat. Before the 2014 amendment, there were generally three types of licences[62]: (1) the original 'undertaker' licences (owners of the main network assets of post-1989 divestitures);[63] (2) New Appointment and Variations (NAV) licences awarded to a particular area, which required variation of the aforementioned undertaker's licence;[64] and (3) water supply licences (WSL) which consisted of either a combined licence or a retail licence containing third party access authorisation to an undertaker's network.[65]

However, this is undergoing some changes as the 2014 amendment expands the current WSL regime so as to include various retail (non-household)

---

61 Water Industry Act 1994 No. 121 of 1994, Version No. 063 s.5
62 See Hendry, 'An Analytical Framework for Reform of National Water Law' (PhD thesis, University of Dundee 2008) pp.303–309 (section 5.2.3) for another detailed account of the licensing regime in England.
63 This is regulated primarily by ss. 6, 7, 11 and 12 of the Water Industry Act 1991 c.56
64 This is regulated primarily by ss. 6, 7, 11 and 12 of the Water Industry Act 1991 c.56
65 This is granted under s.17 F ibid

authorisations and adds a new sewerage licensing regime.[66] The 2014 Water Act also provides undertakers to exit from retails in non-household markets. The new licensing type can be categorised into water supply licences (either combined or retail); sewerage licences (combined or retail); appointment and variations and the original undertaker licence. This book will mainly discuss the transparency of household licences.

In Indonesia, other than industry regulation and the Company Law[67] which require the companies and cooperatives to obtain commercial licences[68] from the Ministry of Trade, the invalidation of the water law and its implementing regulations have created a vacuum on the regulation of water licences.

Both before and after invalidation of the Water Law, however, licence types in Indonesia have never been as detailed and as specific as in England or Victoria. Under the defunct GR-16, there were (1) 'operational' licences for internal use; (2) 'licences' for other uses; and (3) environmental licences in the form of abstraction and discharge licences.

Article 65 of the now *defunct* GR-16 reads:

> Para.3: 'Provisions [of water service] by the cooperatives and privately-owned business enterprises [in order to fulfill their own needs] must be conducted based on licence issued by the government or regional government in accordance with its authority under prevailing laws and regulations'.

This is further reiterated in Article 40 which stipulates that regional governments 'issue licenses for drinking water provisions system in its regions'.[69] In para. 5 of Article 65, the defunct GR-16 only stipulates that the guidelines and procedures of licensing will be regulated by a Ministerial Regulation.

The current draft government regulation only mentions licences for internal use but not other licences. This is unfortunate, since although water utilities are state-owned enterprises, they too still require clarity with respect to their licences types and obligations owed to such licences. It is also unfortunate, given that contracting with the private sector is still possible after the Judicial Review, that there is no clarity on their licensing framework. As such, Indonesia does not have detailed prescription on licence approval criteria and licence conditions.

3.2.2 Criteria for approving licences

In Victoria, the criteria for approving licences *was* contained in the WIA 1994, in which it was determined that the Minister (of Water) has the discretion to

---

66 'Explanatory Notes, Water Act 2014, Chapter 21' <www.legislation.gov.uk/ukpga/2014/21/pdfs/ukpgaen_20140021_en.pdf> accessed 16 November 2015
67 Undang Undang No. 40 Tahun 2007 Tentang Perseroan Terbatas
68 Undang Undang No. 3 Tahun 1982 Tentang Wajib Daftar Perusahaan, Article 11
69 Peraturan Pemerintah No. 16 Tahun 2005 Tentang Pengembangan Sistem Penyediaan Air Minum, Article 40.k The elucidation of this article only stipulates that licences shall be issued in accordance with prevailing laws and regulations. This is the only part of this elucidation which contains the word 'licence'. Others are silent about it.

refuse or grant licence applications for *any reason* that it considers appropriate.[70] The WIA stipulates that the Minister *must not* grant an application unless he or she is satisfied that all of these prerequisites are fulfilled: (a) the applicant is financially viable; (b) the applicant has the technical capacity to comply with the conditions of the licence; and (c) the applicant is a Victorian body corporate or a statutory corporation within the meaning of the State Owned Enterprises Act 1992.[71]

Under the previous licensing regime, any decision by the Minister with respect to a licence application had to be communicated to the applicant in the form of a written notice. If the decision was in the form of a refusal of such application, the Minister was under an obligation to provide reasoning for such refusal.[72] As the retailers are now converted into statutory corporations, the license regime is no longer applicable. The retailers will continue to provide water services unless the legislation is amended.

In England, the rules for the appointment of water and sewerage undertakers are outlined in the legislation. It is required that these take the form of a limited company.[73] A company is appointed by the Secretary of State or by a general authorisation provided by the Secretary of State to Ofwat.[74] An appointed company is subject to duties imposed by enactments.[75]

A new licence which is granted due to the cessation of an incumbent's licences would be a rare circumstance due to takeovers. New appointments or appointments followed by variations of an incumbent undertaker's licences are more common.[76] Ofwat may grant new appointments if one of the following three conditions is fulfilled: (1) the site is unserved, or (2) large user criterion (the site will or is serving over 50 megalitres per year) and the customer would like to change its supplier, or, (3) the incumbent company provides consent.[77]

Applicants must serve notice to existing appointees, local authority and 'appropriate' agencies.[78] Ofwat is also obligated to publish a notice stating its proposals to make appointments or variations, stating the purpose and reason for doing so and specifying the period when representation and objection can be made.[79] Such notices must be published in a manner appropriate to bring attention to any affected parties.

3.2.3 Licence conditions

In Victoria, water corporations are statutory corporations under the Water Amendment Act. They are no longer subject to licence conditions, but are still

---

70 Water Industry Act 1994 No. 121 of 1994,Version No. 063 s.6 (repealed)
71 ibid
72 ibid s.6(5)
73 Water Industry Act 1991 c.56 s.6(5). These are privately financed water companies authorised to supply water under the Water Act, 1945. 8 & 9 GEO. 6. c.42
74 Water Industry Act 1991 c.56 s.6(1)
75 ibid s.6(2)
76 See ibid s.7(4)
77 ibid s.7(4)
78 ibid s.8(2)
79 ibid s.8(3)

required to comply with SOOs issued by the Minister. In Indonesia, there is no clarity with respect to types of licences and, as such, there is no clarity on licence conditions. Since water companies in Indonesia are mostly regionally owned enterprises, they should be subjected to appropriate licence governance and can learn from England with respect to the conditions and enforcement of licences.

In England, the WIA provides Ofwat (and statutorily, the Secretary of State), the power to impose conditions of appointment.[80] The WIA also empowers the Secretary of State to enact standard conditions for WSL and WSSL.[81] The content of such a standard has not yet been determined but Ofwat had conducted a consultation regarding the draft standard in June 2015.[82]

The conditions for NAV licences are essentially the same as undertakers' licences. The conditions of appointment normally comprise of several items. Those with particular importance are: condition B (charges) which embodies the price limit (RPI+K) and periodic reviews; condition F (accounts and accounting information) which includes accounting records, statements, financial ring-fencing, audit and publication of statements; condition G (code of practice for customers and relations with customer service committee); condition H (code of practice and disconnection procedure); and condition J (level of service and service targets).[83] Some of these conditions might be amended in order to facilitate retail market in 2017.[84]

For both WSL and WSSL, the WIA outlines the principal framework of licence conditions[85] and further authorises the Secretary of State to enact a standard licence condition.[86] The existing standard comprises of certain requirements during droughts, the requirement to provide information to relevant undertakers, protocols for transferring customers, definition of areas of operation, the obligation to transact at arm's length, provision of information to Ofwat and conditions which entail the revocation of such licences.[87] In terms of arm's length transaction, the current proposal by Ofwat will remove the requirement to notify Ofwat if the licensee becomes or ceases to be related

---

80 ibid s.11
81 Water Act 2014; 2014 c.21 (England) (n 156). Schedule 7
82 'Licensing and Policy Issues in Relation to the Opening of the Non-Household Retail Market – A Consultation' <www.ofwat.gov.uk/wp-content/uploads/2015/09/pap_con201506retaillicence.pdf>.
83 *Instrument of Appointment by the Secretary of State for the Environment of Severn Trent Water Limited as a water and sewerage undertaker under the Water Act 1989* (1989); *Instrument of Appointment by the Secretary of State for the Environment of Thames Water Utilities Limited as a water and sewerage undertaker under the Water Act 1989* (2005); *Instrument of Appointment by the Secretary of State for Wales of Dwr Cymru Cyfyngedig as a water and sewerage undertaker under the Water Act 1989* (1989)
84 'Licensing and Policy Issues in Relation to the Opening of the Non-Household Retail Market – Appendices' <www.ofwat.gov.uk/regulated-companies/company-obligations/annual-performance-report/> see Appendix B, accessed 15 May 2016
85 Water Industry Act 1991 c.56 s.17 G
86 ibid s.17 H (as amended by Water Act 2014 Schedules 5 and 7)
87 *Water Industry Act 1991 Section 17 H, Standard Conditions of Water Supply Licences* (DEFRA 2005)

to an undertaker. Other amendment may include the removal of customer transfer protocol (replaced by procedure from market operator).[88]

3.2.4 Legal obligation to publish licences

In Victoria, one key transparency mechanism in Victoria's water licensing activities *was* the prohibition of persons to apply for a licence unless the Minister has published in the *Government Gazette* and a newspaper circulating in the licensing area inviting the application for licences and specifying the type of the licence.[89] The WIA contained some obligations on the part of the Minister to announce and publish applications for licences in the newspapers circulating in Victoria.[90] Such announcement must specify the name of the applicants and the area which is intended to be covered by the licence. The Minister was also obliged to invite interested persons to make submissions with respect to the licence applications.[91] There was no requirement on the WIA to publish licences in newspapers, but the Minister must notify the applicant[92] in writing of his decision and, in the event of refusal, the reasoning for such refusal must be provided.[93] There was a requirement to publish notification in the Victorian *Government Gazette* pursuant to the issuance, revocation or amendment of licences under the WIA.[94]

The Water Amendment Act repealed the licensing system. In the new legislation, each retailer's service area is directly specified in the legislation (called 'district').[95] However, the publication mechanism for SOOs are still in place. The Minister is obliged to provide notice for the making and issuance of the SOO to the corporations, or any amendments thereof, in the *Government Gazette*.[96] The SOOs of The Three Retailers contain provisions obligating (1) the document of the SOO itself, (2) information about the services the utility provides and (3) information about water conservation and the efficient and responsible use of water[97] to be 'available to the public' by way of publication on the company website, public inspection at the licencee's offices and provision of the copies of such documents free of charge or at a reasonable charge.[98]

In England, for undertaker and NAV licences, Ofwat is required to 'serve notice of the making of the appointment or variation' to local authorities and

---

88 'Licensing and Policy Issues in Relation to the Opening of the Non-Household Retail Market – Appendices' (n 460). See Appendix
89 Water Industry Act 1994 No. 121 of 1994, Version No. 063 s.5(2) (repealed)
90 ibid, s.6.3.a (repealed)
91 ibid s.6.3.b (repealed)
92 The applicant must be a Victorian body corporate or a statutory corporation See ibid s.6(2)
93 ibid s.6(5) (repealed)
94 ibid, s.13 (repealed)
95 Water Amendment (Governance and Other Reforms) Act 2012 No. 17 of 2012 (n 128) s.16
96 Water Industry Act 1994 No. 121 of 1994, Version No. 063 s.4I
97 ibid
98 'Statement of Obligations (General) 2012' (n 113)

'the appropriate agency' and 'serve the copies' of the appointment and variation to existing appointees.[99] Although the proposal for making appointments must be brought to the attention of any persons likely to be affected by it there are no statutory requirements to publish NAV licences once they are approved. Nevertheless, in practice, both licences of the original undertakers and NAVs are published by Ofwat.[100] The power in publishing these licences comes *not* from a specific statutory obligation to publish licence instruments but from a general empowerment to publish regulatory information under WIA s.201.[101]

Meanwhile, WSLs are different. Ofwat is required to 'serve a copy of the licence or licence as varied' (instead of just a notice) to a number of regulators (EA, DWI, CC Water) including the undertakers, so there is a wider scope of information users targeted by the WIA than for a NAV licence, however, there are no requirements to serve copies of such licences to customers or to publicly disclose them.[102] Ofwat said in its guidance that it 'will retain a copy of the licence or variation of the licence' in its library, in addition to issuing a press notice subsequent to licence approvals and maintain a Register of Licensees on their website.[103] Ofwat's Register of Licencees contains the list of WSL licencees and the copies of its licences and its contact details.[104] To conclude, similar to the publication of undertakers' licences on Ofwat's website, the publication of WSL licences is Ofwat's own initiative rather than a statutory obligation. Nevertheless, statutes do have the role of enabling publication by providing discretionary power to Ofwat to do so, through WIA s.201.

There is no such obligation to publish licences **in Indonesia**, including Jakarta.

3.3 Information flow

3.3.1 *Means for acquiring information*

In Victoria, regulators are empowered by four instruments in acquiring information from regulated companies: the Water Industry Act 1994 (WIA 1994); the Essential Services Commission Act; the WIRO and SOO; and the Safe Drinking Water Act. Each will be discussed below.

---

99 Water Industry Act 1991 c.56 s.8(5)(a) and (b)
100 ibid s.8(4), see also 'Water company licences' (Ofwat, No Year) <www.ofwat.gov.uk/industrystructure/licences/> accessed 13 January 2016
101 Water Industry Act 1991 c.56 s.201
102 ibid s.17(F)(7) as amended by WA 2014
103 'Guidance on applying for a water supply licence Version 3' (Ofwat 2011) <www.ofwat.gov.uk/publications/water-supply-licensees-contact-details/> accessed 13 May 2016, p.9. On its website, it says that 'The Water Supply Licences held on the WSRA's Register may be inspected during normal office hours at OFWAT, 7 Hill Street, Birmingham, B5 4UA (telephone number 0121 644 7500)' 'Water Supply Licences' (Ofwat, No Year) <www.ofwat.gov.uk/regulated-companies/licences/> accessed 13 January 2016
104 'Water Supply Licensees' Contact Details' (Ofwat, No Year) <www.ofwat.gov.uk/competition/wsl/prs_web_wslcontacts> accessed 16 January 2012

Previously, WIA 1994 provided powers to acquire information from the companies, to monitor their compliance with licence conditions. These powers were delegated to 'inspectors' under s.38 and are limited to the following purposes: (a) the planning, construction, operation or maintenance of works; (b) technical performance standards; and (c) water quality standards.[105] The types of powers ranging from the authority to conduct searches of premises, which include the power to inspect, take photographs or samples, seize or open any containers which allegedly contain information.[106] Under s.45 (repealed), WIA 1994 also empowers DSE inspectors to require *persons* to give and/or produce information to the inspectors and to provide reasonable assistance to them in carrying out their duties.[107]

The differences between the 'search' power and the 'power to require information' to be submitted is with respect to its effect on another person. Under search power, other persons remain passive, as their legal obligation is only to allow the inspectors to conduct a search, inspect and seize anything on their premises. Whereas, under the power to require information to be provided, third parties are required to be active in submitting already available information in their possession or in producing information which is not readily available. Failure to do so may entail penalty.[108] Deliberately providing misleading information or documents is also punishable by penalty.[109]

The licensing system is currently abolished and so are the inspector's rights to acquire information as discussed above. Nevertheless, the economic regulator, ESC, still enjoys wide power in acquiring information as discussed below.

While regulatory bodies are typically empowered with the authority to obtain information only from the regulated companies, the ESC has the power to acquire information from both (1) *any person*[110] and (2) the *regulated companies*.[111] Under s.37 (General power to obtain information and documents), the ESC can require *any person* to submit information or documents to them, and to appear before them, if they believe that such person has information or documents which are relevant and necessary for regulatory purposes.[112] In doing so, the ESC must issue a written notice specifying the information or document required, the format in which the information must be submitted to them, the deadline; referral to s.37 and a copy of that section should be included in the notice.[113] If such person fails to comply, it could be considered an offence which entails a penalty.[114] There are some limitations to this

---

105 Water Industry Act 1994 No. 121 of 1994, Version No. 063 s.38(1) (repealed)
106 ibid s.38(2) and s.41 (repealed)
107 ibid s.45(1) (repealed)
108 ibid s.45(2) (repealed)
109 ibid s.45(3) (repealed)
110 Essential Services Commission Act 2001 No. 62 of 2001 s.37
111 ibid s.37A
112 ibid s.37
113 ibid s.37(2) and (3)
114 ibid s.37(4)

power. First, the obligation to submit information does not apply if the person has a 'lawful excuse'[115] and second, the Minister may limit these powers if it is believed that it is being used in an *inquiry* (will be elaborated below) which is not directly correlated with the regulated industry.[116] The ESC Act also protects disclosers by imposing penalties on those who threaten, incite or coerce to cause injuries, losses or disadvantages to them.[117]

Regulated companies must provide information as requested by the ESC in its notice.[118] The ESC may require the companies to enter into arrangements with third parties in order to compel it to submit the information to the ESC.[119] This section also empowers the ESC to enact a *Code of Practice* which specifies the types or classes of information that entities must maintain for regulatory purposes.[120]

Inquiry powers do not include the power to enter utilities' premises, however, the inquiry power is linked with s.37 (General power to obtain information and document) which empowers the ESC to request information from any person as described above.[121] Apart from that, there are no other powers provided by the ESC Act to conduct inquiries.

Inquiries can be conducted through the Minister's referral[122] or on the ESC's own initiative.[123] If the latter is the case, the ESC must first consult with the Minister.[124] The ESC is obliged to publish notice of inquiry in the *Government Gazette*, newspapers and the internet, specifying the purpose of the inquiry, the matters to be inquired, the length of the inquiry, the period when the public may make submissions and the details of public hearings.[125] The Act also specifies that in conducting inquiries, at least one public hearing must be held.[126] If there are commercial confidentiality or public interest concerns, the hearing can be conducted in private.[127] A very important transparency aspect is the requirement to publish the final report (by the Minister). The ESC is obligated to submit its final inquiry report to the Minister[128] and must also dissect and

---

115 ibid s.37(5) A lawful excuse is when the disclosure to the ESC will cause the person to be incriminated or leads to a penalty for any other offence. Presumably, a court action may be required to disclose this type of information. S.37(8) clarifies that a person who discloses in good faith is not liable for any damage, injury or loss suffered by another person.
116 ibid s 41 A. The limitation by the minister is provided through a ministerial direction.
117 ibid s.37(7)
118 ibid s.37A
119 ibid s.37A(1) and (2)
120 ibid s.37A(3)
121 ibid s.41A
122 ibid s.41(1)
123 ibid s.40
124 ibid s.40
125 ibid s.42(1) and (2)
126 ibid s.43(4) The ESC has the discretion to determine whether a person may appear on the hearing or be represented. See s.43(4)(b)
127 ibid s.43(5)
128 ibid s.45(1)

indicate information which is confidential or commercially sensitive.[129] Upon receiving the report, the Minister then must lay the copy to parliament,[130] ensure that the copies are available for public inspection[131] and make the copies publicly available.[132] Only non-confidential reports are laid before parliament and available in the public domain.[133]

So, it is the Minister and not the ESC who is obligated to lay the reports in front of parliament and to make it available to the public. Presumably, this is an exercise of the ministerial responsibility doctrine, in which it is the Minister, as a political appointee, who is ultimately held accountable to parliament. The discretion in determining which part of the report is confidential, however, lies with the ESC and not the Minister.[134]

Two other instruments which enable the Victorian ESC to acquire information are the WIRO and the SOO. There are two categories of powers enjoyed by the ESC in acquiring information from the utilities under the WIRO. The first is with respect to price enactment where the ESC is given the power to request extra information from the utilities, in addition to what they have included in the Water Plan[135] (*Water Plans* will be discussed further in section 4.1).

Second, WIRO also empowers the ESC to conduct an audit against the utilities. An audit is carried out to ensure utilities' compliance with service levels, to verify the reliability and quality of information submitted to the ESC and to ensure its compliance with the SOO.[136] Audits made under WIRO are limited to only once per financial year.[137] WIRO stipulates that all audit results must be publicly reported.[138]

Finally, the Victorian Secretary of State is granted powers under the Safe Drinking Water Act to require water storage managers or water suppliers to provide information.[139] The Secretary can request any information especially in relation to compliance with water quality standards[140] and specify the format and frequency of delivery.[141] In addition, water storage managers and water suppliers are obligated to report on the condition of drinking water quality in Victoria every financial year.[142] The Safe Drinking Water Act also protects

---

129 ibid s.45(2)
130 ibid s.45(5)
131 ibid s.45(6)
132 ibid s.45(7)
133 ibid s.45(3)
134 ibid s.45(3)
135 Water Industry Regulatory Order (WIRO) 2012 (n 121) para 12
136 Water Industry Act 1994, Water Industry Regulatory Order 2003 para 17(b)
137 ibid para 17(d)
138 ibid para 19
139 Safe Drinking Water Act 2003, No. 46 of 2003 (Victoria) s.29(1)
140 ibid s.29(2)
141 ibid s.29(4) and (5)
142 ibid s.32

the quality of information by penalising those who knowingly supply false and misleading information or data.[143]

In England, legislation requires companies to submit information to the regulator and provides discretion for the regulator to disclose any information in its hands, including information provided by the regulated companies, to the public.

The English DWI has the power to enter any of the water companies' premises for the purposes of its investigation and to carry out inspections, measurements and tests, take away samples or articles[144] and it may, at any reasonable time, require water companies to supply it with copies, extracts and records indicating the company's effort to comply with drinking water quality regulations or require 'relevant persons' from the companies to supply them with relevant information.[145]

WIA requires companies to 'furnish the Secretary of State with all such information relating to any matter'[146] related to the company's functions as a water undertaker or any other information considered material by the Secretary of State. The WIA also empowers the director to collect information on utilities' performance.[147] Condition M of the Licence Condition of an undertaker typically contains clauses for the company to furnish an Ofwat director with information he requires for regulatory purposes subject to some exceptions.[148] Condition M further provides discretion to Ofwat to regulate the details of such submission and to require companies to provide reasonable explanation.[149] Ofwat did not propose to amend this condition in future reform.[150]

Furthermore, Condition J of the company's licence requires the submission of 'Levels of Service Information and Service Targets'.[151] The regulator has the power to conduct investigations in order to verify that the reports on service levels are correct. The power allows the regulator to inspect utilities' premises, copy, take extracts and conduct tests and measurements, subject to reasonable prior notice.[152]

---

143 ibid s.55
144 Water Industry Act 1991 c.56 s.86(4)(a),(b)
145 ibid s.86(4)c
146 ibid s.202. Companies are also required to 'comply with any direction given by the Director' in accordance with its licence condition or any other arrangements under s.12(1). See also the duty to report compensation and performance under s.38A. ibid
147 ibid s.38A(2)
148 *Instrument of Appointment by the Secretary of State for the Environment of Thames Water Utilities Limited as a water and sewerage undertaker under the Water Act 1989* (2005) Condition M
149 ibid Condition M. 2: 'Information required to be furnished under this Condition shall be furnished in such form and manner and at such times and be accompanied or supplemented by such explanations as the Director may reasonably require'.
150 'Licensing and Policy Issues in Relation to the Opening of the Non-Household Retail Market – Appendices' (n 460)
151 *Instrument of Appointment by the Secretary of State for the Environment of Thames Water Utilities Limited as a water and sewerage undertaker under the Water Act 1989* (2005) Condition J
152 ibid Condition J para 9

Previously, Ofwat collected information from the companies, consisting of detailed data and information it should submit annually, known as the 'June Return'.[153] If a company misreported its June Return data, it could be held to be in breach of Licence Conditions M and/or J and could therefore be liable for a penalty.[154]

However, the June Return exercise was stopped after Ofwat moved toward a 'risk-based approach'. Under the new 'risk-based' approach, companies must publish four basic pieces of information in their 'annual performance report': regulatory financial reporting, price control and additional segmental reporting, performance summary and additional reporting (including total expenditure analysis, current cost reporting and financeability statement).[155] These reporting requirements are still enabled through conditions M and J in companies' licenses. Thus, although the data collection method has changed, the legal tools for acquiring information remain the same.

As the amount of data submitted by companies in the new risk-based framework significantly decreases, it is likely that Ofwat will rely on their investigative power and incidental information requests to companies for either clarification or investigation purposes should they suspect a utility to be in breach of its licences.[156]

In addition to the above basic information companies will be placed in one of three categories depending on the quality of their publication: 'self-assurance', 'targeted' and 'prescribed'.[157] They can move from one category to another every autumn. Companies also need to submit some information, among other things, on audit procedures and a summary on the outcome of its assurance. There are no further requirements for self assurance companies but targeted companies need to engage with stakeholders to discuss issues.

Meanwhile, prescribed companies, in addition to complying with all the same requirements as companies in other categories, will need to publish assurance plans for all information before they report. They may also be required to conduct a risk, weaknesses and strength exercise to identify areas of greater risk to customers and, in doing so, incorporate independent external assurance. With this categorisation, the compliance cost to companies increases with their risk of misreporting.

---

153 'Reporting requirements' (Ofwat, 2011) <www.ofwat.gov.uk/regulated-companies/company-obligations/annual-performance-report/> accessed 15 May 2016. Other than the June Return, OFWAT acquire information from other reporting duties such as principal statements; charges schemes; regulatory accounts; business plans; customer literature; codes of practice; and cost base information. See Ofwat, *Getting it right for customers, How can we make monopoly water and sewerage companies more accountable?* (2010) p.38

154 See, for example, *Notice of Ofwat's proposal to impose a penalty on United Utilities Water plc* (Ofwat 2007) p.1

155 'Annual Performance Report – Summary of Performance Parameters' <www.ofwat.gov.uk/wp-content/uploads/2015/10/pap_tec201502annperfsumm.pdf> accessed 29 November 2015

156 ibid

157 'Company Monitoring Framework – Final Position' <www.ofwat.gov.uk/wp-content/uploads/2015/11/pap_pos201506comon1.pdf>

84 *Regulator, licences and information flow*

In Jakarta, water services are suffering from ambiguous regulatory arrangements. JWSRB's real mandate under the Cooperation Agreement is only in conducting monitoring and mediating disputes.[158] PAM Jaya also has a regulatory role in supervising[159] and even in enforcing penalties[160] against their private partners. PAM Jaya obviously has a conflict of interest in this sort of regulatory structure, as it is both a regulator (equipped with sanctioning power by the contract) and, at the same time, also a party to the contract. In addition, there is the role of the Governor (with the approval of the regional parliament) who is in charge of determining tariffs.[161]

This fragmented regulatory structure has implications for information flow. As a party to the contract and a 'regulator', most reporting duties imposed on the private sector under the contract are toward PAM Jaya. PAM Jaya, for example, has powers to investigate, review, assess and evaluate the private partner's performance,[162] and inspect and take copies of the assets register.[163] It is also entitled to 'obtain information and data' from the private partners,[164] acquire online access to all information and data,[165] and obtain monthly, quarterly, semi-annual, annual and five-yearly reports.[166] There is also an obligation on the concessionaire to submit reports, quarterly, monthly, semi-annually and five annual reports.

There is also an obligation by the concessionaire to 'maintain transparent accounts' and the corresponding right of PAM Jaya – at any time – to audit such accounts,[167] and to enable other relevant governmental bodies to conduct audits and access, at all reasonable times, 'all relevant books and records'.[168] There is no clarification on what is meant by a 'transparent' account. There is no distinctive regulatory account. The contract only refers to the Indonesian standard generally accepted accounting principles.[169] Meanwhile, there is only one clause in the contract empowering the JWSRB with an audit power and the concessionaires' corresponding obligation to 'provide all requested information and data' for the purpose of such audits.[170]

---

158 Cooperation Agreement Between PAM Jaya and The Concessionaire, 2001 Clause 51
159 ibid Clause 9.1. PAM Jaya has the right to: 'investigate, review, assess and evaluate the performance of the Second Party of its obligations under this Agreement so as to cause the Second Party's achievement of the Technical Targets and Service Standards'.
160 ibid Clause 31
161 ibid Clause 26
162 ibid Clause 35.2.a
163 ibid Clause 13.4.c
164 ibid Clause 35.2.b
165 ibid Clause 35.2.d
166 ibid Clause 35.3 Unfortunately, the content of such reporting obligation is not outlined in the contract as they are stipulated in the 'Procedure on Performance Supervising and Evaluation System Agreement' which is confidential and not available to the author.
167 ibid Clause 50.1.a
168 ibid Clause 50.2
169 ibid Clause 16.3
170 ibid Clause 50.1.b

Since PAM Jaya has a CoI in the regulatory structure, it may have an interest not to share all regulatory information it receives from the private partners with JWSRB. Often there are disagreements between the JWSRB and PAM Jaya. The regulatory structure creates incentives to PAM Jaya not to disclose information to the public, which will be explained in the next section.

Therefore, JWSRB lacks regulatory powers to acquire information and may not receive adequate input of information from its counterpart, PAM Jaya, due to PAM Jaya's interest in non-disclosure. As a result, despite its relatively reformist stance, JWSRB only has a little information to be disclosed to the public.

3.3.2 Means for disclosing information

In Victoria, one of the functions of the ESC according to the WIRO is to 'publicly report the performance of a regulated industry'.[171] However, there are two limitations under the ESC Act to disclose information to the public. The first is a restriction on disclosing information which the ESC acquired by virtue of the powers granted by s.37 and s.37A of the ESC Act[172] and the second is a restriction on disclosure of any information exempted by the FoI Act 1982.[173] Both restrictions come with qualifications.

If the ESC acquires information under s.37 or s.37A and, at the time the information was provided to them, the person giving the information stated that such information is confidential or commercially sensitive, the ESC must ask that person to provide (1) the reason why such information is deemed confidential and (2) the harm or detriment from disclosure.[174] The ESC must not disclose information unless it is certain that disclosure will not cause harm to the person supplying it[175] (or third parties that might be affected by it),[176] or, that in such cases where harm occurs, the public benefit would outweigh its harm.[177] If the ESC eventually decides to disclose such information, it must serve notice to the supplier of the information specifying the nature of the intended disclosure and its rationale in detail.[178] Persons receiving such notices may appeal the ESC's decision of disclosure.[179]

The ESC Act also prohibits the disclosure of information if it is acquired from other 'Ministries or Agencies' and they are exempted under the FoI Act

---

171 Water Industry Act 1994, Water Industry Regulatory Order 2003 para 16
172 Essential Services Commission Act 2001 No. 62 of 2001 s.38
173 ibid s.39
174 ibid s.38(1A)
175 ibid s.38(2)(a)(i)
176 ibid s.38(2)(b)(i)
177 ibid s.38(2)(a)(ii) and (b)(ii)
178 ibid s.38(2) (c) and (d)
179 ibid s.55(1)(b) Interestingly, only those receiving notice under s.38 (2)(c) and (d) have the right to appeal, not all 'aggrieved' parties.

1982.[180] The provision does not apply the FoI Act 1982's exemption clauses to all information in ESC's possession, it only extends to information acquired by the ESC from other public bodies.

This means that an individual may only obtain regulatory information from a public body which acquired it in the first place – subject to some restrictions under FoI – and, on the other hand, the regulatory bodies can only disclose information if it is acquired by itself, after considering the harm and the public interest affected by the disclosure. It appears that this provision seeks to protect the exchange of information among regulatory bodies from disclosure by the ESC and, therefore, promotes uniformity on how FoI exemptions are applied among public bodies.

In England, Ofwat believes that transparency encompasses three elements: (1) consultation, (2) information and (3) reasoned decision. Consultation is achieved through workshops, seminars, media and seeking written responses to published consultations. Information is achieved by publication of regulatory materials and reasoned decision is employed at every level, from dispute determination to price limits.[181]

Legislation is generally silent with respect to the details of the publication of information by Ofwat or the Secretary of State, but acts as an 'enabler' of transparency instead, by providing them with wide discretion to publish.[182] This is reflected, for example, by WIA s.201 which stipulates that the Secretary of State and the Director (of Ofwat) *may* arrange for the publication 'in such form and in such manner as he considers appropriate'[183] of information related to the companies which would be in the *public interest*[184] to be published.[185] When disclosing the information, there is a duty for the Secretary of State and Ofwat to 'have regard' to the need for excluding information related to individual affairs

---

180 ibid s.39
181 *How we do our job: A code of practice governing the discharge of Ofwat's functions* (Ofwat 2003)
182 There are some transparency requirements, such as the requirement to publish performance information to customers under s.93D and 27F, and in publishing water (s.198) and sewer networks (s.199) in the form of a map but these apply to utilities, not OFWAT. There is an obligation for an OFWAT Director to publish utilities' performance information 'in such form and in such manner as he considers appropriate' at least once a year (s. 38A(4)). This clause corresponds to directors' powers in collecting information under s.38A(2) discussed in the previous section. Water Industry Act 1991 c.56
183 ibid s.201(1)
184 The exact wording of s.201(1) is: 'as it may appear to him to be in the public interest to publish'. Hence, the legislation provides discretion to the regulator to judge which matters are considered to be in the public interest. ibid s.201(1)
185 This is further reinforced in the company's licence condition. See Condition M.3. *Instrument of Appointment by the Secretary of State for the Environment of Severn Trent Water Limited as a water and sewerage undertaker under the Water Act 1989* (1989) 'nothing in this paragraph shall prevent the Director from using or disclosing any Information with which he has been furnished under this Condition or any other Condition of this Appointment for the purpose of carrying out his functions under the Act'.

Regulator, licences and information flow 87

or the affairs of a body of persons (corporate or incorporate) if the publication may 'seriously and prejudicially affect' their interests.[186]

The above discretion to publish comes with a caveat. Section 206 of the WIA restricts the disclosure of any information acquired by virtue of the WIA or any information relating to the affairs of individuals or business.[187] Violation of this provision is considered an offence and may result in imprisonment.[188] It was thought that s.206 would be repealed after the FoI Act 2000 came into force,[189] but it turned out that it was preserved.[190] Therefore, information exempt under s.206 can still be exempted even when it is requested to be disclosed under the FoI regime, as the FoI regime contains exceptions preserving information made confidential by other statutes.[191]

Such a restriction under s.206, however, contains many qualifiers; for example, that it does not apply if the disclosure is necessary to facilitate the carrying out of the functions of the regulators (this includes Ofwat, the Secretary of State, CC Water and the Competition Commission, among others)[192] as well as for health, safety, environmental or other regulatory reasons.[193]

June Return data was published by Ofwat until 2011, although some commercial in-confidence information was being excised.[194] Ofwat applied some categories for excision.[195] This is no longer the case. Under the present risk-based approach, companies are required to publish information as mentioned

---

186 Water Industry Act 1991 c.56 s.201(3) The duty of the regulator is only to 'have regard', and so long as it is exercised, the regulator has carried out its statutory obligation. Moreover, in order for disclosure to be considered for exemption, the matter must 'seriously' and 'prejudicially' 'affect' their interest. This gives the regulator wide powers to disclose regulatory information. As we shall see later on in the chapter, when discussing the passive disclosure rule, the causality between disclosure and harm and the severity of harm may be difficult to assess.
187 ibid s.206(1) as amended by WA 2014 For similar provision, see Utilities Act 2000, 2000 c.27 s.105 and Railways Act 1993, 1993 c.43 s.145 also Enterprise Act 2002, 2002 c.40 s.237
188 Water Industry Act 1991 c.56 s.206(7) and (8)
189 'DEFRA have told us that the statutory bar on the provision of information to third parties in s206 of the Water Industry Act 1991 will be amended or repealed to coincide with the full implementation of the FOIA on 1 January 2005.' R D Dunshea, *RD 22/04, Freedom of Information Act 2000* (Ofwat 2004)
190 R D Dunshea, *RD 10/05: Freedom of Information Act 2000 – s206 of the Water Industry Act* (Ofwat 2005) 'The Department of Constitutional Affairs announced on 16 June that s206 of the WIA 1991 will be retained'.
191 Freedom of Information Act 2000, 2000 c.36 s.44(1)(a)
192 Water Industry Act 1991 c.56 s.206(3)(a)
193 See the long list of qualifiers in s.206(b)–(k). ibid
194 Ofwat, 'Publication of the June return 2009' (Ofwat 2009) <http://webarchive.nationalarchives.gov.uk/20090606091533/ofwat.gov.uk/regulating/junereturn/ltr_rd0809_jr09> accessed 22 May 2016
195 See Northumbrian Water Limited, *June Return 2007: Statement to Accompany the Public Domain Version* (Northumbrian Water, 2007); Thames Water Utilities Ltd, *June Return 2006: Statement to Accompany the Public Domain Version* (Thames Water 2006); United Utilities, *June Return 2006: Statement to Accompany the Public Domain Version* (United Utilities 2006) Yorkshire Water, *June Return 2007: Statement to Accompany the Public Domain Version* (Yorkshire Water 2007)

before: regulatory financial reporting, price control and additional segmental reporting, performance summary and additional reporting (including total expenditure analysis, current cost reporting and financeability statement). From the format that Ofwat provides, it appears that although the quantity of data presented to the public domain is significantly reduced (compared to June Returns data), the quality and actionability of data *could* potentially increase significantly as the publication offers simple metrics that could be used by customer and stakeholders to compare information.[196] Indeed, this mechanism would depend on whether the processed data are accurate and honest, which is the reason why various assurances are required.

When the June Return data was published, Ofwat permitted non-disclosure of some data that it considered 'sensitive' by creating several categories:[197] category 1 is price sensitive information whose publication or publication by reference to other information may affect share prices; category 2 is information which could assist contractors or potential contractors in tenders; category 3 is information which has not been approved by affected organisations or individuals for disclosure; category 4 is information that could give third parties a commercial advantage; and category 5 is information that could pose a security risk to the nation or an individual.[198]

Upon making an FoI request to Ofwat,[199] the author discovered that this categorisation was not based on any policy,[200] but probably developed out of practice instead. In MD 135, Ian Byatt (Ofwat's Director at that time) decided that he would not pre-determine what information is confidential.[201] The companies' responses as to which information should be declared confidential varies.[202] Byatt gave some indication of which tables (of the June Return) are likely to be prejudicial if disclosed, but it is up to the companies to decide which information is confidential by marking it in both electronic and hard

---

196 'Annual Performance Report' <www.ofwat.gov.uk/regulated-companies/company-obligations/annual-performance-report/> accessed 30 November 2015
197 Ofwat, 'Publication of the June return 2009' (Ofwat 2009) <http://webarchive.nationalarchives.gov.uk/20090606091533/ofwat.gov.uk/regulating/junereturn/ltr_rd0809_jr09> accessed 22 May 2016
198 See Northumbrian Water Limited, *June Return 2007: Statement to Accompany the Public Domain Version* Northumbrian Water Limited, 'June Return 2007: Statement to Accompany the Public Domain Version' (Northumbrian Water 2007) <www.ofwat.gov.uk/legacy/aptrix/ofwat/publish.nsf/AttachmentsByTitle/JR07_YKY_ExcisionsStatement.pdf/$FILE/JR07_YKY_ExcisionsStatement.pdf> Thames Water Utilities Ltd, *June Return 2006: Statement to Accompany the Public Domain Version* (Thames Water 2006) United Utilities, *June Return 2006: Statement to Accompany the Public Domain Version* (United Utilities 2006) Yorkshire Water, *June Return 2007: Statement to Accompany the Public Domain Version* (Yorkshire Water 2006)
199 P Bennett, *Re: Ofwat's excision policy for the June Return data* (email correspondence 21 June 2011)
200 'I am afraid that there is no source document as such for the categorisation policy'. See ibid
201 I C R Byatt, *MD135, Confidentiality for July Returns and PR99 Information Submission* (Ofwat 1998)
202 RD 29/98 sum up the companies' responses on what information should be made confidential (and not) based on MD 135; R D Dunshea, *RD 29/98, Confidentiality for July Returns and PR99 Information Submission* (Ofwat 1998)

Regulator, licences and information flow 89

copy submission made to Ofwat.[203] In doing so, the companies must set out the justifications for its restriction and this explanation will be published along with other information which is not excised.[204] RD 29/98 makes clear that Ofwat might still need to consider the justification used in excisions, and if it declines the companies' justification, it will provide time for companies to make representations and prepare for publication.[205]

The move toward a risk-based approach to regulation as discussed in the previous section would mean that the above June Return excision 'policy' will no longer be relevant. If Ofwat no longer collects the June Return data, it will have no similar information to be disclosed to the public. However, if disclosure of regulatory accounts becomes mandatory in the future this excision policy could be revisited. Moreover, the excision 'policy' can be used to evaluate each company's consideration in non-disclosure.

In Jakarta, JWSRB, the regulatory body are constrained from disclosing information arising out of the concession due to the confidentiality clause on the Cooperation Agreement. This has been the primary impediment to transparency.

The clause obligates the parties to keep all information arising out of the contract confidential, unless both of the parties agree otherwise. Through some informants, the author is able to confirm that the confidentiality clause reads as follows:[206]

47.1 General Provisions

The parties, officers, directors, experts and/or personnel and agents of each Party are obliged to maintain the confidentiality of all commercial and technical information which they possess and has been obtained from each Party, and are forbidden from using the information except for the purposes intended in this Agreement, except for that categorized as:

a information which was already controlled/possessed by one Party, unless it should have been known by such Party that such information constitutes confidential information of the other Party;

b information which was public knowledge at the time it was revealed under this Agreement; and

c information which became public knowledge after being revealed under this Agreement.

---

203 Byatt, *MD135, Confidentiality for July Returns and PR99 Information Submission* (Ofwat 1998) 'The only areas that I believe could be considered to have a serious and prejudicial effect are Tables 30, 31, 35a, 35b, 36a, 36b and 39 plus the associated commentaries of the standard July Return and table 40 in the enhanced July Return for 1998.'
204 ibid
205 Dunshea, *RD 29/98, Confidentiality for July Returns and PR99 Information Submission* (Ofwat 1998)
206 Cooperation Agreement Between PAM Jaya and The Concessionaire, 2001 Clause 47.1 and 2

47.2 Disclosure of Confidential Material

a   The Parties may disclose the confidential information referred to in Clause 47.1 to a third party for the purpose of implementation of this Agreement, with the stipulation that a written agreement has been made before the information is disclosed to ensure that the third party receiving the information will maintain its confidentiality and only use the information for the purpose for which it was disclosed.

b   In the event of a disclosure of information as intended in Clause 47.2(a), in the interest of the implementation of this Agreement, the disclosure must first be approved by the other Party.

Without any waiver clause or FoI override, such a clause impedes the application of the FoI Law. In Victoria's water project, the confidentiality clause is complemented by a waiver clause, which requires compliance with FoI Act or other legislation.

First, it is relevant to ask: who is bound by this provision? The Cooperation Agreement mandates that all parties (PAM Jaya and the concessionaires) and people affiliated with them (this includes directors, experts, personnel) shall 'maintain the confidentiality of all commercial and technical information which they possess and has been obtained from each Party'.[207] It is to be noted that the term 'party' here refers to the concessionaires and PAM Jaya. It is interesting to ask if the regulatory body (JWSRB) and officials at the Governor's office can also be bound by this clause. Strictly speaking, as a non-party, they cannot be directly bound by the contract. However, as the regulatory body is instituted under the contract, they adopt some of the principles stipulated therein, and this includes the policies to preserve confidentialities. This prompts a question on the transparency impact of the *hybrid* model.[208]

Second, it is relevant to discuss the breadth of this provision. Which information is covered by the confidentiality clause? One must note that the term 'commercial and technical information' covers a wide range of information. In practice, this clause effectively shields all information acquired by PAM Jaya through reports and investigation toward the concessionaires. In other research conducted by the author, not only regulatory information is treated as confidential, but also the Cooperation Agreement itself.[209] The regulator considers that the contract confidentiality clause extends into the contract document itself. This was confirmed by a field interview with Palyja, which also interprets that the confidentiality clause is meant to cover both information arising out of the contract and the contract itself.[210] Finally, this stance was confirmed

---

207   ibid Clause 47.1
208   For discussion on the 'hybrid' model of regulation see Eberhard, 'Infrastructure regulation in developing countries: an exploration of hybrid and transitional models.' (African Forum of Utility Regulators, 3rd Annual Conference, 15–16 March 2006, Windhoek, Namibia)
209   Al'Afghani and others, *Transparansi Lembaga-lembaga Regulator Penyediaan Air Minum Di DKI Jakarta* (ECOTAS/KRuHA/TIFA, 2011)
210   Interview with Palyja in Jakarta, 10 January 2011. Palyja regard that the confidentiality clause may provoke suspicion and erode public trust.

by an official FoI request[211] made by an NGO to PAM Jaya. The NGO request demanded that PAM Jaya disclose (a) Jakarta Water Cooperation Agreements along with its amendments, (b) results of financial audits conducted by the state audit agency and (c) financial projections used in determining water tariffs. However, PAM Jaya, through a letter[212] cited the summary of clause 47 above and refused to disclose the requested information, including the Cooperation Agreement itself. Thus, the private sectors, JWSRB and PAM Jaya all have one voice in this matter: the confidentiality clause extends to the concession contract itself. The case was finally brought to the National Freedom of Information Commission.[213]

This restriction from disclosure under Clause 47 has four qualifiers: (1) disclosure can only be made to 'third parties', (2) disclosure can only be made with the purpose of implementing the Cooperation Agreement, (3) the disclosing party and the third party must enter into a confidentiality agreement prior to the disclosure, and (4) all parties to the Cooperation Agreement must agree to the disclosure.[214] Public disclosure of any regulatory information acquired by PAM Jaya is then virtually impossible, as the contract requires any third parties to enter into a confidentiality agreement with the disclosing party. The qualifiers are only designed to disclose information to specific third parties, such as accountants and auditors but not the public.

Furthermore, this clause primarily serves the interest of the concessionaire, although it is formulated to apply to both parties. This is because all regulatory information tends to flow from the concessionaires to PAM Jaya through the reporting duties and investigative powers as discussed in the previous section, and not the other way around. It is PAM Jaya who has the obligation to be accountable in its dealings with third parties, including the concessionaire, and therefore might be required to disclose some regulatory information.

Pergub-118, which is the primary legal basis for the establishment of the regulatory body outside the Cooperation Agreement, stipulates that the JWSRB is obligated to maintain confidentiality of *all* information and can only utilise information for the purposes of mediating disputes between the contracting parties.[215] This is despite the fact the Pergub-118 refers to the Indonesian Freedom of Information Law. In addition, JWSRB enacted its internal code of conduct on participation and transparency, the Regulatory Body Rule No. 2 Year 2007 on the Mechanism and Procedure of Transparency in Jakarta's

---

211 Muhammad Reza, *Permintaan Dokumen dan Informasi Kontrak Konsesi Layanan Air Minum Jakarta (Freedom of Information Law Request for Documents and Contractual Information Concerning Jakarta's Water Services Concession)*, Letter No. 019/KIP/V/2011 dated 31 October 2011 (KRuHA 2011)
212 Daryanto, *Jawaban Surat KRuHA* (Letter No. 581/DIV.T&P/XI/2011 dated 8 November 2011 on PAM JAYA's response to FoI Request by KRuHA) (PAM Jaya 2011)
213 Rizal, *Tanda Terima Pendaftaran Pengajuan Sengketa Informasi No. A26/RSI/P/XII/KIP/2011, KRuHA v PDAM DKI Jakarta, 07-12-2011* (Komisi Informasi Pusat (KIP) 2011)
214 Cooperation Agreement Between PAM Jaya and The Concessionaire, 2001 Clause 47.2
215 Peraturan Gubernur DKI Jakarta No. 118 Tahun 2011 Tentang Badan Regulator Pelayanan Air Minum Article 5.b. Note that the JWSRB's primary function is mediating disputes. The JWSRB lacks the power normally accorded to independent regulatory bodies, such as in determining tariffs or imposing penalties. This article appears to be drafted in light of that purpose.

Water Services.[216] Since JWSRB's initial mandate is weak, the rule has no legitimate binding power, although in practice it is used as a basis for JWSRB's operation. Despite the word 'transparency' in the rule's title, the rule makes no mention of public disclosure of regulatory information.

To conclude, although the JWSRB and its officials and agents are not a party to the contract, the regulation which establishes them incorporates the contract's confidentiality principles. As a result, public disclosure of regulatory information is constrained.

This is in contrast with other regional-owned waterwork companies which do not engage with PSP, such as Bogor. Unconstrained by any confidentiality obligation to another party, Bogor, a city 60 kilometres south of Jakarta, regulates in its regional by-law that the utility must provide periodical performance reports for the purpose of transparency, to the public.[217]

---

216 Peraturan Badan Regulator Pelayanan Air Minum DKI Jakarta No. 02 Tahun 2007 Tentang Mekanisme Dan Prosedur Transparansi Pelayanan Air Minum Jakarta

217 Peraturan Daerah Kota Bogor Nomor 5 Tahun 2006 Tentang Pelayanan Air Minum Perusahaan Daerah Air Minum Tirta Pakuan Kota Bogor Article 3(2)(c)

4 Regulatory functions

This chapter will discuss the transparency mechanism in five core regulatory functions: investment, tariff and prices, service levels and customer service standard, non-compliance and redress.

4.1 Investment

In Victoria, utilities' Statement of Obligation (SOO) contains obligations for them to manage their assets in a way that allows them to supply their services sustainably, maintain service levels and to minimise their assets' life-costs as well as the environmental, social and economic impacts that may be caused by its operation.[1]

The details of each utility's investment plan are contained in a 'Water Plan', which must be submitted before the next regulatory period commences. The obligation to submit this 'Water Plan' is embodied in the SOO.[2] There is a minimum of information that must be contained in the Water Plan, among others: (a) outcomes to be delivered with respect to service levels, fulfilment of future demand, its compliance with SOO and other relevant legislations,[3] (b) a description of how they propose to deliver those outcomes; (c) the utility's revenue requirements in that regulatory period; (d) the proposed price to be charged.[4] Utilities are also required to describe, in their Water Plan, their proposal to meet their sustainability management plans, which incorporates climate change concerns, maintenance of natural assets and minimisation of environmental impacts.[5]

The WIRO states that there are two ways for prices to be determined by the ESC: by way of approval of a Water Plan submitted by utilities[6] or by

---

1 'Statement of Obligations (General) 2012' (n 113).
2 *Water Industry Act 1994, Statement of Obligation, City West Water Limited* (2008) The SOO also sets the deadline for submitting the Water Plan
3 These are deemed to be the Environment Protection Act 1970, Water Industry Act 1994, Safe Drinking Water Act 2003, the Food Act 1984 or the Health (Fluoridation) Act 1973.
4 *Water Industry Act 1994, Statement of Obligation, City West Water Limited* (2008) para 7.3
5 ibid paras 25.1 and 25.2
6 Water Industry Act 1994, Water Industry Regulatory Order 2003 para 8.a

unilaterally specifying prices if utilities fail to submit the Water Plan.[7] The latter should occur only if the utilities miss the prescribed deadline for the submission of the Water Plan or if it has been formulated without due regard to procedural requirements[8] as set out in the SOO and/or the regulatory principles of the WIRO.[9] The 'regulatory principles' obligate the ESC to allow the utilities to recover their expenditures and rate of return on assets, to provide incentives on sustainable water use and improve efficiency. It also obligates the price setting to have regard and to 'take into account' the interests of vulnerable and low-income customers. In the English water industry, such principles are enshrined in a primary legislation.[10]

The Water Plan consists of outcomes which are expected to be delivered by the retailers, investment programmes required to deliver such objectives, the expenditures involved and the revenue in order to fund the expenditures.[11] An exposure draft is presented to the ESC for review. The ESC must review the consistency between the prices in the Water Plan with WIRO as well as SOO and may also use external resources to review the utilities' expenditure projections.[12]

The Minister of Water (in consultation with the Treasurer) and other regulatory agencies can give comments on the retailers' Water Plan.[13] If the Minister requests it, the retailer must make variation to its Water Plan. There is, at present, no obligation for the Minister to explain the rationale behind variation of the water plan and such a requirement would require amendments of relevant acts.[14]

With respect to other regulatory agencies, the retailer should only 'pay attention' to their comments. The retailers are under a duty to consult with customers but the SOO does not prescribe the detail and timeframe for such consultancies. The timeframe between the Draft Water Plan and the submission of the Final Water Plan to the ESC is one month; meanwhile, the period between final submission and the ESC's obligation to 'have regard' to comments from other regulatory agencies is two weeks.[15] Customer consultation takes place within this one-month period.

One of WIRO's regulatory principles is an obligation on the utilities to enable customers and potential customers to understand pricing and how it is

---

7 ibid para 8.b
8 The so called procedural requirements are no more than the duty to consult the drafting of the Water Plan with relevant regulatory agencies (Environment Protection Authority, the Secretary to the Department of Human Services, and the ESC) with respect to their specific regulatory competences.
9 Water Industry Act 1994, Water Industry Regulatory Order 2003 para 10. The regulatory principles are outlined in para 14
10 Water Industry Act 1991 c.56 s.2
11 See for example Yarra Valley Water, *Water Plan 2009/10–2012/13, Yarra Valley Water, November 2008* (2008) and *Water Industry Act 1994, Statement of Obligation, City West Water Limited* (2008)
12 Water Industry Act 1994, Water Industry Regulatory Order 2003 paras 9, 10 and 13
13 See 'Statement of Obligations (General) 2012' (n 113).
14 Victorian Competition and Efficiency Commission, *WaterWays: Inquiry into Reform of the Metropolitan Retail Water Sector, Final Report February 2008* (2008) p.153
15 ibid

calculated.[16] This one-month period (in the Water Plan) is perceived to be too short to allow agencies and the public to comment on the Draft Water Plan. A four-month timeframe between the Draft Water Plan and the Final Water Plan is perceived to be ideal.[17] It is suggested that the SOO contain an obligation for the Minister to explain and publish his rationale for requiring the variation of the Water Plan. It is also suggested that other regulatory agencies publish their comments on the Draft Water Plan.[18]

Neither the WIRO nor utilities' SOOs contain specific obligations to publish the Water Plan. The SOO, however, requires that utilities 'develop and implement *open and transparent* processes to engage its customers and the community in its planning processes',[19] in addition to some obligations to make available to the public information about water supply, sewerage and recycled water services, water conservation and the efficient and responsible use of water; and also to put educational materials about water conservation into schools.[20] In practice, the Water Plan is published on the ESC's website. The utilities also make available the water plans on their websites in order to ensure consistency with the obligation to develop an 'open and transparent' planning process.[21]

In England, determination of a utility's investment priorities can be a contentious issue. Prices, network expansion, drinking water quality and the environment are the four main concerns of the regulatory trade-off. In EU countries such as England, there is little discretion with respect to drinking water quality and effluent standard and with almost full coverage, network expansion is not as contentious as in developing countries, although sewerage networks that are over capacity are still a problem and require investment to expand and upgrade.

Thus, having almost full coverage does not mean that there will be no other trade-offs with respect to investment made. There are still pressures to curtail carbon emissions, repair leakages, invest in sewers and lower charges. Utilities' duty to invest in sewerage, as discussed by Hendry, is not an absolute duty, as it must be balanced against other duties as discussed above.[22] The Marcic litigation at the House of Lords epitomises this balancing principle. The Court held that the duty to invest is not absolute as it must be balanced against other duties, constrains consumer recourse within available regulatory remedies and

---

16 Water Industry Act 1994, Water Industry Regulatory Order 2003 para 14(1)(a)(vii) If utilities fail to adhere to this provision then the Water Plan may be deemed contrary to 'regulatory principles' and as a result they may need to be revised or the ESC will instead prescribe prices.
17 Victorian Competition and Efficiency Commission, *Water Ways: Inquiry into Reform of the Metropolitan Retail Water Sector, Final Report February 2008* (2008) See Box 7.3
18 ibid see Box 7.3
19 'Statement of Obligations (General) 2012' (n 113).
20 ibid
21 Lower Murray Water, *Lower Murray Water Exposure Draft Water Plan 2008–09 to 2012–13*, October 2007 (2007) Yarra Valley Water, *Water Plan 2009/10–2012/13*, Yarra Valley Water, November 2008 (2008)
22 S Hendry, *Frameworks for Water Law Reform* (Cambridge University Press 2014) p.86

overrules other private law actions.[23] This signifies that utilities' investment decisions in sewerage have winners and losers. Since litigation efforts have been overruled, the most appropriate way is to integrate the losing stakeholders in the participatory mechanism where they can voice their concerns. A prerequisite for this is for the utilities and the regulatory bodies to disclose the reasoning behind their decision not to invest in sewerage capacity expansion and to outline and explain to the losing stakeholders how their concerns are taken into account and reflected in future utilities' investment policy.

The next important issue is leakage. It is occasionally cheaper for companies that have a surplus of water resources (and therefore a low marginal cost) to 'treat and leak' water rather than to repair the leakages.[24] There is no problem with this practice until bulkwater resources become scarce, for example, due to drought, as occurred in Yorkshire in 1995.

The drought that struck Yorkshire in 1995 was rather unanticipated as it was preceded by a wet winter leading to a maximum groundwater level and fully recharged reservoirs.[25] The utilities, Yorkshire Water Services (YWS), had been paying high dividends to its parent companies instead of allocating the funds to manage its *headroom*[26] properly.[27] With leakage level high and customer awareness programmes failing to constrain demand[28] YWS had no other option but to enforce emergency drought orders which authorised them to, among other actions, ban all non-essential water uses[29] and abstract water from other sources.[30] These had significant implications for the environment which prompted the authorities to artificially aerate some rivers and conduct 'fish rescue'.[31]

The legal obligation to repair leakages, however, is never straightforward since 'treat and leak' can be more economical than repairing leakage, and this is also true in legislative terms. The WIA under s.37(1) requires utilities to arrange for (a) the supplies of water to premises in their respective supply area[32]

---

23 *Marcic v Thames Water Utilities Ltd [2003] UKHL 66* (4 December 2003)
24 Bakker, *An uncooperative commodity: Privatizing water in England and Wales* (Oxford University Press, USA 2003) p.90
25 K J Bakker, 'Privatising water, producing scarcity. The Yorkshire drought of 1996' 76 Economic Geography 4
26 *Headroom* is a margin between supply and demand. According to OFWAT, 'Target Headroom' is the minimum amount of headroom needed to meet demand, 'taking into account supply and demand uncertainty such as the temporary loss of a water resource' *Security of supply 2006–07 – supporting information* (Ofwat)
27 Bakker, 'Privatising water, producing scarcity. The Yorkshire drought of 1996' 76 Economic Geography 4
28 See G Haughton, 'Private profits–public drought: the creation of a crisis in water management for West Yorkshire' 23 Transactions of the Institute of British Geographers 419 The utilities' declining popularity may have contributed to the failure of the customer awareness programme designed to curtail water demand.
29 Water Resources Act 1991 s.76
30 Water Resources Act 1991 s.77
31 Bakker, 'Privatising water, producing scarcity. The Yorkshire drought of 1996' 76 Economic Geography 4
32 Water Industry Act 1991 c.56 s.37(1)(a)

and (b) 'maintaining, improving and extending the water undertaker's water mains and other pipes'.[33] However, the provision continues 'as are necessary for securing that the undertaker is and continues to be able to meet its obligations under this Part'.[34] Ofwat's 'translation' of this provision is to impose the policy which requires utilities to fix leakage, to the extent that the cost for doing so is less than the cost of not fixing it, which is calculated from environmental damages and the cost of developing new water sources to offset the leak, known as the SELL (Sustainable Economic Level of Leakage).[35] According to the Water White Paper, the SELL approach will be reviewed, so as to incorporate further externalities into the calculations, further integration with water resources planning and customer engagement for efficiency.[36]

Prior to determining final prices, companies are obligated by Ofwat to submit their 'final business plans'.[37] This document contains investment programmes that companies are making in the following five years after the Price Determination. This includes, for example, network expansion, maintenance of ageing assets, including climate change management plans.[38] For 2014 price review, high quality business plans may qualify for 'enhanced' status, if such companies accept Ofwat risk and reward guidance. Enhanced companies will have a fast track price review process where the substance of the draft determination will not change. Other companies will be labelled with 'standard' (subjected to a standard price review process, adjustment from draft determination) or 'resubmission' (companies resubmit their draft business plan for more scrutiny).[39] Each company publishes their draft business plans on their website and – in the past – Ofwat has supplied links to them on its own website.[40]

The leakage target of each company is a part of the 5 Year Price Determination (published by Ofwat). Under the present system, companies' leakage commitments are associated with its incentive mechanism.[41]

---

33 ibid s.37(1)(b)
34 ibid s.37(1)
35 'Leakage' (Ofwat) <http://goo.gl/wYOOiq> accessed 21 May 2016. This approach is called SELL, which stands for the 'Sustainable Economic Level of Leakage' 'PR09/20: Water supply and demand policy' (Ofwat 2008) <http://goo.gl/MZAVA2> accessed 21 May 2016; see also United Kingdom, *Providing Best Practice Guidance on the Inclusion of Externalities in the ELL Calculation: MAIN REPORT, Appendix 2 (part 1)* (2011)
36 'The Water White Paper; Second Report of Session 2012–13' <www.publications.parliament.uk/pa/cm201213/cmselect/cmenvfru/374/374.pdf> accessed 30 November 2015
37 Ofwat, 'Overview of the Business Plan Information Requirements for PR09' (Ofwat) <http://goo.gl/?GPKTu0> accessed 21 May 2016
38 Anglian Water, 'PR09 Final Business Plan, Part A: The Company Strategy' (Anglian Water) <www.anglianwater.co.uk/_assets/media/Proposed_business_plan.pdf> accessed 18 August 2011
39 'Setting Price Controls for 2015–20 – Risk and Reward Guidance' <www.ofwat.gov.uk/wp-content/uploads/2015/11/gud_tec20140127riskreward.pdf> accessed 6 December 2015
40 Ofwat, 'Periodic review 2009: water & sewerage companies' final business plans – one page summaries' (Ofwat) <goo.gl/TpKQUI> accessed 21 May 2016
41 'Setting Price Controls for 2015–20 – Final Methodology and Expectations for Companies' Business Plans' <www.ofwat.gov.uk/wp-content/uploads/2015/11/pap_pos201307finalapproach.pdf> accessed 6 December 2015

98 *Regulatory functions*

Companies' leakage reduction commitment forms a part of Ofwat's determination, measured on a yearly basis in megalitres per day. The determination (in various consultations with the company) sets categories of penalties and rewards. If a company's leakage is within a certain band, then a penalty will be imposed. If a company leakage is above the penalty band, then financial rewards will follow.[42] If the matter is considered serious, Ofwat can interpret the company's failure to repair leakage as a violation of s.37(1), which provides them with the authority to invoke enforcement action (under ss.18, 19 and 22A). Companies sometimes disagree[43] with Ofwat's interpretation, but choose to accept s.19 enforcement (undertaking) rather than being fined by Ofwat. In the past, Ofwat have announced the names of companies who fail to achieve their leakage target for naming and shaming purposes.[44]

Ofwat 'expect' the companies to publish their actual level of leakage, annually, as a key performance indicator, in addition to total leakage and customer pipe leakage. Ofwat will also publish a comparison of companies' performance on leakage to foster 'reputational incentive'. Presumably, the first publications will be on the companies' website whereas the second will be on Ofwat's.

Disclosure of companies' leakage conditions enables stakeholders to assess if their supply security is threatened and subsequently determine the course of action that is acceptable to them. If the leakage rate is inefficient, more investment will have to be undertaken. If a regulator perceives that the investment will have to be financed by customers through price increases, disclosure could help to increase the acceptability of a price increase. If, on the other hand, companies consistently fail to achieve their leakage target, disclosure would enable customers and other stakeholders to persuade the regulator to take action against the utility.

In Jakarta, the Cooperation Contract stipulates for a five-year investment programme and an annual Investment and O/M programme.[45] The five-year programme must be agreed by PAM Jaya but the yearly investment and O/M programme needs only to be discussed with them.[46] The obligation to invest and extend the network is also formulated in terms of 'technical targets',[47] detailed in schedule 8[48] of the contract, which consists of the volume of water billed, production of potable water, non-revenue water, number of connections and the ratio of service coverage.[49] The companies

---

42 'Setting Price Controls for 2015–20 Final Price Control Determination Notice: Company-Specific Appendix – Affinity Water' <www.ofwat.gov.uk/wp-content/uploads/2015/10/det_pr20141212afw.pdf> accessed 6 December 2015
43 In a letter to Ofwat Chairman accepting s.19 undertaking, RWE Thames Chief Executive stated: 'Although it in no way diminishes the agreement to which I have referred, as you know we cannot accept that the current situation is such to constitute a contravention of s.37'. J Pelczer, *Leakage and Security of Supply, Undertaking Under s.19 Water Industry Act 1991* (2006)
44 Ofwat, *Ofwat: Meeting the demand for water,' Twenty-fourth Report of Session 2006–07* (2007) p.13
45 Cooperation Agreement Between PAM Jaya and The Concessionaire, 2001 Clause 9.4.F
46 ibid Clause 9.1.F
47 ibid Clause 9.4.B
48 ibid Clause 20
49 ibid Schedule 8

have full discretion on how to implement them.[50] By the end of the contract period, the contract target is 100 per cent of coverage, which means that all of Jakarta should be connected to the water network.[51]

Bakker maintained that the system in Jakarta is implicitly 'anti-poor' as it conveys disincentives to both providers and the poor to connect to the network.[52] The disincentives for the poor to connect according to Bakker are:

> insecure tenure, the need for flexibility of payment, convenience, status and high 'transaction costs' which includes the infrastructure costs to build storage because networked water supply is only intermittent; line-ups and time off work to pay bills (for those without bank accounts and regular income); fear of time required to deal with mis-read meters and over-charging).[53]

The concessionaire also faces some disincentives in connecting to the poor. On the face of it, the system of water charges which pays the concessionaire based on the volume of water they sell (in accordance with indexation formula and other variables) should not influence their decision to connect. This assumption was confirmed by the private sector during an interview in Jakarta.[54] Bakker found that disincentives occur because the poor are covered by the lowest tariff band and the income generated by extending the network to them falls below the production cost.[55] Connecting to the poor means reducing PAM Jaya's capability to collect more revenue and this will eventually affect PAM Jaya's ability to pay[56] water charges to the concessionaires.[57] Other disincentives built in to the system are due to the disorderly distribution of homes which raises the transaction costs, and lack of land tenure.[58]

Expansion to poor areas with lack of land tenure has been inhibited by the presence of mafia-like[59] organisations controlling public hydrants, which benefit from very high prices for the amount of water sold from these taps to the

---

50   ibid Clause 9.4.B
51   ibid Schedule 8 Aetra's coverage in 2007 was 66.08% while its target was 74%. See Lanti and others, *The First Ten Years of Implementation of the Jakarta Water Supply 25-Year Concession Agreement (1998–2008)* (Jakarta Water Supply Regulatory Body (JWSRB) 2009)
52   Bakker, 'Conflicts over water supply in Jakarta, Indonesia' in Barraqué and Vlachos (eds), *Urban Water Conflicts: an analysis on the origins and nature of water-related unrest and conflicts in the urban context* (UNESCO Working series SC-2006/WS/19. 2006)
53   ibid p.115
54   The private sector commented that, due to the in-built system of water charges, they extend the water network solely due to demand considerations. PAM Jaya's Concessionaire, *Personal Communication with the Private Sector* (11 January 2011)
55   According to Bakker's research in May 2005, the lowest tariff is IDR 500 whereas the production cost is approximately IDR 3,000
56   See also the discussion on PAM Jaya's debts in section 4.4 below
57   Bakker, 'Conflicts over water supply in Jakarta, Indonesia' in Barraqué and Vlachos (eds), *Urban Water Conflicts: an analysis on the origins and nature of water-related unrest and conflicts in the urban context* (UNESCO Working series SC-2006/WS/19. 2006) p.123
58   ibid p.128
59   L Lovei and D Whittington, 'Rent-extracting behavior by multiple agents in the provision of municipal water supply: a study of Jakarta, Indonesia' 29 Water Resources Research 1965

poor.[60] The flow of money from these activities could also be used to capture policy-making in network expansion to the poor. Bluntly said, not connecting to the poor benefits both the concessionaire (by reducing the risk of non-payment from PAM Jaya and the high risk of transaction costs of connecting to the poor) and also benefits complicit officials through high rent-extraction from selling water from public taps.

A transparent system would enable the public to comment and participate in network expansion and investment plans.[61] Achievement of the concessionaire's technical targets is published partially (but not routinely) by the regulatory body on its website[62] and is discussed widely in books published by them.[63] However, what is urgent for the citizen is the *plan* itself, the outcome of which will have a direct effect on their livelihood. In an interview with Palyja,[64] they pointed out that they voluntarily submitted an investment plan every three months before year-end to PAM Jaya although it is not required by the contract. This is good practice but, unfortunately, this submission is not followed by a public disclosure from PAM Jaya or the regulatory body to the public. There are also no adequate mechanisms for the public to be able to obtain, comment and participate in the concessionaire's investment plan.

4.2 Tariffs and prices

In Victoria, the Water Plan exposure draft is made available for public review. The final drafts are also published. Unless the ESC decides to determine prices on its own, the Water Plan will be the substantial document upon which the prices are based.

Various consultations are carried out in the price-setting process. The ESC has a good practice of making the consultation documents and the public comments and submissions available on its website.[65] Water utilities also conduct various consultations with stakeholders, as they are required by the SOO to develop an *open and transparent* planning process. One of the 'regulatory principles' under WIRO[66] – with which the utilities must comply if they want their Water Plan to be approved by the ESC – is to enable customers to understand pricing. As such, the water utilities' method of consultation is embodied in their Water Plan.

---

60 'Pay Up: How the Water Mafia Controls Access' (*The Jakarta Globe*, 2009) <http://goo.gl/Axg3RY> accessed 21 May 2016
61 In many instances, the high cost of transaction in making the connection can actually be reduced through public work conducted by the poor themselves
62 Jakarta Water Supply Regulatory Body, 'Kinerja Operator' (*JWSRB*) <http://goo.gl/yFJAnS> accessed 21 May 2016
63 Lanti and others, *The First Ten Years of Implementation of the Jakarta Water Supply 25-Year Concession Agreement (1998–2008)* (Jakarta Water Supply Regulatory Body (JWSRB) 2009)
64 Interview with Palyja, Jakarta, 10 January 2011
65 'Melbourne metropolitan water price review 2009–10 to 2012–13, Consultations' (*Essential Services Commission*) <http://goo.gl/rc9Rjp> accessed 21 May 2016
66 Water Industry Act 1994, Water Industry Regulatory Order 2003

ESC's power to make determinations is vested in the ESC Act.[67] The ESC Act obligates that every determination includes a statement of purpose and the reason for making such determination.[68] When a determination is made, a notice must be published in the *Government Gazette*, the daily newspapers generally circulating in Victoria *or* on the internet.[69] Such a notice must contain information on the nature and effect of the determination, the effective date and how a copy of the determination can be obtained from the Commission.[70] The ESC is obliged to send the copies of its determination to regulated entities and to any person who makes inquiries.[71]

In England, legislation regulates price review in broad terms, referring to it together with other matters as 'Determinations made under conditions of appointment'.[72] The company's licence further regulates this in more detail, by stipulating the intervals for price reviews[73] and limiting the increase of standard charges or the 'K' factor.[74]

In the past, price reviews involved several stages, involving large amounts of data collection.[75] Ofwat's approach has been criticised by the Gray review as too burdensome, as it went too much into the detail of company business plan, making companies too 'Ofwat focused' and thereby hindering innovation.[76] The review recommends that Ofwat needs to substantially reduce the regulatory burden and return the ownership of the business plans to the companies.

As a response to this, Ofwat moved further toward implementing a risk-based approach to regulation. As discussed previously, the June Return data collection is now no longer required. The risk-based approach places the onus on each company's board, to own and be accountable for their business plan.[77] Ofwat sets several incentives for companies in order to increase the quality of their business plan: process incentive (regulatory efforts are focused only on parts considered necessary), reputational incentive (giving signals to stakeholders and investors through the quality of their business plans), procedural incentives (earlier draft determination and potentially earlier final determination – for those with 'enhanced' status) and financial incentives (access to enhanced menus with greater shares of cost outperformance).[78]

---

67 Essential Services Commission Act 2001 No. 62 of 2001 s.33
68 ibid s.35(1)
69 ibid s.35(2)
70 ibid s.35(3)
71 ibid s.35(4)
72 Water Industry Act 1991 c.56 s.12
73 *Instrument of Appointment by the Secretary of State for the Environment of Thames Water Utilities Limited as a water and sewerage undertaker under the Water Act 1989* (2005) Condition B (Charges) para 1.2
74 ibid Condition B (Charges) para 1.1
75 Ofwat, 'Price Review 2009' (Ofwat) <http://goo.gl/DDpoVL> accessed 21 May 2016
76 Gray, *Review of Ofwat and consumer representation in the water sector* (Defra and the Welsh Government 2011)
77 'Setting Price Controls for 2015–20 – Final Methodology and Expectations for Companies' Business Plans' (n 637)
78 ibid

102 *Regulatory functions*

Companies can either decide to accept Ofwat's determination or refer their objection to the Competition and Markets Authority.[79] If no referrals are made, Ofwat approves the charging scheme. Finally, the new price limit will take effect and the whole process is evaluated. In all of these phases, information and documents are published by both Ofwat and the companies.

Legislation acts generally as a facilitator to transparency in price reviews. All of Ofwat's research and inquiries, framework and methodology for price review, consultations, information requirement, companies draft business plan, and the Determination (both the draft and final Determination) are available on either Ofwat's website or the company's.

In Indonesia, a regulation from the Minister of Home Affairs issued in 2006 (Permen 23) stipulates that 'transparency and accountability' is one of the principles of tariff setting.[80] It requires tariffs to be 'affordable' to those having wages equal to the regional minimum wage or not comprising more than 4 per cent of the monthly average community's income.[81] Permen 23 also stipulates that the calculation and enactment of tariffs must be transparent and accountable.[82] 'Transparency', according to Article 7 of the Permen 23 is to be achieved by 'clearly delivering information related to the calculation and enactment of tariffs to stakeholders' and by 'wholeheartedly capturing stakeholders' aspirations in connection with the calculation and enactment of tariffs'.[83] 'Accountability' in turn, is to be achieved by 'using calculations which can be easily understood and can be justifiable to the stakeholders'.[84]

The components of costs[85] (including the data to justify such components), types of revenues,[86] types of tariffs,[87] and steps in calculating tariffs, including the procedures and mechanisms for tariff enactment, are all stipulated in Permen 23. The procedures and mechanisms for tariff enactment include the requirement to conduct consultations with customers' representatives and forums and through various media in order to obtain their feedback.[88] This should be done before the proposal is submitted to the mayor/governor.

In Jakarta, presumably because of the Cooperation Agreement, the room for regulating becomes narrower and that leaves the city with a by-law which, after being enacted in 1993, has never been amended or reformed. Regulators

---

79   Ofwat, 'Price review 2009 timeline' (Ofwat) <http://goo.gl/ XXCLGx> accessed 21 May 2016
80   *Peraturan Menteri Dalam Negeri No. 23 Tahun 2006 Tentang Pedoman Teknis dan Tata Cara Pengaturan Tarif Air Minum Pada Perusahaan Daerah Air Minum* Article 2.e
81   ibid Article 3
82   ibid Article 7
83   ibid Article 7.2
84   ibid Article 7.2
85   ibid Articles 12, 13, 14
86   ibid Articles 15, 16
87   ibid Articles 17, 18; It was also revealed in the interview that some customers complained over their arbitrary removal from a tariff band. *Interview with Non Governmental Organizations, Jakarta, 20–30 December 2010*
88   Peraturan Menteri Dalam Negeri No. 23 Tahun 2006 Tentang Pedoman Teknis dan Tata Cara Pengaturan Tarif Air Minum Pada Perusahaan Daerah Air Minum Articles 21.2

and the private sector themselves maintained during interviews that Permen 23 and other guidelines issued by the central government do not apply to the Jakarta concession.[89] In practice, the governing law on tariff setting in Jakarta is limited to By-laws 11 and 13 and the Governor's Decision on automatic tariff adjustment.

By-law 11 stipulates that the number of drinking water tariffs shall be determined by the Jakarta Governor,[90] after being approved by the Ministry of Home Affairs.[91] The calculation of tariffs is based on the classification of consumers multiplied by the volume[92] of water used by the consumer.[93] Details on the cost structure are not known to the public although the component of the water charge[94] is announced by the regulator. As discussed in the previous section, By-law 11 does not contain any provision on disclosure or public participation on tariff setting. On the contrary, in Bogor a city 60 km from Jakarta, the regional by-law requires tariff setting to be based on the principles of affordability, justice, quality, cost recovery, efficiency, transparency, accountability and conservation.[95]

4.3 Service levels and customer service

In Victoria the ESC has the power to make determinations[96] with respect to standards and conditions of service and supply, licensing, market conduct and 'other' economic regulatory matters as stipulated by the *empowering instrument*.[97] Other normative sources for service levels and customer service are found in the WIRO, the Codes of Practice and the approved Water Plan. Drinking water quality standards are regulated directly by legislation.[98]

---

89 Personal Communication, *Field Interview with Palyja, Jakarta, 10 January 2011*
90 Peraturan Daerah Khusus Ibukota Jakarta No. 11 Tahun 1993 Tentang Pelayanan Air Minum di Wilayah Daerah Khusus Ibukota Jakarta Article 16.1
91 ibid Article 16.2 this provision reflects the legal situation before regional autonomy was introduced. Prior to 2001, every regional by-law had to be approved by the central government through the Ministry of Home Affairs, including rules which are politically sensitive, such as determination of water tariffs. After regional autonomy was introduced, this requirement no longer existed. The Jakarta regulator and the private sector maintain that Jakarta is not covered by PP-16 and Water Law 7/2004 and therefore should be covered solely by By-law 11 – which obligates determination of tariffs through the approval of MOHA. This has brought confusion and potential legal challenges to tariff decisions.
92 ibid Article 18
93 ibid Article 17
94 The formula used in water charges and water tariffs is available at JWRSB's website <www.jakartawater.org/< accessed 5 January 2010
95 Peraturan Daerah Kota Bogor Nomor 5 Tahun 2006 Tentang Pelayanan Air Minum Perusahaan Daerah Air Minum Tirta Pakuan Kota Bogor Article 15
96 ibid s.34
97 'Empowering instrument' is defined as other relevant legislations; a Governor's Order, the Tariff Order; or the Water Industry Regulatory Order made under Part 1A of the Water Industry Act 1994, see s.3 of the Essential Services Commission Act 2001 No. 62 of 2001
98 Safe Drinking Water Act 2003, No. 46 of 2003 (Victoria)

104 *Regulatory functions*

The WIRO enables the ESC to prescribe service standards, either by approving companies' Water Plans or by issuing Codes.[99] In practice, quantitative service standards (such as the average time taken to repair leaks or average duration or planned interruption) as well as Guaranteed Service Level payment schemes of each company are approved by the ESC through the Customer Services Code (CSC)[100] as the conditions differ from company to company.

The CSC sets the general standards on what the customer can expect from their utility.[101] It contains the utilities' duty to connect to customers, and the utilities' right to refuse or discontinue connection to waste water service which is not in accordance with the utilities' terms. The Code also regulates charges that water businesses can impose on customers, the complaints and disputes policy and the resolution of disputes. The CSC also requires utilities to provide customer information about referral to EWOV and other external dispute resolution when a complainant is not satisfied with the utility's response.[102] One key transparency mechanism is the obligatory publication of the Customer Charter containing the condensed form of the CSC and explaining the details of service levels and customer service standards that customers can expect from the utilities.[103]

The format of billing is regulated in the Code.[104] It is stipulated that a bill must contain certain information such as the date of issue, the customer's billing address and account number, including the amount, the date and ways for the customer to pay the bill, the total of any payments made by the customer since the last bill, information on concessions available and any concession to which the customer may be entitled, and in the event of financial difficulties, the channels available to resolve the situation.

Bills must be broken down into several parts to increase transparency: any service charge to the property, the usage charge for each service to the property, other charges in connection with the provision of services and rates and other charges.[105] The bill must also contain graphical illustrations of the customer's current water and recycled water usage, the customer's usage for each billing period over the previous 12 months; and a comparison of the customer's usage with the customer's usage for the same period of the previous year.

In case of financial difficulty, a water business is obligated to make flexible payment plans according to the customer's capacity to pay. Other measures such as referral to the Utility Relief Grant Scheme or free financial advice are available. There is also a hardship policy[106] which will be applicable if a customer has the intention but not the financial capability to pay their bill.

---

99 Water Industry Act 1994, Water Industry Regulatory Order 2003 para 15
100 Essential Services Commission, *Customer Service Code Metropolitan Retail and Regional Water Businesses* (Issue No 7, 15 October 2010, 2007) these form Schedules 2 and 1 of the CSC
101 ibid
102 ibid para 3.2
103 See ibid Part C (Customer Charter)
104 ibid part 4, p.5
105 ibid pp.5–6
106 ibid pp.9–10

The Code forbids utilities to employ supply restriction, legal action, or any additional debt recovery costs if a customer is suffering hardship.[107] There is a requirement in the Code that this hardship policy must be published on the utility's website and a copy must be made available to a customer upon request.[108]

As for water quality, the Safe Drinking Water Act requires the publication of water quality monitoring programmes within seven days after the test results are compiled.[109] There are penalties for the publication of knowingly misleading material.[110] The Secretary of State can impose additional reporting duties if there are risks to public health[111] and requires water suppliers to notify customers that treatment might be required before drinking.[112]

Unlike England (will be discussed below), however, the 'Guaranteed Service Levels' schemes are, so far, voluntary. Business is not bound to provide compensation to customers for failures to meet service levels. Lack of clarified service levels[113] and inadequate historical data on service levels are among the reasons why some businesses are reluctant to propose GSL Schemes.[114] All three retailers have GSL schemes.

The CSC obligates utilities to make available to customers all regulatory instruments including the CSC itself.[115] The GSL must be approved by the ESC. After they are approved, they form a part of the ESC-issued Customer Service Code.[116] As every code must be published, the approved GSL schemes are also automatically published along with the CSC.

In England, disconnection for non-payment and the use of limiting devices for household customers is prohibited by the WIA.[117] Vulnerable groups are facilitated with lower tariffs and flexibility of payment.[118] This policy is not applicable to non-household customers.[119] However, when a premise serves

---

107 ibid para 5.4
108 ibid para 5.4
109 Safe Drinking Water Act 2003, No. 46 of 2003 (Victoria) s.23
110 ibid s.23
111 ibid s.34(1) and (2)
112 ibid s.34(3)(b)
113 GSL payments are said to be appropriate when businesses propose higher service levels than is required by regulation. The existing service levels already require compliance. GSL may have disincentives; for example, utilities may choose to pay GSL rather than improving the service. See Gerard Brody, *Policy Proposals for refinements to Essential Services Commission regulatory framework for water* (Prepared for the Department of Sustainability and Environment by the Consumer Law Centre Victoria)
114 Lower Murray Water, *Lower Murray Water Exposure Draft Water Plan 2008–09 to 2012–13*, October 2007 (2007) p.9
115 Essential Services Commission, *Customer Service Code Metropolitan Retail and Regional Water Businesses* (Issue No. 7, 15 October 2010, 2007) para 12.8
116 ibid See Schedule 1 (Approved GSL Schemes)
117 Water Industry Act 1991 c.56 s.61(1A)
118 Water Industry (Charges) (Vulnerable Groups) Regulations 1999 SI 1999/3441 (as amended) See Regulation 2
119 Water Industry Act 1991 c.56 s.61

106 *Regulatory functions*

both non-household customers and household customers, Ofwat categorises this as a 'mixed-use premise' where disconnection is disallowed.[120]

WIA requires that water supplied by the utilities is 'wholesome'.[121] Wholesomeness is accomplished when the water supplied complies with the list of maximum or minimum concentrations or values prescribed by the water quality regulations or, when a prescription is absent, does not contain microorganisms, parasites or substances at concentrations or values which could be potentially dangerous to human health.[122] The supply of water unfit for human consumption is an offence.[123]

When contamination occurs, water undertakers have the power to disconnect and the obligation to serve notices to customers, specifying the steps that need to be undertaken before supply is restored.[124] Legislation does not detail any further how contamination has to be communicated. There is no uniform standard on how companies should deal with contamination, so the mechanism has been developing out of practice. Some companies place alerts on websites, deliver notices by hand door-to-door, ring the customers and contact local doctors to obtain information on sensitive customers, and normally have pre-arranged agreements with local media in the event of emergencies.[125] From the materials collected in one research project, it was revealed that 90 per cent of the notices are 'readable'.[126]

Service and customer service levels in England are contained in a Statutory Instrument[127] separated from that regulating drinking water quality, and is called the Guaranteed Standard Scheme (GSS) which regulates six categories of customers' rights.[128] These minimum standards are subject to some qualifications

---

120 'Disconnection of Mixed-Used Premises For Non Payment of Water Charges, RD 14/04' (2004) <http://goo.gl/UwlmY0> accessed 21 May 2016
121 Water Industry Act 1991 c.56 s.68(1)(a)
122 In most situations, the regulation prescribes a maximum value, acidity (pH) level is the exception, with a minimum value of 6.5 and a maximum of 9.5. See The Water Supply Regulations 2010, SI 2010 No. 1991 This SI is regularly amended. Particularly see Regulation 4(2)(a)
123 Water Industry Act 1991 c.56 s.70
124 Incidents must be immediately notified to the DWI as soon as they come to the attention of the company. The Water Industry (Suppliers' Information) Direction 2009. See Water Industry Act 1991 c.56 s.75(1) and (1A) and s.75(3). Failure to serve notice is considered an offence see s.75(5)
125 Risk Solutions, *Good Practice for Communicating about Drinking Water Quality; A report for The Drinking Water Inspectorate* (D5173/R1, 2009)
126 ibid There are several methods by which to assess the readability of material, namely, through the Flesch-Kincaid grade level, Gunning fog index and Lexical Density Function. See L Si and J Callan, 'A statistical model for scientific readability' (Proceedings of the Tenth International Conference on Information and Knowledge Management)
127 The power to make regulation is conferred on the Secretary of State, see Water Industry Act 1991 c.56 ss.38(2)-(4), 95(2)-(4), 213(2)(d) (e), (2A)(a)-(c), and (2B)
128 The Water Supply and Sewerage Services (Customer Service Standards) Regulations 2008, SI 2008 No. 594 The six categories of customer's rights are: (1) The making and keeping of appointments; the GSS rule sets the obligation to provide notice specifying the exact time of the appointment with customers and the utilities' obligation to keep such appointment. (2) Lack of pressure; the minimum pressure is set at 0.7 bar, violation occurs when a company fails to comply with such requirement more than twice, each more than one hour, within a 28-day period. (3) Supply interruptions; utilities are obliged to provide notice of planned interruptions of supply

such as natural disaster or labour strikes. Violations occur when none of the qualifications apply. This entails financial penalties to be paid directly by the utilities to customers.

Another relevant instrument embodying 'service levels and customer service' is Condition G of the company's licence, which applies the 'Code of Practice for Customers and relations with the Customer Service Committee' (currently CC Water).[129] The Code of Practice must be approved by Ofwat and typically would contain: a description of tariff charges, arrangements for the payment of bills and payment by instalments including budget plans, the procedures for making complaints, testing of meters, methods for meter reading, offences for tampering with meters, emergency conditions and making enquiries with the company, a description of CC Water and its contact information.[130] The existence of the code and any substantive revision thereof must be put to customers' attention.[131] Utilities must also explain how the code can be inspected and copied by the customers.[132] Ofwat require utilities to send, free of charge, the code in its latest form to anyone requesting it.[133]

While the GSS Rule prescribes the minimum amount of payment against violation of service standard, some companies use the Code of Practice to enhance the amount of the compensation.[134]

In Jakarta, service levels and customer service are regulated through several rules which often overlap. The first layer is national legislation and its implementing regulations enacted by the central government, which includes regulations from the Ministry of Health on drinking water quality[135] and rules from the Ministry of Public Works[136] on the drinking water supply provision system.

---

at least 48 hours before it occurs, specifying the time when supply will be restored, any alternatives of supplies that can be obtained and the telephone number of the utilities where queries can be made. If a utility fails to restore supplies by the time stated on the notice provided to customers it may be subjected to fines. (4) Queries on charges; when customers make queries (in writing) about the accuracy of their bill, utilities have the obligation to provide a substantive response. (5) Complaints in general; any written complaints must be responded to within 10 working days. (6) Sewer flooding; effluent from utilities' sewers must not enter customers' buildings and land properties. See ibid, Regulations 6, 10, 8, 9, 7, 11 and 12

129 *Instrument of Appointment by the Secretary of State for the Environment of Thames Water Utilities Limited as a water and sewerage undertaker under the Water Act 1989* (2005) Condition G
130 Thames Water, 'Code of Practice: important helpful information and advice for household customers' (*Thames Water*) <http://goo.gl/q4pUIj> accessed 21 May 2016
131 *Instrument of Appointment by the Secretary of State for the Environment of Thames Water Utilities Limited as a water and sewerage undertaker under the Water Act 1989* (2005) Condition G.6(2)
132 ibid
133 ibid Condition G.6(4)
134 Thames Water, 'Code of Practice: important helpful information and advice for household customers' (*Thames Water*) <http://goo.gl/q4pUIj> accessed 21 May 2016, p.7. See also Thames Water, 'Our guarantees to you: Customer Guarantee Scheme' (*Thames Water*) <http://goo.gl/gljzxZ> accessed 21 May 2016
135 *Peraturan Menteri Kesehatan Republik Indonesia No. 492/Menkes/PER/IV/2010 Tahun 2010 Tentang Persyaratan Kualitas Air Minum*
136 Indonesia, *Peraturan Menteri Pekerjaan Umum No.18/PRT/M/2007 Tentang Penyelenggaraan Pengembangan Air Minum Sistem Penyediaan Air Minum* (2007)

108 *Regulatory functions*

In the second layer, there is the 1993 pre-concession Jakarta regional by-law on 'Drinking Water Services in Jakarta Region' (By-law 11)[137] and several regulations issued by the Governor, such as Pergub-118[138] regulating the JWSRB and some other Governor's regulations on automatic tariff adjustments. In the third layer, there is the Cooperation Agreement[139] along with its addenda and annexes, which contain prescriptions on service levels to which the concessionaire must adhere.

These rules often overlap and contradict each other. As previously discussed, both the regulator and the concessionaire believe that the national regulation on drinking water, the now defunct GR-16 was not applicable to the Cooperation Agreement.

After the Water Law was invalidated in the 2015 Judicial Review, GR-16 is regarded as no longer binding and as of this moment, there is no legal umbrella for water services at the national level. Nevertheless, since the provisions on service levels and customer service were not regarded as contentious during the Judicial Review, such provisions may be reinserted with minimum modification in future legislations. As such, the provisions will be discussed below.

The now-defunct GR-16 obligated cooperatives and privately owned business enterprises involved in drinking water provision to follow planning, management, monitoring and evaluation guidelines issued by the minister and to provide the regional or central government with information on their service delivery.[140] Article 67 of the GR guarantees all customers the right to obtain drinking water services which fulfil the quality, quantity and continuity standards,[141] to obtain information on the structure and the amount of tariffs and bills, to lodge a lawsuit for any harm resulting from the service, to obtain compensation against any negligence in service delivery and to obtain sewerage services or on-site sanitation services.[142]

Water services providers are obligated to: (a) guarantee services based on the prescribed standards, (b) provide information to all interested parties on any occurrences or specific circumstances which have the potential to alter the quantity or quality of service and (c) provide information on the implementation of service.[143] GR-16 did not provide examples of what sort of circumstances might potentially alter service levels. However, the wide formulation of the clause would mean that all sorts of deviation from service levels, including

---

137 Peraturan Daerah Khusus Ibukota Jakarta No. 11 Tahun 1993 Tentang Pelayanan Air Minum di Wilayah Daerah Khusus Ibukota Jakarta
138 Peraturan Gubernur DKI Jakarta No. 118 Tahun 2011 Tentang Badan Regulator Pelayanan Air Minum
139 Cooperation Agreement Between PAM Jaya and The Concessionaire, 2001
140 Article 66, Peraturan Pemerintah No. 16 Tahun 2005 Tentang Pengembangan Sistem Penyediaan Air Minum Ministerial guidelines are available but not sufficiently clear Indonesia, *Peraturan Menteri Pekerjaan Umum No.18/PRT/M/2007 Tentang Penyelenggaraan Pengembangan Air Minum Sistem Penyediaan Air Minum* (2007)
141 Article 67.1, Peraturan Pemerintah No. 16 Tahun 2005 Tentang Pengembangan Sistem Penyediaan Air Minum
142 ibid
143 ibid Article 68

disruptions or contamination, would require the water utility to inform and warn customers.

Under the Indonesian Freedom of Information Law there is also an obligation to announce to the public any information about situations that might threaten the 'livelihood' of many people and 'public order'.[144] Such information must be disclosed in manners accessible to the community and in an understandable language.[145] According to the government drafter of the Indonesian FoI Law UU No. 14/2008, 'livelihood' is to be understood as the 'society's needs' and 'public order' is to be understood as 'concerning a person's life'.[146] This formulation renders it certain that vital information concerning contamination of water supplies falls under this clause.

The next layer regulating service level and customer service in Jakarta is By-law 11. By-law 11/1993 stipulates that the Jakarta Governor appoints PAM Jaya as a caretaker in undertaking the provision and distribution of drinking water[147] and that PAM Jaya has the obligation to provide the service to the community.[148] By-law 11 regulates the prerequisites for connecting to the mains network[149] and the boundaries on liability for maintenance of assets.[150] The consumer's rights and obligations are also regulated in By-law 11/93, however, they put weight on consumer's obligations toward the utilities and not their rights. GR-16 and Water Law 7/2004 (both now defunct) could have been implemented in the regions when they are incorporated in regional legislations. Nevertheless, the Jakarta by-law has never been amended since its enactment in 1993, thus, it was disconnected from those national legislations.[151]

The final layer for service level and customer service regulation in Jakarta is The Cooperation Agreement. The Agreement obligates the concessionaires

---

144 Undang Undang No. 14 Tahun 2008 Tentang Keterbukaan Informasi Publik, Article 10
145 ibid
146 See Anotasi Undang Undang Nomor 14 Tahun 2008 Tentang Keterbukaan Informasi Publik, Edisi Pertama, Komisi Informasi Pusat, 2009, p.136
147 Article 2.1 Peraturan Daerah Khusus Ibukota Jakarta No. 11 Tahun 1993 Tentang Pelayanan Air Minum di Wilayah Daerah Khusus Ibukota Jakarta
148 ibid Article 2.2
149 Inter alia, that the request to connect has to be in writing, Article 4.2. Other prerequisites are listed in Article 7 ibid
150 Consumers are responsible for pipes existing in their parcels of land, although prior checking by PAM Jaya is obligatory, Articles 7.b and 8 of ibid
151 The concession might be one of the reasons why the by-law has never been amended to ensure compliance with national legislations in the water sector. Changing the by-law would require changing key terms in the concession contract which directly affects the contract's economics. The cost for renegotiation is high, meanwhile, the government's and the parties' concern is to keep the contracts afloat, by insulating it from sudden changes. This begs the question of whether regulation by contract, and concession especially, will have the effect of restraining sectoral reform. See Mohamad Mova Al'Afghani, 'When it comes to water services, Jakarta is living in the distant past' *The Jakarta Globe*, 16 October 2011 <http://goo.gl/p5b08e> accessed 21 May 2016; also Mohamad Mova Al'Afghani, 'Anti-privatisation debates, opaque rules and "privatised" water services provision: some lessons from Indonesia' in A Nicol, L Mehta and J Allouche (eds), *IDS Bulletin: 'Some for All?' Politics and Pathways in Water and Sanitation*, vol. 43.2 (Institute of Development Studies, Wiley-Blackwell 2012)

110 *Regulatory functions*

to meet certain service levels.[152] Concessionaires are given the liberty to determine the *means and method* for delivering the service standards as set on the contract schedule. There is also an obligation to conduct sampling and testing of water quality in accordance with standards agreed by the Ministry of Health, complemented by the obligation to deliver the test results to PAM Jaya, every month. PAM Jaya is allowed to exercise its own testing on the condition that it does not hinder the concessionaire's daily operation. The parties may refer examination to an independent expert should disagreement concerning compliance of water quality arise.

Service levels[153] consist of ambient water quality standards, drinking water standards, pressure at customer connection, maximum response time to answer phone calls, attendance time to respond to complaints, time for completion of repairs, and the obligation to connect in areas where mains are available. Categorisation of these standards is made available on JWSRB's website,[154] but the details have never been officially disclosed by the authorities and the concessionaire. Hence, there is no way for customers in Jakarta to directly know the services to which they are entitled, despite the obligation under GR-16 that private water undertakers are obligated to provide information on the implementation of service.[155] In 2007, the regulatory body insisted to the media that the Cooperation Agreement contains a clause mandating compensation to consumers in the amount of IDR 50,000 (approximately USD 5) if a disruption occurs for more than one day. A member of the regulatory body stated: 'The JWSRB has requested, over the last 6 months, that customer rights should be published. However, the operators always refuse. Without publication on the mass media, Jakartans will never know their rights with respect to service disruption'.[156]

---

152 Cooperation Agreement Between PAM Jaya and The Concessionaire, 2001 Schedule 8
153 ibid Clauses 31.1 and 31.2
154 Jakarta Water Supply Regulatory Body, 'Kinerja Operator' (*JWSRB*) <www.jakartawater.org/index.php?option=com_content&view=article&id=96&Itemid=257&lang=en> accessed 18 August 2011
155 Peraturan Pemerintah No. 16 Tahun 2005 Tentang Pengembangan Sistem Penyediaan Air Minum does not expressly obligate the disclosure of the service standard itself, only its *implementation* is obligated to be disclosed. The obligation to disclose service standards is implied. ibid Article 68.2(a) guarantees services based on the prescribed standards, (b) provides information to all interested parties on any occurrences or specific circumstances which has the potential to alter the quantity or quality of service and to (d) provide information on the implementation of service. The Public Service Law also obliges public bodies to inform communities of the content of any cooperation agreement entered into between them with third parties. The information should at least explain important issues that should be known to the community such as the type of the outsourced project, identity of the provider, the contract period, and the work commenced by the provider in accordance with service standard. Undang Undang No. 25 Tahun 2009 Tentang Pelayanan Publik Article 13.1.b and its elucidation.
156 Statement of Dr Riant Nugroho as quoted by Kompas See 'Hak Pelanggan Disembunyikan (Customer's Rights are Concealed)' *Daily Kompas* (Jakarta, 27 November 2007). In a Personal Communication with the author, Dr Nugroho confirmed this statement.

Note that JWSRB is constrained from publishing the contract due to a confidentiality clause[157] and its statute[158] which – pursuant to the contract – prohibits the disclosure of regulatory information.

Such a stance was also supported by the JWSRB Chairman at that time, Ahmad Lanti, who suggested that disclosure of consumers' rights would enable the community to file class action suits in order to obtain such compensation.[159] The PAM Jaya Director, however, denied that such a compensation scheme exists.[160]

A group of civil society launched a Freedom of Information campaign requesting the disclosure of the Cooperation Agreement. After the case went all the way to the Supreme Court, the contract disclosure request was granted, with minor exemption.[161] The copy contract was finally provided by the Jakarta Governor to the NGOs requesting it, but the document never entered the public domain.[162] The details of compensation, therefore, remain unknown to the public. The FoI and Court decisions cover only the contract documents but not other information arising out of or in connection with the contract. This information remains confidential.

In order to avoid the presumption that such a problem is typical in developing countries where there is a general lack of governance, it is relevant to briefly provide another Indonesian case study. Bogor is a municipality 60 km south of Jakarta where the company is publicly owned. The city's population is a lot smaller, 750,000, compared to Jakarta's 10 million. Unlike Jakarta, which relies on 1992 and 1993 by-laws, and has never reformed these even after the concession was concluded, Bogor's water services by-laws were modified in 1996 and 2006. The 2006 amendment is a particularly distinctive one as it contains many guarantees on service levels and customers' rights. The regional autonomy, which delegates the management of drinking water services to regional governments, might have been the driver for these reforms. This can be seen from the tendency in several other regions to conduct utilities' reform after autonomy was introduced in 2001.[163]

In Jakarta's by-laws there is a duty to serve connection requests from industry, residential properties, tourism, etc.[164] imposed on the regional-owned

---

157 Cooperation Agreement Between PAM Jaya and The Concessionaire, 2001 Clause 47
158 Peraturan Gubernur DKI Jakarta No. 118 Tahun 2011 Tentang Badan Regulator Pelayanan Air Minum Article 5b
159 'Hak Pelanggan Disembunyikan (Customer's Rights are Concealed)' *Daily Kompas* (Jakarta, 27 November 2007)
160 ibid
161 *Kruha v PAM Jaya, Putusan 172/G/2012/PTUN JKT* (Mahkamah Agung Republik Indonesia)
162 Interview with NGO activists in Jakarta, May, 2012
163 See regional by-laws enacted in various regions, for example, Peraturan Daerah Kabupaten Maros No. 4 Tahun 2011 Tentang Perusahaan Daerah Air Minum; Peraturan Daerah Kabupaten Sragen No. 8 Tahun 2004 Tentang Perusahaan Daerah Air Minum Kabupaten Sragen; Peraturan Daerah Kabupaten Takalar No. 15 Tahun 2003 Tentang Perusahaan Daerah Air Minum; Peraturan Daerah Kendal No. 13 Tahun 2011; Peraturan Daerah Provinsi Kalimantan Barat No. 2 Tahun 2006 Tentang Pendirian Perusahaan Daerah Air Minum Provinsi Kalimantan Barat
164 Peraturan Daerah Khusus Ibukota Jakarta No. 11 Tahun 1993 Tentang Pelayanan Air Minum di Wilayah Daerah Khusus Ibukota Jakarta

112 *Regulatory functions*

waterwork company that is a partner of the concession contract to the private sector. However, there is no duty directly imposed on the private sector to connect the customer. In Bogor, there is a general duty 'to serve' water services for Bogor residents and a specific duty to extend the network to regions with inadequate groundwater quality.[165]

In terms of service levels, the Jakarta by-laws refer to the Ministerial Decree on drinking water quality;[166] but in practice, changes to the Decree are not automatically applicable. Due to the concession, changes in water quality regulation must be *negotiated* with the private sector. On the other hand, any changes to water quality regulation are directly applicable in Bogor. The Bogor regional by-law also contains provisions regulating service disruptions, the general obligation for the regional waterwork company to supply water with a certain quality, continuity and quantity (except on the event of *force majeure*) and a 24-hour call centre and mailbox for customer service.[167] These service levels are clearly stipulated in the Bogor regional by-law and are therefore published. As discussed in the previous section, in Jakarta, the service levels are regulated in Schedule 8[168] of the Cooperation Agreement and are subject to contractual confidentiality.

In terms of customers' rights, the only 'right' available under the Jakarta regional by-law is the 'right' to object to PAM Jaya about an incorrect water meter,[169] the 'right' to object to the imposition of penalties by the Governor and the 'right' to request an examination of a water meter – discussed earlier. Even these are not directly formulated as rights. The word used is 'may' (i.e. 'dapat mengajukan keberatan'/i.e. 'may' propose objection). The Cooperation Agreement contains some stipulation on customers' rights including compensation payments for violation of service level standards in 'Schedule 15' of the contract as argued by the regulator, but this schedule, as it forms a part of the contract, is also confidential.

On the other hand, the Bogor regional by-law contains provisions guaranteeing the right to (1) obtain results on the examination of water quality, accuracy of metering device, calculation of water bill, (2) obtain explanation of the agreed terms when submitting new connection requests, (3) obtain information on the structure and price of tariffs, (4) receive a 50 per cent discount on monthly fee if water supply is disconnected for three consecutive days without prior notice, (5) receive a discount if the water company fails to respond within three days after a leakage occurs, which causes elevation of customers' bills,

---

165 Peraturan Daerah Kota Bogor Nomor 5 Tahun 2006 Tentang Pelayanan Air Minum Perusahaan Daerah Air Minum Tirta Pakuan Kota Bogor Article 3 hereinafter 'By-law 5 (Bogor)'
166 Peraturan Daerah Khusus Ibukota Jakarta No. 11 Tahun 1993 Tentang Pelayanan Air Minum di Wilayah Daerah Khusus Ibukota Jakarta Article 19.1
167 Article 5, ibid
168 Cooperation Agreement Between PAM Jaya and The Concessionaire, 2001 Schedule 8
169 Article 15, Peraturan Daerah Khusus Ibukota Jakarta No. 11 Tahun 1993 Tentang Pelayanan Air Minum di Wilayah Daerah Khusus Ibukota Jakarta

(6) obtain replacement of water meter if the installed meter is not working and (7) to convey their complaints on water bills, water distribution, quality and other matters related to water services.[170] All of these rights and compensation mechanisms are stipulated in the by-law and, by default, a published document.

4.4 Non-compliance

Transparency is required, not only with respect to the content of the service levels and customer service, but also with respect to violation of such standards by the utilities and any enforcement measures by the regulator in response to such violations. The reason is because information on non-compliance is vital for investors and creditors as it may influence their investment decisions, as well as for the public to create pressure to hold the regulator accountable and for the utilities to take action. It is also used to compel other companies to change behaviour in addition to maintaining a sense of fairness.[171]

In Victoria, the ESC publishes performance reports on the retailers regularly. The performance report synthesises data from each retailer's Key Performance Indicator set by the ESC and through audits made by ESC.[172] Water utilities' compliance with service levels is outlined in the performance report.

The ESC has enforcement powers against contraventions with WIRO, Codes or Determinations made by it, applicable only when such contraventions are deemed to be of a 'non-trivial' nature.[173] There are two kinds of enforcement orders: provisional and final. The purpose of such orders is to ensure compliance with WIRO, Codes and Determinations or in rectifying the occurrence of contraventions.[174] A final order is not required if the utilities provide an undertaking or if the ESC is satisfied with their actions.[175] Inquiries might be established before any sanctioning is imposed.

Penalties are available for not complying with the orders.[176] There is room for objection and submission.[177] One key transparency mechanism of non-compliance is the publication of the orders in the *Government Gazette*.[178]

In England, the system on enforcement of non-compliance follows Macrory's recommendations on enforcement which include some transparency

---

170 Article 20, Peraturan Daerah Kota Bogor Nomor 5 Tahun 2006 Tentang Pelayanan Air Minum Perusahaan Daerah Air Minum Tirta Pakuan Kota Bogor
171 According to OFWAT: 'Use of these enforcement tools and transparency about their use may also incentivise other companies to change their behaviour'. United Kingdom, *Ofwat's Approach to Enforcement* (2009) para 19 <http://goo.gl.NFb4YJ> accessed 21 May 2016
172 Essential Services Commission, *Water performance report: Performance of urban water businesses 2009–10* (December 2010)
173 Essential Services Commission Act 2001 No. 62 of 2001 s.53(1)
174 ibid s.53(2)
175 ibid s.53(5)
176 ibid s.53(9)
177 ibid s.53(6)
178 ibid s.53(7)

principles,[179] namely: (1) the publication of enforcement policy,[180] (2) the justification on the choice of enforcement action,[181] (3) transparency on which formal enforcement activities have been undertaken[182] and (4) transparency in the methodology for calculating penalties.[183]

Ofwat categorises[184] formal enforcement action into several layers: the securing of formal undertakings from the companies (s.19),[185] the 'enforcement order' (s.18)[186] and, finally, the imposition of financial penalties (s.22A).[187] 'Enforcement Orders' (s.18) can be imposed on utilities that contravene their licence conditions[188] or any other statutory requirement.[189] The s.18 order requires them to do or not to do things which the order specifies.[190] An enforcement order must be preceded by a notice, specifying the purpose of the order, its effect, the requirement to secure compliance, the acts or omission which constitute contravention and other supporting facts justifying the order.[191] Such notices must be published[192] and copies served on the utilities.[193]

The alternative to s.18 enforcement orders is applicable in circumstances where Ofwat perceives the contravention to be of a trivial nature[194] or where a company has agreed to provide an undertaking to Ofwat to secure compliance.[195] If the utility provides an undertaking, such undertaking will be perceived as a statutory requirement enforceable under s.18.[196] This, too, requires Ofwat to serve notice to companies and to publish a copy of such notice.[197]

---

179 The other framework is in measuring the outcome of enforcement actions and to follow-up enforcement actions. United Kingdom, *Regulatory justice sanctioning in a post-Hampton world: consultation document* (2006) p.8
180 This is to signal to all stakeholders what the expected behaviours are, and what the consequences will be if they breach such expectation. See ibid p.21
181 This is to increase confidence in how regulatory non compliance is being dealt with. See ibid p.21
182 This is in order to keep stakeholders and the public up to date with regulatory action. Macrory considers that when and against whom the enforcement action is taken should be disclosed. See ibid p.22
183 If the methodology for imposing fines is published, firms will have awareness of each mitigating or aggravating factor considered by the regulator, leading to the overall amount of the penalty. See ibid p.22
184 See United Kingdom, *Ofwat's Approach to Enforcement* (2009) <http://goo.gl.NFb4YJ> accessed 21 May 2016. There are also 'special administration orders' for violation of 'principal duties' or where the utility is unable to pay its debts. Water Industry Act 1991 c.56 ss. 23–25), but this occurs only in extraordinary circumstances and is not a part of day-to-day regulation.
185 Water Industry Act 1991 c.56 s.19
186 ibid s.18
187 ibid s.22A
188 ibid s.18(1)(a)(i)
189 ibid s.18(1)(a)(ii)
190 ibid s.18(5)(a)
191 ibid s.20(1)
192 ibid s.20(2)(a) The provision continues by explaining that the purpose of such publication is to bring the matters to the attention of persons who may be affected.
193 ibid s.20(2)(b)
194 ibid s.19(1)(a)
195 ibid s.19(1)(b)
196 ibid s.19(2)
197 ibid s.19(3)

Regulatory functions 115

Finally, Ofwat has the authority to impose financial penalties on the utilities for contravention of their licence conditions or for failing to achieve performance standards.[198] There is an obligation to serve notice on three occasions: before the penalty is made[199] (as a Proposal to Impose Penalty), when it is decided that such proposal is to be varied[200] and after imposing the penalty.[201] These notices should contain information, *inter alia*, on the amount of penalty (this should not be more than 10 per cent of the utilities' annual turnover), the acts or omission which are deemed to constitute a contravention, supporting facts and justification and the period for the utilities to make objection with respect to the penalties issued.[202]

Publication of these notices is obligatory as well as the serving of copies of such notices to the utilities and other regulatory bodies.[203] Ofwat carries out good practice by publishing these notices on its website.[204] Its enforcement policy and statement of policy on financial penalty[205] policy is also published. Hence, most of Macrory's sanctioning framework (with respect to transparency) above has been incorporated by legislation[206] and also practised by Ofwat, an example being that which concerns Thames Water[207] and United Utilities.[208] Responses from the utilities and their representations expressing disagreement or objection with respect to facts, circumstances and methodologies raised by Ofwat are also available in the public domain, as a matter of good practice.[209]

In Jakarta, the Cooperation Agreement obliges the concessionaire to complete repairs following any interruption, at a maximum, within 24 hours after it occurs. Failure to comply with such a requirement may trigger a penalty and, in addition, the obligation to pay compensation to consumer.[210] Schedule 15 reads:

---

198 ibid s.22A(1)(a)
199 ibid s.22A(4)
200 ibid s.22A(5)
201 ibid s.22A(1)(a)
202 See Water Industry (Determination of Turnover for Penalties) Order 2005 SI 2005/ 477, ibid s.22A(4)(b),(c) and (d)
203 ibid s.22A(8)(a),(b),(c),(d)
204 For example 'Notice of Ofwat's imposition of a penalty on Thames Water Utilities Limited' (OFWAT, 2008) <www.ofwat.gov.uk/consultation/notice-of-ofwats-proposal-to-impose-a-penalty-on-thames-water-utilities-limited/> accessed 21 May 2016
205 United Kingdom, *Ofwat's Approach to Enforcement* (2009) <http://goo.gl.NFb4YJ> accessed 21 May 2016; also *Section 22A Water Industry Act 1991: Statement of policy with respect to financial penalties* (Ofwat)
206 Regulatory Enforcement and Sanctions Act 2008, 2008 c.13 contains lengthy transparency requirements on enforcement (see s.64) but this Act is binding to Ofwat, only with respect to ss.72–73: 'Duty not to impose or maintain unnecessary burdens'.
207 The notice is divided into several sections, among others: Identification of relevant regulatory provisions, facts and matters giving rise to the contravention, penalties, OFWAT's reasons for considering it appropriate to impose a penalty, assessment of the amount of the penalty and summary of representations received by OFWAT and OFWAT's response to these representations. *Notice of Ofwat's proposed variation to its proposal to impose a penalty on Thames Water Utilities Limited* (Ofwat)
208 *Notice of Ofwat's proposal to impose a penalty on United Utilities Water plc* (Ofwat 2007)
209 Cristopher Wright, *Memorandum: United Utilities Water Proposed Penalty – Representations of United Utilities Water ('UUW')* (2007)
210 Cooperation Agreement Between PAM Jaya and The Concessionaire, 2001 Schedule 15

> Every Customer who complains in writing to the Second Party shall be entitled to a rebate in the next month's Customer bill of 10% of the Customer's bill for the month in which the complaint arose – with a minimum rebate of Rp.10,000 and a maximum rebate of Rp.50,000.
>
> If a Customer claims compensation in excess of Rp.50,000, the Customer shall only be entitled under this Schedule to a maximum of Rp.50,000 with the balance of any claim to be settled by mutual agreement between the Second Party and the Customer or through some other mediation, arbitral or court process.
>
> Rebates will be made directly to the Customer in the next month's Customer bill, without affecting project revenue.

When water quality is not in compliance with the prescribed standard, the Cooperation Agreement obliges the parties to hold 'discussions' *'for the purposes of establishing the reason for the non-compliance'*.[211] Only when it is found that the concessionaire is at fault will it be responsible to repair the service and pay a penalty. The italicised clause above implies that non-compliance is permissible if it is not due to the first party's fault.[212]

With only three healthy rivers flowing to Jakarta (out of 19), the supply of bulk water is in a critical situation. During certain seasons silt causes damage to water pumps and treatment installations and eventually causes disruptions. As the contract places the risk of bulk water supply on PAM Jaya, the clause above often effectively shields the concessionaire from its obligation to pay penalty fees caused by the disruption.

In 2009, news emerged that Aetra offset IDR183 billion worth of penalty fees to PAM Jaya. Even with such offset, PAM Jaya still owes Aetra another IDR237 billion, which if not paid, will be billed by the time the concession ends in 2022.[213] Thus, as a result of the 'water charge' system and bulk water insecurity, PAM Jaya has a large amount of debts toward the private partners. If customers are compensated, the funds generated from penalty payments will not be available to offset the repayment of such debts.

---

211 ibid Clause 21.g
212 There are possibilities that the supply of bulk water might decrease in terms of quality and quantity. Such a condition is beyond the reach of the concessionaire's abilities. This clause protects the concessionaire from being penalised for failures in bulk water supplies. See ibid Clause 11
213 In the Jakarta concession system, PAM Jaya pays the concessionaires based on the volume of water sold to consumers calculated through an indexation formula, taking into account exchange rate and inflation rate (this is called 'water charge'). Tariff, on the other hand, is set by the Governor, and is divided into several bands, depending on the customer's economic situation. If collection of tariff payment is unable to meet the water charge, PAM Jaya owes money to the Concessionaire ('shortfall'). Apparently, the set-off was to pay the amount of shortfall PAM Jaya owes to Aetra. What is not known is whether there are portions of money for consumers in that transaction. The concession contract obliges that compensation to consumers is paid directly. See ibid definition of 'Water Charge' and clause 35

There is no obligation to disclose non-compliance by the concessionaire and the JWSRB has no discretionary power to do so. The confidentiality clause also impairs PAM Jaya from disclosing information on non-compliance.

4.5 Redress

In Victoria, dispute resolution was previously regulated in the Water Industry Act, water utility's operational licence which obligated the utility to enter into a dispute resolution scheme.[214] With the current status as statutory corporations, similar obligation is regulated under the 1989 Water Act, which also does directly refer to a specific dispute settlement body.[215] In practice, utilities enter into contractual agreements with EWOV to resolve disputes.

The obligation to inform the public of the existence of a dispute resolution body lies with both the utilities and the EWOV itself – by virtue of its Charter. Utilities are obligated under the ESC Code to 'provide to customer, information about referral to [EWOV] and other relevant external dispute resolution', in the event that the customer is not satisfied by the response from the water utility.[216] The EWOV Charter, meanwhile, contains the obligation to promote its dispute resolution scheme and to make available to the public 'an accurate and up-to-date list of all Participants'.[217] It appears from the Code that the obligation to inform a customer of the existence of a dispute resolution body is triggered only when the customer is not satisfied with the utility's explanation. When a customer is satisfied, the obligation to inform them of existence of the EWOV scheme does not arise.

The Decision by the Ombudsman shall be made in writing and should provide rationales.[218] The Decision must be published but the names of the parties must not be identified.[219] From the perspective of the complainant, this requirement is understandable, since water disputes may involve the indication of a financial problem which is a matter of a complainant's privacy. For the utilities, however, water disputes with complainants may reveal their compliance with service level and customer rights. Disclosure of such information may be in the public interest. The EWOV Charter stipulates that in the event of a dispute utilities should provide all relevant information to the Ombudsman, except for confidential information of a third party, after a reasonable effort

---

214 Government of Victoria, *Water and Sewerage Licence, City West Water Limited A.B.N. 70 066 902 467, Reprinted incorporating amendments as at 28 July 2004* (2004) Government of Victoria, *Water and Sewerage Licence, Yarra Valley Water Limited A.B.N. 93 066 902 501, Reprinted incorporating amendments as at 28 July 2004* (2004) para 7b
215 Water Act 1989 No. 80 of 1989, Version 102. S122ZG
216 Essential Services Commission, *Customer Service Code Metropolitan Retail and Regional Water Businesses* (Issue No. 7, 15 October 2010, 2007) para 3.1.d
217 Energy and Water Ombudsman Victoria, *Energy and Water Ombudsman Charter 30 May 2006* (2006) para 2.2
218 ibid para 6.2
219 ibid para 6.1

by the utilities to acquire it.[220] There is an obligation for the Ombudsman 'to act in accordance with accepted privacy principles'.[221] It is not clear to whom this privacy concept is applicable, since the corporation could also, to a certain extent, invoke some privacy protection.

Finally, EWOV's form as a private entity – a company limited by guarantee – has cultivated criticism in the literature.[222] EWOV's private status means that the FoI Act will not be applicable to it – this will be discussed in another section below. However, in terms of the active disclosure rule the redress mechanism provided by EWOV is adequately transparent.

In England, there is a detail mechanism on redress to both regulated companies and customers.

Regulated companies have access to a redress mechanism if they are not satisfied by the price determination, sanction or penalty imposed by Ofwat and by other regulatory decisions such as mergers. As discussed above, Ofwat may impose financial penalties on the utility for contravention of its licence condition or for failing to achieve performance standards.[223] Companies can appeal to the High Court if they do not accept the penalty imposition by Ofwat, or with respect to its amount and date of payment.[224]

Companies can also disagree with the Price Determination made by Ofwat for reasons such as the need to invest more in assets or in conducting operation and maintenance programmes.[225] The right for such 'appeal' is actually not direct as the company cannot directly commence proceedings against Ofwat at the CMA. What the legislation does is to enable the companies to require Ofwat's Director to refer the case to the CMA[226] and this facility is further elaborated in the Licence condition.[227]

Finally, the companies can appeal to the Competition Appeal Tribunal (CAT) against any merger decision made by the CMA. The CMA is tasked

---

[220] ibid para 5.1.c
[221] ibid para 5.1.d
[222] Criticism on the existence of EWOV as a 'creature of contract' (Company Limited by Guarantee) and its accountability implications has been raised in the literature. See P O'Shea and C Rickett, 'In defence of consumer law: the resolution of consumer disputes' (2009) 28 Sydney Law Review 139; A Stuhmcke, 'How good is private justice?' 71(1) The Law Institute Journal 6; S Zifcak, 'Complaint resolution in government owned corporations and privatised utilities: some legal and constitutional conundrums' in M J Whincop (ed.), *From bureaucracy to business enterprise: legal and policy issues in the transformation of government services* (Ashgate 2003)
[223] Water Industry Act 1991 c.56 s.22A(1)(a)
[224] ibid s.2E(1)
[225] This was the reason behind Bristol Water's rejection of Ofwat's Price Limit for the 2010–2015 period. See Bristol Water, 'Bristol Water Rejects Ofwat Price Decision' (*Bristol Water*) <http://goo.gl/i2ddCo> accessed 21 May 2016
[226] Water Industry Act 1991 c.56 ss.12(2) and (3)
[227] *Instrument of Appointment by the Secretary of State for the Environment of Thames Water Utilities Limited as a water and sewerage undertaker under the Water Act 1989* (2005) Condition B (Charges)

with referring water companies' mergers to further stages of investigation,[228] except if they are excluded.[229] The CMA can decide to entirely prohibit the proposed merger or impose partial prohibition or compel divestiture. When the companies disagree with this decision, they can appeal to the CAT for a review, which in turn may either dismiss the application, or quash the whole or part of the decision.[230]

Customers are entitled to service standards as outlined in the GSS Regulation.[231] Complaints about bad service should be directed to the companies, which in many cases would entitle customers to receive a certain amount of money within the limits as prescribed by the GSS Regulation. Although customers can contact CC Water at any stage of their complaints, only when they have exhausted measures available at the water company will CC Water or Ofwat carry out measures to settle their dispute.

Ofwat has the power to settle disputes on some matters.[232] Some of the disputes are settled by Ofwat by making 'Determinations'.[233] 'Determinations' made under s.30A by Ofwat are considered to be final and enforceable 'as if it were a judgment of a county court'.[234]

Ofwat maintains a record of every dispute brought to it. A Report on a GSS Dispute typically consists of several parts: Ofwat's power to issue the Determination,[235] the factual background and chronology, the relevant part of the GSS regulation applicable, the views of the disputants and Ofwat's

---

228 Water Industry Act 1991 c.56 s.32. Among the considerations made by the CC is whether the merger will hinder Ofwat's task in comparing different water enterprises against the benefits of the merger to consumers. See schedule 4ZA of ibid 1991. See also Hendry, 'An Analytical Framework for Reform of National Water Law' (PhD thesis, University of Dundee 2008) p.59
229 Water Industry Act 1991 c.56 s.33 also 'Water and Sewerage Mergers: Guidance on the CMA's Procedure and Assessment' <www.gov.uk/government/uploads/system/uploads/attachment_data/file/476839/Water_merger_guidance.pdf> accessed 6 December 2015
230 Enterprise Act, s.120
231 The Water Supply and Sewerage Services (Customer Service Standards) Regulations 2008
232 This includes disputes on expenses incurred when making connections with mains, conditions imposed by water utilities before a connection is made, requirements for metering, the terms and conditions for non domestic customers, financial requirements to connect to a sewer or lateral drain, location and timescale for providing sewer or lateral drain, appeals regarding the adoption of private sewers, refusal of the right to connect to public sewers, the cost to connect to public sewers, right to be charged by reference to volume, and the laying of pipes on private land. See, respectively, Water Industry Act 1991 c.56 ss.45(6A), 47(3A) and (3B), 49(3)(b), 56, 99, 101, 105(1) (Not all sewers belong to the companies, some of them are owned by individuals or are 'Private Sewers'. The owners of such sewers or lateral drains may ask the company to 'adopt' the sewers – or they can object to the company's initiative in adopting their sewer. This clause provides mechanism to settle any dispute arising from such adoption. Also ss.106(4); 150A(6b), 107(4A), 144A(4), 181(1) and (2)
233 ibid s.30A
234 ibid s.30A(5)(b)
235 The Water Supply and Sewerage Services (Customer Service Standards) Regulations 2008, SI 2008 No. 594 s.17

120 *Regulatory functions*

considerations and Determination.[236] Although the value of each case may be economically insignificant, these reports are important in two respects. First, they create incentives for companies to comply since they make clear that even seemingly economically insignificant disputes will be processed. Second, they create a sense of fairness among the disputants as the reasoning of the Determination and the relevant legal provisions are considered.

Customers can also refer their problem to CC Water in their area. The Water Act 2003, amending the WIA 1991, provided wide authority to CC Water to conduct investigations into customer complaints, except for some situations which are within Ofwat's authority to investigate,[237] or which constitute an offence.[238] If the matter can be solved under Ofwat's power to make Determinations, CC Water can refer such matter to Ofwat if the complainant agrees.[239] CC Water is not required to investigate if the water companies have not been given a reasonable opportunity to address the complaint.[240] In practice, customers are required first to exhaust remedies provided to them by the companies.[241] Despite its wide powers to conduct investigation, unlike Ofwat which announces the results of its enquiries, there is no clarity as to CC Water's investigations procedure and its results.

Access to the Ombudsman is available for customers who are not satisfied by Ofwat's or CC Water's performance, including that relating to complaints or disputes. The Ombudsman makes sure that complaints about water services are addressed to CC Water before they are brought to them.[242] DWI, DEFRA and the Environment Agency may also receive complaints in accordance with their respective jurisdictions.

Jakarta lacks a redress mechanism. On the contrary, the provisions are set to penalise customers. Under By-law 11/1993, other than the consumer's right to ask for examination of a water meter,[243] the right to complain against inaccurate water metering, the compensation of which, if hard to measure,

---

236 *Ofwat's Final Report on a Dispute Between Dr Lashley and Anglian Water About Entitlement to Payment Under the Guaranteed Standard Scheme (GSS)* (2005)
237 Water Industry Act 1991 c.56 s.29(3) and (4). These are matters such as the alleged violation of licence conditions, imposition of penalty, the laying of pipes or conducting sewerage work on the street
238 ibid s.29(5). This matter should be referred to the Secretary of State or the Welsh Assembly (for Wales)
239 ibid s.29(6)
240 ibid s.29(8)(b)
241 'How do I complain about my water and/or sewerage company?' (*CC Water* 2010) <http://ccwater.custhelp.com/app/answers/detail/a_id/417> accessed 31 May 2011 'If you have followed your company's complaints procedure but remain dissatisfied, you can ask us to look at your complaint. We will tell you how we can take your matter forward and what resolution, if any, you can expect from your company'.
242 'Gas, electricity and water' (*Parliamentary and Health Service Ombudsman*) <www.ombudsman.org.uk/make-a-complaint/if-we-cant-help/gas-electricity-and-water> accessed 31 May 2011
243 Peraturan Daerah Khusus Ibukota Jakarta No. 11 Tahun 1993 Tentang Pelayanan Air Minum di Wilayah Daerah Khusus Ibukota Jakarta Article 20.1

will be arbitrarily discussed by PAM Jaya,[244] and the right to object to the Governor against PAM Jaya's penalty decision for some type of violations and 'crimes', there are no references whatsoever to any other redress mechanism. The Governor's Decision on penalty for water theft, according to the by-law, is 'binding'.[245] This is actually incorrect since redress to the courts was, and is, possible through the law on judicial powers.[246] Failure to clarify access to justice for consumers in By-law 11 is a grave omission. This is contrary to the case of Bogor, a city neighbouring Jakarta, which regulates referrals to arbitration and alternative dispute resolution as a redress mechanism.[247]

---

244 ibid Article 19.4
245 ibid Article 28.3
246 Undang Undang Pokok Kekuasaan Kehakiman No. 14 Tahun 1970; Undang Undang Pokok Kekuasaan Kehakiman No. 48 Tahun 2009. When By-law 11/1993 was enacted, Indonesia was under an authoritarian rule and the courts, although available, were not the custom for settling disputes. Access to court at that time was actually available through Law No. 14 Year 1970 on Judiciary Power (this law has been revoked. The prevailing rule is Law No. 48 Year 2009). Everyone could, in theory, have brought the case to Court if they disagreed with the arbitrary determination by PAM Jaya in compensating for its substandard service or by the Governor's decision on water theft penalty.
247 Article 22.4, By-law 5 (Bogor)

5 Transparency in utilities' corporate governance

The Three Retailers in Victoria *were* Public Company Limited by Shares, subject to certain disclosure requirements under the Australian Corporations Act of 2001 and the State Owned Enterprise Act 1992. In 2012, they were reformed into Statutory Corporations under the Water Act 1989.[1] In addition, The Three Retailers are also regulated by the Water Industry Act 1994 (Vic), the ESC Act of 2004, WIRO and a set of codes prescribed by the ESC.

In England the Companies Act of 2006 imposes tough disclosure rules on companies. As water and sewerage undertakers have to be in the form of a company,[2] they are also covered by this rule. In Jakarta, two types of companies involved in the water services sector need to be evaluated; PAM Jaya: the regional state-owned enterprise and PT Aetra and PT Palyja as concessionaires, both privately owned companies.

PAM Jaya, the owner of Jakarta's water services assets and a party to the concession contract, is a regional-owned SOE established under Regional SOE Law UU No. 5/1962. Its corporate governance is regulated under the 1962 Act and By-law 13/1992 which also acts as PAM Jaya's statute.

Palyja and Aetra are both privately owned companies. Their corporate governance is regulated primarily by UU No. 40/2007 on Corporations. Both have issued bonds which are actively traded on the Indonesian Stock Echange (IDX). As long as they remain listed in the IDX, they are obligated to comply with capital market regulations, UU No. 8/1995, as well as rules enacted by the Indonesian Capital Market Supervisory Agency (Bapepam) and the stock exchange rules.[3] The capital market rule contains a number of corporate governance requirements with which the companies need to comply.

---

1 Water Amendment (Governance and Other Reforms) Act 2012 No. 17 of 2012 (n 128).
2 Water Industry Act 1991 c.56 s.6(1)
3 Palyja and Aetra fit the definition of 'Issuer' under UU No. 8/1995. UU No. 8 in Article 1, para 6 states: 'An Issuer is a Person who makes a Public Offering', para 15: 'A Public Offering is an offer to sell Securities to the public, made by an Issuer in ways stipulated in this Law and its implementing regulations' and para 5: 'Securities are promissory notes, commercial paper, shares, bonds, evidences of indebtedness, Participation Units of collective investment contracts, futures contracts related to Securities, and all derivatives of Securities'.

Transparency has always been a part of the corporate governance debate. The problem with this is that the original idea of 'corporate governance' has primarily been centred upon the relationship between management and shareholders while leaving other stakeholders such as consumers somewhat as 'outsiders' to the company.[4] Consumers of a utility company, on the other hand, hold a very important stake in the company. Their stakes might not be in the form of shares, but a guaranteed purchase of the utility product. In addition, the product itself, water, is essential to the consumer and cannot be substituted with other goods. In a regulated natural monopoly setting, a water consumer has no choice but to buy from the company and the company has no choice but to sell to them.

5.1 Corporate structure and the board

In Victoria, when The Three Retailers were under the Corporations Act 2001 there were obligations for companies to lodge to ASIC personal details of a new secretary or director of the company.[5] It obligated companies to report to their *members*, (1) the financial report, (2) the directors' report, and (3) the auditor's report.[6] There was no public disclosure requirement, although if members elected, they could choose that companies publish these reports on their websites, which would render them available to the public at large.[7]

Since they were reconstituted as statutory corporations, their appointment and dismissals are regulated by the Water Act (and its amendments).[8] The basic structure consists of at least 2–9 board directors, appointed by the Minister, one of whom must be the chairperson.[9] They are obligated, under Financial Reporting Directives (FRD) to disclose certain information, including their corporate structures and accountable executives.[10] The FRDs are empowered by the Financial Management Act and statutory corporations must comply.

When they were still under the Corporations Act, the SOE Act required the Treasurer to present accounts and report to Parliament on (1) the retailers' memorandum and articles of association as well as its amendments, (2) financial reports, directors' reports and auditor's report and (3) every report by the Auditor General with respect to the company.[11] After they become statutory corporations, the Water Amendment Act 2012 became their statute, which

---

4 B Hannigan, *Company Law* (Oxford University Press 2009) p.115
5 Corporations Act 2001 s.205B The details include their given and family names; all of their former given and family names, date and place of birth; and addresses.
6 ibid s.314
7 ibid s.314(1AA)
8 Water Act 1989 (Vic) (n 811); Water Amendment (Governance and Other Reforms) Act 2012 No. 17 of 2012 (n 129). See ss.97, 101
9 Water Amendment (Governance and Other Reforms) Act 2012 No. 17 of 2012 (n 128) ss.9 and 13
10 See Financial Reporting Directive (FRD) 22G and FRD 22F (repealed)
11 State Owned Enterprises Act 1992 (Victoria), No. 90 of 1992, Version No. 036 s.75

directly delineated their services area.[12] The content of their annual reports is regulated by the Financial Management Act[13] and FRDs. FRD 30B requires annual reports to be published in electronic format on their website.[14]

In the past, the appointments of board members of The Three Retailers has been quite transparent. The Department of Sustainability and Environment issues an advertisement accessible through its website, outlining the vacant position, its duties and challenges, links to the remuneration rules, the selection criteria and its process and the procedures to apply.[15] After being shortlisted and endorsed by the cabinet, the Minister for Water announces the result of the selection process.[16]

In England, the 2006 Companies Act (CA 2006) obligates companies to maintain registers, among others, a register of directors[17] containing their names,[18] date of birth, their service address[19] and other information, which should be available for company members at no charge or by any other person in accordance with a prescribed fee.[20] The directors' residential addresses,[21] however, should be kept in the register but not disclosed, except under certain circumstances.[22]

Rules on appointment under CA 2006 are very general, and are concerned primarily with age.[23] For removal before the term of office is ended, a resolution is required[24] and a director can defend himself against such removal at the meeting.[25] There is no requirement of ex-ante public disclosure, but there is a duty to notify Companies House when a person ceases to be a director.[26] This register of directors at Companies House is available for public access for a fee.

The Companies Act also obligates companies to keep a register of members,[27] containing their names and addresses,[28] their shareholdings[29] – including the

---

12 Water Amendment (Governance and Other Reforms) Act 2012 No. 17 of 2012 (n 128) s.16
13 Financial Management Act 1994 No. 18 of 1994 (Victoria), Version No. 061 1994.
14 'Standard Requirements for the Publication of Annual Reports (April 2015) Financial Reporting Directive 30B'
15 Department of Sustainability and the Environment, 'Melbourne Water Retailer Board Director' <http://goo.gl/Pwu061> accessed 21 May 2016
16 State Government of Victoria, 'Appointments to Melbourne region water boards' (6 September 2011) <http://goo.gl/3b2eBF> accessed 21 May 2016
17 Companies Act 2006 c.46 s.162(1)
18 ibid ss.163 and 164
19 ibid s.163(1)(b)
20 ibid s.162(5)
21 ibid s.165
22 ibid ss.240, 243(2), see also The Companies (Disclosure of Address) Regulations 2009, SI 2009/214
23 Companies Act 2006 c.46 ss.154–161
24 ibid s.168(1)
25 ibid s.169(3)
26 ibid s.167
27 ibid s.113(1)
28 ibid s.113(2)
29 If companies issue shares based on classes and designation, or vary rights attached to sharers, or create a new class of shares, information containing their class and designation and its variations must be notified to the registrar, see ibid ss.636–640.

type of shares and the amount paid[30] – which must be kept available for inspection (free of charge for members and for a fee for anyone else).[31] Refusal to disclose must go through an application to the court by the company which decides whether the request is 'not sought for a proper purpose'.[32] There is also a restriction for persons who obtain such information not to disclose it to another person who would use it for 'a purpose that is not a proper purpose'.[33] What is deemed to be a 'proper' or 'improper' purpose is not explained on the CA 2006, but it has been suggested that those which are intended for fraud, intimidation or harassment, mass mailings or which relate to the offering of securities are improper.[34] Ultimately, this is something that the court must decide on a case-by-case basis.

A large chunk of information shall be included in the 'Directors' Report', the contents of which are similar from company to company although small companies can be exempted from some disclosure duties.[35] The Director's Report must contain the identities of directors, the company's principal activities and a business review. The implementing regulation to the CA 2006[36] adds some more information to be disclosed, among others, the company's asset value and political donations and expenditure.[37] For quoted companies there are obligations to include directors' salaries and remuneration policy, some details of its service contracts and, if the shares which are traded have voting rights, the rights, privileges and limitations attached to it such as restriction on transfer of securities.[38]

Such information is included in companies' 'Annual Accounts and Reports' which must be circulated to companies' members, holders of debentures and any other parties entitled to receive notices of the general meetings. The duties for disseminating the report for quoted companies are extended: its annual account and report must be available on a website, the access to which must be free of charge.[39]

In Jakarta, due to the concession, three companies are involved, one company, PDAM, is a regional state-owned enterprise and two other companies, the private partners are private enterprises. Each of the categories is subject to different corporate governance standards and, by implication, different transparency mechanisms.

---

30 ibid s.113(3)
31 ibid s.116(1)
32 ibid s.117(3)
33 ibid s.119(2)
34 Institute of Chartered Secretaries and Administrators, 'ICSA Guidance on Access to the Register of Members: Proper Purpose Test' (2007) <www.icsa.org.uk/assets/files/pdfs/Policy/PP2.pdf> accessed 21 May 2016
35 Companies Act 2006 c.46 s.415A(2). Under s.417(1) small companies are exempted from the obligation to create a business review under its Director's Report.
36 SI 2008/410 The Large and Medium-sized Companies and Groups (Accounts and Reports) Regulations 2008
37 SI2008/410, Schedule 7
38 SI2008/410, Schedule 8
39 Companies Act 2006 c.46 s.430(3)

PAM Jaya's corporate structure comprises of a Board of Directors, a Supervisory Body and an internal audit task force which reports directly to the President Director. Directors are appointed by the Governor.[40] The Governor can temporarily suspend the directors from their position, but permanent removal must be conducted through an assessment by the Supervisory Body,[41] which then delivers its recommendation to the Governor for a decision. The Governor will have the final say unless the director decides to appeal to the Ministry of Home Affairs.[42]

The directors are responsible to the Governor, and must deliver the 'profit and loss account' to the Governor, through the Supervisory Body.[43] The 'profit and loss account' is the only accountability report that the directors need to deliver to the Governor. By-law 13 also contains no obligation of parliamentary supervision. There are no obligations for the Governor to table this 'profit and loss account' to parliament. This weak reporting mechanism is due to Indonesia's anachronistic regulation on regional SOEs. The statute governing PAM Jaya has not been reformed since it was enacted in 1993.

The Supervisory Body is chaired by the Governor himself (or a person appointed to represent him)[44] and its members are appointed from Jakarta's government officials.[45] The President Director coordinates the Board of Directors and is responsible to the Governor of Jakarta.[46] There is no requirement for the names of the BoD and the Supervisory Body to be disclosed to the public, but since they are appointed by a Governor's Decision,[47] in theory, the document should be in the public domain and the public should have access to their names. In practice, the names of the directors – but not the members of the Supervisory Body – are available on JWSRB's website.[48] This is unfortunate since the Supervisory Body is tasked and empowered with the authority to supervise, audit and monitor PAM Jaya and even has the power to request explanations from the directors in all matters related to PAM Jaya's operations, and in requesting the directors to be present at their meetings.[49] The Supervisory Body conducts meetings once every three months and such meetings should be recorded.[50] There is no obligation that such minutes of meetings should be available to the public, but an FoI request for the minutes is possible.

---

40 Peraturan Daerah Khusus Ibukota Jakarta No. 13 Tahun 1992 Tentang Perusahaan Daerah Air Minum Daerah Khusus Ibukota Jakarta (PAM Jaya) Article 17.1
41 ibid Article 18
42 ibid Article 18
43 ibid Articles 39 and 40
44 ibid Article 25.1
45 ibid Article 24.1
46 ibid Article 12
47 ibid Article 17.1
48 PAM Jaya, 'Direksi PAM Jaya' (*PAM Jaya*,) <www.pamjaya.co.id/Direksi.html> accessed 3 March 2011
49 Peraturan Daerah Khusus Ibukota Jakarta No. 13 Tahun 1992 Tentang Perusahaan Daerah Air Minum Daerah Khusus Ibukota Jakarta (PAM Jaya), Article 22
50 ibid Article 23.4

PAM Jaya's directors can be dismissed by the Governor for several reasons, such as when they 'act or behave' to the detriment of PAM Jaya, or the Jakarta region or the state.[51] The termination must be preceded with a temporary suspension by the Governor, through a letter stating the rationale of such suspension.[52] By-law 13 states that such a letter must be directed to the person being suspended, other members of the Board of Directors and the members of the Supervisory Body. The by-law also regulates that a special session needs to be convened by the Supervisory Body, that the person being suspended be given the opportunity to defend himself and that the Supervisory Body recommend the decision to the Governor, i.e. whether the person's membership shall be terminated or not.[53] The person is given the right to object to the decision to the Minister of Home Affairs, who has the authority to overturn the Governor's Decision.[54] In a case where the decision of the Governor on the suspension is overturned by the Minister, the said director should be publicly reinstated.[55]

In all stages of suspension, information as to the rationale of suspension and those related to the special session are only disclosed internally among the members of the Board of Supervisors, the Governor and the Minister of Home Affairs. This is quite understandable since the disclosure of such processes may contradict the 'presumption of innocence' principle. The name(s) of the new director, if the suspension is approved, will presumably be made available to the public since such change of directorship needs to be enacted through a Governor's Decision, which is a public document. There is no obligation to disclose the rationale behind the Governor's Decision.

PAM Jaya must deliver its budget plan to the Governor to obtain approval; the Governor is deemed to have approved the plan if, within three months after its submission, he does not express his objections or refusals.[56]

By-law 13 also obligates PAM Jaya to deliver its profit/loss account to the Governor, which shall be evaluated by the state auditor or public accountants, based on prevailing accounting rules. The report will be legalised by the Governor once it is audited and such legalisation indemnifies PAM Jaya's directors against future liabilities.[57] The regional SOE Law also requires the Governor to appoint an auditor and stipulates that the result of its audits shall be reported to the regional House of Representatives.[58] Furthermore, the state budget law requires the Governor to report regional SOEs' financial accounts to the regional parliament, as part of its accountability report.[59]

---

51 ibid Article 18.2.b and c
52 ibid Article 18.3
53 ibid Article 18.4
54 ibid Article 18.4.e
55 ibid Article 18.5
56 ibid Article 38
57 ibid Article 40
58 Undang Undang No. 5 Tahun 1962 Tentang Perusahaan Daerah Article 27.1
59 Undang Undang No. 17 Tahun 2003 Tentang Keuangan Negara

Nevertheless, there is a discrepancy in accounting rules between those required by the regional SOE law and the state budget law. The former is simpler, requiring only a profit/loss account and this is the rule that prevails. Except for some accountability reporting mentioned before, there are no requirements to disclose regional SOEs' annual budget plans or their annual reports in By-law 13 and UU No. 5 although this is actually mandatory under the Public Service Law and the FoI Law.[60] There are no other accountability obligations other than what is outlined above. Thus, the Governor's accountability reporting with respect to PAM Jaya is limited only to reporting its profit and loss account, and not toward other aspects such as overall performance or the success of its concession arrangements.

The private concessionaire in Jakarta, Palyja and Aetra is regulated under Indonesian Company Law. The company organs in Indonesia consist of the General Meeting of Shareholders (GMS), the Board of Directors and the Board of Commissioners.[61] The Corporation Law obligates the Minister of Law and Human Rights to keep the register of companies,[62] containing information on, *inter alia*, name and domicile, purpose and objective and business, activities, period of incorporation, and capitalisation; the Company's full address, data on number and date of the deed of establishment (including its amendments) and the Minister's ratification of the Company, and the full names and address of members of the Board of Directors and members of the Board of Commissioners.[63] The Corporation Law obligates that such registers of companies 'shall be open to the public'.[64] However, the company register is not automatically available in the public domain. In order for a person to obtain information about a company, it must log a request with the Directorate General on General Legal Administration and pay a fee.[65]

There is an obligation under company law for the directors to produce an annual report but these are only delivered to the companies' shareholders.[66] As Palyja and Aetra are listed companies (due to their bond issue), they are obligated to disclose their audited financial accounts annually to the public, through publication in newspapers.[67] However, there is no obligation to disclose their annual report to the public.

Law 40 on Corporations obligates the rules for appointment, replacement and dismissal of members of the Board of Directors and Board of Commissioners to be stipulated in the company's Articles of Associations.[68] Anyone who is capable

---

60 Undang Undang No. 25 Tahun 2009 Tentang Pelayanan Publik Article 23.4 and Undang Undang No. 14 Tahun 2008 Tentang Keterbukaan Informasi PublikArticles 9.2 and 9.3
61 Undang Undang No. 40 Tahun 2007 Tentang Perseroan Terbatas, Article 1 paras 2, 4, 5 and 6
62 ibid Article 29.1
63 ibid Article 29.3
64 ibid Article 29.6
65 Peraturan Menteri Hukum dan Hak Asasi Manusia Nomor M.HH-03.AH.01.01 Tahun 2009
66 Undang Undang No. 40 Tahun 2007 Tentang Perseroan Terbatas Articles 66 and 67
67 Capital Market and Financial Institutions Supervisory Agency (Bapepam-LK) Rule X.K.2
68 Undang Undang No. 40 Tahun 2007 Tentang Perseroan Terbatas, Article 15.f

of performing legal actions is eligible to be appointed except if they, within five years before appointment, have been declared bankrupt; have been members of a Board of Directors or a Board of Commissioners declared to be at fault in causing a company to be declared bankrupt, or have been sentenced for crimes which caused losses to the state and/or were related to the finance sector.[69] This requirement, the law suggests, 'is without prejudice to the possibility of the authorised technical agencies determining additional requirements'.[70] The GMS shall appoint members of the Board of Directors[71] and determine their remuneration.[72] Directors can be dismissed at any time by the GMS, through a resolution stating its rationale.[73] Alternatively, the Board of Commissioners may suspend a member of the Board of Directors.[74] Such suspension must be confirmed or revoked by the GMS within one month.[75] There is no public disclosure rule for change of board members in the Company Law. However, for listed companies, Bapepam Rule XK1 obligates public disclosure and reporting to Bapepam for events, information or material facts, that may reasonably affect the price of securities or investors' decisions such as 'a change in control or significant change in management'[76]

The corporation law obligates companies' directors to compile an annual work plan before the start of the new financial year, which should also contain annual budgets.[77] These plans must be delivered to the Board of Commissioners and/or the shareholders – depending on the company's Articles of Association.[78] Annual reports should be delivered within a period of not more than six months after the company's financial year ends and must contain a financial report and other types of report. The financial report must contain at least the last balance sheet for the financial year just ended in comparison with the previous financial year, a profit and loss statement, a cash flow report, a report on changes in equity and notes accompanying the financial report.[79] There is also an obligation on CSR reporting: a report on the details of problems which arose during the financial year which influenced the company's business activities; a report on the duty of supervision performed by the Board of Commissioners during the financial year just ended; the names of the members of the Board of Directors and members of the Board of Commissioners and salaries and allowances for members of the Board of Directors and salaries or

---

69 ibid Article 83.1
70 ibid Article 83.2
71 ibid Article 94.1
72 ibid Article 96.1
73 ibid Article 105.1
74 ibid Article 106.1
75 ibid Article 106.4
76 Capital Market and Financial Institutions Supervisory Agency (Bapepam-LK) Rule XK1, Article 2.f.
77 Undang Undang No. 40 Tahun 2007 Tentang Perseroan Terbatas Article 63
78 ibid Article 63
79 ibid Article 66

130 *Transparency in corporate governance*

honoraria and allowances for members of the Board of Commissioners of the company for the year just ended.[80]

Certain companies, such as those collecting and/or managing public funds, issuing bonds or with assets of more than Rp.50 billion,[81] must refer their financial report to public accountants to be audited. The law forbids the GMS to ratify the financial report of such a company if it is not audited by public accountants.[82] Within seven days of being ratified by the GMS, the law obligates the financial report to be published in one daily newspaper.[83] Members of the Board of Directors and commissioners are jointly and severally liable to the aggrieved party for any misleading or inaccurate financial report they sign, except if they can prove that any losses are not due to their fault.[84] During an interview with Palyja, they stated that they deliver an annual report and investment plan to PAM Jaya every three months before year-end, although such is not required by the contract.[85]

5.2 Related party transaction

In Australia, the Corporations Act requires compliance with accounting standards[86] and mandates the Australian Accounting Standards Board (AASB) to issue such accounting standards.[87] The AASB's[88] definition of 'related party'[89] is broader than the Corporations Act and it requires public disclosure of transactions entered into with them in the companies' annual reports.[90] The 2015 edition of AASB 124 permits commitments with entities controlled/jointly controlled with government or entities to which government has significant control, to be exempted from public disclosure.[91]

Although the retailers are now statutory corporations, they should remain compliant with AASB provisions, if they are adopted by the government. The Financial Management Act allows the government to adopt AASB (and other accounting standards).[92] At present, FRD 21B (responsible persons) contains very detailed disclosures on related party transactions, including payments to

---

80 ibid Article 66
81 Under this category are if: a. the Company's business is to collect and/or manage the public's funds; b. the Company issues acknowledgements of indebtedness to the public; c. the Company is a Public Company; d. the Company is a state-owned liability company; e. the Company has assets and/or a business turnover worth at least Rp.50,000,000,000 (50 billion Rupiah); or f. it is obligatory under legislative regulations. See ibid
82 ibid Article 68
83 ibid Article 68.4 and 5
84 ibid Article 69.4
85 Interview with Mr Philippe Pedrini, Palyja's Contract Manager, Jakarta, 10 January 2011
86 Corporations Act 2001 s.296(1)
87 ibid s.334
88 Australian Accounting Standards Board, *AASB 124, Related Party Disclosures* (2009)
89 ibid
90 ibid para 18
91 'AASB 124: Related Party Disclosure (July 2015)'
92 Financial Management Act 1994 (Vic) (n 856). See s.59

personnel who can be considered as a related party.[93] Such disclosures are made by the retailers and published on their annual report, on their website.[94]

The Victorian ESC enacted the Regulatory Accounting Code (RAC), which regulates both transactions with a 'related party' and with a 'third party'. A related party is defined as any other entity subject to control or significant influence by the water business whereas a third party is a term used to cover transactions with any party which is not categorised as a related party.[95] The definition of 'related party' in the RAC is a simple one and covers the relationship between the water businesses and a daughter company or any other company within its influence. This is because, unlike the English water utilities with multiple layers of ownership, the Victorian Government is the ultimate shareholder of the companies.

In conducting transactions with a related party, water businesses are required to disclose the names of the related party, the water businesses' interest in them, the value of payment, a description of how the payment is reflected through RAC and a description on how shared costs are allocated.[96] Similar to the English June Return Reporting Manual,[97] information on related party transactions is confidential. For transactions with any third parties worth more than USD1 million of Opex or USD10 million of Capex, the names of the third parties, description of the service, the values of payments made to them, a description of the basis of the payment made and how they are reflected in RAC must be provided.[98]

In England, under the CA 2006, directors have a duty to avoid CoI[99] and to declare interest in a planned[100] or existing[101] transaction or arrangements at directors' meetings or through written[102] or 'general' notices.[103] There are obligations that companies must note with respect to related undertakings and preparing group accounts.[104] Disclosure[105] of companies' accounts is required

---

93 'FRD 21B Disclosures of Responsible Persons, Executive Officers and Other Personnel (Contractors with Significant Management Responsibilities) in the Financial Report'
94 'City West Water Annual Report 2015' <www.citywestwater.com.au/documents/Annual_Report_2015.pdf>
95 Essential Services Commission, *Water Industry Regulatory Accounting Code, October 2009, Issue No. 4* (2009) p.11
96 ibid part B.12
97 Ofwat, *Chapters 30 & 31: Transactions with Associated Companies, June return reporting requirements and definitions manual 2011, Issue 1.0 – January 2011* (Ofwat 2011)
98 Essential Services Commission, *Water Industry Regulatory Accounting Code, October 2009, Issue No. 4* (2009) part B.11
99 Companies Act 2006 c.46 s.175(1)
100 ibid s.177(1)
101 ibid s.182(2)
102 ibid s.184 The notice will be regarded as forming a part of the directors' next meeting and the document forms a part of the minutes of the meeting.
103 ibid s.185 This applies only when given at a directors' meeting. This is also applicable when the parties affiliated with the director are deemed to have an interest in that transaction. See s.252 on the explanation of affiliated persons.
104 ibid s.409
105 The Large and Medium sized Companies and Groups (Accounts and Reports) Regulations', Statutory Instrument, SI 2008/410 para 72(1). The SI obligates disclosure of the nature of related party relationships and amount of transactions.

if material transactions are entered into with related parties not 'under normal market conditions'.[106]

Ofwat takes further measures to ensure that the utilities it regulates are appropriately ring-fenced and transact in an arm's length manner. This is conducted by imposing some ring-fencing requirements directly in the company's licence condition[107] and by issuing a series of Regulatory Accounting Guidelines (RAG). The RAGs themselves are not binding per se but facilitate compliance as they are used by the companies as a reference when submitting their regulatory accounts.[108] Submission of the regulatory accounts is a part of the licence condition[109] and failure to comply with this requirement may trigger penalty sanctions.[110]

A Related Party Transaction *was* part of the data that utilities were required to submit to Ofwat in their June Return, forming Chapters 30 and 31 ('Transactions with Associated Companies').[111] These chapters were drafted in accordance with RAG 5.04 on Transfer Pricing.[112] Chapters 30 and 31 reiterate the company's duty – under its Licence Condition F[113] – to trade at arm's length from associate companies to ensure that no cross subsidy occurs and requires the companies' directors to provide a statement of compliance with condition F.[114] Information submitted under Chapters 30 and 31 *were* labelled 'Commercial in Confidence'.[115]

---

106 See also Accounting Standards Board, *Amendment to FRS 8 Related Party Disclosures: Legal Changes 2008* (2008) which has a higher threshold as it requires disclosures of all related party transactions, even if made under normal market conditions.

107 *Instrument of Appointment by the Secretary of State for the Environment of Thames Water Utilities Limited as a water and sewerage undertaker under the Water Act 1989* (2005) Condition F: Accounts and accounting information. In para 1.1 of Condition F, it is stipulated that the purpose of the licence condition is to separate the financial affairs of the 'Appointed Business', to ensure that no cross subsidy between the regulated company and its 'Associated Companies' exists and to ensure that any transfer of assets or financial support to its associated companies does not affect the regulated companies' function as an undertaker.

108 They are occasionally referred to in the licence condition. See ibid Condition B para 13.3(3) and Condition F para. 6.8(i)

109 ibid Condition F: Accounts and accounting information, para 9.3 obligates companies to send regulatory accounts to OFWAT's Director 'as soon as reasonably practicable' and in any event no later than 15 July of each year.

110 Water Industry Act 1991 c.56 s.22A

111 Ofwat, *Chapters 30 & 31: Transactions with Associated Companies, June Return reporting requirements and definitions manual 2011, Issue 1.0 – January 2011* (Ofwat 2011). The definition of 'Associated Companies' refers to Financial Reporting Standard 8 and International Accounting Standard 24

112 *Guideline for transfer pricing in the water industry; Regulatory Accounting Guideline 5.04* (Ofwat 2007)

113 *Instrument of Appointment by the Secretary of State for the Environment of Thames Water Utilities Limited as a water and sewerage undertaker under the Water Act 1989* (2005) Condition F

114 Ofwat, *Chapters 30 & 31: Transactions with Associated Companies, June Return reporting requirements and definitions manual 2011, Issue 1.0 – January 2011* (Ofwat 2011). Companies are also required to enact procurement procedures which comply with RAG 5.04. The chapters also provide guidelines on how to record and report transactions with associated companies. See p.3

115 ibid p.1

Transparency in corporate governance 133

In most statements issued by the utilities (for example, Sutton & East Surrey,[116] United Utilities[117] and Yorkshire Water[118]) to accompany the public domain version of the June Return data, companies categorise Chapters 30 and 31 under category 1, that is, information which if disclosed in conjunction with other materials (on the June Return data), will have an effect on share prices.[119] Northumbrian Water,[120] in the 2007 June Return, considers such information to fall under both category 1 and 2 (category 2 is for information which the affected organisation or individual disagrees to disclose) while Thames Water,[121] in its 2006 June Return, considers such information to fall under category 4, that is, that the excised information can give potential competitors or a third party a commercial advantage. The invocation of such categories by the companies therefore appears to be arbitrary as there is little consistency between them with respect to the same information, i.e. related party transaction.

The June Return was no longer required in 2012, as Ofwat was moving toward a risk-based approach. Ofwat was proposing several sets of information requirements, including the publication of regulatory accounts.[122] Ofwat compiled links to each company's reports in its website and graded the companies' submission.[123] Only few companies disclosed their related party transactions and the others opted for excision, as permitted by the Financial Reporting Standard.[124] From 2016 onward, companies must produce an annual performance report. Unfortunately Related Party Transaction *is not* included in the summary of performance parameters issued by Ofwat.[125]

One of the purposes of related party transaction disclosure in utilities regulation is to enable customers to track the inflow and outflow of money from the regulated utility to an associated company and to level the playing field for prospective entrants. If related party transaction information is withheld, consumers and other interested parties will not be able to track possible transfer pricing.

---

116 Sutton and East Surrey Water plc, *Annual Report to the Water Services Regulatory Authority June 2010, Public Domain Submission*
117 United Utilities, *June Return 2006: Statement to Accompany the Public Domain Version* (Northumbrian Water 2006)
118 Yorkshire Water, *June Return 2007: Statement to Accompany the Public Domain Version* (Yorkshire Water 2006)
119 This is relevant only with respect to companies listed on the capital market
120 Northumbrian Water Limited, *June Return 2007: Statement to Accompany the Public Domain Version*
121 Thames Water Utilities LTD, *June Return 2006: Statement to Accompany the Public Domain Version* (2006)
122 Ofwat, 'Regulatory compliance – a proportionate and targeted approach, a consultation' (2011) <http://goo.gl/ezfhI2> accessed 21 May 2016
123 'Companies' Performance 2014–15 – Ofwat' <www.ofwat.gov.uk/regulated-companies/comparing-companies/performance/companies-performance-2014-15/> accessed 12 December 2015
124 Anglian Water disclosed its related party transaction, see 'Anglian Water Annual Report and Accounts 2015'; Severn Trent is among those who choose to exempt related party transaction from disclosure 'Severn Trent Water Limited Report and Financial Statements for the Year Ended 31 March 2015'
125 'Annual Performance Report – Summary of Performance Parameters' <http://goo.gl/W0T26l> accessed 29 November 2015

In Jakarta, under By-law DKI 13/92 on Regional SOEs, family ties among the directors, up to the third degree vertically or horizontally including husband/wife and in-laws, are prohibited.[126] The only exception to this rule is when the ties occur after appointment, in which case the director(s) may continue to hold office after approval by the Governor based on the consideration of the Minister of Home Affairs.[127] Directors are also forbidden from holding another office [at another institution]; the by-law does not explain which offices are prohibited.[128] Directors are also prohibited from having a 'personal interest' in another business whose purpose is for profit, unless permitted by the Governor.[129] The lack of clarity on what is meant by 'personal interest' and 'another business' may mean that the directors are barred from activities such as investing in capital markets. The rules for 'related party' and 'double office' are drafted in the same terms for the board of supervisors.[130] However, there is no clause prohibiting them from engaging in business activities. There is no public disclosure rule for potential or manifested CoI.

The private concessionaire in Jakarta is subject to the Indonesian Company Law. In terms of regulating related party transaction, the Indonesian Company Law is weaker than the Company Laws of Victoria or England. The closest to this is the term 'personal interest' which appears a few times in the Corporation Law, among others, on the provision regulating the exception toward limitation of legal liability for shareholders.[131] Evidence that directors do not have any CoI in the action of management that causes losses to the company can free the directors from personal liability.[132] The members of the Board of Commissioners can also be personally liable for actions that cause losses to the companies, unless they can prove, among other things, that they *do not have any direct or indirect personal interest* in the actions of management of the Board

---

126 Peraturan Daerah Khusus Ibukota Jakarta No. 13 Tahun 1992 Tentang Perusahaan Daerah Air Minum Daerah Khusus Ibukota Jakarta (PAM Jaya)
127 ibid
128 ibid
129 ibid
130 ibid Article 24
131 Shareholders are not personally liable for legal relationships entered into on behalf of the Company and are not liable for the Company's losses in excess of the shares they own except if they directly or indirectly exploit the Company in bad faith in their own personal interest. Undang Undang No. 40 Tahun 2007 Tentang Perseroan Terbatas, Article 3
132 As is commonly found in Corporation Law around the world, directors in Indonesian corporations could be held personally liable – jointly and severally – for the company's losses, except if they can prove that the losses were not caused through their fault or negligence, that they carried out the management in good faith and with prudence in the interests of and in accordance with the purpose and objectives of the Corporation, that they do not have a direct or indirect conflict of interest in the action of management that caused the losses; and that they took action to prevent the losses from arising or continuing. This provision exempting the directors from liabilities is cumulative, which means that all of its elements have to be fulfilled. This does not prevent other members of the Board of Directors and Commissioners from filing suit on behalf of the company, ibid Article 97

of Directors which caused the losses.[133] Existence of a conflict of interest bars the directors from representing the company in or out of court.[134] There are no public disclosure requirements for related parties and related party transactions under the company law.

The Capital Market Law UU No. 8/1995 does not provide any definition of 'conflict of interest', however, it defines 'affiliation' and obligates some reporting and disclosure on their transactions. Affiliation is defined as:

> a family relationship by marriage and descent to the second degree, horizontal as well as vertical; a relationship between a Person and its employees, directors, or commissioners; a relationship between two Companies with one or more directors or commissioners in common, a relationship between a Company and a Person that directly or indirectly, controls or is controlled by that Company'.[135]

Rule IXE1 of the Bapepam LK (Capital Market Supervisory Agency) however defines 'conflict of interest' as:

> a difference between the economic interests of a Company and the personal economic interests of the director, commissioner, or the major shareholder of the Company in a Transaction that may inflict financial loss upon the Company because of unfair pricing'[136]

The rule is subject to some exception, for example, if the subsidiary is 99 per cent owned by the parent company.

Affiliated transactions (subject to some exceptions) have to be notified to Bapepam LK and disclosed to the public within two working days after they occur, accompanied by some explanations, *inter alia*, the justifications for commencing such transactions, the report from independent appraisal and the identities of the parties involved.[137] Transactions with CoI (subject to some exemptions) must be approved by independent shareholders[138] in a general

---

133 ibid Article 115.5.b. The conditions so that they can be exempted from personal liability are cumulative: a. they have carried out their supervision in good faith and prudence in the interests of the Company and in accordance with the Company's purpose and objectives; b. they do not have any direct or indirect personal interest in the actions of management of the Board of Directors which caused the losses; and c. they have given the Board of Directors advice to prevent the losses arising or continuing.
134 ibid Article 99.2
135 Undang Undang No. 8 Tahun 1995 Tentang Pasar Modal Article 1.1
136 Capital Market and Financial Institutions Supervisory Agency (Bapepam-LK) Rule IXE1 Article 1.e
137 ibid Rule IXE1 para 2 (Latest amendment 25 November 2009)
138 ibid Rule IXE1, Article 1.f: Independent shareholders are the shareholders who do not have any Conflict of Interest with respect to a particular Transaction and or who are not an affiliated Party of the director, the commissioner, or the substantial shareholders that have a Conflict of Interest on certain Transaction.

meeting of shareholders and confirmed in notarial deeds. The notice of GMS must contain information on the object, value, parties, nature of CoI, appraisal report concerning the transaction involved[139] and must be delivered through registered mail or fax in addition to newspaper announcements.[140]

The purpose of this Bapepam LK rule is to provide room for the independent shareholders to voice their objections against transactions that could be detrimental to their investment value at the company. Independent shareholders have an economic interest that the company engages in fair transactions, and that the benefits from the transactions are passed onto them in the form of higher share value. In water utilities regulation, consumers (and potential consumers) also benefit from the utility's arms-length transactions as its benefits can be reflected in lower tariffs or taxes. However, unlike the English regulatory accounts[141] and licence condition,[142] the Bapepam LK Rule does not explicitly require the company to engage in an arm's length manner. What it regulates is if the transaction(s) inflict financial loss on the company (the definition of CoI above) and hence is detrimental to independent shareholders.[143] Insofar as independent shareholders approve such a transaction (presumably since they are compensated) nothing prevents that transaction from occurring, although such transactions would be detrimental to consumers.

Company law requires companies to draft their financial account *based on the generally accepted accounting standard*.[144] The linkage between accounting standards and company laws are weak as, unlike Victoria,[145] there is no direct mandate under company law that a particular body should enact and safeguard accounting standards with which companies must comply.[146]

The accounting standards, known as PSAK, require the disclosure of related parties.[147] In 2010 Aetra reported its related party transactions in its financial

---

139 ibid Rule IX.E1, para 4.f
140 ibid
141 *Guideline for transfer pricing in the water industry; Regulatory Accounting Guideline 5.04* (Ofwat 2007) also Ofwat, *Chapters 30 & 31: Transactions with Associated Companies, June Return reporting requirements and definitions manual 2011, Issue 1.0 – January 2011* (Ofwat 2011)
142 For example, *Instrument of Appointment by the Secretary of State for the Environment of Severn Trent Water Limited as a water and sewerage undertaker under the Water Act 1989* (1989) Condition F para 6.1. 'The Appointee shall ensure that every transaction between the Appointed Business and Associated Company (or between the Appointed Business and any other business or activity of the Appointee) is at arm's length, so that neither gives to or receives from the other any cross-subsidy. In the Indonesian case, receiving cross subsidy would be allowed.
143 The author would like to thank Pramudya Oktavinanda for the discussion on the interpretation of Bapepam Rule IX.E.1
144 Undang Undang No. 40 Tahun 2007 Tentang Perseroan Terbatas Article 66(3). Elucidation of Article 66(3) refers to accounting standards issued by the Indonesian Association of Accountants
145 See s.334 Australian Accounting Standards Board, *AASB 124, Related Party Disclosures* (2009)
146 Undang Undang No. 40 Tahun 2007 Tentang Perseroan Terbatas Article 66(3) and Elucidation of Article 66(3). In addition, in compliance with Article 66(3) it carries no liability, except if they mislead or misreport their financial account (see Article 69(3))
147 Ikatan Akuntan Indonesia, *Pernyataan Standar Akuntansi Keuangan (PSAK) No. 07: Pengungkapan Pihak Pihak Berelasi* (2010)

account, specifying the identities of the parties, their relationship with the company, the amount of the transaction and its nature[148] and this was published on its website. Palyja, however, only published its consolidated account[149] and there is only one line mentioning receivables to related parties.

The Jakarta Cooperation Agreement provides flexibility for the concessionaires to arrange procurements with third parties. There is a general obligation to enter into fair, transparent and competitive procurement procedures under the contracts but this is not enumerated in more detail. Palyja commented that they have their own internal procurement rule from Suez GDF.[150] Such a rule, if it exists, could be helpful in promoting efficient competition, but without sufficient regulation on procurement, its enforcement depends entirely on the utilities' discretion.

Given such regulatory structures, utilities procurement in Jakarta is not sufficiently regulated. Capital market rules obligate public disclosure and reporting to Bapepam for some affiliated transactions,[151] but this reporting rule occurs *ex post facto* (two working days after it occurs). CoI transactions obligate the approval of independent shareholders and require disclosure through a GMS mechanism specifying the details of the intended transaction.[152] This requirement requires ex-ante disclosure but unfortunately is not applicable to Palyja and Aetra since they only list their bonds in the capital market and not their shares.

Capital market disclosure rules are, therefore, only applicable conditionally upon the type of instruments traded in the capital market; some disclosure rules – such as that requiring approval of independent shareholders and disclosure on the nature of the transaction to be approved – are applicable to listing of shares, but not for bond issue. The rules are also applied incidentally. Palyja and Aetra will be bound by disclosure rules as long as their bonds are still listed on the market. Once all of their bonds are matured, they will no longer be obligated to adhere to the rules. Responding to this possibility of a regulatory vacuum following the delisting of bonds, a proponent of PSP commented that more permanent regulation should be emphasised by the state.[153] Indeed, the capital market rules cannot be relied on to promote transparency without any additional public utility regulation. In the UK, Ofwat utilises the capital market rule to promote disclosure by obligating utilities to adhere to it, irrespective of whether their shares or bonds are being traded.

5.3 Corporate restructuring

In Victoria, when the retailers were subject to the Corporations Act, the SOE Act prescribed in the Articles of Association that no offering, allotment issuance

---

148 PT Aetra Air Jakarta, *Financial Statement, December 31, 2010 and 2009* (2010) Schedule 5
149 PT PAM Lyonnaise Jaya, *Laporan Keuangan* (2011)
150 Personal Communication, *Field Interview with Palyja, Jakarta, 10 January 2011*
151 Capital Market and Financial Institutions Supervisory Agency (Bapepam-LK) Rule IX.E.1 para 2.a
152 ibid Rule IX.E.1 para 3
153 Interview with Gerard Payen and Jack Moss of Aquafed, Jakarta, 28 January 2010

of shares, disposal or sale of a main undertaking and involvement in acquisition, or disposal of shares in a subsidiary was possible without a 'special resolution'.[154] As the Victorian government was the sole owner of The Three Retailers, they retained ultimate control of such resolutions. Any changes to the company's Memorandum or Articles of Association must be tabled at Parliament.[155]

At present, the retailers are statutory corporations. Thus, the question of change of ownership is irrelevant. Furthermore, the Australian Constitution requires that water utilities are a 'public authority', accountable to the Minister.[156] This provision is 'entrenched' as it can only be modified if a special majority is achieved.[157] Therefore, every corporate restructuring measure that would affect the status of the water utility as a Public Authority would require a constitutional change by parliamentary vote. As such a plan would require parliamentary scrutiny and provoke a public debate, it is a transparency mechanism in itself.

In England, the regulator generally has two concerns over the restructuring of a regulated utility: (1) the question of probity, capacity of the new owner and its role in a regulated utility, and, if the restructuring involves the delisting of publicly traded shares, (2) the effect of utilities 'going private' on the loss of comparative information and the absence of capital market pressures on managerial efficiency.

In the UK, Ofwat has no power to block acquisition (although it can refer it to the Competition and Market Authority). Hence, the reputation of the new owners and its perceived capacity in the water industry will have no impact on the legality of the acquisition.[158] Thus, the only thing the English regulator can do is to manage utilities' licence conditions and require them (as part of the licence condition) to provide undertakings from their 'ultimate controller'.[159] Consultations are employed so that Ofwat will have sufficient information in modifying the utility's licence and in understanding the customer's view.[160] This requires the publication of 'consultation papers' containing detailed information surrounding the restructuring.[161]

---

154 SOE Act 1992, Exhibit I, paras 3, 4, 5
155 State Owned Enterprises Act 1992 (Victoria), No. 90 of 1992, Version No. 036 s.75
156 Constitution Act 1975, No. 8750 of 1975, Version No. 196 s.97(1)(2)
157 ibid s.18(2)(h)
158 One of the consultation responses, for example, questions the multi-layered structure of 'Macquarie Investors' and doubts their ability to be responsible, reliable and accountable utility owners. See T Martin Blaiklock, *Consultation: 'The Completed Acquisition of Thames Water Holdings plc by Kemble Water Limited' (Consultation Response)* (2007)
159 This is in order to tackle the complexities of layers of ownerships.
160 CC Water's response was: 'We fear that Thames Water will be seen as a cash cow to be milked for all it is worth ... The ownership structure for Thames Water is unwieldy, its corporate governance proposals seriously flawed, and the financing arrangements deeply suspect'. CC Water, *Consultation: 'The completed acquisition of Thames Water Holdings plc by Kemble Water Limited' (CC Water Thames' Response)* (2007)
161 For example, *The completed acquisition of Northumbrian Water Limited, a consultation paper by Ofwat* (2003) *The completed acquisition of Thames Water Holdings plc by Kemble Water Limited, a consultation paper by Ofwat* (2007)

With respect to new ownership, Ofwat's regulatory safeguard is in securing various undertakings from the utility's UK holding company.[162] The undertakings cover (1) the supply of all information from the holding company to the regulated utility necessary to comply with its licence condition, (2) a requirement to refrain from any action that will cause the regulated utility to breach its licence condition and any other statutory obligations, and (3) guarantee that the regulated utility has no fewer than one independent non-executive director with specific qualifications.[163]

If the restructuring causes the delisting of shares (as was the case with Thames' acquisition by RWE), the stock exchange public disclosure rules will no longer apply and the company's performance will no longer be scrutinised by analysts and shareholders. This will, according to Ofwat,

> remove the Director's ability to compare the market's ratings [of the company] with other listed owners of licensed water and sewerage utilities [and] would also affect his ability to make judgements about an appropriate cost of capital for the water and sewerage industries.[164]

One of the basic assumptions behind the divestiture of water utilities was that water utilities' management will not live a 'quiet life' because of the threat of acquisition and that the market, as reflected by the value of stocks listed on the capital market, will provide input to Ofwat on the 'true' value of the company. The capital market and its institutions,[165] therefore, is an important factor in regulation, without which Ofwat may lose information essential for regulating the companies.

Ofwat's response to this is to require the company to either publish its financial information as if it were listed and subject to the rules of the stock exchange, or re-list its shares or some class of its shares or the parent company of the regulated business list bonds or other financial instruments which would provide some market information, although less than a listed equity.[166] Although not listed in the stock exchange, Thames publishes its interim and final financial accounts as if it were a listed company.[167] This is reflected in its modified licence condition.[168] Thames also retains bonds.[169] The obligation

---

162 *Water Industry Act 1991, Section 13(1) Modification of the Conditions of Appointment of Thames Water Utilities Limited* (2007) Condition P
163 ibid Condition P
164 *The proposed takeover of Thames Water plc by RWE AG: a consultation paper by the Office of Water Services* (Ofwat 2000) p.5
165 These include the public shareholders, investment banks and appraisals
166 *The proposed takeover of Thames Water plc by RWE AG: A consultation paper by the Office of Water Services* (Ofwat 2000) p.5
167 Thames Water, *Thames Water Utilities Limited interim report and financial statements for the six month period ended 30 September 2010* (2010) p.8
168 *Instrument of Appointment by the Secretary of State for the Environment of Thames Water Utilities Limited as a water and sewerage undertaker under the Water Act 1989* (2005) Condition F, 6A.5B
169 ibid Condition F, 6A.5C: '(effective 2 May 2001) The Appointee shall maintain a Bond and shall use all reasonable endeavours to retain its listing on the London Stock Exchange'.

to retain bonds – although subjected to a lesser disclosure and governance requirement compared to listed shares – will compel the companies to comply with some rules of the stock exchange.[170] In a licence modification for Thames, Ofwat also imposes a condition whereby utilities' accounting statements and auditors' reports sent to Ofwat (with some exceptions) are published together with its annual accounts (which are prepared under the Companies Act) and copies are made available to customers upon request.[171]

In Dwr Cymru's restructuring, asset ownership of the new company was separated from its operation. The company owning the assets is Dwr Cymru's parent company, Glas Cymru, a company limited by guarantee which raises finance through debts. The change from equity to entirely debt financing raised a number of important regulatory questions. Among others, Ofwat was concerned that the absence of shareholders means that there is no buffer for 'shocks' in case emergency financing is required, unless Dwr Cymru has adequate reserves[172] and that resort to debt financing means that its credit rating must remain at least at an 'investment grade'.[173] Both of these problems were resolved through amendments of its licence condition, the former by obligating the companies to have adequate financial and management resources and certifying it to Ofwat,[174] and the latter by obligating Dwr Cymru and companies issuing debt on its behalf to, at all times, maintain an investment grade rating.[175]

Without shares listed on the capital market, however, there will be no incentive for Dwr Cymru's management to be competitive, as there is no threat of acquisition or pressures from shareholders. There may be pressure from lenders, but this could be limited in the form of securing the return of

---

170 *The proposed takeover of Thames Water plc by RWE AG: a consultation paper by the Office of Water Services* (Ofwat 2000) p.5
171 *Instrument of Appointment by the Secretary of State for the Environment of Thames Water Utilities Limited as a water and sewerage undertaker under the Water Act 1989* (2005) Condition F, 9.4 (2007 Modification) *Water Industry Act 1991, Section 13 (1) Modification of the Conditions of Appointment of Thames Water Utilities Limited* (Ofwat 2005)
172 *The proposed acquisition of Dwr Cymru Cyfyngedig by Glas Cymru Cyfyngedig: a consultation paper by Ofwat* (2000) p.12
173 Companies with 'investment grade' rating guarantees are considered to be able to meet their payment obligations. It is a BBB– rating or higher according to S&P's standard or Baa3 according to Moody's.
174 *The proposed acquisition of Dwr Cymru Cyfyngedig by Glas Cymru Cyfyngedig: a consultation paper by Ofwat* (2000) p.22. See also Dwr Cymru's Licence *Instrument of Appointment by the Secretary of State for Wales of Dwr Cymru Cyfyngedig as a water and sewerage undertaker under the Water Act 1989* (1989) Condition F, 6A.1(1)(a):'The Appointee shall at all times act in the manner best calculated to ensure that it has adequate ...financial resources and facilities', also Condition F 6A.2A and 6b.2B(1) obligating Dwr Cymru's directors to submit a certificate that it has the financial resources needed to carry out its task for the next 12 months accompanied by statements explaining the main factors justifying it, and Condition F 6A.2B(2) obligating the directors to immediately notify OFWAT as soon as they become aware that they may be in financial difficulty.
175 *Instrument of Appointment by the Secretary of State for Wales of Dwr Cymru Cyfyngedig as a water and sewerage undertaker under the Water Act 1989* (1989) Condition F, 6A.6(1)

their investment and not to contribute to the long-term efficiency as shareholders would normally demand capital growth.[176] Appointment and dismissal of Dwr Cymru's board – due to the absence of shareholders and acquisition pressures – will, therefore, depend solely on the mechanism provided by Glas Cymru, its parent company. Ofwat was concerned that the Members of Glas Cymru might in the future be captured by a special interest group.[177]

In response to the above problem, Ofwat's strategy was to require Dwr Cymru to publish periodical financial information in line with London Stock Exchange Rules, as if its shares were listed there,[178] to require that Glas Cymru maintain an incentive scheme to attract a highly qualified board and to have such a scheme be made publicly available and formalised in its Articles of Association.[179] This disclosure obligation is a part of Ofwat's series of efforts to 'intervene' in Dwr Cymru and Glas Cymru's corporate governance[180] as a result of the loss of capital market pressures. Dwr – as with Thames following RWE's acquisition – was also required to maintain the listing of a financial instrument[181] and to publish its accounting statements with its annual accounts and the auditor's report to Ofwat and to make copies available to customers.[182]

Of all 10 water and sewerage companies only one, United Utilities, is, at the moment of writing, a plc. The rest are Ltds and one company, Yorkshire Water, is a company limited by guarantee. Although United Utilities is a plc, and therefore automatically subject to listing rules, its licence condition contains clauses requiring it to comply with London Stock Exchange listing rules *as if* it were a listed company,[183] presumably to ensure continuity of information publication and reporting in the event of the company going private.

In Jakarta, corporate restructuring rules of two companies: PAM Jaya (a regionally owned company constituted under By-Law 13/92) and Palyja/Aetra (concessionaire companies set up under ordinary Indonesian Company Law) will need consideration.

---

176 *The proposed acquisition of Dwr Cymru Cyfyngedig by Glas Cymru Cyfyngedig: a consultation paper by Ofwat* (2000) p.15
177 ibid p.17
178 ibid p.19 *Instrument of Appointment by the Secretary of State for Wales of Dwr Cymru Cyfyngedig as a water and sewerage undertaker under the Water Act 1989* (1989) Condition F 6A.5B(1)
179 *The proposed acquisition of Dwr Cymru Cyfyngedig by Glas Cymru Cyfyngedig: a consultation paper by Ofwat* (2000) p.15
180 ibid OFWAT requires Dwr Cymru's board to have a majority of non executive directors and to secure undertakings from Glas Cymru, that it will (i) consult OFWAT on any modification of its Articles of Association, (ii) provide information as reasonably required by OFWAT directors as to its activities and finances, (iii) provide necessary information to Dwr Cymru so that it can comply with its licence, and (iv) refrain from any action that will result in Dwr Cymru's breach of its licence.
181 *Instrument of Appointment by the Secretary of State for Wales of Dwr Cymru Cyfyngedig as a water and sewerage undertaker under the Water Act 1989* (1989) Condition F 6A5C(1)
182 ibid Condition F 9.4
183 *Water Industry Act 1991 Section 13(1) Modification of the Conditions of Appointment of United Utilities Water plc* (2005) Condition F 1.1; see also 6A.5b; 6A.5(c)(1)

PAM Jaya

PAM Jaya's initial composition of capital is determined by By-law 13/92.[184] There is no publicly accessible information as to whether PAM Jaya has ever raised its capital after its inception. By-law 13 does not stipulate that its capital is comprised of shares, hence, there is no issue about the identity of shareholders. All capital belongs to the regional government.[185]

By-law 13 does not regulate any provision on company restructuring and the law on Regional SOE in which the by-law is based has actually been revoked.[186] Under the new SOE Law, the rules on corporate restructuring for '*Perseroan Daerah*' will follow the rules for ordinary limited liability companies (discussed below) whereas the rules for '*Perusahaan Umum Daerah*' (general public utility company) will be detailed in a government regulation (not yet enacted).[187] Since the by-law has yet to be amended, it is not clear if water utility companies are intended to be in the form of a *Perseroan Daerah* or *Perusahaan Umum Daerah*, for which the legal regimes differ.

If the government decides that regionally owned water utility companies take the form of ordinary companies, then all the rules for ordinary limited liability companies (as discussed below) will apply to them, complementary to the rules for state-owned enterprises.

Palyja / Aetra

Both Palyja and Aetra are ordinary limited liability companies serving as concession partners to PAM Jaya. Under the company law, the merger of a company requires the approval of the GMS of a Merger Plan, containing the name, domicile of the company, procedures for share valuation, financial report and methods of settlements for the BoDs and BoCs and non-approving shareholders.[188] There is no public disclosure requirement in corporation law. For listed companies, however, there are reporting and public disclosure obligations for mergers. A detailed *merger plan* for listed companies must be delivered to the company's shareholders 28 days prior to the GMS approving the merger.[189] An abridged *merger plan* must be publicly disclosed through two daily newspapers.[190] Companies are obligated to report to Bapepam LK (the capital market supervisory agency) on the occurrence of a merger within two days of it taking place.[191] Similar rules apply for acquisition of shares, if conducted by a legal entity, but not if the acquisition

---

184 Peraturan Daerah Khusus Ibukota Jakarta No. 13 Tahun 1992 Tentang Perusahaan Daerah Air Minum Daerah Khusus Ibukota Jakarta (PAM Jaya)
185 ibid Article 8.1
186 Undang Undang No. 5 Tahun 1962 Tentang Perusahaan Daerah
187 Undang Undang Nomor 23 Tahun 2014 Tentang Pemerintahan Daerah. Chapter XII
188 Undang Undang No. 40 Tahun 2007 Tentang Perseroan Terbatas, Article 123
189 Capital Market and Financial Institutions Supervisory Agency (Bapepam-LK) Rule IX.G.1
190 ibid Rule IX.G.1
191 ibid Rule XK1

is done by natural persons.[192] The tender offer rule, which also contains some disclosure requirements, could also be applicable to some types of acquisitions, but is nevertheless not applicable to Palyja and Aetra since only their bonds and not their shares are listed on the capital market.

The acquisition of TPJ (the former name of Aetra) by a Singaporean consortium involved various layers of ownership and the use of Special Purpose Vehicles.[193] PAM Jaya has the ability to block the acquisition if it involves a transfer of more than 51 per cent of shares to third parties.[194] The layers of SPVs caused the ownership structure to become obscured. It is unlikely that PAM Jaya and the Jakarta Government were able to obtain detailed information concerning the new owner. The assurance only came in the form of a 'legal opinion' from the buyer's lawyers, which certified the link between the acquirer and its ultimate owners. This is different from the UK regulatory practice of securing legally enforceable undertakings from the utility's UK holding company.[195]

There is no requirement to disclose existing ownership and shareholders' rights to the public under the Cooperation Agreement and the Jakarta Governor decree regulating the concession. Even today, the regulator has inadequate information as to the actual ownership of Aetra, other than what is clarified by the 'legal opinion'.

---

192 Undang Undang No. 40 Tahun 2007 Tentang Perseroan Terbatas, Article 125
193 The ultimate owner of Aetra through Aquatico is said to be Recapital Advisors (80%) and Glendale Partners (20%). Both companies own Aquatico through layers of Special Purpose Vehicles (SPV): Arrosez (Recapital) and Praeo (Glendale), both of which are British Virgin Island SPVs. Sawitri, 'Committee questions Acuatico's suitability as tap water operator' *The Jakarta Post* (Jakarta, 30 November 2006) <http://x.crpg.info/1YpdVwj> accessed 13 May 2016; Sawitri, 'Regulatory body casts doubt on takeover bid' *The Jakarta Post* (Jakarta, 14 December 2006)
194 Cooperation Agreement Between PAM Jaya and The Concessionaire, 2001 Clause 7.2.a (iii) also Lanti and others, *The First Ten Years of Implementation of the Jakarta Water Supply 25-Year Concession Agreement (1998–2008)* (Jakarta Water Supply Regulatory Body (JWSRB) 2009) and Ardhianie, *Kontroversi Penjualan PT Thames Pam Jaya (TPJ)* (Amrta Institute for Water Literacy No Year)
195 Cooperation Agreement Between PAM Jaya and The Concessionaire, 2001 Condition P

6 The role of the Freedom of Information Law

6.1 Applicability of freedom of information rules

The Freedom of Information laws are supposed to bring greater transparency to water services. In the heyday of PSP in public services, literature on the diminishing values of public law emerged. Earlier critics such as Minow argued that 'Access to information about services and results also decreases if the information becomes private'.[1] Meanwhile, Swyngedouw argued that water privatisation dispossesses the public from data and information that is normally available.[2]

Realising that the focal point of power had shifted from the state to corporations, champions of access to information law such as Calland advocated the idea that corporations that are playing a quasi-public role should also be covered by access to information laws.[3] Privatised water utilities, due to their natural monopoly and the essential nature of their product, are considered by him to be corporations of this kind and should, therefore, be covered by access laws.[4]

However, the public/private debate in the water sector also blurs the public/private distinctions in Freedom of Information (FoI) legislations. FoIs are supposed to be applicable only to 'public' bodies.

In Victoria, the range of actors involved in water services are as shown in Table 6.1.

The Victorian FoI Act is applicable to 'Agencies',[5] which could be in the form of a Government Department, Council or a Prescribed Authority. 'Prescribed Authorities' under the FoI Act cover (a) a body corporate for a public purpose or a body unincorporated created by the Governor in Council or

---

1 Minow, 'Public and private partnerships: accounting for the new religion' Harvard Law Review 1229
2 '... the privatized nature of crucial parts of the water cycle diminishes the transparency of decision-making procedures and limits access to data and information that could permit other social groups to acquire the relevant information on which to base views, decisions, and options' Swyngedouw, 'Dispossessing H_2O: the contested terrain of water privatization' 16 Capitalism Nature Socialism 81
3 R Calland, 'Transparency in a Profit Making World' (*Institute for Policy Dialogue*, 2006) <www0.gsb.columbia.edu/ipd/pub/Calland_Private_Sector.pdf> accessed 29 February 2010
4 ibid
5 '*agency* means a department council or a prescribed authority', '*council* has the same meaning as in section 3(1) of the Regional Government Act 1989'; '*department* means a department within the meaning of the Public Administration Act 2004 or an office specified in section 16(1) of that Act'; Freedom of Information Act 1982 (Victoria) No. 9859 of 1982 Version No. 066, s.5(1)

Table 6.1 Actors involved in water services in Victoria

Institutions	Role	FoI applicable?
Minister of Water; Department of Environment, Land, Water and Planning (Victoria)	General policy/direction and licensing	Yes
Treasurer at the Department of Treasury	Financial management	Yes
Secretary at the Department of Health	Drinking Water	Yes
Essential Services Commission	Pricing and monitoring of performance	Yes
Environment Protection Authority	Environmental protection, waste water discharges	Yes
Energy and Water Ombudsman	Consumer dispute	No
Victorian Ombudsman	Public service complaints	Yes
City West Water	Retail water supply and sewerage services in Melbourne metropolitan area	Yes
South East Water		Yes
Yarra Valley Water		Yes
Melbourne Water	Bulk water supplier	Yes
AquaSure	Consortium of Suez-Degremont *et al.*, water desalination plant, concessionaire	No

by a Minister,[6] (b) any other body declared by the regulations to be a prescribed authority either because they are supported directly or indirectly by government funds or through other assistance or over which the State is in a position to exercise control or a body established by or under an Act of Parliament.[7]

A branch of the executive in Victoria is covered by the FoI Act as a government department. The Minister of Water, Department of Sustainability and Environment, Treasurer at the Department of Treasury, Secretary at the Department of Health, Essential Services Commission and Environment Protection Authority all fall under this category.[8]

Melbourne Water, The Three Retailers: City West Water, South East Water and Yarra Valley Water, are covered under the Act as a Prescribed Authority, a body established under an Act of Parliament.[9] The Three Retailers are also considered a Prescribed Authority under the Victorian FoI Act as confirmed by the Freedom of Information Regulations 2009.[10]

Not covered by the FoI Act are the Victorian Energy and Water Ombudsman (EWOV) and AquaSure. EWOV is not covered by the FoI (Vic) Act as it is a company limited by guarantee and is not yet determined as a Prescribed

---

6 ibid s.5(1)(a)
7 ibid s.5(1)(b)
8 ibid s.5(1)
9 Freedom of Information Act 1982 No. 9859 of 1982 Section 5a
10 Freedom of Information Regulations 2009 S.R. No. 33/2009 Section 5b

146 *The role of the FoI Law*

Authority through the Freedom of Information Regulations. AquaSure, the consortium partnering with Victorian government to provide desalination services to Melbourne Water, is a purely private entity. AquaSure is not covered by the Victorian FoI Act although information it submits to the government during the tender process and in the course of routine regulatory activities can be subjected to FoI requests. This reveals that the 'privatisation' of services (be that in the form of dispute resolution or provision of bulk water) hinders the application of the FoI Act.

In England, the situation is much more complicated. As discussed, England divested its water utilities. *Full privatisation* is thus in force. The question becomes: are the privatised utilities a public body within the meaning of the FoI Act and the Environmental Information Regulation (EIR)? The answer to this question is not straightforward and the court had to go a very long way in order to decide whether English water utilities are a public body.

In England and Wales, entities can be covered[11] by the FoI based on (1) the list of public authorities under Schedule 1 of the FoI Act 2000 or (2) further designation by the Secretary of State (s.5 designation).[12] Schedule 1 of the Act specifies some of the public bodies which are covered by the Act[13] but others are covered through more general terms. For example, the Schedule covers 'Any government department'[14] and this is meant to include both ministerial departments (such as DEFRA) and non-ministerial government departments, such as Ofwat and the EA. The DWI would also fall under this definition, as part of DEFRA, although it has a distinct organisational structure and some degree of independence accorded to it by sectoral water regulations. The Consumer Council for Water, which is an executive non-departmental public body is specifically named by Part VI of Schedule 1.[15]

The EIR is (or was intended to be) much broader compared to the FoI Act 2000 in terms of its coverage. The EIR covers (1) government departments,[16] (2) public bodies listed in schedule 1 of the FoI Act 2000 (but with some exceptions),[17] (3) any other body that carries out functions of 'public administration',[18] (4) any other body or person under the control of the previous categories which has public responsibilities relating to the environment, or exercising functions of a public nature relating to the environment or provides public services relating to the environment.[19] If an entity is not covered under the first category, it may be covered under the other categories. The third and fourth categories have been the subject of controversy for water utilities.

---

11 Freedom of Information Act 2000, 2000 c.36, s.3 on the definition of 'Public Authorities'
12 ibid s.5
13 See ibid Schedule 1, Part VI: Other Public Bodies and Offices: General
14 ibid Schedule 1, para 1
15 ibid Part VI: Other Public Bodies and Offices: General
16 Environmental Information Regulation 2004, SI 2004/3391, Regulation 2(2)(a)
17 ibid Regulation 2(2)(b). The special forces and any other special units are included (they are excluded under Freedom of Information Act 2000, 2000 c.36), insofar as it concerns environmental information
18 Environmental Information Regulation 2004, SI 2004/3391, Regulation 2(2)(c)
19 ibid Regulation 2(2)(d)

Table 6.2 Application of FoI/EIR to water regulators

Institution	Function	Legal basis of applicability
Ofwat	Regulation of the water industry in general: price setting, consumer protection, competition	FoI Act 2000 s3(1)(a)(i), Schedule 1, para 1; EIR Reg 2(2)a
Environment Agency	Pollution control, management and conservation of water resources, issuance of abstraction licence and discharge permits	FoI Act 2000 s.3(1)(a)(i), Schedule 1, part VI; EIR Reg 2(2)b
Drinking Water Inspectorate (acts on behalf of DEFRA)	Water quality regulator, technical audit on water companies, investigating consumer complaints and water quality incidents	FoI Act 2000 s.3(1)(a)(i), Schedule 1, para 1; EIR Reg 2(2)a
Consumer Council for Water	Representing consumers' interests, taking complaints, investigating water industry on consumer complaints	FoI Act 2000 s, 3(1)(a)(i), Schedule 1, part VI; EIR Reg 2(2)b
Competition Commission	Accepting referrals on merger issues, adjudicating breaches of competition law concurrently with Ofwat	FoI Act 2000 s.3(1)(a)(i), Schedule 1, part VI; EIR Reg 2(2)b
DEFRA	Standard setting, drafting of legislations and policies, appointment of regulators, industry restructuring	FoI Act 2000 s.3(1)(a)(i), Schedule 1, para 1; EIR Reg 2(2)a

The application of the UK FoI Act and EIR to the institutions above appears to be straightforward. All of them adopt model publication schemes as required by the FoI Act (s.19). The idea to expand the coverage of FoI to privatised utilities had been considered in the UK and regained public attention when the Secretary of State proposed to include other bodies to be covered by the FoI through its s.5[20] designation.[21] In addition to the view that utilities including water are essential services, it was generally perceived by the respondents on the s.5 designation consultation that there is a public interest in obtaining information on the decisions made by those companies regarding how their services are delivered.[22] The UK government considered that information about utilities is already available through regulatory bodies, which are subject to the FoI Act 2000. Thus, they considered that the current access rights were already adequate, without an urgent need to directly cover water utilities under the FoI Act. Eventually, the UK Government abandoned the

---

20 Freedom of Information Act 2000, 2000 c.36 s.5
21 United Kingdom, *Freedom of Information Act 2000: Designation of additional public authorities, consultation paper* CP 27/07 (2007)
22 United Kingdom, *Freedom of Information Act 2000: Designation of additional public authorities, response to consultation* CP(R) 27/07, 16 July 2009 (2009) p.10

idea of including the utilities under the initial s.5 designation, although they plan to commence another consultation in order to include some or all of the utilities under subsequent s.5 orders or to amend the FoI Act 2000 in some way so as to incorporate privatised utilities.[23]

There is a stronger argument for including water utilities under the FoI Act's coverage: the move toward risk-based regulation. The UK Government's argument that access to regulatory information is adequate is only relevant to the present day situation where Ofwat has wide powers in acquiring detailed information from utilities, and does so, and subsequently publishes this. However, Ofwat is planning to move to a risk-based regulation and will no longer require utilities to submit their annual June Return. This will result in the significant decrease of regulatory information published by Ofwat. As discussed in previous sections, Ofwat's plan is to have utilities publish their own regulatory account. Thus, the focal point for transparency in British water utilities regulation will slowly move from Ofwat to the regulated company. As the UK Government's justifications for exempting utilities from the FoI Act will no longer be relevant in the near future, it is only appropriate that water utilities are included as a 'Public Body' in the next s.5 designation or through an FoI Act amendment. Failure to include water utilities under FoI coverage will result in the disconnection between 'active' and 'passive' disclosure policies. Ofwat will subject utilities to some active disclosure policies by obligating them to publish their regulatory account (and presumably other regulatory information). However, if the FoI Act is not applicable to them, there is no way that the public would be able to verify detailed background information which underlies the companies' reports.

One author, Birkinshaw, notes that utilities may want to reject the effort of extending FoI for reasons of 'unjustified state intervention, damage to profitability, undermining competitive capability, and producing an uneven playing field especially in relation to overseas competitors'.[24] Unlike other utilities, however, many of the world's and indeed the EU's water utilities are state-owned and, therefore, could fall under FoI or similar access to environmental information laws given the application of the Aarhus Convention and Directive 2003/4/EC.[25] Even within the UK there is Scottish Water, which is state-owned, and is covered by the Freedom of Information (Scotland) Act.[26] Scottish Water – despite its FoI coverage – performs quite well if compared to its English counterparts, which are not covered by FoI or EIR, and charges customers even less than the majority of English water utilities.[27]

---

23 ibid
24 P Birkinshaw, 'Freedom of information and its impact in the United Kingdom' 27 Government Information Quarterly 312
25 Directive 2003/4/EC of the European Parliament and of the Council of 28 January 2003 on public access to environmental information and repealing Council Directive 90/313/EE, O.J. L 041, 14/02/2003 P. 0026–0032
26 Freedom of Information (Scotland) Act 2002, 2002 asp 13
27 *Performance Report 2010* (Water Industry Commission for Scotland, 2010) Scottish Water is benchmarked against other English and Welsh water utilities. Its Overall Performance Assessment (OPA) score for 2010 fits well with the average English water utilities' OPA. In terms of average

For EIR, its application or disapplication to water utilities is not straightforward. Initially, it was thought by some authors that EIR would, without much controversy, be automatically applicable to water utilities.[28] DEFRA guidance on EIR – reiterating the Aarhus Implementation Guideline – specifically mentions that private companies may fall under EIR 2(2)(c) or (d), and the guideline also provides private entities conducting 'water management functions' or waste collection companies under contract with local governments as examples.[29] The DEFRA guidance added a caveat though, that either the elements of 'public administration' or 'under the control' accompanied by any of the sub paragraphs (i), (ii) or (iii) of the above Regulation 2(2) has to be fulfilled. Interestingly, it adds that 'under the control' could mean

> a relationship constituted by statute, *regulations*, rights, licence, contracts or other means which either separately or jointly confer the possibility of directly or indirectly exercising *a decisive influence* on a body. Control may relate, not only to the body, but also to control of the services provided by the body (emphasis added).[30]

These predictions, that the EIR will likely cover water utilities, had been partially strengthened by earlier ICO analysis in *Sutton and East Surrey Water plc* (2008) which consider water utilities 'carrying out the functions of public administration' since water companies are appointed by the Secretary of State (or indirectly by the Director General of Water Services/Ofwat), and can have their licence terminated.[31] Second, the ICO deemed that they can also be categorised as entities which are 'under the control' of other public bodies, in this case Ofwat, through specific duties under the Water Industry Act 1991.

However, in 2010, in *FishLegal* and *Smartsource*, the ICO changed their position.[32] The crux of the dispute remains the phrases 'functions of public administration' and 'under the control' in EIR Regulation 2(2)(c) and (d). The case went all the way to the UK Upper Tribunal (UKUT) and the European

---

household bills, Scottish water is among the lowest if compared to England and Wales water companies, with seven English companies charging higher than Scottish Water. *Costs and performance 2008–09* (Water Industry Commission for Scotland, 2009)

28 See DWI's website: 'Water companies are themselves obliged to comply with the Environmental Information Regulations.' 'Access to Information' (*Drinking Water Inspectorate*, 2010) <http://dwi.defra.gov.uk/about/access-to-info/index.htm> accessed 13 June 2011; R W Davis, 'The Environmental Information Regulations 2004: limiting exceptions, widening definitions and increasing access to information?' 8 Environmental Law Review 51 and M M Al'Afghani, 'The transparency agenda in water utilities regulation and the role of freedom of information: England and Jakarta case studies' 20 Journal of Water Law 129

29 *Environmental Information Regulations 2004 detailed guidance* (Defra 2005)

30 ibid Guidance 2.19

31 *FER0118853 (Sutton and East Surrey Water plc)* (Information Commissioner's Office)

32 Respectively, FER0269130 and FER0272665. *Case Reference Numbers FER0269130 & FER0272665 (Yorkshire Water Services and United Utilities), ICO Decision 12 March 2010* (Information Commission) The author has the copy.

Court of Justice (ECJ) (as the EIR implements an EC Directive 2003/4[33] and the Aarhus Convention[34]).

After very lengthy, complicated but quite profound arguments in the UKUT and ECJ, the interpretation eventually boils down to two primary issues: (1) the 'special powers' test to determine whether water utilities are 'public authorities' under the EC Directive 2003/4 vis-à-vis 'public administrative functions' under EIR and (ii) the 'control test' – both considered by the ECJ[35] and applied by the UKUT.[36]

The special power test requires that an entity have powers 'beyond those which result from the normal rules applicable in relations between persons governed by private law'. Some of the 'special powers' considered by the ECJ and the UKUT are the power of compulsory purchase of land, the power to make by-laws for public use for private land (and to enact criminal sanctions) and the power to discharge water including into private watercourses, the right to impose hosepipe bans and the power to (subject to strict conditions and only to certain customers) disconnect the supply of water.[37] Each of these powers has actually been argued in the UKUT before referral to the ECJ was made but apparently only gained some weight after the ECJ reconsidered it. The UKUT considered that these powers would not be available under private law, and thus, eventually decided that water companies have 'special powers', which qualify them as 'public authorities' under EIR, Directive 2003/4 and the Aarhus Convention.

The second test was with regard to control. In earlier UKUT proceedings before referral was made, there was a lengthy debate as to whether a 'regulation' would constitute 'control'. According to the ECJ, the question would be whether the entity performs its function in the environmental field 'in a genuinely autonomous manner', since the public authority is 'in a position to exert decisive influence on the entity's action in that field.'[38] The UKUT considered several propositions of 'control' in the case, including Ofwat's enforcement power (s.18 WIA), 'the use of highway drains as sewers [by highway authority or the company] and vice versa' in which the company cannot 'unreasonably refuse to enter into agreement' (s.115 WIA). UKUT eventually rejected the arguments, reasoning that such regulation is a substitute for effective monopoly and thus still consistent with their genuine autonomy. As for the threat of enforcement, UKUT consider it ubiquitous in many instances. The final and

---

33 Directive 2003/4/EC of the European Parliament and of the Council of 28 January 2003 on public access to environmental information and repealing Council Directive 90/313/EE, O.J. L 041, 14/02/2003 P. 0026–0032 1990 4

34 Convention on Access to Information, Public Participation in Decision Making and Access to Justice in Environmental Matters 25 June 1998 (Aarhus Convention) 38 International Legal Materials (ILM) (1999) 515 1998

35 Case C-279/12 OJ C 250, 18.8.2012 (European Court of Justice)

36 *Fish Legal v Information Commissioner* UK Upper Tribunal GIA/0979 and 0980/2011, [2015] UKUT 0052 (AAC)

37 Respectively, ss.165, 168, 171; s.157; s.165; s.76; ss.60, 61 and 63 of the Water Industry Act

38 Case C-279/12 (n 1077)

most important part of UKUT consideration was the fact that the companies are fully privatised and each run by independent directors responsible under the Companies Act 2006.

Here, UKUT's conception of 'control' appears to be influenced by the notion of control under Corporation Law. The UKUT said that if companies are under control, they would in effect be run by 'shadow directors'.[39] The UKUT acknowledges influence is exerted, and can be extensive, but nevertheless is still 'relatively marginal compared to the extent of the actual freedom exercised.[40] Thus, the UKUT does not consider stringent regulation in a water utilities setting to constitute a 'control' under EIR. The outcome of the case this far is that EIR is applicable to water companies, as they satisfy the 'special power' test. At the time of writing, it is not known if the companies will appeal the decision.

In Indonesia, the Indonesian FoI Law, UU No. 14/2008 is applicable to public bodies, which are defined as:

> any branches of the executive, legislative and judiciary as well as other bodies whose functions and main tasks are related to the organization of the state, whose funds are derived partially or in entirety from the state and/or regional government's budget, or non-governmental organizations insofar as part or all of its budget is derived from the state or regional government's budget, community's contribution and/or foreign funds.[41]

It is thus quite clear that FoI Law UU No.14/2008 is applicable to all governmental bodies, including those involved in regulating water services such as the Department of Public Works, the National Planning Agency, Jakarta regional government and the Governor and the Ministry of Environment. What about the JWSRB?

Being an entity set up by a contract,[42] the JWSRB claim that they are neither a branch of the executive, legislative nor the judiciary. They consider themselves a private body or, at the very least, a non-governmental organisation.[43] The JWSRB does regularly receive its funding directly from the collection of water tariffs and not the state/regional budget. It is also questionable if the JWSRB's *present*[44] functions in mediating disputes, supervising the contract

---

39 See Companies Act 2006 c.46 2006 s.251(2)
40 *Fish Legal v Information Commissioner* UK Upper Tribunal GIA/0979 and 0980/2011, [2015] UKUT 0052 (AAC)
41 Undang Undang No. 14 Tahun 2008 Tentang Keterbukaan Informasi Publik Article 1(3)
42 Cooperation Agreement Between PAM Jaya and The Concessionaire, 2001 Clause 51
43 Al'Afghani and others, *Transparansi Lembaga-lembaga Regulator Penyediaan Air Minum Di DKI Jakarta* (ECOTAS/KRuHA/TIFA, 2011)
44 See JWSRB's 'Present' Functions under Clause 51.1: coordinating governmental entities and conducting a supervisory role in the enforcement of the contract, closure of deep wells, tariff levels, enforcement of PAM Jaya's rights and in developing consumer dispute mechanisms and in mediating disputes between PAM Jaya and its concessionaires.

152 *The role of the FoI Law*

and developing consumer dispute mechanisms, would categorise it as a Public Body. However, its *future*[45] functions in preventing the misuse of dominant position, protecting consumer interests and ensuring sustainability of water supplies are much more manifest in reflecting public functions.

It is also important to note that JWSRB's *present* functions, although not yet enabled by legislation, are enabled by a Governor's Regulation.[46] The Regulation established that the members of JWSRB are appointed and removed by the Governor. Hence the JWSRB is accountable to the Governor and PAM Jaya and, in turn, the Governor is accountable to the local parliament. JWSRB's regulatory function forms a part of the Governor's accountability to the local parliament, as a direct accountability line between JWSRB and the parliament does not exist.

Moreover, the rationale of the Governor's Regulation is not only in materialising the contract but also in protecting the greater public interest which exists independently from the contract. This is well reflected in the preamble of the Governor's Regulation which cites various legislations, including the laws on regional autonomy, the competition law and the law on consumer protection.[47] The Regulation also clarifies the purpose of the establishment of JWSRB, which is to safeguard the implementation of the concession contract in accordance with principles of transparency, justice and accountability and in guaranteeing service levels and affordability.[48] These aspects may give weight to the arguments that JWSRB is a public body. However, the Governor's Regulation is by no means an adequate legal framework as it does not have much power compared to legislation.[49] This reasoning was considered in the 2011 *Kruha vs PAM Jaya* case, in which the FoI Commission considered the JWSRB as an 'official body' as it was appointed by the Governor.[50] Unfortunately, as JWSRB was not a party to the case, there was no conclusion as to whether JWSRB's status is a public body.

In another case related to the disclosure of oil and gas Production Sharing Contract (PSC), the Southern Jakarta District Court decided that the state's oil and gas regulatory body, the Badan Pelaksana Minyak dan Gas or 'BP Migas' (which during the Court proceeding was transformed into Satuan Kerja Khusus Pelaksana Kegiatan Usaha Hulu Minyak dan Gas or 'SKK Migas') was not a public body. The Court decided that, as the BP Migas is financed from

---

45 The contract at Clause 51.2 stipulates that the parties intended that JWSRB shall have the functions of preventing the misuse of dominant position, protecting consumer and community interest in terms of charges and service levels, ensuring that customers benefit from improved efficiency as well as ensuring 'the provision of an efficient and economically sustainable water supply'. All of these functions have to be enabled by legislation. These have not materialised up to now. Cooperation Agreement Between PAM Jaya and The Concessionaire, 2001
46 Peraturan Gubernur DKI Jakarta No. 118 Tahun 2011 Tentang Badan Regulator Pelayanan Air Minum
47 ibid see Preamble paras 1–12
48 ibid
49 Undang Undang No. 10 Tahun 2004 Tentang Pembentukan Peraturan Perundang Undangan
50 *Kruha v PAM Jaya, Putusan Nomor 391/XII/KIP-PS-M-A/2011* Komisi Informasi Pusat

the percentage of oil and gas sales and not from the state budget – as stipulated by the Indonesian FoI Law – it is not a public body.[51] Indeed, the Indonesian FoI Law can only regard bodies other than executive, legislative or judicative as public bodies if their (i) 'main tasks are related to the organisation of the state' and whose (ii) 'funds are derived partially or in entirety from the state and/or regional government's budget'.[52] It is unfortunate that the Court did not try to extend the interpretation further to apply public body status to BP Migas (SKK Migas) using only the *performing state functions* criterion as it is very clear that BP Migas/SKK Migas tasks are related to the organisation of the state. The BP Migas was formed through a government decree and was in charge of signing PSC contracts with private contractors on behalf of the state. It was clearly a 'public' duty.

Applicability of the FoI Law to SOE

Whether or not an SOE should be covered by the FoI Law was one of the central issues debated in the parliament during the enactment process of the FoI Law. The government draft of the FoI Law did not include SOEs in the definition of 'Public Body' (although the parliament's draft did)[53] for the reason that the separation of assets in an SOE reflects the transformation of such an entity from public into private. The remaining public component in an SOE, the government maintained, is the portion of fund used for *Public Sector Obligations* or PSO.[54] Second, according to the government, an SOE must comply with various public sector rules, such as the laws on state budget, state finance, state auditor, corporation law, capital market law, etc., which make them more transparent than the private sector.[55] The Government's arguments appear to be unsound as, on the one hand, they maintain that the separation of assets means that SOEs are governed by purely 'private' rules and, on the other hand, that SOEs are already transparent since in addition to being governed by 'private' rules, the SOE is also regulated by the rules on the public sector.

The parliament's draft which explicitly included 'SOE' in the definition of 'public bodies' did not make it to the final reading and the agreed formulation of Article 1(3) is what is mentioned in the beginning of this chapter. The final draft of Article 1(3) contains the phrase 'whose funds are derived partially or in entirety from the state and/or regional government's budget' which nevertheless could be interpreted to cover SOEs. Even though the term 'SOE' is missing in Article 1(3) in the definition of a public body, Article 14 of the

---

51 *Putusan Pengadilan Negeri Jakarta Selatan No. 450/PdtG/2012/PNJktSel; KIP v BP Migas* (Pengadilan Negeri Jakarta Selatan)
52 Undang Undang No. 14 Tahun 2008 Tentang Keterbukaan Informasi Publik 2008
53 Komisi Informasi Pusat Republik Indonesia, *Anotasi Undang Undang Nomor 14 Tahun 2008 Tentang Keterbukaan Informasi Publik* (1st edn, Indonesian Center for Environmental Law dan Yayasan Tifa 2009)
54 ibid pp.32–33
55 ibid pp.32–33

154 *The role of the FoI Law*

FoI Law specifies the list of information which must be published by an SOE: among others, its financial and annual report and the remuneration system of its executives.[56]

With this interpretation, there should be no debate that all SOEs, owned by both central government and regional government such as PAM Jaya, which were set up under UU No. 5/1962,[57] fall under the definition of 'public body' under Article 1(3) of the Indonesian FoI Law. In addition, the Indonesian Information Commission Rule listed 'Perusahaan Daerah Air Minum' (Regional Waterwork Companies) as a Public Body covered by the FoI.[58]

In practice, however, this can be problematic. Some lawyers admitted the applicability of the Indonesian FoI Law on the one hand, but argue that such applicability precludes information which is generated by the SOE in its dealings with the private sector as they should be entirely governed by 'private' rules. This was argued in a 2010 *BHP Case*.[59] In this case an applicant sought a Cooperation Agreement on oil and gas between the Respondent, *BHP*, an SOE owned by Blora regional government PT Blora Patragas Hulu, and two private entities. The copy of the Agreement was deemed important following the plan to divest 49 per cent of Blok Cepu's participating interest to a private entity. The respondent rejected the request to disclose the contract on several grounds, among others, that: (1) the obligation to disclose agreement with third parties under the Indonesian FoI Law does not apply to them[60] and that only certain obligations of disclosure for SOEs are applicable;[61] (2) the Cooperation Agreement between Respondent and ABSJ is a trade secret;[62] (3) disclosure of Cooperation Agreements are exempted by the Indonesian FoI Law as 'Information which shall not be disclosed pursuant to legislations';[63] (4) the Applicant is not a party to the concession contract and therefore has no legal standing to request the contract document; (5) based on the *Pacta Sunt Servanda* principle under Indonesian Civil Code,[64] the agreement shall be perceived as the *lex specialis* to the disclosure obligation

---

56 Undang Undang No. 14 Tahun 2008 Tentang Keterbukaan Informasi Publik, Article 14
57 Undang Undang No. 5 Tahun 1962 Tentang Perusahaan Daerah
58 Attachment I of Indonesian Information Commission Rule 1/2010, para G
59 *LPAW v BHP, Keputusan Komisi Informasi Pusat No 001/VII/KIP-PS-A/2010*, 7 October 2010
60 This is despite the fact that Undang Undang No. 14 Tahun 2008 Tentang Keterbukaan Informasi Publik, Article 11.e stated that: 'Public Bodies are obligated to provide information which should be available at all time, which covers ...The agreements entered into with third parties'.
61 ibid Article 14 lists types of information which should be disclosed by regional SOEs and SOEs owned by the central government, among others, results of audit by external auditors, credit rating agencies, remuneration system for directors and commissioners and procurement mechanisms, but there is no obligation to disclose agreement with third parties under Article 14. The relation between Article 11.e and Article 14 under the Indonesian FoI Law is not clearly established. It is posssible to argue that Article 11.e covers the disclosure obligation for all public bodies (including SOEs) whereas Article 14 lists the *additional obligation* for SOEs. See also the parliamentary debate on the definition of 'public body' above.
62 ibid Article 17.b protects trade secrets
63 ibid Article 17.j. The applicant does not detail which Indonesian legislations forbids the disclosure of contracts.
64 Indonesian Civil Code, the 'Burgerlijk Wetboek' Article 1338

arising under Indonesian FoI Law; (6) the Cooperation Agreement between Respondent and ABSJ is regulated under Book III of the Indonesian Civil Code and is not regulated by the Indonesian FoI Law, hence the Indonesian FoI Commission has no authority to adjudicate the case; (7) the Criminal Code at Article 322(1) restricts public officials from disclosing secrets; (8) the Corporations Law at Article 97(3) holds directors liable for the losses sustained by the company, hence the Respondent's directors are justified in not disclosing the information; (9) by withholding the information, the Respondent's Directors are acting pursuant to the Business Judgment Rule as regulated by the Indonesian Company Law. The Indonesian FoI Commission eventually rejected all the Respondent's arguments and decided the case on behalf of the Applicant.[65]

The position of SOE as a public body was relatively unopposed in the 2011 *PAM Jaya case*, in which, an applicant sought the regional waterwork company to disclose its concession contract ('Cooperation Agreement') with private entities. Presumably, since after *BHP* several cases involving SOE have been submitted to the FoI Commission, there is almost no disagreement that PAM Jaya, the respondent, is a public body which must abide by FoI rules. Thus, unlike the *BHP Case* the *PAM Jaya Case* did not give much consideration as to PAM Jaya's public body status.[66]

Applicability of FoI Law to Palyja and Aetra

Are Palyja and Aetra 'Public Bodies' under Indonesian FoI Law? This question can be approached from two directions. First, by interpreting the part of Article 1(3) of the FoI law which reads 'or non governmental organizations insofar as part or all of its budget is derived from the state or regional government's budget, community's contribution and/or foreign funds'[67] and second, by looking at Palyja and Aetra as a private entity exercising governmental functions through the concessions.

Nature of the Budget

One method for applying administrative law to private entities is by looking at the origins of its financing. If an entity is financed partly or entirely through public funds, it may provide justification for state bodies, such as the state audit body and the ombudsman, to exert authority on the entities. Article 1(3) of the Indonesian FoI Law provides that the Law is applicable to 'non governmental organisations insofar as part or all of its budget is derived from the state and/or regional government's budget, and contribution from the community, and/or foreign sources'.[68]

---

65 *LPAW v BHP, Keputusan Komisi Informasi Pusat No 001/VII/KIP-PS-A/2010*, 7 October 2010
66 *Kruha v PAM Jaya, Putusan Nomor 391/XII/KIP-PS-M-A/2011* (n 1092)
67 Undang Undang No. 14 Tahun 2008 Tentang Keterbukaan Informasi Publik, Article 1(3)
68 ibid Article 1(3)

156 *The role of the FoI Law*

In the Jakarta concession system, PAM Jaya pays Palyja and Aetra based on the volume of water sold to consumers multiplied by an indexation formula linked to other things such as exchange rate and inflation rate ('water charge'). If the tariff charged to consumers is unable to meet the water charge, PAM Jaya still needs to pay the remaining 'shortfall'. If the payment of shortfall is made through the regional government's budget, the FoI Law would apply. This would be a rare situation since PAM Jaya still owes the concessionaires a large amount of debt and any payments are made by offsetting PAM Jaya's debt with the concessionaire's penalty.

Using the budget as a means of categorising an entity as a 'public body' faces some other challenges. It brings about several technical questions of amount, timeframe and applicability to types of information. During the parliamentary debates, the government was cautious on how this article would be applied and queried whether entities with only minuscule financing from the public should be covered by this provision. This also sparks another question: when the entity is no longer covered by public funds, will it still be listed as a public body? If the answer is no, there is then a question of timeframe: at which point in time will the FoI Law be applicable to the entity, when they are receiving public funds? State budget funds could be disbursed for only one time, but used over a period of time. Finally, if the entity also operates commercially, using private funds, some information that it generates, in theory, results purely from private financing. The FoI Law might not be applicable to this information. The law is silent with respect to the hybrid function of these entities and how the FoI Law can apply to that situation. Due to difficulties in categorising which information is derived from which funds, we can assume that once an entity becomes a public body, the FoI Law will be applicable to all sorts of information that it generates, whether it is related to the use of public funds or not.

Furthermore, there is also confusion on what 'non governmental organization' really meant; does it cover only NGOs in the common sense of the term or also corporations and other private entities? KIP regulation lists a number of 'public bodies' to which the Indonesian FoI Law would be applicable. PDAM (state-owned regional water companies, PAM Jaya is also in this category) is listed as a Public Body, however, its concessionaires are not. The KIP regulation does not overrule the possibility that other bodies not listed on the attachment of its rule can still be covered. At the time of writing, there has been no clarity on whether the proportion of public funds on the entities budget matters for the determination of such an entity as a public body.

Nature of the Concession

Adapted from continental Europe's administrative legal tradition, Indonesian doctrines in Administrative Law recognise several kinds of 'licences' that would allow the private sector to be involved in public service: *Dispensasi* (dispensation), *Lisensi* (licence), and *Konsesi* (concession).

Atmosudirdjo wrote that a concession is '*suatu penetapan administrasi negara yang secara yuridis sangat kompleks karena merupakan seperangkat dispensasi-dispensasi, izin-izin, lisensi-lisensi, disertai pemberian semacam "wewenang pemerintahan" terbatas kepada konsesionaris*' ('an administrative decision which is legally very complex as it contains a set of dispensations, permits and licences followed by some kind of limited "governmental authorities" to the concessionaires').[69] Since concessionaires hold some form of governmental powers, some authors[70] even consider them to be 'public officials'.

Since Palyja has been granted a monopoly to provide water to western Jakarta, and Aetra to the eastern part, together with the power to collect tariffs and decide on matters such as investment, network expansion and the connection and disconnection of customers from the water network, they are exercising a delegated governmental authority in the water services sector.

Article 1(3) of the Indonesian FoI Law defines a Public Body as:

> any branches of the executive, legislative and judiciary as well as other bodies whose functions and main tasks are related to the organization of the state, whose funds are derived partially or in entirety from the state and/or regional government's budget'.[71]

Both Palyja and Aetra could fit under the part 'as well as other bodies whose functions and main tasks are related to the organization of the state' as their main function is to deliver water services on behalf of the regional government.[72]

If such logic is followed, Palyja and Aetra are public service institutions, their officials are, therefore, public officials acting on a delegated authority, their decisions on investment, connection and disconnection issues are administrative decisions (subject to reviews at the administrative court) and any documents resulting from their activities are public information.

This interpretation, however, is rarely implemented in practice. Although concessions are common in Indonesia and have been implemented in almost every sector such as mining, oil and gas, forestry and infrastructure, concessionaires are always seen as a private entity. Concession contracts tend to be seen as purely private contracts and, in practice, any disputes resulting from them are often referred to a private court, not the administrative court.

Table 6.3 summarises the applicability of the FoI Law to institutions involved in water utilities regulation:

---

69 Atmosudirdjo, *Hukum administrasi negara* (Ghalia Indonesia 1981) p.98
70 See Indroharto, as quoted in Ridwan HR, *Hukum Administrasi Negara* (Yogyakarta: UII Press, 2003), p.59 and S F Marbun, *Peradilan Administrasi Negara dan Upaya Administratif di Indonesia*, (Yogyakarta: Liberty, 1997), p.60
71 Undang Undang No. 14 Tahun 2008 Tentang Keterbukaan Informasi Publik Article 1.3
72 Determination of the status of an entity as a public body can be conducted by looking at several criteria as follows: The legal entity obtains authority through attribution, delegation, mandate or concession, which objectives are in serving the public interest. Such authority can be derived from laws and regulations, entrustment of task from the government or such authority can also be derived from *cooperation* between the government and the entity in performing state functions. Komisi Informasi Pusat Republik Indonesia, *Anotasi Undang Undang Nomor 14 Tahun 2008 Tentang Keterbukaan Informasi Publik* (1st edn, Indonesian Center for Environmental Law dan Yayasan Tifa 2009) p.39

158 *The role of the FoI Law*

Table 6.3 Applicability of the FoI Law to institutions involved in water utilities regulation

Institutions	Role	FoI applicable?
Department of Public Works, The National Planning Agency	General policy/direction	Yes
Ministry of SOE Governor	Financial management	Yes
Ministry of Health	Drinking water regulator	Yes
Jakarta Governor/Jakarta Regional Government	Tariff determination Monitoring of performance Financial management Operational licence	Yes
Jakarta Water Sector Regulatory Body (JWSRB)	Mediation and conciliation of consumer disputes, monitoring of performance Adviser to Jakarta Governor in tariff determination	Very likely. JWSRB denied that it is applicable
Ministry of Environment/ Bappedal Badan Pengendalian Dampak Lingkungan Daerah DKI	Environmental licences, enforcement of environmental matters	Yes
PT Jasa Tirta	Bulk water supplier	Yes
Perusahaan Daerah Air Minum Jakarta (PAM Jaya)	Contract and performance monitoring	Yes
PT PAM Lyonnaise Jaya	Retail water supplier	No, although in theory it is possible
PT Aetra	Retail water supplier	No, although in theory it is possible
Perum Jasa Tirta	Bulk water supplier	Yes

6.2 Exemption clauses

Freedom of information legislations are subject to exemption clauses. For water utilities, three exemption clauses are deemed most relevant: those which relate to law enforcement and investigation, commercial information and obligation of confidence.

6.2.1 Law enforcement and investigations

In Victoria's FoI Law, law enforcement documents are protected from disclosure (s.31). This exemption includes documents containing information on investigation of breach or possible breach of law, proper 'administration of the law', fair trial and fair adjudication, disclosure which may endanger the life of police informants and law enforcement officers and methods of crime prevention or law enforcement.[73]

The clause covers both 'investigation of a breach or possible breach' of the law and 'proper administration of the law'. The latter has been argued to encompass 'something concerned with the process of the enforcement of legal rights or duties' and covers both civil and criminal law.[74] Investigation by the Ombudsman or any other regulatory bodies may be covered by this exemption, but the harm must be sufficiently argued if the exemption is to be granted.

In England, s.30 of the FoI Act 2000 exempts information related to investigations and proceedings conducted by a Public Authority if such information had been or is being held by a Public Authority for the purpose of investigation. As such, it also covers closed and abandoned investigations conducted by public authorities.[75] The term 'investigation' here is quite broad, as it covers information related to questions as to whether a person should be charged with an offence, whether a person charged with an offence is guilty or if it amounts to criminal and/or civil proceedings.[76]

Ofwat has wide investigation and enforcement powers[77]. Those which relate to 'offences', for example, are the unauthorised use of an undertaker's network,[78] the supply of water unfit for human consumption,[79] and water contamination.[80] The term 'charged with an offence',[81] is not defined in the Act. In practice, the ICO expanded this into anything that could lead to the commencement of criminal proceedings including police cautions.[82] It is likely that investigation leading to a penalty decision may be covered by this exemption. S.30(2)(iii)[83] referring to s.31(2), lists various types of investigation which would effectively cover investigations undertaken through all layers of enforcement action by Ofwat, including (s.19), the 'enforcement order' (s.18) and, financial penalties (s.22A).[84]

---

73 s.31(1)
74 *Accident Compensation Commission v Croom [1991] VicRp 72; [1991] 2 VR 322* (24 September 1990)
75 'Information held by a public authority is exempt information if it has at *any time* been held by the authority for the purposes of' (italics added) s.30(1) Freedom of Information Act 2000, 2000 c.36 *The exemption for criminal investigations, criminal proceedings and confidential source* (Information Commissioner Office 2009)
76 Freedom of Information Act 2000, 2000 c.36 s.30
77 This is imposed in the licence condition, for example, see para 8–9 *Instrument of Appointment by the Secretary of State for Wales of Dwr Cymru Cyfyngedig as a water and sewerage undertaker under the Water Act 1989* (1989)
78 A Collins and R Fairchild, 'Sustainable food consumption at a sub-national level: an ecological footprint, nutritional and economic analysis' 9 Journal of Environmental Policy & Planning 5s.66I-L
79 ibid s.70
80 ibid s.73
81 Freedom of Information Act 2000, 2000 c.36 s.30(1)(a)
82 *The exemption for criminal investigations, criminal proceedings and confidential source* (Information Commissioner's Office 2009)
83 This section refers to the Freedom of Information Act 2000, 2000 c.36 s.31(2)
84 Water Industry Act 1991 c.56 19, 18 and s.22A

160 *The role of the FoI Law*

Section 30 contains a public interest test and is a 'class exemption' where the harm test is not necessary. As for public interest test, the right to a fair trial is generally accepted as a public interest which needs protection from disclosure.[85]

EIR provides exemption for disclosure of information which 'adversely affects' (1) the course of justice, (2) the ability of a person to receive a fair trial and (3) the ability of a public authority to conduct an inquiry of a criminal or disciplinary nature.[86] A public interest test is mandatory to all exemptions made under EIR, including this one.[87]

The term 'adversely affect' means that there should be a harm test and the threshold for non-disclosure is a high one.[88] The term 'course of justice' has been interpreted widely so as to include law enforcement.[89] 'Proper administration of the law' such as prevention, investigation or detection of crime, and apprehension or prosecution of offenders is also deemed to come within the exemption,[90] as well as legal professional privilege.[91]

The application of this type of exemption to a water utilities regulator is likely to be similar to the FoI, the difference being the former obligates a harm test with a high threshold, whereas s.30 of the FoI Act 2000 contains no harm test and s.31 contains a harm test but with a lower threshold, compared to the EIR.

In Indonesia, the Indonesian FoI Law recognises an exemption on law enforcement,[92] but this covers only criminal law enforcement. Furthermore, the exemption is only applicable if a disclosure is deemed to obstruct criminal investigation,[93] reveal the identity of witnesses or informants or endanger the safety of law enforcers or their infrastructure. Investigations into civil or administrative matters are not covered in the exemptions.

As it can be considered a crime[94] to distribute drinking water which is unfit for consumption or jeopardise human health, cases on water contamination

---

85 *The exemption for criminal investigations, criminal proceedings and confidential source* (Information Commissioner's Office 2009)
86 Environmental Information Regulation 2004, SI 2004/3391 Regulation 12(5)(b). This exemption applies when the public authority is not exercising its legislative or judicial function, as bodies exercising those functions are beyond the scope of EIR's applicability see ibid Regulation 3(3)
87 ibid Regulation 12(b)
88 See *Archer v The Information Commissioner and Salisbury District Council, EA/2006/0037* (Information Tribunal) para 51
89 *Environmental Information Regulations 2004 detailed guidance* (Defra 2005) Guidance 7
90 ibid Guidance 7
91 *Freedom of Information Act, Environmental Information Regulations: The exemption for legal professional privilege* (Information Commissioner's Office 2008)
92 Undang Undang No. 14 Tahun 2008 Tentang Keterbukaan Informasi Publik, Article 17.a
93 'Investigation' under the Indonesian Criminal Justice System consists of two stages: *penyelidikan*, a stage where no suspect has been declared by the police and the case has not been determined as a criminal offence and *penyidikan*, a later stage where a suspect has been declared, the case is declared by the police as a crime and the dossier is being completed for a transfer to the prosecutor's office
94 Peraturan Pemerintah No. 16 Tahun 2005 Tentang Pengembangan Sistem Penyediaan Air Minum prohibits the distribution of water unfit for human consumption (see article 6.2) however there are no criminal liabilities attached to this. If contamination occurs, then it will be dealt with by ordinary criminal law, the investigation of which might be covered by FoI exemption.

could be covered by this exemption, as long as they are being investigated by the police and the disclosure of information related to the case may obstruct the criminal investigation. Violation of another service level, as long as they are not under police investigation, is not likely to be covered by this exemption.

6.2.2 Commercial information

In Victoria, s.43 regulates the exemption related to trade secret or commercial information. This section regulates two kinds of documents: documents obtained by the minister or agency from a third party and documents within an agency or ministry.

Documents acquired from a third party containing (a) trade secrets or (b) other business, commercial or financial information is protected from disclosure. However, exemptions under category (b) contain a further qualification, namely, that it must expose an undertaking to a disadvantage. Trade secret information (category (a)) is an absolute exemption since according to s.34(2) the elements in weighing disclosure are applicable only to category (b).

In determining whether disclosing information may cause disadvantages to an undertaking, the Act lays down several elements, namely, whether the information is already generally available to competitors, whether it would be an exempt matter if it were generated by an agency and whether disclosure could be possible without causing substantial harm to the competitive position of an undertaking. Finally, there is a requirement to determine if there are any public interest considerations in favour of disclosure which outweigh considerations of competitive disadvantage. In order to qualify for exemption, information must have the 'essential quality or character of the matter business, commercial or financial'.[95]

A harm test is applicable to this exemption and demonstrated through the use of the phrase 'would be likely to expose the undertaking unreasonably to a disadvantage'.[96] 'Reasonable expectation' that a harm would exist would be adequate.[97] *Attorney-General's Department v Cockcroft*[98] is a leading authority and concludes that the harm tests 'require a judgment to be made by the decision-maker as to whether it is reasonable, as distinct from something that is irrational, absurd or ridiculous.'

Subsequent decisions such as *Alan Sunderland v the Department of Defence*,[99] *Organon v Department of Community Services v Health and Public Interest Advocacy Centre*,[100] *Queensland and Department of Aviation*[101] and *Maksimovic and*

---

95 Re Croom and Accident Compensation Commission (1989) 3 VAR 441
96 Freedom of Information Act 1982 (Victoria) No. 9859 of 1982 Version No. 066 s.34(1)b
97 Re Actors' Equity Association of Australia and Australian Consumers Association and Australian Broadcasting Tribunal and Federation of Australian Commercial Television Stations [1985] AATA 69
98 Re Peter Cockcroft and Attorney-General's Department and Australian Iron and Steel Pty Limited [1985] AATA 224
99 Re Alan Sunderland and the Department of Defence [1986] AATA 278 (19 September 1986)
100 Re Organon (Australia) Pty Limited and Department of Community Services and Health and Public Interest Advocacy Centre [1987] AATA 396
101 Re Queensland and Department of Aviation [1986] AATA 142

162   *The role of the FoI Law*

Commonwealth Director of Public Prosecutions and Anor[102] all refer to and reiterate *Cockroft*. Hence, so long as a disclosure can be expected to cause negative consequences, it will fulfil the likelihood element, without needing much proof.

Goodwill can be categorised as a commercial interest and the loss of goodwill considered a form of 'harm' if it leads to the loss of the consumer. In one case invoking exemption under s.45(1)(c) of the Queensland's FoI Act, (equivalent to the Victorian FoI s.34(b) on the protection of commercial, business and personal interest) the Queensland FoI Commission decided that[103] 'adverse effect on a corporation's business reputation or goodwill . . . is feared ultimately for its potential to result in loss of income or profits, through loss of customers'. Hence, a harm caused to a corporation could either be direct, in the form of decreasing profit, or indirect, such as in the form of goodwill which leads to the loss of customers and, eventually, profit. This would certainly be interesting if argued in a water utility context. More importantly, the FoI Commission considered whether the company is operating in a monopoly context which would influence its assessment of 'harm':

> A relevant factor in this regard would be whether the agency or other person *enjoys a monopoly position for the supply of particular goods or services* in the relevant market (in which case it may be difficult to show that an adverse effect on the relevant business, commercial or financial affairs could reasonably be expected), or whether it operates in a commercially competitive environment in the relevant market.[104]

In England, under the FoI Act there are two sub categories under commercial interest exemption: (1) trade secrets and (2) prejudice to the commercial interests of any person (including the public authority holding the information).[105] For trade secrets, there is a duty to confirm or deny if such information is being held, whereas for commercial interests, such duty can be removed, if there is a prejudice to the disclosure of the requested information.[106] That also means that the trade secret exemption is a class-based one, not requiring a harm test, whereas the commercial interest exemption does require it. In both cases, there is a public interest test. Both exemptions are aimed at protecting competitive advantage.[107]

While what may constitute as a trade secret is fairly clear,[108] 'commercial interest' is extremely broad. Birkinshaw notes that the usual term employed

---

102   Maksimovic and Commonwealth Director of Public Prosecutions and Anor [2009] AATA 700
103   Cannon and Australian Quality Egg Farms Ltd [1994] QICmr 9; (1994) 1 QAR 491 (30 May 1994)
104   ibid para 84
105   Freedom of Information Act 2000, 2000 c.36, s.43
106   FoI Act 200, s.43(3)
107   *Freedom of Information Act Awareness Guidance No. 5, Commercial Interests (Version 3)* (Information Commissioner's Office 2009)
108   See Law Commission of Great Britain, *Legislating the criminal code: misuse of trade secrets; a consultation paper* (HMSO 1997) para 1.29 See also Patrick Birkinshaw, *Freedom of information* (Cambridge University Press 2010) p.168 and *Freedom of Information Act Awareness Guidance No. 5, Commercial Interests (Version 3)* (Information Commissioner's Office 2009)

is 'commercial confidences' which signifies some degree of confidentiality and that in other legislation[109] the term used is 'prejudiced to an unreasonable degree'.[110] This is not the case with the FoI Act 2000 where prejudice alone is sufficient.

As a part of the exercise in determining 'prejudice', the ICO guideline suggested that the level of competition within the industry needs to be weighed. 'Where a company enjoys a monopoly over the provision of the goods or services in question it is less likely that releasing the information will have a prejudicial impact on that company.'[111]

Since cases involving Ofwat are quite rare[112] it would be useful to weigh another case under the FOISA,[113] which concerns a water utility. This case is also relevant for the English experience because Scottish Water (SW) is a regulated company (with Water Industry Commission for Scotland or WICS as the regulator) despite the fact that it is owned by the government.[114] WICS also uses the RPI-X incentive-based regulation in determining prices and also benchmarks SW's performance with their England and Wales counterparts.

S.33(1)(a) and (b) (respectively, trade secret and commercial interest) of the FOISA mimic the UK FoI Act 2000 s.43(1) and (2) governing the same things, the exception being that the FOISA adds the words 'prejudice substantially' with respect to commercial interest exemption, whereas the English FoI Act contains only the word 'prejudice'.

In *MacRoberts and the City of Edinburgh Council*,[115] The Scottish FoI Commissioner had to consider whether city councils should release a copy of the list of the properties in respect of which the council collects water and waste water charges on behalf of Scottish Water. MacRoberts, the complainant (a firm of solicitors), does not require the details of the owner, proprietor or occupier of the premises.[116] The councils denied the request by citing a number of exemptions, one of them is 'Commercial Interest', under s.33(1)(b) of the FOISA, which mimics s.43(2) of the UK FoI Act 2000, except with respect to the use of the word 'substantial' as discussed above.

SW argued that it may levy charges, at a reasonable fee, to obtain copies or extracts from the records it keeps.[117] It further explains that it fixes the charges

---

109 Clean Air Act 1993, s.37; Control of Major Accident Hazard Regulations 1999, sch. 8, para. 18 See Birkinshaw, *Freedom of information* (Cambridge University Press 2010) p.169
110 ibid p.169
111 *Freedom of Information Act Awareness Guidance No. 5, Commercial Interests (Version 3)* (Information Commissioner's Office 2009) p.6
112 Case search – up to 2011 – on the English FoI Commissioner's website reveals only one result which involves OFWAT, the case concerns 'legal professional privilege. See *FS50273866 (Water Services Regulation Authority)* (Information Commissioner's Office). The exemption under s.42(1) was upheld by the IC. Case search at the Information Tribunal reveals 'none'.
113 Freedom of Information (Scotland) Act 2002, 2002 asp 13
114 See Hendry, 'An Analytical Framework for Reform of National Water Law' (PhD thesis, University of Dundee 2008) for a complete account of the Scottish water industry.
115 *Decision 056/2006 MacRoberts and the City of Edinburgh Council* (Scottish Information Commissioner)
116 ibid para 3
117 Water Industry (Scotland) Act 2002, 2002 asp 3 See s.58(5)(b)

for property search certificates, in the amount of 40 GBP, and that amount is routinely paid by search companies or solicitors wishing to know whether a property is connected to SW's water supply, sewerage, whether they are charged using household, business or metered rates and whether any mains are located in a property, which may impact any future building plans.[118]

The first question to be assessed was whether there is 'substantial prejudice to commercial interest'.

Although not elaborated in detail on the case, *MacRoberts* actually concerns two different markets: first, is the market of information provision in which SW would benefit from disclosure and second, the market in natural monopoly of water supply, which may suffer prejudice because of disclosure due to the increase of charges. The prejudice from disclosure toward SW would be in the form of loss of income in the first market. This may also affect customer charges in the second market.

The Scottish FoI Commissioner suggested that such a service (of SW providing property search certificates) is conducted 'in competition' with search companies.[119] Actually it is not exactly clear how this came to be, since, if all information generated by search companies comes from SW, then SW will not be in direct competition with the search companies. What is true is that the provision of such information entails a search cost resulting from the use of GIS map data and access to records of connection consents.[120] It was argued that the charge imposed to the public helped them to relieve the burden of its operational cost.[121] The Scottish FoI Commissioner agreed that SW's commercial interest would or would be likely to be 'substantially' prejudiced.[122]

The second question is the public interest test. There is clearly a public interest in maintaining exemption, since it contributes to decreasing SW's operational cost which may eventually lead to a reduction of actual price charges incurred to customers. There may also be a public interest in disclosure, since it reduces search costs incurred by search companies or other individuals.

There is a public interest in both markets (the market of information and the market of water supply), however, the Scottish FoI Commission was not satisfied that the public interest from disclosure of information – which would be directly enjoyed by companies – would outweigh the public interest in charges enjoyed by customers.[123] It believes that SW is legally entitled to reap

---

118 *Decision 056/2006 MacRoberts and the City of Edinburgh Council* (Scottish Information Commissioner) paras 40 and 41. SW does not charge land owners who inspect records related to their own properties. They also do not charge inspections which are aimed at minimising damages to pipelines due to construction works on the site area. See para 44
119 ibid para 40
120 ibid para 90
121 ibid para 98
122 ibid para 92
123 ibid para 100

the benefit of information that it provides according to the charging schemes as approved by WICS and that the beneficiaries, if the information is released, will only be the commercial companies.[124]

It is interesting that the Scottish FoI Commissioner seemed inclined to dismiss the argument that benefit to the search companies from disclosure would be a 'public interest'. The public interest test would require 'the consideration of whether or not release of the information would be in the interests of the public as a whole'.[125] For the Scottish FoI Commissioner it seems a benefit to the search companies is not 'the public as a whole', therefore not the 'public interest', it would only be an 'individual interest or . . . sectional interest to particular groups in society'.[126] Some writers argue that there is a lack of justification for a natural monopoly industry to possess commercial confidentiality[127] and that such is considered an oxymoron.[128] In England, a DTI Green Paper also considered that information about a monopoly business should generally be disclosable, whereas for markets opening up to competition, the extent of disclosure required should be correlated with the degree to which a company has market power.[129] It is suggested that the more market power a player has, the more barriers there should be to non-disclosure.[130]

All of those statements above might hold true, but not categorically true, since consumers' interests or public interest could be asserted through non-disclosure, as *MacRoberts* demonstrated as discussed above. SW's argument can stand because they have no private shareholders to serve. Hence, the fact that SW is publicly owned played a role.

---

124 ibid para 97
125 ibid para 98
126 ibid para 98 See also M Feintuck, *'The public interest' in regulation* (Oxford University Press 2004) which suggests public interest in regulation as a 'linkage between constitutional values and semi-autonomous legal and regulatory systems' conducted by restraining capital and individualistic values and justifying social regulation and existing independently from the economic argument of market intervention.
127 'Consumer's International argued in TC 224 that in a natural monopoly there is no justification for commercial confidentiality during the life of a contract, and we were not convinced that it is necessary even during a period of competitive tender, which is the justification usually presented.' See R Simpson, 'Down and dirty: providing water for the world' 14 Consumer Policy Review 146. TC 224 (Technical Committee 224) is the ISO committee in charge of setting the standard for water and waste water services. Note that Simpson's argument here correlates with long-term contracts (concessions, lease or the like) and not fully divested companies.
128 G Palast, J Oppenheim and T MacGregor, *Democracy and regulation: how the public can govern privatised essential services* (Pluto Press 2002) p.185
129 Department of Trade and Industry, *A Fair Deal for Consumers: Modernising the Framework for Utility Regulation* (CM 3898, London, The Stationery Office 1998) at Proposal 7.6
130 Baldwin and Cave, *Understanding regulation: theory, strategy, and practice* (Oxford University Press 1999) p.308. See also DGT Submission at para 5.20: 'Review of Utility Regulation, Submission by the Director General of Telecommunications' OFCOM, <www.ofcom.org.uk/static/archive/oftel/publications/1995_98/index.htm> accessed 11 February 2010

Had SW been a privately owned company, as many of the water utilities in England are, would there be a public interest in maintaining exemption? Probably not, since the income from charging for the release of information and records could be channelled to the shareholders through dividends, while the cost for information gathering is still charged to the customers. In this case, maintaining exemption would only serve 'sectional interest to particular groups in society',[131] namely, water utilities' private shareholders.[132]

Is downstream competition not a public interest? MacRoberts was accusing SW of exploiting its statutory monopoly on water and water information.[133] The question of competition was mentioned, but it was not considered to be relevant and not the *lex lata*[134] since the case was adjudicated in 2006 whereas retail competition for non-household customers was intended to be opened in 2008.[135]

Presumably, there would be a public interest toward increasing competition *only if* the disclosure in the first market (the market of information in the form of a list of properties) will have the benefit of increasing competition in the second market (the market of water supply). This distinction is important because disclosure in the first market (market of the commodified information) may or may not increase competition in the second market (market for water supply). This argument also depends on the statutory mandate for opening up water services to competition.

It is to be noted that in some practices of English FoI, the functioning of competition has been noted as a public interest. This occurred in procurement related cases in which there is a public interest in protecting fair market competition in public sector contracts (Welsh Development Agency)[136] and in encouraging private sector participation in procurement (Her Majesty's

---

131 *Decision 056/2006 MacRoberts and the City of Edinburgh Council* (Scottish Information Commissioner) para 98. See also Feintuck, *'The public interest' in regulation* (Oxford University Press 2004) which suggests public interest in regulation as a 'linkage between constitutional values and semi-autonomous legal and regulatory systems' conducted by restraining capital and individualistic values and justifying social regulation and existing independently from the economic argument of market intervention. Coppel argued that the scope of the Public Interest in the FoI Act 2000 (England) may not be as wide as those normally considered in ordinary courts. See also P Coppel, 'The Public Interest and the Freedom of Information Act 2000' 10 Judicial Review 289 and *Your right to know: the government's proposals for a Freedom of Information Act* (Stationery Office 1997) para 3. wider.
132 That is, if the English Information Commissioner, Tribunals or the Courts consider shareholders as only 'a particular group of the society', and not 'the public as a whole'
133 *Decision 056/2006 MacRoberts and the City of Edinburgh Council* (Scottish Information Commissioner) para 99
134 'Although the retail market for non-domestic customers is being opened up to competition from 2008, I must consider the law as it now stands' ibid para 99
135 The Water Services etc. (Scotland) Act 2005, 2005 asp 3
136 There is 'an inherent public interest in ensuring that companies are able to compete fairly and in ensuring that there is fair competition for public sector contracts'. Welsh Development Agency Case, Reference FS50097376 <https://ico.org.uk/media/action-weve-taken/decision-notices/2006/381738/DECISION_NOTICE_FS50097376.pdf> accessed 22 May 2016

Revenue and Customs (HMRC)).[137] In one case, the IC mentioned the public interest to protect a newly liberalised state-owned company (*The Royal Mail*).[138] However, in all of these cases, the public interest toward the functioning of a competitive market is served by *maintaining* the exemptions.

However plausible it might seem, arguing the functioning of a competitive market as the rationale of public interest disclosure might be a difficult one. As was argued in *MacRoberts*, the direct beneficiary from the disclosure by an 'upstream' utility company is likely to be the 'downstream' companies, not the public as a whole. Public interest toward disclosure may arise, only if such disclosure would improve the development of competition, which leads to the expansion of consumer choice.

In order to invoke the proper working of competition as a public interest in disclosure, the following factors might need to be considered:

1   The causality between disclosure and enhancement of consumer choice. Unless the new market is matured, however, this may be difficult to ascertain.
2   The existence of specific legislation mandating liberalisation; competition in the market, or retail competition. The Cave Review was asked to be considered in *Smartsource* but was dismissed as the Upper Tribunal is concerned only with the water industry as it is today, 'not as it may look in the future'.[139] Retail competition was also considered in *MacRoberts* but was dismissed as it was considered not to be the law as it stands today.[140]
3   Interpretation of specific sections in the legislation, which leads to the conclusion that disclosure would be required. This will help with contextualising public interest. It is likely that liberalisation would be conducted through legislative reforms, and followed by 'active disclosure rules'. The role of FoI/EIR will be picking up what was left by sectoral rules, for example, in a bid to improve an entrant's decision *whether, where and how to enter* the market.[141]

---

137 'However the Commissioner recognises that there is also a strong public interest in encouraging the wider involvement of the private sector in public procurement, to increase competition'. Her Majesty's Revenue and Customs. Reference FS50157117, para 57 <https://ico.org.uk/media/action-weve-taken/decision-notices/2009/485520/FS_50157117.pdf> accessed 22 May 2016
138 The information is commercially sensitive. Royal Mail no longer has a monopoly over postal delivery and must now operate in a fully liberalised market place. Disclosure of the requested information is likely to harm its *competitive position*. *The Royal Mail Case*. Reference: FS50126145, para 18(i) <https://ico.org.uk/media/action-weve-taken/decision-notices/2007/396634/FS_50126145.pdf> accessed 22 May 2016
139 *Smartsource Drainage & Water Reports Limited v The Information Commissioner, Upper Tribunal Case No. GI/2458/2010* (The Upper Tribunal (Administrative Appeals Chamber)) para 73
140 'Although the retail market for non-domestic customers is being opened up to competition from 2008, I must consider the law as it now stands' *Decision 056/2006 MacRoberts and the City of Edinburgh Council* (Scottish Information Commissioner) para 99
141 With respect to upstream bulk water supply, Cave commented that there are significant barriers of entry: 'there are significant information asymmetries, alternative suppliers often have little information on which to decide whether, where and how to enter'; Cave, *Independent review of competition and innovation in water markets: final report* (Department for Environment Food and Rural Affairs (Defra), 2009) p.46

168 *The role of the FoI Law*

The English EIR Regulation 12(5)(e) exempts information if its disclosure 'would adversely affect' the confidentiality of commercial or industrial information where such confidentiality is provided by law to protect a legitimate economic interest.[142] Like any other EIR exemption, a public interest test is mandatory. A four-stage test from *Bristol City Council*[143] is invoked by the ICO guideline[144] in determining if the exemption is engaged. It comprises of the questions: (1) Is the information commercial or industrial in nature? (2) Is the information subject to confidentiality provided by law? (3) Is the confidentiality provided to protect a legitimate economic interest? (4) Would the confidentiality be adversely affected by disclosure? The test is cumulative.

The striking difference between FoI and EIR is that the EIR attached confidentiality to commercial information, whereas confidential obligation is a separate exemption under FoI. Such confidentiality can only arise out of common law, contract or statute.

The EIR also contains a separate clause specifically exempting Intellectual Property Rights (IPR) information (subject to the harm and public interest tests). The understanding of IPR covers anything from copyright, patents and trade secrets to new chemical constituents.[145] For FoI only, trade secret was categorised specifically, whereas the other types of IPR will come under 'commercial information' or 'obligation of confidence'.

Customers' databases (for the parts which are not covered by Data Protection legislation, but contain some form of 'database') and utility underground network assets data may be covered by this exemption.[146] However, as the threshold for harm is higher than the FoI Act 2000 and there is a public interest test, the ICO *in University of East Anglia*[147] and *Ofcom*[148] has been quite generous with respect to disclosures.

In Indonesia, the Indonesian FoI Law[149] exempts all sorts of Intellectual Property Rights (IPR) and information which, if disclosed, undermines protection against unfair business competition.[150] The formulation of the FoI Law is unnecessarily wide as IPR covers a range of rights from patents, industrial designs and trade secrets to copyright. Some types of IPR such as patents and copyright already entail an element of publication and, as such, their

---

142 Environmental Information Regulation 2004, SI 2004/3391 Regulation 12(5)(e)
143 *Bristol City Council v IC and Portland and Brunswick Squares Association, EA/2010/0012* (Information Rights Tribunal) para 8
144 *Confidentiality of commercial or industrial information, LTT160* (Information Commissioner's Office 2010)
145 *Environmental Information Regulations 2004 detailed guidance* (Defra 2005) Guidance 7
146 Copyright, Designs and Patents Act 1988, 1988 c.48 s.3A protects databases, insofar as they are original
147 See the two recent cases involving the University of East Anglia Climatic Research Unit *University of East Anglia (FER0282488)* (Information Commissioner's Office); *University of East Anglia (FER0280033)* (Information Commissioner's Office)
148 *Ofcom (FER0072933)* (Information Commissioner's Office)
149 Undang Undang No. 14 Tahun 2008 Tentang Keterbukaan Informasi Publik Article.17.b
150 ibid

exemptions are irrelevant. Some relevant IPR-related exemptions are for trade secrets, industrial design[151] and plant varieties.[152]

In the aforementioned *BHP* case[153] adjudicated by the Indonesian FoI Commission, the respondent tried to argue that the Cooperation Agreement between BHP and ABSJ contained trade secrets and, therefore, should be exempted from disclosures. As the Respondent did not provide evidence for this, the FoI Commission rejected the Respondent's claim that the contract contained trade secrets. When it comes to utility, however, as the majority of the data submitted to the regulator is rarely traditional technological trade secrets but merely business information, the trade secret argument is rather rare in cases involving utilities.[154]

The second category in the exemption clause is: *'information which, if disclosed, undermines the protection against unfair business competition'*.[155] Arguments pertaining to *healthy competition* were considered in the *BP Migas* case regarding the disclosure of a Production Sharing Contract (PSC). The Indonesian FoI Commission considered that information pertaining to *domestic market obligation* does not warrant exemption. Similarly, neither does information on the accounting method used in cost recovery, since, the FoI Commission argued, they can only reveal a company's financial capacity if equipped with data regarding volume and realisation of the company's finances. Accounting information such as depreciation and amortisation is also considered disclosable, but not information on Earning Before Interest, Tax and Depreciation (EBITDA).[156] Although the FoI Commission's arguments were solid, it was finally quashed by the Courts, for the reason that BP Migas/SKK Migas was not a public body, as previously discussed.

Under Indonesian FoI, there is only one public interest clause (the terminology used in the FoI Law is the *greater*[157] interest) which applies generally throughout the whole law. The idea of 'public interest', however, is not well developed in the legal system, although some legislation does contain a public

---

151 The obligation of confidentiality is only enforced on employees of the Directorate General of Intellectual Property Rights, the Ministry of Law and Human Rights, during the registration process pending announcement. See Undang Undang No. 31 Tahun Tahun 2000 Tentang Desain IndustriArticle 23
152 The obligation of confidentiality is only enforced on consultants, employees of the Office on Protection of Plant Variety and the relevant government officials, the Ministry of Farming, during the registration process pending announcement See Undang Undang Nomor 29 Tahun 2000 Tentang Varietas Tanaman, Articles 13, 22, 23, 30
153 *LPAW v BHP, Keputusan Komisi Informasi Pusat No 001/VII/KIP-PS-A/2010*, 7 October 2010
154 See J T O'Reilly, 'Confidential submissions to utility regulators: reconciling secrets with service' 18 Ohio Northern University Law Review 217
155 Undang Undang No. 14 Tahun 2008 Tentang Keterbukaan Informasi Publik
156 *Putusan Nomor: 356/IX/KIP-PS-M-A/2011; YP2IP v BP Migas* (Komisi Informasi Pusat)
157 Indonesian FoI Law, Article 2(4) and 19. The clause is not clear on what is meant by *consequence* and *greater interest* but its elucidation confirms that consequence refers to the interests which are protected under prevailing regulations and greater interest refers to public interest. Undang Undang No. 14 Tahun 2008 Tentang Keterbukaan Informasi Publik

interest clause.[158] The system of codified law, where judges are considered only as interpreters of rules and shall refrain from making laws[159] probably constrains the development of the notion of 'public interest'.

The meaning of public interest is also influenced and constructed by the state's ideology toward the market. In Judicial Reviews of the water law, oil and gas law[160] and the electricity law,[161] it was revealed that market competition for vital services is not emphasised by the Indonesian Constitution. In its water law ruling, the Constitutional Court affirms that regional waterwork companies (PDAM) should not position themselves as profit-oriented companies.[162]

The Indonesian Competition Law states: 'Business actors shall be prohibited from conspiring with other parties to obtain information regarding the business activities of their competitors classified as company secrets which may result in unfair business competition.'[163] Meanwhile under the FoI Law, exemption from disclosure is granted only if it undermines protection from *unfair business competition*.[164] Elucidation of the Indonesian FoI clarifies that the clause aims to protect business practices which are dishonest, illegal or undermine competition.[165] In order to maintain an exemption, therefore, respondents will need to argue that the information request is illicit, or motivated by commercial gains.

The articles above will only apply *if* there is competition in the sector. Unlike in other competitive sectors, when it comes to *natural monopoly* however, the argument should be different. Here, the notion of a 'public interest' toward the functioning of the market should be treated with great caution. This is not to suggest that competition is not protected. Given that private operators are given a legal monopoly over certain regions by the regional government (and since direct competition is not foreseeable for the moment) claiming exemption on grounds of public interest might be difficult.[166] The idea that a concession is a form of licence and that the operators themselves as concessionaires are public officials mandated with some form of governmental authorities would weaken the argument toward secrecy. *If* a concession – by

---

158 Indonesian Criminal Code Article 14.h grants authority to public prosecutors to drop charges for *public interest* reasons
159 S Mertokusumo, *Mengenal Hukum, Suatu Pengantar* (5 edn, Liberty 2003)
160 *Judicial Review of Law Number 22 of 2001 Concerning Oil and Gas, Judgment of 15 December 2004, No. 002/PUU-I/200* (Constitutional Court of the Republic of Indonesia)
161 Mohamad Mova Al'Afghani, 'Constitutional Court's Review and the Future of Water Law in Indonesia' 2 Law, Environment and Development (LEAD) Journal (2006)
162 *Judicial Review of Law Number 7 Year 2004 regarding Water Resources, Judgment of 13 July 2005, No. 058-059-060-063/PUUII/2004* (Constitutional Court of the Republic of Indonesia): 'PDAM has to position itself as the state's operational unit to realize the state's obligation as stipulated in Article 5 of the Water Resources Law, and not as the company which is economically profit-oriented' (Official translation).
163 Undang Undang No. 5 Tahun 1999 Tentang Praktek Monopoli dan Persaingan Usaha Tidak Sehat Article 23. Translation by the Indonesian Commission for the Supervision of Business Competition
164 Undang Undang No. 14 Tahun 2008 Tentang Keterbukaan Informasi Publik Articles 6.3.b and 17.b
165 ibid elucidation of Article 6(3)b
166 See *Decision 056/2006 MacRoberts and the City of Edinburgh Council* (Scottish Information Commissioner)

definition – is a public service, then any information generated from it would be public information, the non-disclosure of which can only be justified if the public is put at harm. One of the public service functions of a concession is 'institutional learning'.[167] In addition to obtaining value for money for the delivered service, the regional waterwork companies or other water companies in another region need to learn from the concessionaire. Such a learning process requires a certain degree of openness.

Competition *for* the market in the form of tender for an exclusive legal monopoly to distribute water can enjoy such protection and this is confirmed by the procurement rule. But once the tender process is over and the winner is pronounced, there is no more justification to keep the information secret. In fact, there is a demand for accountability and transparency of the tender process in the form of an explanation by the tender committee as to the rationale of their decision.

It is possible that a water company already entrusted with a legal monopoly feels that disclosure of its tender information is harmful since it decreases its competitiveness to bid for another project in another region. In this case, the task of the FoI Commission and the Court is to define and construct the meaning of 'public interest'. On the one hand, there is the interest of the bidding company, to maintain its dominant position by withholding information and, on the other hand, there is a public interest to open up the market to allow the delivery of public services at efficient cost.

6.2.3 Obligation of confidence

In Victoria, materials obtained in confidence by an agency or a Minister are protected from disclosure.[168] The key feature of this clause is that the information must be communicated 'in confidence' to an agency or a Minister. Section 35 excludes information acquired by an agency or a Minister from a business, commercial or financial undertaking and that which relates to trade secrets or other matters of a business's commercial or financial nature, presumably as this has already been covered in s.34.

The Russell Report[169] concludes that exemptions are deemed to apply only where information is submitted to the government in confidence (s.35) and not when the information is generated jointly between the government and a third party.[170] The Victorian Administrative and Appeals Tribunal Decision *Thwaites and MAS* emphasised: 'the documents do not so much consist of information

---

167 See J Colin and H Lockwood, 'Making innovation work through partnerships in water and sanitation projects' (2002) <http://aguaconsult.co.uk/assets/Uploads/Publications/BPD-WASHInnovation-2002.pdf> accessed 22 May 2016
168 Freedom of Information Act 1982 (Victoria) No. 9859 of 1982 Version No. 066 s.35
169 E W Russell, E Waterman and N Seddon, *Audit Review of Government Contracts: Contracting, Privatisation, Probity and Disclosure in Victoria 1992–1999, An Independent Report to Government* (State Government of Victoria May 2000)
170 Similar condition applies to s.34 exemption

172 The role of the FoI Law

acquired by the agency from a business, commercial or financial undertaking but rather constitute the record of the transaction between the parties'.[171] Hence, if this interpretation is taken, any contracts between a government and a third party, such as the Victorian Desalination Contracts, will not fall under the exemptions provided in s.34 and s.35 of the Victorian FoI Act.

In England, Section 41 of the FoI Act 2000 exempts information if it was obtained by the public authority from any other person (including another public authority) and the disclosure of which by the public authority holding it would constitute a 'breach of confidence' actionable by that person.[172] As s.41 contains the conjunction 'and', both the elements of 'obtained' and the likelihood of breach of confidence should occur. This exemption is absolute, which means, no balancing test is required. However, a public interest test can be employed as a court defence for a breach of confidence.

One of the criticisms against this exemption in the FoI Bill was that it gives too much flexibility and control on the part of utilities to declare information as confidential.[173] This may confuse regulators in separating those which are 'commercial in confidence' and those which are not.

One can imagine several scenarios where regulators 'obtain' information about utilities, for example, passively, by way of voluntary submission of information from the utilities or obligatory submission due to licence conditions[174] or statutory[175] requirements, and actively through the process of information gathering by the regulator in the course of an investigation.[176] However, a contract concluded between a Public Authority and a third party does not constitute information 'obtained' by it.[177]

A three-step test was developed in *Coco v A.N. Clark (Engineers) Limited*[178] in order to determine the essential elements that will cause an actionable breach of confidence, and these are: (1) the necessary quality of confidence (i.e. the information is not publicly known), (2) the confider is receiving information in which obligation of confidence can be inferred and (3) disclosure not

---

171 *Thwaites v Met Ambulance Service (1995/04289) [1994] VICCAT 6* (3 May 1994). The Victorian Administrative and Appeals Tribunal is the former name of VCAT.
172 Freedom of Information Act 2000, 2000 c.36, s.41
173 Fitch and Graham 'The draft Freedom of Information Bill – implications for utilities' 10 Utilities Law Review 257. The UK's Information Commission guidelines acknowledge the 'flexibility' and contextual nature of the law on confidence in common law. *Freedom of Information Act awareness guidance 2: Information provided in confidence* <http://goo.gl/pnoAEQ> accessed 22 May 2016
174 *Instrument of Appointment by the Secretary of State for the Environment of Thames Water Utilities Limited as a water and sewerage undertaker under the Water Act 1989* (2005) Condition M
175 Water Industry Act 1991 c.56 s.202
176 For example, *Instrument of Appointment by the Secretary of State for Wales of Dwr Cymru Cyfyngedig as a water and sewerage undertaker under the Water Act 1989* (1989) Condition J
177 See *Derry City Council v Information Commissioner, EA/2006/0014* (Information Tribunal) Para 32(c) and (d) 'the correct position is that a concluded contract between a public authority and a third party does not fall within section 41(1)(a) of the Act'.
178 *Coco v A.N. Clark (Engineers) Limited [1968] F.S.R. 415* Anne Lyons

The role of the FoI Law 173

authorised by discloser may amount to damage to confider. This test is well adopted by the IC in its guidance,[179] as well as case-law.[180]

In *MacRoberts*, the Scottish FoI Commissioner adopted the three-step test.[181] The Commissioner concluded that the list of properties served by SW, whose charges are collected by local authorities, had been compiled by SW and is, therefore, not publicly known information. This was deemed to satisfy the first limb of the *Coco* test above. It was revealed that the agreement between SW and the Council contained a confidentiality clause[182] and that SW threatened to sue the Council if it released information to MacRoberts.[183] Respectively, this was deemed to satisfy the second and third limbs of the *Coco* test. Finally, the public interest defence toward disclosure was also considered in *MacRoberts*, which reached the conclusion that it was not adequate to trump the public interest in maintaining exemption.

The Information Tribunal in *Ofcom* considered the confidence test in *Coco*. The Information Tribunal found that some detailed information about individual base stations had been released through another channel, without any confidentiality duty attached to it, through a roll-out programme organised between the mobile operator association and local planning authority.[184] The information disclosed to local planning authorities is not exactly as requested by the applicant, but it is possible to match up information disclosed in the roll-out programme with that which is disclosed in the Sitefinder website. This significantly erases the quality of confidence which would otherwise be attached to the information.[185] This would entail that even if the information is protected as a database and/or by copyright, it still has to be disclosed, since it has no more quality of confidence.[186]

In Indonesia, there is no specific exemption on the confidentiality obligation as the law does not recognise a 'duty of confidence'. In England, the duty to hold information confidential arises out of equity or contract.[187] Nevertheless, under Indonesian Law, the obligation of confidence may arise out

---

179 *Awareness guidance 2, Information provided in confidence* (Information Commissioner's Office 2009) also *FOI Policy Knowledge Base, Test of confidence, LTT93* (Information Commissioner's Office 2009)
180 See for example *Derry City Council v Information Commissioner*, EA/2006/0014 (Information Tribunal) para 34
181 *Decision 056/2006 MacRoberts and the City of Edinburgh Council* (Scottish Information Commissioner) para 70
182 ibid The clause prohibits the release of any information relating to the agreement. Data supplied by SW to the Council and data provided and received by the Council in relation to billing and collection of charges are also confidential, para 67.
183 ibid
184 *The Office of Communication (Ofcom) v Information Commissioner and T-Mobile (UK) Limited*, EA/2006/0078 (Information Tribunal) paras 4, 9, 55, 64
185 ibid para 64
186 ibid para 66
187 A Coleman, *The legal protection of trade secrets* (Sweet & Maxwell 1992) p.12

of contractual obligation[188] or be mandated by the regulatory statute. In Jakarta, JWSRB is obligated under its mandate to maintain secrecy of *all*[189] information and must use information in the regulatory process only for the purpose of mediating potential disputes arising out of the concession. Similarly, PAM Jaya is bound by contractual confidentiality obligations[190] and has refused an FoI request to disclose the contract document and other regulatory information.[191]

As demonstrated in *BHP*, Respondents often use obligation of contractual confidentiality to argue for exemptions. In this case they were trying to argue that disclosure of information would trigger liability by way of 'breach of contract' under the Indonesian Civil Code. Directors of a company, therefore, according to the Respondent, must be careful not to disclose information that could cause litigation and bring losses to the company.[192] A similar argument about contract sanctity was used in the *BP Migas* case.[193]

The 'MALE' (Maximum Access, Limited Exemption) principle under Indonesian Law requires that exemption can only be given under very limited and narrow exemption clauses provided in Article 17. The FoI Law at Article 17.j. does provide exemptions for *Information which shall not be disclosed pursuant to legislations*. The FoI Commission and the Court may require that the referred legislation explicitly states which information is intended to be withheld. Since Indonesian Corporations Law does not mention any specific information that should be withheld from the public, Article 17.J of the FoI Law cannot be used. A mere construction or interpretation that the company law infers non-disclosure is not sufficient.

The possibility that litigation for breach of contract could arise due to disclosure by government officials as a result of FoI requests, however, poses another problem. The FoI disclosure case and the breach of contract will be dealt with as separate cases involving different judges. The FoI case will be adjudicated by the FoI Commission and in case of appeal either to an Administrative Court (if the respondent is a state entity) or a State Court (if the respondent is not a state entity),[194] while the breach of contract litigation or shareholders' litigation will be dealt with by the private law chamber of the State Court. It is possible to submit evidence from the previous FoI tribunals to the private law proceeding,

---

188 All contracts are legally binding as law on the parties. Indonesian Civil Code, the 'Burgerlijk Wetboek' Article 1338.
189 Peraturan Gubernur DKI Jakarta No. 118 Tahun 2011 Tentang Badan Regulator Pelayanan Air Minum, Article 6.b
190 See Cooperation Agreement Between PAM Jaya and The Concessionaire, 2001 Clause 47
191 Daryanto, *Jawaban Surat KRuHA (Letter No. 581/DIVT&P/XI/2011 dated 8 November 2011 on PAM JAYA's response to FoI Request by KRuHA)* (PAM Jaya 2011); Reza, *Permintaan Dokumen dan Informasi Kontrak Konsesi Layanan Air Minum Jakarta (Freedom of Information Law Request for Documents and Contractual Information Concerning Jakarta's Water Services Concession), Letter No. 019/KIP/V/2011 dated 31 October 2011* (KRuHA 2011); Rizal, *Tanda Terima Pendaftaran Pengajuan Sengketa Informasi No. A26/RSI/P/XII/KIP/2011, KRuHA v PDAM DKI Jakarta, 07-12-2011* (Komisi Informasi Pusat (KIP) 2011)
192 The Corporation Law 40 Year 2007 at Article 97(3) holds directors liable for the losses sustained by the company. Undang Undang No. 40 Tahun 2007 Tentang Perseroan Terbatas
193 *Putusan Nomor: 356/IX/KIP-PS-M-A/2011;YP2IP v BP Migas* (n 1198)
194 Undang Undang No. 14 Tahun 2008 Tentang Keterbukaan Informasi Publik Article 47

but since the Indonesian Judiciary recognises no *stare decisis*, there is nothing to prevent the judges in deciding otherwise and, in turn, inflicting damages on the company.

Bearing this in mind, it is thus better to regulate FoI disclosure as part of mandatory provision in the procurement contract, as shown by the Victoria case study, as this will deter 'breach of contract' litigation.

6.2.4 *Memorandums and internal documents*

Memorandums and internal working documents can be used as an argument in favour of exemption from disclosure involving water companies.

In Victoria the FoI Act provides exemption for internal working documents in s.30. However, the sentence in s.30 contains the conditional 'if' and the conjunction 'and'.[195] Hence, non-disclosure would be triggered only when the two prerequisites are fulfilled: first, the document contains advice, recommendation, consultation or deliberation of the officials *and* second, that such disclosure is contrary to public interest. The burden of proof for arguing that non-disclosure is in the public interest lies with the agencies. This provision does not contain a harm test.

The public interest which is often argued in favour of non-disclosure is the free and frank deliberation of government officers, as it is feared that without sufficient protection from disclosure, the quality of decisions arrived at by deliberation will decrease.[196] However, this 'candour and frankness' has been treated with scepticism.[197] Only when an office is at a sufficiently high level (such as ministerial level) where frankness and candour exist with regard to policy making, is the exemption considered appropriate.[198]

In England, s.35(1)(a) of the English FoI Act exempts 'formulation' or 'development' of government policy from FoI disclosure[199] and s.36 exempts information which, if released, will prejudice the effective conduct of public affairs. The difference between s.35 and s.36 is that the latter contains a prejudice test (as well as a public interest test) whereas the former contains only a public interest test. The rationale for exempting the information, however, is more or less similar, namely, to protect the quality of public policy.[200] When information is not caught under s.35, it may be caught under s.36.

---

195 Freedom of Information Act 1982 (Victoria) No. 9859 of 1982 Version No. 066 s.31
196 *Re News Corporation Limited, Mirror Newspapers Limited, Nationwide News Pty Limited and Control Investments Pty Limited and National Companies and Securities Commission [1983] AATA 311; 8 Aclr 316* (14 September 1983) (Administrative Appeals Tribunal)
197 Re Robyn Frances Murtagh and Commissioner of Taxation [1984] AATA 249 (5 July 1984) *Department of Premier and Cabinet v Hulls [1999] VSCA 117* (11 August 1999) (Supreme Court of Victoria – Court of Appeal) Re Howard and the Treasurer of the Commonwealth (1985) 3 AAR 169
198 *Sankey v Whitlam [1978] HCA 43; (1978) 142 CLR 1* (9 November 1978) (High Court of Australia) para 39
199 This section is to be read in conjuction with s.36
200 *Awareness guidance 24: Policy Formulation, Ministerial Communications, Law Officers' Advice, and The Operation of Ministerial Private Office* (Information Commissioner's Office 2008); *Awareness guidance 25, section 36: Effective conduct of public affairs* (Information Commissioner's Office 2008)

The term 'policy' in s.35(1)(a) is deemed to have been well understood in practice.[201] The term 'government policy' is intended to cover any policies coming out of Whitehall and Westminster including policies endorsed by individual ministers, although they have not been signed inter-departmentally.[202]

Timing appears to be a crucial issue in this exemption as it seeks only to protect 'formulation or development' of government policy and not after it has been concluded and implemented. The Information Tribunal has rejected the idea that a policy is like a 'seamless web', in that it is a continuing process. The Tribunal considers that there is a beginning and an end to a policy's formulation and an interval between the end of the formulation and its development.[203] What signals the end of the formulation period is, then, a question of fact and must be considered on a case-by-case basis. This could be a mere parliamentary announcement, or a Bill receiving Royal Assent.[204]

What this means is that the current policy-making activities on the restructuring of the English water industry, apart from papers and reports already released to the public, may be exempted from FoI disclosure. Until the water White Paper is turned into legislation,[205] the deliberation forming the policies might not be able to be disclosed using FoI. Deliberation between Ofwat's board members may also be exempted either under s.35 or s.36.[206]

The danger of this exemption is that it might provide influence to a particular party in shaping policies through lobbying. There is, however, a public interest test to both s.35 and s.36. The public interest consideration includes (1) the understanding of the role of lobbyists, its mechanics and the relationship between government and a particular lobbyist including the influence they exert, (2) the scrutinising of the probity of public officials and (3) in providing the opportunity to present opposing views during policy development.

EIR Regulation 12(4)(e) protects internal communication from disclosure. The rationale of the clause and the public interest consideration is similar to FoI Act 2000 s.35 and s.36, as discussed above. EIR 12(4)(e) obligates a no harm test.

---

201 'Policy making is the process by which governments translate their political vision into programmes and actions to deliver "outcomes" – desired changes in the real world'. T Blair and J Cunningham, *Modernising Government* (Prime Minister and Minister for the Cabinet Office 1999) p.15; P Waller, R M Morris and D Simpson, *Understanding the formulation and development of government policy in the context of FOI* (2009) p.15

202 Waller, Morris and Simpson, *Understanding the formulation and development of government policy in the context of FOI* (2009) p.15

203 ibid para 75(v)

204 LTT62

205 A White Paper turned into legislation is one of the examples which signals that a formulation stage has ended. See Waller, Morris and Simpson, *Understanding the formulation and development of government policy in the context of FOI* (2009)

206 Fitch and Graham, 'The draft Freedom of Information Bill – implications for utilities' 10 Utilities Law Review 257

In Indonesia, the FoI Law has no specific exemption for policy formulation. Such exemption is possible if the information is presented in the form of a 'confidential memorandum' (Article 18i).[207] The elucidation elaborates that such exemption is meant to protect 'frankness and candour' in the decision-making processes and the premature revelation of a future policy which could impede the success of an ongoing or future negotiation.[208] However, since the exemption covers only information presented in the form of a confidential memorandum, it cannot be applied to other forms of documents such as meeting notes.

In practice, this exemption was used successfully in the *PAM Jaya* case in order to prevent financial projections contained in the annex of the Cooperation Agreement (water concession contract) from being disclosed. In the FoI proceedings, PAM Jaya tried to argue that Article 17h(3) exempts 'a *person's* financial conditions, assets, income and bank account' from disclosure, as according to the law, this may reveal personal secrets.[209] The original intention of this clause is to protect an individual's privacy, as stipulated in other parts of Article 17(h) which seeks to protect 'family' condition (point 1), health, treatment and physical treatment (para 2). Thus, the Respondent's argument attempted to conflate this and extend the understanding of a *person* into corporation. This would certainly be impossible considering points 1 and 2 above. The Respondent's argument was later dismissed by the FoI Commission without further considering its merit.

Unfortunately, the FoI Commission then resorted to Article 17(i) which exempts memorandums and letters between public bodies, which are considered classified. The FoI Commission approved the Respondent's request to exempt Palyja's financial projection contained in the attachment of the Cooperation Agreement, under the reason that a negotiation process (to discuss costs and tariff between PAM Jaya and Palyja, the concessionaire) is under way. The FoI Commission cited the elucidation of Article 17i which elaborates that exemption of a memorandum is required if it might impede the success of an ongoing or future negotiation.[210] On the other hand, the FoI Commission rejected PAM Jaya's request to exempt financial projections contained in the contract with Aetra, on the grounds that the negotiation process for tariff rebasing has taken place.

Although the FoI Commission is correct in applying the elucidation of Article 17(i) which exempts negotiation, it failed to explain why a contract annex can be considered a 'memorandum'. The annex in the Palyja contract has been signed – it is not a draft annex – thus, the condition is similar to Aetra's contract in which the FoI Commission decided to disclose in full. Finally, the

---

207 Undang Undang No. 14 Tahun 2008 Tentang Keterbukaan Informasi Publik Article 18i
208 ibid Elucidation of Article 18i
209 Undang Undang No. 14 Tahun 2008 Tentang Keterbukaan Informasi Publik (n 1094) Article 17h
210 *Kruha v PAM Jaya, Putusan Nomor 391/XII/KIP-PS-M-A/2011* (n 1210)

FoI Commission failed to adequately apply the harm test as required by the FoI Law. The only consideration concerning harm was found in para 4.38 of the decision: fear of public resistance and fear of affecting diplomatic relations (without mentioning which country, but presumably it meant France, since Palyja is the subsidiary of Suez Environnement, a French company). None of these 'harms' have been validated. In places such as England and Victoria discussed above, cost components are regularly disclosed by regulators without any problem. More importantly, even if these harms can be validated, the FoI Commission failed to weigh the public interest. Presumably the public may resist if they discover the annex of the contract signifies a price hike. However, there is certainly a public interest in understanding cost components.

7 Conclusion

As explained in Chapter 1, the water sector is suffering from various forms of 'governance failure'. Enhancing transparency would improve overall governance, fulfil the human right to water prerequisite and facilitate economic regulation. In Section 1.4 this book developed a framework for transparency which consists of: policy in involving the private sector, regulators' internal governance, licensing and information flow, regulatory functions, utilities' corporate governance and the role of Freedom of Information law. Each of these components was assessed by comparing and applying it to three jurisdictions: Victoria (Australia), England (United Kingdom) and Jakarta (Indonesia).

7.1 Policy in involving the private sector

Whether or not water services provision can be delegated to the private sector, the extent of such delegation, the body which has the power to delegate and how the delegation is carried out are sensitive issues in water utilities regulation. Such concern is embodied in General Comment 15 on the Human Right to Water which recommends 'full and equal access of information' concerning water held by states or third parties and reports from the Independent Expert (now Special Rapporteur) of the Human Right to Water which emphasises that any decision toward delegation should be democratic, participatory and transparent. Similarly, a human rights framework requires transparency in tendering, bidding and the contract negotiation processes. The Independent Expert specifically outlined that 'Commercial confidentiality must not jeopardize the transparency requirements provided for under the human rights framework'.

For England, the question of delegation is resolved by parliament. Through the 1989 Water Act, parliament decided to fully privatise water utilities through assets divestiture. Since the UK parliament is the highest political forum in the country, the enactment of the 1989 Water Act – which contained divestiture clauses– is deemed to be sufficiently democratic. The follow-up questions of procurement and government contract are to this extent less relevant to England which divested its assets through flotation. Only in Victoria and Jakarta (as with many states around the world) where contracting is employed as an instrument of delegation, do the questions of public procurement and

180 *Conclusion*

government contract become relevant. In these jurisdictions, the question of democracy arises because there is a distance between the parliament, which is accountable to the public through elections and other means, and the decision to delegate water services. Both in Victoria and Jakarta, the decision to delegate water services lies within the discretion of the executives.

7.1.1 The decision to delegate

Both in Victoria and Jakarta, there is a legislative 'entrenchment' of public ownership. The Victorian Constitution mandates that a 'public authority' which is accountable to the Minister be responsible for ensuring the delivery of water services. Meanwhile the Indonesian Constitutional Court emphasises that water should remain under 'state control' and that state-owned enterprises should be prioritised in water services. Full divestiture of assets will not be compatible with either jurisdiction. However, PSP is possible. The most common PSP is implemented only in specific parts of the water cycle, such as a treatment plant in Victoria. However, some PSPs, such as Jakarta's Cooperation Agreement, range from treatment to distribution, completely removing the incumbent utility (PAM Jaya) from its operational duties and positioning it as a quasi-regulator and contract supervisor. As demonstrated in the preceding chapters, such PSPs have far reaching consequences toward public accountability. Thus, despite the 'entrenchment' of public ownership in Victorian and Indonesian legislation, there is always scope for PSPs and this scope is vague. In order to provide clarity and transparency, legislation must be comprehensible, it must clarify the type of PSP allowed and differentiate the delegation procedure according to the scope of the water services cycle that it wishes to delegate. If most parts of the water services cycle (from abstraction to distribution) are subjected to delegation, it will have far reaching accountability consequences and, as such, may require specific procedures prescribed by the legislation which could be in the form of a referendum or a parliamentary approval.

7.1.2 Procurement

In both Indonesia and Australia, there are rules pertaining to CoI in the procurement team. In Australia, the disclosure of such CoI must be made, albeit internally, however, in Indonesia such disclosure is not mandatory. In both countries, all types of procurements must be announced through the procuring institution's website, official announcement board and the national procurement tender portal. The purpose is to allow interested parties to bid. There are no other transparency, accountability or public participation mechanisms.

Similar to Jakarta (Indonesia), in Victoria the 'Expression of Interest' should be published through the procurement website. In Victoria, however, there is emphasis on public accountability and transparency of procurement. The National Guideline also mentions the need to 'consider' access, accountability and consumers' rights. Accountability – including the applicability of the FoI

Act to procurement is considered as 'risk' to be borne by the government, but there is no adequate guidance on how it should be assessed and mitigated. Full disclosure is a general principle, but in order to protect competitiveness and sensitive information it only applies to the PPP Contract and not during the bidding process. The government should guarantee that information on project performance is available for release after contract execution.

An important lesson from Victoria is the effort to integrate the FoI Act with procurement. It requires private parties to agree that disclosure by way of FoI will not amount to a breach of confidentiality. In practice, this is formulated in a 'waiver' clause which serves as an exception to the contract's general confidentiality provisions. Such a 'waiver' clause may be efficient in protecting liabilities arising out of contractual confidentiality, but will not be applicable to confidentiality obligations arising from outside the contract, such as equity law.

In both Victoria and Indonesia, there is a sense that transparency in procurement is still focused mainly on particular stakeholders, in this case the bidders and other market players interested in bidding, rather than the public. Thus, transparency is perceived only as a tool to facilitate fair competition and generate value for money in procurement. This kind of transparency lays emphasis on the disclosure of information required for those interested in bidding, such as the call for tender, the specification of the goods or services to be procured and the prerequisites for participating in tenders. On the other hand, the notion of 'public interest' is certainly greater than the mere agenda to facilitate competition or in achieving value-for-money for the project and this may require disclosure of other kinds of information, such as the rationale and consideration of the procurement team on why it arrives at certain decisions. In this respect, Victoria fares better than Indonesia as there is already an attempt to integrate FoI with procurement rules and there is an acknowledgement that the accountability problem is a kind of risk, although it still lacks in outlining of how it should be assessed and weighted. Victoria enables transparency in procurement not through legislation, but through guidelines, which influence the procurement process including the contract drafting.

7.1.3 *Publication of contract*

In Indonesia, both the Law on Public Service and the Law on Freedom of Information require contracts entered into by the government with the private sector to be published. Similar requirements are imposed on Victorian public bodies as a matter of policy. However, although only a matter of policy, the requirement to disclose a contract in Victoria is enumerated in greater detail than in Indonesia. For example, the Victorian contract publication policy is clear in that it intends to publish in full and in readily accessible format, contracts over USD10 million of value and requires only the publication of headlines of contracts worth more than USD100,000. In Indonesia there is no clarity on the policy of contract publication. The Indonesian FoI Law requires contracts to be published, but does not set the value threshold. The Indonesian Public

Service Law, on the other hand, also does not provide clarity as it requires only the publication of key contractual terms.

A good practice in Victoria – something that Indonesia could learn from – is the high level of integration of disclosure policies with general administrative law as well as sectoral law and policies, especially the procurement policy. The Indonesian procurement rule does not contain any clause mandating contract disclosure although legislations, the aforesaid FoI Law and the Public Service Law, do. This creates a disharmony between parliamentary legislations and the practice of procurement. In Victoria, the procurement guidelines specifically refer to the principles of the FoI Act. Premier Bracks' contract publication requirements are also referred to in the Procurement Guideline.

In addition, the contract disclosure policy in Victoria is also embodied and interlinked with public sector accounting. The Victorian Department of Treasury and Finance regularly issue Financial Reporting Directions (FRD) to the public sector. The contract disclosure policy is embodied in FRD 12A which also sets the guidelines for exclusion from publication by referring to FoI Act exemptions.

Finally, there is a role for formal institutions: the VGPB and the Victorian Auditor-General. The VGPB as Victoria's centralised procurement board administers and announces every call for tender in the Victorian public sector. At the same time, the VGPB also publishes contracts which result from the procurement. The Victorian Auditor General has wide powers under the Audit Act 1994 and also has the mandate to oversee the implementation of contract disclosure policies. With such powers, the Auditor General is able to have access to documents in the possession of agencies, conduct audits and report them to the parliament and the public.

Nevertheless, the Victorian ways of managing government contract publication through a set of fragmented policies (the Policy Statement and Guideline, the Procurement Guidelines and FRD12A) have some compliance problems. The initial policy statement requires that any excisions from disclosure should be given explanations. This was not implemented in some instances as it is deemed to be required only by the policy statement and not by FRD 12A. If the contract publication requirement was embodied in statute as well as properly reflected in policies, its enforcement would have been more coherent.

7.2 The regulators' internal governance

In all three jurisdictions, legal frameworks regulate the composition, structure, term of office, appointment and removal mechanisms for members of the regulatory bodies. The power to appoint and remove members of the regulatory bodies is vested in the executive. In England, the power to appoint and remove rests with the Secretary of State, whereas in Jakarta, it rests with the Governor. In Victoria, the power to appoint rests with the Governor in Council but removal must be approved by parliamentary resolution. Presumably, this is meant to reinforce the regulatory body's insulation from the executive's political interference.

With the exception of Victoria, transparency mechanisms are used when filling positions as members and chairpersons of the regulatory body. In Jakarta, selection for JWSRB members must be announced to the public. There is, however, no explanation of whether this obligation falls to the Governor and no clarification on how the publication needs to be carried out. The Victorian legal framework lacks a transparency mechanism in the appointment of ESC members. The ESC Act contains provisions on appointment, as discussed previously, but is silent on the transparency mechanism. The best practice of the three jurisdictions compared is in England. Ofwat's board appointments by the Secretary are subject to transparency requirements imposed by The Commissioner for Public Appointments. The selection is carried out by setting up a recruitment website and candidates may be required to appear before a parliamentary select committee.

Other than appointments, removal of members from the membership of a regulatory body is also an important issue. This is mainly because the creation of 'independent' regulators needs to calculate any possible conflict between the executive and the regulatory body and the abuse of the executive's statutory powers in removing them from their membership. Victoria addresses this by requiring parliamentary approval, and Jakarta by requiring suspensions (which precede removal) to be announced transparently to the public. However, in Jakarta, there is no parliamentary intervention in the removal process, so the position of the regulators in the face of the Governor is significantly weaker than in Victoria. England, while faring best among the three on its transparency in appointing Ofwat board members, does not regulate in detail the procedure of removal of Ofwat members by the Secretary.

Conflict of Interest management is another important topic in the regulator's internal governance and transparency mechanisms play an important role. England has good practice in defining clearly what is meant by 'prohibited interest' and requiring its disclosure. What is lacking in England is that Ofwat's rule of procedure does not really clarify to whom the CoI should be disclosed: the public or Ofwat's Chairman and Secretary. Nevertheless, some memberships, positions and relationships which may trigger CoI must be disclosed in the The Register of Board Members' Disclosable Interests, which – according to Ofwat's procedure – is a public document. The register is a powerful transparency instrument of Ofwat's internal governance as it allows the public to immediately scrutinise any possible CoI. Jakarta, on the other hand, is lacking in terms of CoI management. CoI is nowhere mentioned, defined or regulated in the legal frameworks applicable to JWSRB. There are only minimal regulations on appointment and dismissal of regulators. In Victoria, CoI is regulated in primary legislation, but it lacks definition and transparency requirement. There are only two provisions relevant in the context of CoI in Victoria: the obligation for the ESC Chairperson not to take paid employment and the obligation of all members to disclose existing or foreseeable pecuniary interest to the Minister. However, there is no requirement to publicly disclose these interests.

7.3 Licence governance

Crucial to the transparency of licences are specifications on the types of licences, the criteria for application, the licence conditions and whether there is an obligation or policy to publish licences in the public domain. Water utilities might be subjected to various kinds of licences, but when this book uses the term 'licence' it means 'operational' licences which contain some authorisation by the state for the water utility to carry out the delivery of water services in its service area. The procedure for obtaining such operational authorisation, including the publication of such authorisation in the form of licences, is important due to the natural local monopoly nature of the water industry.

Each of the three jurisdictions has a different understanding of what a 'licence' is and, therefore, the role of licences varies from one jurisdiction to another. England – for the time being – is very much a licence-based regime, so the majority of regulatory arrangements in the English water industry are stipulated in the utilities' licences. Victoria no longer uses licences since the companies were reconstituted as statutory corporations, however, several other instruments, the Statement of Obligation and Water Industry Regulatory Order are still in place. Jakarta has a parallel and somewhat conflicting regulation: The 'Cooperation Agreement' system which dates from 1997 and the new water law regime which has applied throughout Indonesia, including Jakarta, since 2004. Both the Jakarta contract system and the new Indonesian water law applicable to Jakarta are problematic in terms of licensing.

The type of licences applicable in the water services sector is clarified by legislation in England but not in Indonesia. The criteria for approving licences are also well defined in England but not so in Indonesia. This is because there are ambiguous provisions in the revoked Indonesian Water Law and its implementing regulations with respect to the extent to which PSP would be permissible. Before 2015, Indonesia, through a government regulation, limited private sector involvement by allowing them to participate only in a 'region which is not yet covered' by services provided by SOE or regional SOEs'. This creates confusion as to whether the rule only intends to allow greenfield projects in water services or whether non-greenfield projects can be allowed in some cases. In practice, a large number of brownfield projects have been approved or are in the process of tender. The ambiguity leads to lack of clarity on the type of licences, the conditions attached to them, and ways to obtain them. This obviously opens up opportunities for corrupt dealings. Since the water law was revoked, the position is not yet clear but future legislations can specify licences based on the scope of water services being delegated and incorporate licensing transparency mechanisms in England.

Ofwat's (England) licensing practices are quite ideal, although different transparency requirements are applied differently to different types of licences. Criteria for approval and the licence conditions in England are well defined in the legislation. Thus, the private sector knows what is expected of them by the regulators. The English licensing practice has several important transparency mechanisms that could be implemented in other regions. The transparency mechanism in the English licensing regime includes, a statutory obligation for the regulator to issue guidelines on how to apply a licence, obligations for applicants to 'serve notice' to relevant persons and an obligation for Ofwat to publish and declare its intention of making an appointment and variations, which must be published in a manner appropriate to bring attention to any affected persons and also in providing opportunities for any interested stakeholders to express their objections. Legislation does not specify reason-giving for NAV licences, but Ofwat has a policy to disclose the rationale behind the rejection of applications. Conversely, for WSL, there is a specific reason-giving obligation imposed on Ofwat in the legislation, through a notice to unsuccessful applicants, although there is no requirement to publicly disclose it.

Before 2012, similar ex-ante publication requirements are also imposed on applicants in Victoria, where legislation provides that no persons can apply for a licence unless the Minister has published the call for the application in the *Government Gazette* and local newspaper. This kind of requirement is beneficial for minimising corruption. This mechanism is also important to make the public (and any competitors) aware that the government is planning to entrust the delivery of water services in their region to a local monopolist.

What are lacking in all jurisdictions are ex-post legal requirements to publish licences. When Victoria used a licensing mechanism, there were gazette requirements to publish licences. At present, service areas are stipulated in legislation and the SOO must be available on each utility's website and copies must be prepared for inspection. For England, the lack of legal obligation to publish licences is mitigated by an Ofwat discretion (which is enabled by the WIA s.201) on publishing licences.

In Indonesia, neither the national regulation (under the revoked Water Law 7/2004 and GR 16/2005 or the existing Irrigation Law) nor the regional by-laws and the Cooperation Agreement provide clarity on the publication of licences. Another complicating problem in Jakarta, is the categorisation of the Cooperation Agreement with the private sector. If the contract is regarded as a '*concessie*' (concession but in the 'legal' sense of the term) then it may be treated as if it is a licence and some of the decisions made by the concessionaire holders could be subjected to public scrutiny through judicial review by the Administrative Court. This does not apply if the contract is categorised as a common private contract 'made by the government in the course of its daily activities'. If the contracts are kinds of licences, then the public would have more claims in asking for disclosure, because licences should be subject to public scrutiny and evaluation by the state. On the other hand, if it is regarded as a purely private contract, then there is more justification for non-disclosure.

In later sections we will see that licence-based regimes are generally more transparent than contractual regimes. This is because in licence-based regimes, the regulatory arrangements are stipulated in licences, which are public documents. In contractual regimes, the regulatory arrangements such as service levels, customer service and investment planning, are stipulated in contracts which – unlike licences – could be subjected to confidentiality clauses. Licence-based regimes, such as in England, also require that legislation properly specifies in detail the ways to obtain licences and the conditions attached to them.

186 *Conclusion*

7.4 Information flow

7.4.1 Means of acquiring information

The regulators' means for acquiring information from utilities carry important transparency implications since, if regulators lack power in obtaining information from the utilities, it will not have much to disclose to the public. However, even with stronger power to demand information, there is no guarantee that regulators will publicly disclose all information they acquire from the utilities. Their propensity to disclose will depend on their disclosure policy – to be discussed in the next section.

The legal framework used for acquiring information differs across the three jurisdictions compared and is dependent upon the regulatory model. In Jakarta, the primary instrument is the Cooperation Agreement. In Victoria, it is the legislation, the WIRO and each company's SOO. In England, it is legislation and licences.

The content of the power to acquire information is quite typical, although the empowering instrument varies as discussed above. The most common is 'reporting duties'. This method must be supplemented by specification of information and data to be submitted, usually stipulated through the 'regulatory' accounting guidelines but can also be through other means.

In Victoria, the regulatory account is empowered by the ESC Act. The Commission may also request another set of information not specified in the ESC Act, by a written notice which contains direction as to the details of information that needs to be submitted to them. In England, the power to acquire information is outlined in the WIA 1991 and each company's licences. The annual data requirement was known as the 'June Return' –but this is no longer required since they moved to 'risk-based' regulation. The misreporting of information to Ofwat entails penalty. Ofwat also obligates the companies to follow the Regulatory Accounting Guideline, which is not prescribed by statutes, but is referred to in the company's licence conditions. The position of the regulatory account in England is thus different from Victoria. In Victoria, the regulatory accounts are directly stipulated in the ESC Act whereas, in England, they become binding because they are referred to in each company's licence. In Jakarta, the private sector is obligated under the contract to submit reports to PAM Jaya monthly, quarterly, semi-annually, annually and every five years. On the other hand, the private sector is under no duty to submit any report to the regulatory body, the JWSRB. There is also an obligation to 'maintain transparent accounts' but this is not followed by any reference to regulatory accounts. Hence, in Jakarta, there is no obligation to submit reports based on a prescribed regulatory account, although this could have been done by inserting a clause in the contract.

The second most common feature is the 'investigative power'. In this feature, the regulator does not rely on data submitted by utilities, but may appropriate data and information that it finds in the utility's premises. Hence, the role of the legal framework is in enabling the regulator to enter the premises, investigate or even confiscate materials. In England, this is enabled, for example, through licence condition J though applicable only on several matters. The power includes the authority to inspect, make photocopies and take extracts from any books and records, carry out inspections, measurements and tests on any premises or plants, and take equipment onto such premises and plants.

In Jakarta, this is enabled by the contract, but limited to copying and verifying of the assets register and any documents directly related to it. Concerning utilities' accounts, PAM Jaya and JWSRB have the power to conduct audits and the concessionaire has the corresponding obligation to 'provide all requested information and data', but there is no mention of the power to enter premises. The contract enables external audit by state audit agencies, and requires that they are given 'access at all reasonable times to the relevant books and records'.

Victoria's Department of Sustainability and Environment Inspectors were granted broad powers via the WIA 1994 to ensure companies' compliance with licences. This includes the authority to conduct searches in premises, to inspect, take photographs or samples, seize or open any closed containers, but they are limited to (a) matters on planning, construction, operation or maintenance of works; (b) technical performance standards; and (c) water quality standards. This is no longer applicable since the licensing system was abolished and the retailers converted into statutory corporations. Presumably, none of these powers are required given the statutory corporation status. The ESC also has audit power under WIRO, but the WIRO makes no mention that it enjoys the power to enter premises.

The third type is the power to acquire information from unregulated third parties. Jakarta regulates this in the contract by guaranteeing that PAM Jaya (but not JWSRB) shall obtain any data and information it requires from the concessionaire 'or, through the Second Party, from any of its agents, contractors, and representatives associated with the performance of this Agreement'. England, on the other hand, lacks this approach, despite the fact that for governing ring fencing, Ofwat has required utilities to procure undertakings from their parent companies, which include the provision of necessary information. In Victoria, the DSE inspector's power, as mentioned earlier, is exercisable against a *person*, not just the regulated company. The ESC also enjoys wide powers. It has the power to acquire information from (1) *any person* – albeit with some possible limitations – and (2) the regulated companies. In addition, the ESC may require the companies to enter into an arrangement with third parties to submit information to the ESC.

It is important to note that although Victoria has the strongest legal means in acquiring regulatory information, England has the most detailed regulation on information acquisition. Strong legal empowerment means that the regulator enjoys broad power (i.e. it can request information from *any* person, not just the regulated company, it can inspect premises or there is a harsh punishment for violating reporting duties) but unless this power is accompanied by adequate expertise and resources, it is no more than a paper tiger. Knowing which information is relevant to be asked for from utilities requires special expertise.

7.4.2 Means for disclosing information

As mentioned, a regulator who has powerful means to acquire information will have the most opportunity to disclose regulatory information to the public. This, however, depends on whether legislation and each regulator's policies allow them to disclose such information.

In England, a disclosure policy is mostly the result of Ofwat's own initiative, as legislation is generally silent on the details of publication of information. Legislation acts as an 'enabler' of transparency by providing regulators with wide discretion to publish information that they believe to be in the public interest. This discretion is further reinforced in the company's licence which enables Ofwat to publish any regulatory material for the purpose of carrying out of its functions. This discretion has some restrictions. Regulators should have regard to private affairs and caution if publication will 'seriously and prejudicially affect' the private parties' interests. Another good practice from England *was* the policy to publish major regulatory information submitted by the utilities in their 'June Return' data, allowing a small category of information to be excised. These excision categories developed out of practice and are only to be used as a guideline. If a company invokes some of the excision rules, it must be able to justify its excision and such justifications will be published along with the rest of the data. Ofwat has the final say as to whether or not to accept the utilitiy's rationale in invoking excision. In addition, the FoI channel is still available even if Ofwat has granted the company's request for excision.

However, the collection and publication of the June Return were regarded as burdensome and, as such, are no longer required in the current risk-based approach to regulation. As utilities will be required to publish regulatory accounts and key performance indicators, the locus for transparency in England water regulation will slowly shift from regulators to utilities. Ofwat will require companies to publish four main pieces of regulatory information to their stakeholders under their annual performance reporting mechanism: regulatory financial reporting; price control and additional segmental reporting; performance summary; and additional regulatory information. From the Ofwat data template it appears that although the quantity of data reduces (compared to June Return), its quality and actionability will increase as the metrics presented are much simpler for benchmarking purposes.

In contrast to England, regulators in Victoria and Jakarta lack empowerment to publicly disclose regulatory information. Jakarta's regulator has no obligation to disclose. On the other hand, it has the obligation to keep regulatory information secret. In Victoria, the closest thing to a requirement of public disclosure is the WIRO's general mandate for the ESC to 'publicly report the performance of a regulated industry'. This is more of a specific publication requirement of information related to performance rather than a general discretion to disclose regulatory information.

Legal frameworks often mandate regulators with the duty of non-disclosure. This is found in all of the three jurisdictions. The regulator's duty of non-disclosure is often perceived as a counter balance to its powers in acquiring information discussed earlier. However, if the duty of non-disclosure is too broadly construed, it may act as an impediment toward transparency.

In England, restriction from disclosure is imposed through WIA. WIA s.206 clearly indicates that information acquired by virtue of the regulator's powers under the Act which pertains to the affairs of individuals or businesses shall not be disclosed. A similar restriction applies in Victoria, for information acquired through the powers granted by s.37 and s.37A of the ESC Act. The restrictions come with qualifiers, for example, if consent is given by the supplier of information (England) or if it is required to facilitate the performance of the regulators' functions (England) or if the 'public benefit' outweighs the harm (Victoria).

In Jakarta, the strict formulation of the confidentiality clauses renders public disclosure virtually impossible. The contract only allows the disclosure of technical and commercial information to third parties if such third parties enter into a confidentiality agreement with the discloser. Furthermore, such engagements must be approved by all parties to the Cooperation Agreement. As a result, only limited and specific disclosure to third parties is permitted, but 'public' disclosure is impossible. The regulatory body, JWSRB, is instituted under the contract and reinforces this confidentiality policy in its mandate. Hence, although it is not a party to the contract, it is prohibited by its statute from disclosing information.

7.5 Regulatory functions

7.5.1 Investment and price determination

In Victoria, every investment plan for the upcoming regulatory period is stipulated in each utility's 'Water Plan'. Utilities are required by their SOO to submit a Water Plan, for the purpose of price determination. The Water Plan is published on each utility's website and the ESC, although there is no specific obligation to do so, but each utility's SOO contains an obligation for the utility to 'develop and implement open and transparent processes' in its planning stage. As a matter of regulatory practice, the draft Water Plan is released for discussion for a one-month period to provide opportunities for commenting before the final draft Water Plan is submitted to the ESC. There is no exact mechanism regulating the publication of this draft Water Plan and the one-month period is considered too short to allow informed participation. When the ESC finally makes its determination, there is a legal obligation to include a statement of purpose and the reason for making such determination and the notice must be published in the *Government Gazette*, a daily newspaper generally circulating in Victoria *or* on the internet.

In England, the primary transparency tools in investment and price determination are the publication of companies' Business Plans, and (*previously*) the annual June Return. At the moment, Ofwat expects the companies to take ownership of their business plan and companies publish them on their websites. Ofwat also publishes each company's leakage reduction commitment in its Price Determination.

In Jakarta, there is no such investment planning process. Unlike in Victoria and England, Jakarta concessionaires are not required to submit periodical investment plans that the regulator must approve for the purposes of price determination, because they are paid directly based on the volume of water delivered to consumers' taps. Investment targets are not determined periodically in the regulatory process like in Victoria and England, but are already contained in the Cooperation Agreement. This includes a five-year investment programme and an annual Investment and O/M programme (which must be approved by PAM Jaya – not JWSRB). There are obligations to extend the network which forms a part of 'technical targets'. This five-yearly and annual investment plan is not disclosed to the public and there is an impediment to doing so due to the confidentiality clause. Tariffs are determined separately by the Governor. The national law has a relatively transparent method for setting tariffs but this is deemed inapplicable to the Jakarta concession.

Ideally, investment (and service levels) should reflect consumer demand and therefore be appropriately reflected in prices, as is done through various stakeholder participation mechanisms preceding price determinations in England and Victoria. However, in Jakarta, the 'water charge' system and the contractually pre-determined investment targets disconnect prices from politics, as they put investment matters into the hand of PAM Jaya themselves without public involvement. This situation can be slightly improved if, at the very least, the five-year approval process of investment targets is conducted publicly and all investment plan documents are published. However, such a measure would require contractual amendment on the part of the confidentiality clauses and the reforming of Jakarta's regional by-laws regulating PAM Jaya and water services in Jakarta. The former would require agreement from the private sector and the latter requires strong political will from the local councillors.

7.5.2 Service levels and customer service

The transparency of service levels and customer service standards is required so that customers are able to exercise their rights and utilities have an incentive to comply. In both England and Victoria, there are obligatory publication requirements on service standards and customer service.

In England, both service levels and customer service standards are regulated in a Statutory Instrument (the 'GSS') and so they are available to the public. In addition, utilities must enact a code of practice, based on the GSS, to be approved by Ofwat. An important transparency mechanism in England is that, in the company's licence condition, Ofwat requires that this code, and any substantive amendment thereof, be put to the attention of customers, with

Conclusion 191

copies made available for inspection and anyone requesting it should be able to obtain it free of charge.

In Victoria, the service standard is regulated through the Customer Service Code (CSC). Utilities must enact and publish a customer charter which is formulated based on the CSC. The guaranteed service level compensation, however, is not mandatory. If utilities choose to enact them, they must be approved by the ESC and published as a part of the CSC.

Jakarta has no published service levels and customer service standards. Jakarta has by-laws regulating water services, but the by-laws barely regulate service standards. Albeit with less detail than England and Victoria, the national law broadly regulates some guarantee on service levels but this is deemed inapplicable to the concession. The Cooperation Agreement regulates some service standards and guaranteed payments on service levels, but it is subject to contractual confidentiality. The contract, with some exceptions, was declared by the FoI Commission and the Court as public information, but at the time of writing, has never been officially disseminated.

Service levels and customer service standards in England and Victoria are transparent, partly because they are part of the regulatory instruments. The GSS (England) is a Statutory Instrument, and the CSC (Victoria) is a code enacted by the regulatory body, empowered to do so by the ESC Act. Conversely, in Jakarta, they form part of the Cooperation Agreement. Even without the confidentiality clause, as a private arrangement, a contract would be less transparent compared to a secondary legislation (the English GSS) or a code (Victoria's CSC) due to the negotiatory nature of any service level improvements which restricts direct involvement from the public. On the other hand, there is greater opportunity for public involvement if service levels are regulated in instruments such as the English GSS and Victoria's CSC.

Another reason why England and Victoria are more transparent than Jakarta is because in addition to stipulation of service standards in a regulatory instrument (in a Statutory Instrument or in a Code), there is a legal obligation to further disseminate the service standard information in the form of a customer charter (Victoria) or code of practice (England). These charters and codes are drafted based on the empowering regulatory instrument, but in language that is simpler and more understandable than a legal instrument.

7.5.3 Non-compliance

In Victoria, the two types of enforcement mechanisms, provisional and final 'orders', require publication in the *Government Gazette*. In England, it is much more detailed as transparency is applied to every enforcement stage and type of order. Enforcement Orders must be preceded by a published notice, clarifying the violations, points of the licence condition or other regulatory instrument being breached and what is required to cease the violation. If an undertaking is to be provided, a published notice is also required. Likewise, if a fine is to be

192 Conclusion

imposed, a notice must be published specifying the proposed amount of penalty, the acts or omissions which are deemed to constitute a contravention, supporting facts and justification and a period for the utilities to make an objection.

Jakarta is the least transparent. The Cooperation Agreement regulates that concessionaires are obligated to pay penalties for violation of customer service and service level standards, and such payment must be made *directly* (by the concessionaire) to the consumer, in the form of rebates. However, this has never been disclosed and has prompted a polemic between the regulatory body and PAM Jaya. PAM Jaya may have incentives toward non-disclosure since the payment of compensation could decrease its income from the concession, which is used to repay its debt to the concessionaire, despite the fact that such compensation and rebates must be paid directly to the customer. The Cooperation Agreement contains no obligation to publish non-compliance or enforcement. Disclosure on non-compliance is also prohibited by the confidentiality clause. Matters of non-compliance are settled bilaterally between PAM Jaya and its concessionaires.

7.5.4 Redress

Victorian water utilities are obligated by legislation to enter into a dispute resolution scheme. The industrial ombudsman EWOV is currently referred to as the dispute settlement body in the Customer Service Code. The existence of EWOV as a private body may pose an accountability problem on its own; however, to the extent that information pertaining to redress is communicated, Victoria is relatively transparent. The CSC requires utilities to inform customers about referral to EWOV and other available dispute settlement mechanisms.

In England, both Ofwat and CC Water have complaint handling functions. CC Water will only interfere if water companies have been given the opportunity to address the complaint. Similar to Victoria, there is an obligation for the utilities to describe how complaint handling works in the water industry, the functions of CC Water and how they can be contacted.

In Jakarta, a regulatory redress mechanism is virtually non-existent, except for some issues related to inaccurate water metering and water theft penalties. By-law 11 also provides no alternative recourse mechanism for customers to go to court. The previous sections mentioned that there are some service level guarantees and compensation mechanisms in the Cooperation Agreement. However, customers have no direct recourse to this, as they are not a party to the contract.

Service levels, customer service standard, non-compliance and a redress mechanism are a continuum. The first two determine the content of the rights and the last two determine how they can be enforced. Jakarta is lagging behind in all of the four aspects, but especially in a redress mechanism: it hardly exists. In order to be transparent, the content of the rights and how they can be enforced must be communicated to the public. This is a legal obligation in England and Victoria, but not in Jakarta.

7.6 Utilities' corporate governance

7.6.1 *The board and its accountability*

From all three jurisdictions, basic corporate information is available through the companies themselves or the company regulator (or other administering body) for a fee. Listed companies generally have more disclosure requirements than privately owned companies. However, statutory corporations can have a high degree of public disclosure if required by regulations. In England, quoted companies must publish their annual account and report on their corporate website free of charge. If the utilities are not quoted companies, they are not subject to these rules, unless they are required by Ofwat to comply with capital market disclosure rules as if they are listing their equities.

In Victoria, the Financial Reporting Directives provide stringent disclosure and publication requirements for the water retailers, which include the disclosure of responsible persons, corporate structure, functions and board.

In Indonesia, directors of a company must produce an annual report but these are only delivered to the shareholders, unless they are listed (which is the case – for the time being – for Palyja and Aetra due to their bond issue), then they are required to disclose their audited financial accounts annually in newspapers. However, there is no obligation to disclose their annual report to the public. PAM Jaya – which is governed by the regional SOE Law – has even lower reporting standards compared to the concessionaires, which are governed under general company law. PAM Jaya is only required to report to the Governor its 'profit and loss account' and this should later be reported to the parliament as part of the Governor's general accountability report. This may change due to enactment of the new SOE Law but will take some time before adopted by PAM Jaya.

In Victoria, as statutory corporations, the rules on appointment and dismissals are regulated under the Water Amendment Act. There is a general requirement that persons appointed must be familiar with the water sector.

Jakarta's By-law 13 only prescribes that directors are appointed by the Governor, and there are no rules governing the prerequisite of directorship and the appointment process. For Palyja and Aetra, their directors are appointed by the General Meeting of Shareholders, and can be dismissed through a resolution. According to the capital market rule, a change in directorship in Palyja and Aetra must subsequently be announced to the public.

There are three important lessons. First, as demonstrated by the Jakarta case of PAM Jaya, public ownership of water utilities is not a guarantee for transparency if the rules governing public utilities are under-reformed. In order to increase transparency, the Jakarta by-law regulating PAM Jaya needs to be reformed in order to raise the reporting threshold, followed by the public disclosure of such reports and tabling at the local parliament. Second, corporatisation may indeed increase disclosure by water utilities, but the transparency mechanism in general corporate law is geared toward *members*, and not the public at large. As such, corporation law can be used to facilitate transparency, only when there are further requirements to publicly disclose information which is disclosed to members. Third, listed companies do have more disclosure requirements compared to ordinary companies, both in terms of the types of information which should be disclosed and the obligation to disseminate such information, but statutory corporations can also have a high degree of disclosure provided the public law require them to do so.

Utilities may no longer be bound by capital market disclosure rules if they delist themselves. Hence, capital market rules can be used to facilitate disclosures in utilities, but in order for transparency to be sustainable, regulators must have powers (or contracts must contain provisions) to impose requirements that utilities would still be subjected to those capital market rules, even when they decide to delist themselves.

7.6.2 Related party transactions

In all three jurisdictions, accounting standards generally impose higher disclosure requirements for related party transactions, compared to the default disclosure requirement found in each country's company laws. In Indonesia, the Company Law does not require disclosure of related parties but the accounting standards do. In the UK, disclosure is required by the company law, for a related party transaction made not under normal market conditions, however, the FRS 8 requires disclosure of all types of related party transactions, irrespective of market conditions.

Capital market rules also generally require higher disclosure than company law, as is the case in Jakarta, but its applicability to water utilities will cease when they delist their equities or debt from the capital market. Thus, subjecting water utilities to accounting standards may increase transparency on related party transactions. Company laws generally refer to each jurisdiction's accounting standards; such linkage is strong in England and Victoria but is weak in Indonesia. Public finance rules can empower government with the authority to adopt and regulate statutory corporations to comply with accounting standards, so that statutory corporations show a high degree of disclosures like private companies. Therefore, ideally, regulators should be empowered with the ability to require utilities to comply with certain accounting standards.

Regulators in Victoria and England impose regulatory accounts on utilities. In Victoria, related party transactions are a part of regulatory accounts which are confidential. In England, individual companies can choose to disclose their regulatory accounts. At the time of writing there was no sign that Ofwat would consider disclosure of regulatory account information as mandatory. In Jakarta, there are no specific regulatory accounts which utilities must submit to regulators; the Cooperation Agreement subjects utilities to prevailing general accounting standards. This is unfortunate, as regulatory accounts are much more specific in focusing on business and industry information rather than general corporate information as imposed by statutory accounts.

In Victoria, related party transactions form the confidential part of the regulatory account issued by the ESC. However, water retailers are required to disclose related party transactions under the financial reporting directive.

When Ofwat was still collecting the June Return, related party transactions were among the excised part for many companies. The excision of related party transaction documents in England was subject to some categories developed out of regulatory practice. Such invocation, however, appears to be arbitrary, as there is no consistency between companies although the information for confidentiality is sought is similar, i.e. information on related party transactions. Some categories such as 'security risk' are arguably reasonable, but other categories such as those where disclosure will provide third party commercial advantage (Category 4) should have been subjected to a balancing test with the general purpose of regulatory account disclosure discussed above. Should disclosure of regulatory accounts become mandatory in the future, the old 'excision policy' can be developed for reference.

7.6.3 *Corporate restructuring*

Regulators and other stakeholders have an interest in gathering sufficient information about a company's ultimate owners (or beneficiaries) who may be affected due to restructuring. Transparency mechanisms are used in the regulatory process to gather information from the public on the credibility of the new owners, in understanding the consumers' views and to deal with the effects of corporate restructuring.

In England, there is a good practice of publishing 'consultation papers' detailing the process of restructuring. Ofwat does not have any power to block acquisition, but information and views generated from the consultation process is then used by the regulator in modifying utilities' licences. Moreover, utilities are obligated through licence conditions to furnish all information deemed necessary by Ofwat from its holding company.

The Jakarta regulator has the power to block acquisition if the transfer of shares involves more than 51 per cent of total shares. Unfortunately, it did not conduct any consultation process during past acquisitions. In Victoria, there is constitutional entrenchment in retaining the status of public ownership.

Some restructuring in England has caused the delisting of equities from the stock exchange. To compensate for the loss of information used in comparison, Ofwat requires the publication of the utility's financial information as if it were listed and subject to the rules of the stock exchange. In England, an undertaker's licence require that utilities' accounting statements, auditors' report and annual accounts be published and copies made available to customers upon request.

7.7 Passive disclosure rules

7.7.1 *Applicability*

Regulators in England (including Ofwat) and Victoria (including ESC) are subject to the provisions of FoI laws, but in Jakarta there is disagreement whether the FoI law applies to JWSRB. The main reason for this is because, unlike Ofwat and ESC, the JWSRB is an entity established under a contract. The JWSRB does have a legal mandate under a Governor Regulation, but it suffers from some problems, namely, that the mandate itself lacks regulatory power and this prevents it from being categorised as 'related to the organization of the state', the legal form of the mandate, as a Governor Regulation is weak under the Indonesian legal system and there are technical legal defects which may cause the mandate to be unenforceable. Due to the above, the argument that JWSRB is a public body becomes less compelling.

Victorian water utilities, being statutory corporations, are covered by Victorian FoI laws. Conversely, FoI is not applicable to water utilities where services are carried out by the private sectors such as in England and Jakarta. This appears to support the thesis that 'privatisation' decreases the level of transparency of the decision-making process in the water sector. Nevertheless, there are various dimensions to 'transparency'. Delegation to the private sector does not necessarily result in the decrease of all of those dimensions. 'Availability' of information to regulators may actually increase, as demonstrated by the England case study. Thus it is more suitable to say that delegation to the private sector has the potential to obstruct information from being accessible to the public.

In England, water utilities are not covered by the FoI Act, but there is growing pressure for utility companies to be covered by it, through designation by the Secretary of State. The rationale is that utilities, including water, provide essential services and there is a public interest in knowing how the companies deliver their services. At the moment the UK Government still considers that information about utilities is adequately accessible via regulators and, therefore, has not included utilities in the initial s.5 designation, although they are strong candidates for inclusion in the future. Another strong point for subjecting water utilities to the FoI Act is because Ofwat's move toward risk-based regulation would mean a decrease in the amount of regulatory information made available in the public domain, as utilities are no longer required to submit their June Return. With fewer regulatory burdens and more reliance on self-regulation, additional public scrutiny via the FoI Act is the appropriate counter-balance.

The application of the UK's EIR to water utilities was quite controversial. This is because, unlike the FoI Act which lists a number of public bodies in its schedule, the EIR relies on the legal interpretation of several terminologies, namely, whether the body carries 'functions of public administration' or it is acting 'under the control' of other public bodies with some environmental functions.

After several legal proceedings in the Information Commission Office, the UK Upper Tribunal (UKUT), referral to the ECJ and back to the UKUT, the current position is that water companies have 'special powers' (such as on compulsory purchase of land, hosepipe bans and some disconnection powers) which would make them 'public authorities' under EIR/EC Directive 2003/4 and the Aarhus Convention. As for the 'under the control' part, the UKUT find it not applicable to water utilities. There was a lengthy debate into whether strict regulation under a natural monopoly setting constitutes a 'control' under EIR and the UKUT position was that it does not. Thus, as water utilities are public authorities, the current position in the UK is that the EIR is applicable to them.

The status of the concessionaires in Jakarta is also similarly elusive. While they are not straightforwardly covered by the Indonesian FoI Law as a government entity, the FoI Law could also be applicable to 'non-governmental' entities whose budget is derived partially or in its entirety from the state or regional budget or from foreign contributions. This is possible in the Cooperation Agreement, in cases where the tariffs collected are smaller than the 'water charge' that must be paid to the operators. The remaining 'shortfall' must be paid by PAM Jaya. If the payment of such a shortfall is derived from the state or regional budget, then this will trigger application of the FoI Law. Indeed, PAM Jaya currently owes a great deal of money to the concessionaires, the repayment of which can only be derived from state or regional budgets.

Second, the concessionaires can be categorised as bodies (other than the executive, judiciary or the legislative), whose 'main tasks are related to the organization of the state'. Unlike in the UK, there has never been any decision to entirely delegate water services to the private sector as it is constitutionally forbidden. Any authority vested in the concessionaires is derived from the Cooperation Agreement, but can only exist if it is sourced from public law. The primary sources of these are the regional by-laws. Hence, the concessionaires are effectively exercising a function 'related to the organization of the state'. This argument, however, is dependent upon whether the concessionaires receive portions of the state or regional budget.

Comparing the three jurisdictions above, we can tell that jurisdictions which rely on the applicability of FoI by way of definition (UK's EIR and Indonesia's FoI) will require lengthy legal interpretation in determining whether non-state entities involved in regulation of water services are covered by its access to information regimes. The situation becomes difficult when it involves the delegation of public services to non-state entities. On the one hand, there is a public policy problem of accountability arising out of the delegation of water services to the private sector in which such service is crucial to the fulfilment of human rights and, on the other hand, the fact that its users often have limited or no ability to switch to another provider/seller was not considered. Such public policy concerns would have been more effectively considered through public consultations carried out by a 'designation' system such as the UK's FoI, rather than debates on statutory definitions.

Such an inapplicability problem, in a way, mirrors the concern of authors such as Swyngedouw and Minow on the possibilities of information being 'privatised' following the 'privatisation' of services. The crux of the problem, however, lies not with the decision to delegate services to non-state actors, but with the unpreparedness of the access to information regimes and the body of administrative law in answering such delegation challenges. The general view is 'either-or': either an entity is an extension of the state and therefore covered

198 *Conclusion*

by an access to information law, or it is not. This was shown in the debates on whether the EIR was applicable to water utilities. What about non-state entities with state-like power? The jurisprudence does not seem to have an adequate answer to this because they were created in the age where the state was the centre of accountability, whereas these cases emerge in the age where the state is in 'retreat' and the locus of power is partially transferred from the state to corporations.

Since water utilities are already faced with a high degree of regulation and accountability requirements under sectoral rules, it is only reasonable that general access to information regimes follow suit. Legal interpretation of the phrase 'public bodies' with the backing of case law cannot be relied on for the reasons mentioned above. Any reform measures to cover non-state actors under access to information laws or any other accountability generating mechanisms must be specifically stipulated in legislation.

7.7.2 Exemptions

From the three jurisdictions compared, the Indonesian FoI Law is generally the most pro-disclosure. The law has narrow exemption clauses, balancing tests applicable for all of its exemptions and allows no exemption on information obtained in confidence. The Victorian and UK FoI Acts have broad exemptions, some of which may be either absolute or qualified (do not require harm and/or public interest test) and, as common law countries, contain exemptions on obligation of confidence.

Four types of exemption clauses were compared, as they are deemed to be relevant in water utilities regulation: law enforcement and investigation, decision making and policy formulation, obligation of confidence and commercial information.

7.7.2.1 *Law enforcement and investigation, decision making and policy formulation*

For law enforcement and investigations, Indonesian water utilities' stakeholders will benefit from the narrow exemption clause, as it only deals with criminal proceedings or if the exemption endangers the life of law enforcement officials or jeopardises law enforcement facilities. Civil and administrative (including regulatory) investigations are not covered by the exemption. Conversely, in England and Victoria they are covered as it uses broad terminologies such as 'proper administration of the law' (Victoria) or 'investigation' and 'charged with an offence' (England) and this covers investigation for 'regulatory offences'.

Indonesia has no exemption on policy formulation, although it has exemption for 'confidential memorandums'. In practice, this exemption has been broadly applied to cover draft contracts under negotiation. Victoria has exemptions for 'internal working documents' which comprise of recommendation, advice, opinion, consultation or deliberation. The UK FoI and EIR also have exemptions for 'formulation' or 'development' of government policy and 'the effective conduct of public affairs'. The exemptions in Victoria and England are wide, and may cover all sorts of formulation and development of policies on water services. Conversely, Indonesia's FoI exemption is narrow, as it only protects memorandums, but not other policy documents.

7.7.2.2 Obligation of confidence, commercial information

'Obligation of confidence' can be a serious deterrent to transparency in water utilities regulation, as it is applicable not only to natural persons, but also to corporations. Again, Indonesian stakeholders benefit from the non-existence of a law of confidence in its legal system. In both Victoria and England, this law exists and as such their FoI Acts provide for its exemption. Both in England and Victoria, information generated jointly by the government and a third party is not considered to be 'submitted in confidence'.

All three jurisdictions compared have an exemption for 'commercial information' and all are subject to the 'harm' test. A leading case in Australia is from Queensland, in which the Information Commission interpret harm to include the loss of 'goodwill' if it amounts to the loss of customers to a competitor and eventually leads to the loss of profit. In all three jurisdictions there is a reference to a company's 'competitive edge' in considering harm, but this is not clearly manifested in the UK. The consideration of competitive edge is particularly interesting given that water utilities operate in a natural monopoly environment: there is no competition in its service area. This may change, however, due to liberalisation.

An important note on the Queensland case is that it considered if the company is operating in a monopoly context, which renders 'harm' caused by disclosure to become less relevant. Victoria's FoI Act requires that 'substantial harm to the competitive position' or 'competitive disadvantage of an undertaking' is one of the elements to be considered in maintaining the exemption. The Indonesian FoI Law only provides exemption where disclosure would 'jeopardize the protection of intellectual property rights and protection from unhealthy competition' and the elucidation clarifies that the purpose of such exemption is to protect healthy competition. The English FoI Act contains no such consideration, although the guideline requires weighing the industry's competition level and recommends that prejudice to commercial interest is less likely to occur if the company enjoys a monopoly. An earlier DTI Green Paper on utility regulation also proposed that the degree of disclosure should be linked to the entity's degree of competition and that a monopoly business should be generally disclosable.

As such, the English FoI Act exemption is the broadest compared to Victoria and Indonesia as it only requires that disclosure 'would, or would be likely to prejudice' commercial interests, without requiring any consideration as to whether the market is competitive. A 'prejudice' would suffice.

In practice, the idea that the utilities' natural monopoly is a perfect justification for disclosure is not always true, as demonstrated by a Scottish case. The Scottish FoI Commissioner maintained exemption in a case involving a disclosure request to Scottish Water – a state-owned company – as the charges collected from the information request are considered for the public interest: it may contribute in decreasing the overall water and sewerage charges. Contrary to what critics often said, the commodification of information in this particular case may actually serve the public interest, in the form of lowering consumer charges.

A challenge for the FoI Commissioner is in determining the 'relevant market' since the market for information could be distinguishable from, and may not necessarily influence, the market for water supply. If disclosure serves only the particular undertaking whose business is confined to services in the market of information, and it has no influence whatsoever in expanding consumer choices or in increasing competition in the market of water supply, then the exemption would be justified. Conversely, if disclosure has implications for the increase of competition in the water supply market or in decreasing consumer charges, then exemption should not be justified. Nevertheless, any public interest argument toward increasing competition in the water supply market would require sufficient backing from a liberalisation policy – such as the 2014 Water Act (England).

7.8 The impact of ownership and regulatory model on transparency

The ownership and regulatory model of water utilities has implications on how transparency can be enabled through the legal frameworks. Aquafed, The International Federation of Private Water Operators is of the opinion that PSP 'ensures key requirements related to transparency and accountability' as the contract or licence defines

> the respective roles of the public authority and the operator; the content of a regular detailed reporting, at least annual, on achievements and performance and that the private operator is permanently regulated by an authority, which checks its compliance with the contract/licence.[1]

Despite such a statement, Jakarta is the least transparent of all of the jurisdictions compared in almost every aspect of the analytical framework although its FoI is the most transparent. Chapter 4 demonstrated that the publicly owned Bogor water utilities are relatively more transparent than Jakarta, in terms of general disclosure policy, service levels and customer service, tariff setting and redress mechanisms. Why is it that Bogor's water services – in some of the aspects mentioned before – are more transparent than Jakarta's, despite the fact that both are covered under similar legislations at national level?

---

1 Payen, Moss and Waeyenberge, *private water operators contribute to making the Right to Water & Sanitation real, AquaFed's submission, Part 3 Avoiding misconceptions on private water operators in relation to the Right to Water and Sanitation* (AquaFed 2010)

Before we deal with the answer, we must first identify what are the causes of non-transparency? The first culprit would be the confidentiality clause, which is interpreted to cover all regulatory information (including regular reporting and performance) and the contract itself which includes basic information such as service level and customer service standards contained within it. If Jakarta is run completely by a publicly owned company like Bogor, the service levels and customer service standards would have been stipulated by law which, by default, is a public document. The Cooperation Contract (including that which contains service levels and customer service standards) in Jakarta has been declared public information by the Indonesian FoI Commission and the Court, except for some parts. However, there has never been any active dissemination of the contract document. Moreover, the FoI decision does not affect regulatory information outside the contract, such as information on performance and compliance with service standards.

So far, the private sector's position is that it generally does not object to disclosure,[2] but disclosure is not a one-sided decision as PAM Jaya's approval is required. Nevertheless, PAM Jaya (and the Governor's office) may regard some regulatory information to be politically sensitive and therefore refrain from being transparent.[3]

Victoria has an innovative solution in manipulating the confidentiality clause in a concession contract so that it will become unenforceable in the event of an FoI request or disclosure made by regulators. Notwithstanding PAM Jaya's approval and political will from the regional government, this could be implemented in Jakarta (it would require contract amendment) and may tackle the contractual confidentiality question.

However, non-transparency which is caused by the regulatory structure in Jakarta, in which there are three overlapping 'regulators', each empowered to supervise the contract (PAM Jaya, the Governor and JWSRB), cannot simply be tackled by modifying the contract's confidentiality clause. PAM Jaya is the most privileged 'regulator' under the Cooperation Agreement but at the same time is also a party to the contract and evidently has a CoI in the form of repayment of its debts to the concessionaires. When the institution which has a regulatory function is also the player, and has a certain CoI, transparency would be very difficult to implement. A way to solve this problem is by altering the regulatory structure which reduces PAM Jaya's and the Governor's powers and transfers them to JWSRB as envisioned by Clause 51.2 of the Cooperation Agreement. However, more powers mean that it must be balanced by credible and highly qualified regulators. Thus, reforms could be conducted in phases and could start with reforms on the regulator's internal governance.

---

2 *Correspondence with one of Jakarta's Private Sector Concessionaires Concerning Confidentiality Clause and The Publication of Contract (9–20 October)* (2011)

3 Payen, Moss and Waeyenberge, *Private water operators contribute to making the Right to Water & Sanitation real, AquaFed's submission, Part 3 Avoiding misconceptions on private water operators in relation to the Right to Water and Sanitation* (AquaFed 2010)

Last but not least, is the position of the supposedly independent regulator, the JWSRB as the 'creature of contract'. As demonstrated in the Indonesian case study, the position of JWSRB as a 'creature of contract' could render the application of the FoI Law problematic. It is a very odd situation, in which a regulator which is supposed to represent the public interest turns out not to be a 'public body' under the FoI Law. This is contrary to the situation in the UK and Victoria where Ofwat and the ESC must comply with FoI Acts. In order to solve this, application of the Indonesian FoI Law could be extended to private entities carrying out delegated governmental functions. This sort of reform will expand the reach of the FoI not only to JWSRB but to other private entities including the concessionaires. Furthermore, inapplicability of the FoI will no longer become a problem if, in the future, the JWSRB's statute is formalised in a regional by-law.

However, reforms might be difficult for Jakarta. The Bogor municipality has been able to reform its by-law several times, the latest amendment being in 2006 but regulatory reform in Jakarta has stalled as there has been no reform since 1993. The rationale of why reforms can be carried out in Bogor is because their hands are not tied to the contract. In Jakarta, every reform project will have to be negotiated with the private sector, otherwise the government might be in breach of its contractual obligation. This also means that any regulatory reform project undertaken at national level, which purports to enable accountability, transparency and participation, will have no meaning in Jakarta, because those changes will also need to be negotiated with the private sector. This is evident from the views of both the private sector and the Jakarta Water Sector Regulatory Body that ministerial and other guidelines issued by the central government are deemed not to apply to the Jakarta concession.

Jakarta's water service lacks transparency in almost every dimension considered. Information is not really 'available' to regulators (and hence cannot be available to the public) due to a lack of means by the regulator to acquire information (e.g. no regulatory accounting standard, no reporting duties to JWSRB). Finally, information in the possession of regulators, which is minimal due to the aforementioned reason, also cannot be disclosed to the public, because of the confidentiality provision, the CoI of PAM Jaya in the regulatory structure that provides an incentive for it not to disclose information and the inapplicability of the FoI law to JWSRB and to the private sector. This thesis, through the case study of Jakarta, thus confirms the criticisms of several authors that regulation by contract can potentially have some transparency problems. However, the thesis suggests that this could be avoided when regulation by contract is done by previously strengthening and preparing the public law infrastructure.

Thus, it might not be accurate to conclude that – as many authors[4] have suggested – 'privatisation' per se decreases transparency. The English case study

---

4 Hall and Lobina, 'Private to public: International lessons of water remunicipalisation in Grenoble, France' (American Water Resources Association, Dundee, 6–8 August 2001); Minow, 'Public and private partnerships: accounting for the new religion' Harvard Law Review 1229; Psiru, 'Undermining Democracy and the Environment, PSI Briefing, The Hague World Water Forum' <www.psiru.org/reports/2000-03-W-Htrans.doc> accessed 25 December 2011; Swyngedouw, 'Dispossessing H_2O: the contested terrain of water privatization' 16 Capitalism Nature Socialism 81

has clearly demonstrated that the full divestiture accompanied by 'regulation by agency' implemented by English water utilities is fairly transparent in almost all parts of the analytical framework, the passive disclosure rule being an exception. Indeed, the major contribution of transparency in the English system is on the creation of information. The English system makes information more 'available' to regulators and, hence, also potentially available to the public. On the second dimension, the 'public disclosure' of the aforementioned 'available' information, England is also – to date – transparent. This is due to legislation that provides discretionary powers to regulators to publish information that is deemed to be in the public interest and the practices of Ofwat in publishing regulatory information. Unlike in Jakarta, the legal frameworks in England (legislation and licence conditions) enable transparency by providing the discretionary power to disclose, whereas, in Jakarta, the legal frameworks (the concession contract and the governor's regulation) constrain transparency.

The drawback of the English system is probably that the information is too voluminous, thus requiring sufficient expertise and resources to interpret it.[5] Therefore, there is an increase in the quantity of information but, without resourceful intermediaries, this might not necessarily translate into quality information. This might change under the current risk-based approach, in which the quality of information might increase but the quantity and details available to the public decrease.

Ownership choice clearly has an impact on transparency in several ways. Access to information laws are directly applicable to Victorian water utilities and Jakarta's PAM Jaya which are state-owned, but (except for EIR and only after a lengthy court battle) not to 'privatised' English water utilities or the private concessionaires in Jakarta and Victoria. Ownership choice may also determine the outcome of adjudication in FoI cases. The Scottish FoI Commissioner opted for non-disclosure because there is a public interest in lowering Scottish Water's customer charges. Charging information requests would help it in doing so whereas disclosure would deprive them of such income. The situation could be different if the utility was fully divested, in which case any additional levies might not necessarily correspond to lower customer charges.

Market structure will also impact on transparency. If there is a clear legislative mandate to liberalise the water sector, then it would help to define the content of the 'public interest' toward disclosure, which would be in the form of lower charges and expansion of consumer choice through competition. As competition requires information, disclosure might be in the public interest, although it could prejudice the incumbent's commercial position. There are two questions which deserve their own in-depth research: can such disclosure be regarded as a form of 'regulatory taking' or confiscation, and what would be the appropriate methodology for the 'balancing test' by public bodies?

---

5 S M Hendry, 'Ownership models for water services: implications for regulation' in A McHarg and others (eds), *Property and the law in energy and natural resources*, vol. 1 (Oxford University Press 2010)

204 Conclusion

Finally, regulatory style will also impact on transparency. Ofwat is currently moving forward with risk-based regulation which removes the requirement of utilities to submit June Returns and other information. Thus, there is a reduction of detailed information on the part of the regulator and, as a consequence of that, a decrease in the volume of regulatory data in the public domain. Nevertheless, although the detail of information may decrease, the comprehensibility of the information disclosed *may* increase due to various levels of scrutiny and certification processes. This would be a trade-off between detail of information versus higher quality of information (and *presumably* lower cost of regulation). The move toward risk-based regulation, which reduces data gathering by the regulator and places the onus on water utilities, should be complemented by applying FoI Law to water utilities.

Appendix
Framework for transparency in water utilities regulation

Chapter	Section	Indicators for transparency
2 Policy in involving the private sector	2.1 The decision to delegate	To what extent can the water sector be delegated to the private sector? Who has the authority to decide on the question of delegation? To what extent is the public involved in deciding the delegation question?
	2.2 Procurements	Are there any rules on the disclosure of CoI in procurement? What are the rules for publishing expression of interest or tender announcements? Are there standard confidentiality clauses in procurement contracts and, if yes, are there exceptions to such clauses due to the operation of FoI rules? Are final contracts published? If yes, are the rules for excision of terms in final contract consistent with access to information principles?
3 The regulator, licences and information flow	3.1.1 Selection and removal of regulators	How are regulators selected, remove or suspended? Are there transparency requirements for the selection, removal or suspension of regulators?
	3.1.2 Conflict of interest	How is CoI within the regulatory body regulated? Are there public disclosure requirements when a CoI arises in a particular case? Are members of the regulatory body required to list their potential CoIs? Is such a list publicly disclosed?
	3.2.1 Criteria for approving licence	Is there clarity on the *types* of licences for water utilities? Does regulatory framework clearly stipulate the prerequisite for applying such licences and the criteria whereby regulators approve (or deny) such application? Is there an obligation to provide explanation if licence application are rejected?

(continued)

(continued)

Chapter	Section	Indicators for transparency
	3.2.2 Licence conditions	What are the conditions (to which the company must adhere) attached to those licences? Are the implications for violating such conditions clearly stipulated in the legislations?
	3.2.3 Publication of licences	Is there a legal obligation to publish licences? Are licences published?
	3.3.1 Means for acquiring information	How do legal frameworks empower regulator(s) to: (i) compel entities to submit regulatory information to them on a regular basis, (ii) obtain information from regulated entities (incidental) (iii) obtain information from third parties associated with regulated entities or *any person* not directly associated with regulated entities, (iv) enter premises, take samples, confiscate documents
	3.3.2 Means for disclosing information	Are there legal obligations or discretionary powers to (i) publish regulatory information, (ii) share regulatory information with other regulators? Are there restrictions or qualifications to these powers? Are there any duties for the regulator to maintain confidentiality?
4 Regulatory functions	4.1 and 4.2 Investment, tariffs and prices, determination	Are there legal obligations to disclose investment plans? Are there legal obligations to publish business plans? Are there incentives for regulated entities in publishing truthful and accurate plans? Are there obligations for regulators to explain their decision behind prices, tariff and determinations?
	4.3 Service levels and customer service	Are there requirements for publishing service levels and customer service? Are service levels legislated or prescribed in a publicly disclosable code? If service levels are regulated in contracts, are they published?
	4.4 Non-compliance	When investigations or inquiries are made, does regulatory framework require regulators to (i) clarify which provisions of the legislations or licence condition the company breaches, (ii) what is required to cease the violation, (iii) what undertaking the company provides, (iv) the amount of penalty or other sanctions given, (v) the time period to provide explanation and objections? Are there obligations to ensure that these are published?

	4.5 Redress	Are there obligations to ensure that redress mechanism and available compensations are published? Are there obligations to ensure that regulators disclose their responses to complaints and what measures are being taken?
5 Utilities' corporate governance	5.1 Corporate structure, board and accountability	Does legal framework require the disclosure of corporate structure and identities of board members? Is there a legal obligation to publish annual accounts and reports? If the utility is state owned, are appointment and dismissals of board members published?
	5.2 Related-party transaction and regulatory accounts	Are regulatory accounts published? Do utilities publicly disclose related-party transactions?
	5.3 Corporate restructuring	Is there a legal obligation to publicly disclose a company's ultimate owners and/or beneficial owners – especially, in the event of corporate restructuring?
6 Passive disclosure rules	6.1 Applicability of access of information rules	Are access of information regulations applicable to these entities – irrespective of whether they are 'public' or 'private': (i) regulators, (ii) consumer representative body and (iii) water companies themselves?
	6.2 Exemptions to access of information rules	Are there harm tests and public interest tests to exemptions applicable in access to information rules? Does investigation by a regulatory body constitute an exemption? To what extent can a public interest consideration toward competition be used to support (or prevent) disclosure? Is information submitted to regulators or acquired by them exempted from disclosure? Will contractual confidentiality hinder the application of access to information regime?

Bibliography

AASB 124: Related Party Disclosure (July 2015)

Access to Information (Drinking Water Inspectorate 2010) <http://dwi.defra.gov.uk/about/access-to-info/index.htm> accessed 13 June 2011

Accident Compensation Commission v Croom [1991] VicRp 72; [1991] 2 VR 322 (24 September 1990)

Accounting Standards Board, *Amendment to FRS 8 Related Party Disclosures: Legal Changes 2008* (2008)

Al'Afghani MM and others, *Transparansi Lembaga-lembaga Regulator Penyediaan Air Minum Di DKI Jakarta* (ECOTAS/KRuHA/TIFA, 2011)

Al'Afghani MM, 'Anti-privatisation debates, opaque rules and "privatised" water services provision: some lessons from Indonesia' in A Nicol, L Mehta and J Allouche (eds), *IDS Bulletin: 'Some for All?' Politics and Pathways in Water and Sanitation*, vol 43.2 (Institute of Development Studies, Wiley-Blackwell 2012)

Al'Afghani MM, 'Constitutional Court's review and the future of water law in Indonesia' 2 Law, Environment and Development (LEAD) Journal (2006)

Al'Afghani MM, 'The transparency agenda in water utilities regulation and the role of freedom of information: England and Jakarta case studies' 20 Journal of Water Law 129

Al'Afghani MM, 'When It Comes to Water Services, Jakarta Is Living in the Distant Past' *The Jakarta Globe*, 16 October 2011 <http://goo.gl/p5b08e> accessed 21 May 2016

Alternative Financing For Water Utilities in Indonesia: A Review of Lessons and Challenges (Report by Development Alternatives, Inc for review by the United States Agency for International Development under Contract No 497-M-00-05-00005-00, 2008)

An Act to Constitute the Commonwealth of Australia (taking into account alterations up to Act No. 84 of 1977)

Anglian Water Annual Report and Accounts 2015

Anglian Water, 'PR09 Final Business Plan, Part A: The Company Strategy' (Anglian Water) <www.anglianwater.co.uk/_assets/media/Proposed_business_plan.pdf> accessed 18 August 2011

Annual Performance Report <www.ofwat.gov.uk/regulated-companies/company-obligations/annual-performance-report/> accessed 30 November 2015

Annual Performance Report: Summary of Performance Parameters <www.ofwat.gov.uk/wp-content/uploads/2015/10/pap_tec201502annperfsumm.pdf> accessed 29 November 2015

Annual Report and Accounts 2010–11 For the Period 1 April 2010 to 31 March 2011 (Water Services Regulation Authority (Ofwat) 2011)

AP, 'Govt's desal figure misleading: Brumby' (24 November 2010) <http://news.smh.com.au/breaking-news-national/govts-desal-figure-misleading-brumby-20100917-15ewb.html> accessed 5 August 2011

Archer v The Information Commissioner and Salisbury District Council, EA/2006/0037 (Information Tribunal)

Ardhianie N, *Kontroversi Penjualan PT Thames Pam Jaya (TPJ)* (Amrta Institute for Water Literacy, 2006)

Argo TA, 'Thirsty downstream: the provision of clean water in Jakarta, Indonesia' (University of British Columbia 2001)

Aronson M, 'A public lawyer's response to privatization and outsourcing' in M Taggart (ed.), *The province of administrative law* (Oxford, UK: Hart Publishing 1997)

Atmosudirdjo P, *Hukum administrasi negara* (Ghalia Indonesia 1981)

Audit Act 1994, No. 2 of 1994 (Victoria), Version No. 051

Australian Accounting Standards Board, *AASB 124, Related Party Disclosures* (2009)

Australian Government, *National Public Private Partnership Guidelines, Volume 2: Practitioners' Guide* (2011)

Awareness Guidance 2: Information Provided in Confidence (Information Commissioner's Office 2009)

Awareness Guidance 24: Policy Formulation, Ministerial Communications, Law Officers' Advice, and The Operation of Ministerial Private Office (Information Commissioner's Office 2008)

Awareness guidance 25: Section 36: Effective Conduct of Public Affairs (Information Commissioner's Office 2008)

Bakker K, 'Conflicts over water supply in Jakarta, Indonesia' in B Barraqué and E Vlachos (eds), *Urban water conflicts, an analysis on the origins and nature of water-related unrest and conflicts in the urban context* (UNESCO Working series SC-2006/WS/19. 2006)

Bakker K, 'Paying for water: water charging and equity in England and Wales' 26 Transactions of the Institute of British Geographers 143

Bakker K, 'Trickle Down? Private sector participation and the pro-poor water supply debate in Jakarta, Indonesia' 38 Geoforum 855

Bakker KJ, 'Privatising water, producing scarcity. The Yorkshire drought of 1996' 76 Economic Geography 4

Bakker KJ, *An uncooperative commodity: privatizing water in England and Wales* (Oxford University Press, USA 2003)

Baldwin R and Cave M, *Understanding regulation: theory, strategy, and practice* (Oxford University Press 1999)

Baldwin R, 'Regulation lite: the rise of emissions trading' 2 Regulation & Governance 193

Ballance T and Taylor A, *Competition and economic regulation in water: the future of the European water industry* (IWA Publishing 2005)

Bedner A, *Administrative courts in Indonesia: a socio-legal study* (Martinus Nijhoff Publishers 2001)

Behn RD, *Rethinking democratic accountability* (Brookings Institution Press 2001)

Bernstein JL, 'Price cap regulation and productivity growth' 1 International Productivity Monitor 23

Better Regulation Executive, 'Better Regulation' (Department for Business Innovation and Skills 2008) <http://webarchive.nationalarchives.gov.uk/+/www.berr.gov.uk/whatwedo/bre/index.html/index.html> accessed 21 May 2012

Better Regulation Task Force, *Regulation – Less is More. Reducing Burdens, Improving Outcomes* (London: Cabinet Office 2005)

210 Bibliography

Birkinshaw P, 'Freedom of information and its impact in the United Kingdom' 27 Government Information Quarterly 312

Birkinshaw P, *Freedom of information* (Cambridge University Press 2010)

Blaiklock TM, *Consultation: 'The Completed Acquisition of Thames Water Holdings plc. by Kemble Water Limited' (Consultation Response)* (2007)

Blair T and Cunningham J, *Modernising government* (Prime Minister and Minister of the Cabinet Office 1999)

Boehm F and Olaya J, 'Corruption in public contracting auctions: the role of transparency in bidding processes' 77 Annals of Public and Cooperative Economics 431

Boehm F, *Regulatory capture revisited – Is there an anti-corruption agenda in regulation?* (Internet Centre for Corruption Research (ICGG) Working Paper No. 22, 2007)

Boehm F, *Anti-corruption strategies as safeguard for public service sector reforms* (Internet Centre for Corruption Research (ICGG) Working Paper No. 22, 2007)

Boehm F, *Regulatory capture revisited – lessons from economics of corruption* (Internet Centre for Corruption Research (ICGG) Working Paper No. 22, 2007)

Booker A, 'Incentive regulation in water – case study' (Utility Regulation Training Program 1997)

Bovis C, *EC public procurement: case law and regulation* (Oxford University Press 2006)

Braadbaart O, 'Privatizing water. The Jakarta concession and the limits of contract' in P Boomgaard (ed.), *A world of water: rain, rivers and seas in Southeast Asian histories* (KITLV Press 2007)

Bracks S, *Ensuring Openness and Probity in Victorian Government Contracts, A Policy Statement* (Victorian Government 2010)

Bracks S, *Ensuring Openness and Probity in Victorian Government Contracts, Implementation Guidelines* (Victorian Government 2010)

Brennan B and others, *Reclaiming Public Water! Participatory Alternatives to Privatization* (Transnational Institute (TNI) 2004)

Bristol City Council v IC and Portland and Brunswick Squares Association, EA/2010/0012 (Information Rights Tribunal)

Bristol Water, 'Bristol Water Rejects Ofwat Price Decision' (Bristol Water) <http://goo.gl/i2ddCo> accessed 21 May 2016

Brody G, *Policy proposals for refinements to Essential Services Commission regulatory framework for water* (prepared for the Department of Sustainability and Environment by the Consumer Law Centre Victoria)

Burns P and Estache A, 'Infrastructure concessions, information flows, and regulatory risk' 203 Public Policy for the Private Sector

Byatt ICR, *MD135, Confidentiality for July Returns and PR99 Information Submission* (Ofwat 1998)

Cadbury A, *Report of the committee on the financial aspects of corporate governance* (Gee Publishing, London 1992)

Calland R, 'Transparency in a Profit Making World' (Institute for Policy Dialogue 2006) <www0.gsb.columbia.edu/ipd/pub/Calland_Private_Sector.pdf> accessed 28 February 2010

Cameron D and Clegg N, *The Coalition:our programme for government* (2010)

Cannon and Australian Quality Egg Farms Ltd [1994] QICmr 9; (1994) 1 QAR 491 (30 May 1994)

Capital Market and Financial Institutions Supervisory Agency (Bapepam-LK)

Case C-279/12 OJ C 250, 18.8.2012 (European Court of Justice)

Bibliography 211

Case C-56/90, *Commission of the European Communities v United Kingdom of Great Britain and Northern Ireland* – Directive 76/160/EEC – Bathing water, European Court reports 1993 Page I-04109

Case Reference Numbers FER0269130 & FER0272665 (Yorkshire Water Services and United Utilities), ICO Decision March 12, 2010 (Information Commission)

Cave M, *Independent review of competition and innovation in water markets: final report* (Department for Environment Food and Rural Affairs (Defra) 2009)

CC Water, *Consultation: 'The Completed Acquisition of Thames Water Holdings plc. by Kemble Water Limited' (CC Water Thames' Response)* (2007)

Center for Public Procurement Policy Development, *Model National Procurement Document* (2007)

City West Water Annual Report 2015 <www.citywestwater.com.au/documents/Annual_Report_2015.pdf>

Coco v A.N. Clark (Engineers) Limited [1968] F.S.R. 415 Anne Lyons

Coleman A, *The legal protection of trade secrets* (Sweet & Maxwell 1992)

Colin J and Lockwood H, 'Making innovation work through partnerships in water and sanitation projects' (2002) <http://aguaconsult.co.uk/assets/Uploads/Publications/BPD-WASHInnovation-2002.pdf> accessed 22 May 2016

Collins A and Fairchild R, 'Sustainable food consumption at a sub-national level: an ecological footprint, nutritional and economic analysis' 9 Journal of Environmental Policy & Planning 5

The Commissioner for Public Appointment, *Code of Practice for Ministerial Appointments to Public Bodies* (2009)

The Commonwealth of Australia and others, *Intergovernmental Agreement on a National Water Initiative* (2004)

The Commonwealth of Australia and others, *The Council of Australian Governments' Water Reform Framework* (1994)

Companies Act 2006 c.46, 2006

The Companies (Disclosure of Address) Regulations 2009, SI 2009/214

Companies' Performance 2014–15 – Ofwat <www.ofwat.gov.uk/regulated-companies/comparing-companies/performance/companies-performance-2014-15/> accessed 12 December 2015

Company Monitoring Framework: Final Position <www.ofwat.gov.uk/wp-content/uploads/2015/11/pap_pos201506comon1.pdf>

Competition Act 1998 c.41

The completed acquisition of Northumbrian Water Limited, A Consultation Paper by Ofwat (2003)

The completed acquisition of Thames Water Holdings Plc by Kemble Water Limited, A Consultation Paper by Ofwat (2007)

Confidentiality of commercial or industrial information, LTT160 (Information Commissioner's Office 2010)

Constitution (Water Authorities) Act 2003, Act No. 37 of 2003

Constitution Act 1975, No. 8750 of 1975, Version No. 196

Convention on Access to Information, Public Participation in Decision Making and Access to Justice in Environmental Matters 25 June 1998 (Aarhus Convention) 38 International Legal Materials (ILM) (1999) 515

Cooperation Agreement Between PAM Jaya and The Concessionaire, 2001

Coppel P, 'The Public Interest and the Freedom of Information Act 2000' 10 Judicial Review 289

Copyright, Designs and Patents Act 1988, c.48, 1988

Bibliography

Corporations Act 2001

Correspondence with One of Jakarta's Private Sector Concessionaire Concerning Confidentiality Clause and The Publication of Contract (9–20 October) (2011)

Costs and performance 2008–09 (Water Industry Commission for Scotland 2009)

Council Directive 76/160/EEC of 8 December 1975 concerning the quality of bathing water, Official Journal L 031, 05/02/1976 P. 0001–0007

Council Directive 80/778/EEC of 15 July 1980 relating to the quality of water intended for human consumption, Official Journal L 229, 30/08/1980 P. 0011–0029

Daryanto A, *Jawaban Surat KRuHA (Letter No. 581/DIV.T&P/XI/2011 dated November 8 2011 on PAM JAYA's response to FoI Request by KRuHA)* (PAM Jaya 2011)

Davidson K, 'Water plans drift behind a veil of secrecy' <www.smh.com.au/opinion/politics/water-plans-drift-behind-a-veil-of-secrecy-20100411-s0os.html> accessed 14 November 2010

Davis RW, 'The Environmental Information Regulations 2004: limiting exceptions, widening definitions and increasing access to information?' 8 Environmental Law Review 51

de-Albuquerque C, *Report of the independent expert on the issue of human rights obligations related to access to safe drinking water and sanitation, A/HRC/15/31* (2010)

Decision 056/2006 MacRoberts and the City of Edinburgh Council (Scottish Information Commissioner)

Department for Environment Food and Rural Affairs, 'Water White Paper' (Defra) <www.official-documents.gov.uk/document/cm82/8230/8230.pdf> accessed 16 February 2011

Department for Environment, Food and Rural Affairs, *Water for Life (White Paper)* (Stationery Office 2011)

Department of Premier and Cabinet v Hulls [1999] VSCA 117 (11 August 1999) (Supreme Court of Victoria – Court of Appeal)

Department of Sustainability and the Environment, 'Melbourne Water Retailer Board Director' <http://goo.gl/Pwu061> accessed 21 May 2016

Department of Trade and Industry, *A Fair Deal for Consumers: Modernising the Framework for Utility Regulation* (CM 3898, London: The Stationery Office 1998)

Department of Treasury & Finance (Victoria), *FRD 12A Disclosure of Major Contracts* (2005)

Department of Treasury & Finance (Victoria), *National PPP Guidelines, Partnerships Victoria Requirements* (2010)

Department of Treasury & Finance (Victoria), *Partnerships Victoria Requirements, Annexure 7, Public Interest* (2009)

Derry City Council v Information Commissioner, EA/2006/0014 (Information Tribunal)

DeWitte K, 'On Analyzing Drinking Water Monopolies by Robust Non-Parametric Efficiency Estimations' (PhD, University of Leuven 2009)

Directive 2003/4/EC of the European Parliament and of the Council of 28 January 2003 on public access to environmental information and repealing Council Directive 90/313/EE, O.J. L 041, 14/02/2003 P. 0026–0032 1990

Directive 2004/18/EC of the European Parliament and of the Council of 31 March 2004 on the coordination of procedures for the award of public works contracts, public supply contracts and public service contracts O.J. L. 134, 30.4.2004, pp114–240

Directive 98/83/EC of 3 November 1998 on the quality of water intended for human consumption, O.J. 330 pp32–54

Disconnection of Mixed-Used Premises For Non Payment of Water Charges, RD 14/04 (2004) <http://goo.gl/UwlmY0> accessed 21 May 2016

DTF, 'Victorian Desalination Project' (*Contract Publishing System, Department of Treasury and Finance, Victoria*) <www.old.tenders.vic.gov.au/domino/Web_Notes/eTenders/etdrPublishing.nsf/ContractsByCategory/6CC923E330DE8F5CCA25767A00109C1E?OpenDocument#Downloads> accessed 10 November 2010

Dunshea RD, *RD 10/05: Freedom of Information Act 2000 – s206 of the Water Industry Act* (Ofwat 2005)

Dunshea RD, *RD 22/04, Freedom of Information Act 2000* (Ofwat 2004)

Dunshea RD, *RD 29/98, Confidentiality for July Returns and PR99 Information Submission* (Ofwat 1998)

DWI, 'About Us' (Drinking Water Inspectorate UK) <http://dwi.defra.gov.uk/about/index.htm> accessed 20 April 2010

Dyck A, 'Privatization and corporate governance: principles, evidence, and future challenges' 16 The World Bank Research Observer 59

Eberhard A, 'Infrastructure regulation in developing countries: an exploration of hybrid and transitional models' (African Forum of Utility Regulators, 3rd Annual Conference, 15–16 March 2006, Windhoek, Namibia)

Elnaboulsi JC, 'Organization, management and delegation in the French water industry' 72 Annals of Public and Cooperative Economics 507

Elyda C, 'Court Decision Ends Privatization of Water in Jakarta' <www.thejakartapost.com/news/2015/03/24/court-decision-ends-privatization-water-jakarta.html> accessed 15 July 2015

Energy and Water Ombudsman Victoria, *Constitution of Energy and Water Ombudsman (Victoria) Limited* (2010)

Energy and Water Ombudsman Victoria, *Energy and Water Ombudsman Charter 30 May 2006* (2006)

Enterprise Act 2002, 2002 c.40

Enterprise and Regulatory Reform Act 2013, 2013 c.24

Environment Act 1995, c.25

Environmental Information Regulation 2004, SI 2004/3391

Environmental Information Regulations 2004 detailed guidance (Defra 2005)

The Environmental Permitting (England and Wales) Regulations 2010; 2010 No. 675

Essential Services Commission Act 2001 No. 62 of 2001

Essential Services Commission, *Customer Service Code Metropolitan Retail and Regional Water Businesses* (Issue No. 7, 15 October 2010, 2007)

Essential Services Commission, *Water Industry Regulatory Accounting Code, October 2009, Issue No. 4* (2009)

Essential Services Commission, *Water performance report: Performance of urban water businesses 2009–10* (December 2010)

Estache A and Wren-Lewis L, 'Towards a theory of regulation for developing countries: Insights from Jean-Jacques Laffont's last book' 47 Journal of Economic Literature 729

The exemption for criminal investigations, criminal proceedings and confidential source (Information Commissioner's Office 2009)

Explanatory Notes, Water Act 2014, Chapter 21 <www.legislation.gov.uk/ukpga/2014/21/pdfs/ukpgaen_20140021_en.pdf> accessed 16 November 2015

Feintuck M, *'The public interest' in regulation* (Oxford University Press 2004)

FER0118853 (Sutton and East Surrey Water Plc) (Information Commissioner's Office)

Financial Management Act 1994 No. 18 of 1994 (Victoria), Version No. 061 1994

Finger M and Allouche J, *Water privatisation: trans-national corporations and the re-regulation of the water industry* (Taylor & Francis 2002)

214 Bibliography

Fish Legal v Information Commissioner UK Upper Tribunal GIA/0979 and 0980/2011, [2015] UKUT 0052 (AAC)

Fitch M and Graham C, 'The draft Freedom of Information Bill – implications for utilities' 10 Utilities Law Review 257

FOI Policy Knowledge Base, Test of Confidence, LTT93 (Information Commissioner's Office 2009)

FRD 21B Disclosures of Responsible Persons, Executive Officers and Other Personnel (Contractors with Significant Management Responsibilities) in the Financial Report

Freedom of Information (Scotland) Act 2002, 2002 asp 13

Freedom of Information Act 1982 (Victoria) No. 9859 of 1982 Version No. 066

Freedom of Information Act 1982 No. 9859 of 1982

Freedom of Information Act 2000, 2000 c.36

Freedom of Information Act Awareness Guidance No. 5, Commercial Interests (Version 3) (Information Commissioner's Office 2009)

Freedom of Information Act, Environmental Information Regulations: The exemption for legal professional privilege (Information Commissioner's Office 2008)

Freedom of Information: Every Expense Spared | The Economist (19 December 2006) <www.economist.com/node/8459574> accessed 16 May 2016

Freedom of Information Regulations 2009 S.R. No. 33/2009

Freiberg A, 'Commercial confidentiality, criminal justice and the public interest' 9 Current Issues in Criminal Justice 125

FS50273866 (Water Services Regulation Authority) (Information Commissioner's Office)

Fyfe M, 'Voters out of loop in ALP's Victoria: a state of secrecy' *The Age* <www.theage.com.au/national/voters-out-of-loop-in-alps-victoria-a-state-of-secrecy-20101009-16d3b.html> accessed 15 November 2010

Gas, Electricity and Water (Parliamentary and Health Service Ombudsman) <www.ombudsman.org.uk/make-a-complaint/if-we-cant-help/gas-electricity-and-water> accessed 31 May 2011

Global Water Partnership, *Towards water security: a framework for action* (Global Water Partnership; World Water Forum 2000)

Godbole M, *Public accountability and transparency: the imperatives of good governance* (Orient Longman 2003)

Government of Victoria (Department of Sustainability and Environment), *Annual Report 2010* (2010)

Government of Victoria (Strategy and Policy Government Services Group Department of Treasury and Finance), *Good Practice Guidelines, Conduct of Commercial Engagements* (July 2011)

Government of Victoria, *Victoria's NWI Implementation Plan* (2006)

Government of Victoria, *Water and Sewerage Licence, City West Water Limited A.B.N. 70 066 902 467, Reprinted incorporating amendments as at 28 July 2004* (2004)

Government of Victoria, *Water and Sewerage Licence, Yarra Valley Water Limited A.B.N. 93 066 902 501, Reprinted incorporating amendments as at 28 July 2004* (2004)

Government Resources and Accounts Act 2000, 2000 c.20

Graham C and Prosser T, *Privatizing public enterprises: constitutions, the state, and regulation in comparative perspective* (Clarendon Press, Oxford 1991)

Graham C, *Regulating public utilities: a constitutional approach* (Hart 2000)

Gray D, *Review of Ofwat and consumer representation in the water sector* (Defra and the Welsh Government, 2011)

Great Britain Committee on Standards in Public Life, *Standards in public life: First Report of the Committee of Standards in Public Life (Nolan Report)* (1995)

Green R and Pardina MR, *Resetting price controls for privatized utilities: a manual for regulators* (World Bank Publications 1999)

Green R, 'Has price cap regulation of UK utilities been a success?' 132 Public Policy for the Private Sector

Greenbury R, *Directors' remuneration: report of a study group chaired by Sir Richard Greenbury* (Gee Publishing 1995)

Guidance on Applying for a Water Supply Licence, Version 3 (Ofwat 2011) <www.ofwat.gov.uk/publications/water-supply-licensees-contact-details/> accessed 13 May 2016

Guideline for transfer pricing in the water industry; Regulatory Accounting Guideline 5.04 (Ofwat 2007)

Hadipuro W and Ardhianie N, *Amandemen Kontrak Konsesi Air Jakarta* (2008)

Hadjon PM and others, *Pengantar Hukum Administrasi Indonesia (Introduction to Indonesian Administrative Law)* (Gadjah Mada University Press 1993)

Hak Pelanggan Disembunyikan (Customer's Rights are Concealed) *Daily Kompas* (Jakarta, 27 November 2007)

Hall D and Lobina E, 'Private to Public: International lessons of water remunicipalisation in Grenoble, France' (American Water Resources Association, Dundee, 6–8 August 2001)

Hall D, 'Introduction' in Brennan B and others (eds), *Reclaiming public water: achievements, struggles and visions from around the world* (Transnational Institute and Corporate Europe Observatory 2005)

Hall D, 'Secret Reports and Public Concerns. A Reply to the USAID Paper on Water Privatisation "Skeptics"' (London: Public Services International Research Unit (PSIRU))

Hampel R, *Committee on Corporate Governance: final report* (Gee 1998)

Hannigan B, *Company law* (Oxford University Press 2009)

Hantke-Domas MP, 'Economic Regulation of Public Utilites with Natural Monopoly Features. A Study of Limitations Imposed by Property Rights from a Legal & Economic Approach' (Dissertation, University East Anglia 2005)

Harris K, *Improving regulatory reporting and compliance* (Report for Ofwat 2010)

Harsono A, 'Water and Politics in the Fall of Suharto' The Center for Public Integrity <www.publicintegrity.org/2003/02/10/5725/water-and-politics-fall-suharto> accessed 16 May 2016

Harsono A, 'When Water and Political Power Intersect' Nieman Reports <www.nieman.harvard.edu/reportsitem.aspx?id=101044>

Hassan J, *A history of water in modern England and Wales* (Manchester University Press: Distributed in the USA by St. Martin's Press 1998)

Haughton G, 'Private profits–public drought: the creation of a crisis in water management for West Yorkshire' 23 Transactions of the Institute of British Geographers 419

Havlicek R, 'Learning from privatisation of water services in Trencin, Slovakia' in B Brennan and others (eds), *Reclaiming public water: achievements, struggles and visions from around the world* (Transnational Institute and Corporate Europe Observatory 2005)

Hendry S, *Frameworks for water law reform* (Cambridge University Press 2014)

Hendry SM, 'An Analytical Framework for Reform of National Water Law' (PhD thesis, University of Dundee 2008)

Hendry SM, 'Ownership Models for Water Services: Implications for Regulation' in A McHarg and others (eds), *Property and the law in energy and natural resources*, vol. 1 (Oxford University Press 2010)

Hern R and others, *Regulatory transparency: international assessment and emerging lessons a final report for the World Bank* (NERA Economic Consulting, 2005)

House of Commons – Environmental Audit – Seventh Report <http://goo.gl/7DHxt3> accessed 22 May 2016

216 Bibliography

How do I complain about my water and/or sewerage company? (CC Water 2010) <http://ccwater.custhelp.com/app/answers/detail/a_id/417> accessed 31 May 2011

How we do our job: a code of practice governing the discharge of Ofwat's functions (Ofwat 2003)

Hurstel D and Pecquet-Carpenter M, 'Public interest and private management: incompatible partners?' in S Cotter and D Campbell (eds), *Comparative Law Yearbook of International Business 1995* (Kluwer Law International 1995)

Ikatan Akuntan Indonesia, *Pernyataan Standar Akuntansi Keuangan (PSAK) No. 07: Pengungkapan Pihak Pihak Berelasi* (2010)

Indonesia, 'Undang Undang No. 32 Tahun 2004 Tentang Pemerintahan Daerah'

Indonesia, *Peraturan Menteri Pekerjaan Umum No. 18/PRT/M/2007 Tentang Penyelenggaraan Pengembangan Air Minum Sistem Penyediaan Air Minum* (2007)

Indonesian Civil Code, the 'Burgerlijk Wetboek'

Infrastructure Australia Act 2008 No. 17, 2008

Institute of Chartered Accountants in England and Wales, *Internal control: guidance for directors on the combined code (Turnbull Report)* (Institute of Chartered Accountants in England & Wales 1999)

Institute of Chartered Secretaries and Administrators, 'ICSA guidance on access to the Register of Members: Proper Purpose Test' (2007) <www.icsa.org.uk/assets/files/pdfs/Policy/PP2.pdf> accessed 21 May 2016

Instrument of Appointment by the Secretary of State for the Environment of Severn Trent Water Limited as a water and sewerage undertaker under the Water Act 1989 (1989)

Instrument of Appointment by the Secretary of State for the Environment of Thames Water Utilities Limited as a water and sewerage undertaker under the Water Act 1989 (2005)

Instrument of Appointment by the Secretary of State for Wales of Dwr Cymru Cyfyngedig as a water and sewerage undertaker under the Water Act 1989 (1989)

International Monetary Fund, 'International Monetary Fund Reports on the International Financial Architecture by the G22 Working Group on Transparency and Accountability, Working Group on Strengthening Financial Systems and Working Group on International Financial Crises (Group of 22)' <www.imf.org/external/np/g22/index.htm> accessed 28 May 2009

Inter-Regulatory Working Group, *The role of regulatory accounts in regulated industries: a joint consultation paper by the Directors General of Oftel, Ofgem, Ofwat, Electricity & Gas Supply (Northern Ireland), Rail Regulator and Civil Aviation Authority* (2001)

Interview with Non Governmental Organizations, Jakarta, 20–30 December 2010

Iwanami M and Nickson A, 'Assessing the regulatory model for water supply in Jakarta' 28 Public Administration and Development 291

Jakarta Court Cancels World's Biggest Water Privatisation after 18 Year Failure (Transnational Institute) <www.tni.org/en/pressrelease/jakarta-court-cancels-worlds-biggest-water-privatisation-after-18-year-failure> accessed 13 November 2015

Jakarta Water Supply Regulatory Body, 'Kinerja Operator' (*JWSRB*) <http://goo.gl/yFJAnS> accessed 21 May 2016

Jensen O and Blanc-Brude F, 'The Handshake: Why do Governments and Firms Sign Private Sector Participation Deals? Evidence from the Water and Sanitation Sector in Developing Countries' SSRN eLibrary

Jensen O, 'Troubled Partnerships: Problems and Coping Strategies in Jakarta's Water Concessions' (4th Conference on Applied Infrastructure Research Berlin)

Jeremy Pelczer, *Leakage and Security of Supply, Undertaking Under s.19 Water Industry Act 1991* (2006)

Jouravlev A and United Nations. Economic Commission for Latin America and the Caribbean, *Water utility regulation: issues and options for Latin America and the Caribbean* (Economic Commission for Latin America and the Caribbean 2000)

Judicial Review of Law Number 22 of 2001 Concerning Oil and Gas, Judgment of 15th December 2004, No. 002/PUU-I/200 (Constitutional Court of the Republic of Indonesia)

Judicial Review of Law Number 7 Year 2004 regarding Water Resources, Judgment of 13th July 2005, No. 058-059-060-063/PUUII/2004 (Constitutional Court of the Republic of Indonesia)

Keputusan Presiden No. 18 Tahun 2000 tentang Pengadaan Barang/Jasa Instansi Pemerintah

Keputusan Presiden No. 11 Tahun 1973 tentang Pedoman pelaksanaan Anggaran Pendapatan dan Belanja Negara tahun 1973/1974

King S, 'Principles of price cap regulation' in M Arblaster and M Jamison (eds), *Infrastructure regulation and market reform: principles and practice* (ACCC and PURC 1998)

Komisi Informasi Pusat Republik Indonesia, *Anotasi Undang Undang Nomor 14 Tahun 2008 Tentang Keterbukaan Informasi Publik* (1st edn, Indonesian Center for Environmental Law dan Yayasan Tifa 2009)

Kooy MÉ, 'Relations of power, networks of water: governing urban waters, spaces, and populations in (post) colonial Jakarta' (University of British Columbia 2008)

Kothari M, 'Privatising human rights – the impact of globalisation on adequate housing, water and sanitation' Social Watch Report <http://unpan1.un.org/intradoc/groups/public/documents/APCITY/UNPAN010131.pdf> accessed 16 May 2016

Kruha vs PAM Jaya, Putusan 172/G/2012/PTUNJKT (Mahkamah Agung Republik Indonesia)

Kruha vs PAM Jaya, Putusan Nomor 391/XII/KIP-PS-M-A/2011 Komisi Inf Pus

Laffont JJ and Tirole J, *A theory of incentives in procurement and regulation* (MIT Press 1993)

Laffont JJ, *Regulation and development* (Cambridge University Press 2005)

Lanti A and others, *The First Ten Years of Implementation of the Jakarta Water Supply 25-Year Concession Agreement (1998–2008)* (Jakarta Water Supply Regulatory Body (JWSRB) 2009)

Lanti A, 'A regulatory approach to the Jakarta Water Supply concession contracts' 22 International Journal of Water Resources Development 255

The Large and Medium sized Companies and Groups (Accounts and Reports) Regulations, Statutory Instrument, SI 2008/410

Law Comission of Great Britain, *Legislating the criminal code: misuse of trade secrets; a consultation paper* (HMSO 1997)

Leakage (Ofwat) <http://goo.gl/wYOOiq> accessed 21 May 2016

Licensing and Policy Issues in Relation to the Opening of the Non-Household Retail Market – a Consultation <www.ofwat.gov.uk/regulated-companies/company-obligations/annual-performance-report/> accessed 15 May 2016

Licensing and Policy Issues in Relation to the Opening of the Non-Household Retail Market – Appendices <www.ofwat.gov.uk/wp-content/uploads/2015/09/pap_con201506retaillicence.pdf> accessed

Lobina E and Hall D, 'The comparative advantage of the public sector in the development of urban water supply' 8 Progress in Development Studies 85

Lobina E, 'Problems with private water concessions: a review of experiences and analysis of dynamics' in AK Biswas and C Tortajada (eds), *Water pricing and public-private partnership* (Routledge 2005)

Lodge M and Stirton L, 'Regulating in the interest of the citizen: towards a single model of regulatory transparency' 50 Social and economic studies 103

Lovei L and Whittington D, 'Rent-extracting behavior by multiple agents in the provision of municipal water supply: a study of Jakarta, Indonesia' 29 Water Resources Research 1965

Lowe LH, Jones P and Brown R, *Liquid Assets. Responsible Investment in Water Services* (ICCR 2009)
Lower Murray Water, *Lower Murray Water Exposure Draft Water Plan 2008–09 to 2012–13, October 2007* (2007)
LPAW v BHP, Keputusan Komisi Informasi Pusat No 001/VII/KIP-PS-A/2010, 7 October 2010
Majone G, 'The regulatory state and its legitimacy problems' 22 West European Politics 1
Maksimovic and Commonwealth Director of Public Prosecutions and Anor [2009] AATA 700
Marbun SF, *Peradilan administrasi negara dan upaya administratif di Indonesia* (UII Press 2003)
Marcic v Thames Water Utilities Ltd [2003] UKHL 66 (4 December 2003)
Marin P, *Public-private partnerships for urban water utilities: a review of experiences in developing countries* (World Bank Publications 2009)
McKinley D, 'Water is life: the anti-privatisation forum and the struggle against water privatisation' (Public Citizen 2003)
Melbourne Metropolitan Water Price Review 2009–10 to 2012–13, Consultations (Essential Services Commission) <http://goo.gl/ rc9Rjp> accessed 21 May 2016
Mertokusumo S, *Mengenal Hukum, Suatu Pengantar* (5th edn, Liberty 2003)
Millar R and Schneiders B, 'Desal plant a $570m-a-year drain' *The Age* <www.theage.com.au/victoria/desal-plant-a-570mayear-drain-20100916-15enu.html> accessed 20 September 2011
The Minister for Water of the State of Victoria and others, *Project Deed Schedule I* (2009)
The Minister for Water of the State of Victoria and others, *Victorian Desalination Project D&C Direct Deed* (2009)
Minow M, 'Public and private partnerships: accounting for the new religion' Harvard Law Review 1229
Mulgan R, 'Contracting out and accountability' 56 Australian Journal of Public Administration 106
Mulgan, R., 'Comparing accountability in the public and private sectors' 59 Australian Journal of Public Administration 87
Myners P, *Developing a winning partnership: how companies and institutional investors are working together* (Department of Trade and Industry 1996)
Myners P, *Report on institutional investment* (London: HM Treasury 2001)
Northumbrian Water Limited, 'June Return 2007: Statement to Accompany the Public Domain Version' (Northumbrian Water 2007)
Notice of Ofwat's Imposition of a Penalty on Thames Water Utilities Limited (Ofwat 2008) <www.ofwat.gov.uk/consultation/notice-of-ofwats-proposal-to-impose-a-penalty-on-thames-water-utilities-limited/> accessed 21 May 2016
Notice of Ofwat's proposal to impose a penalty on United Utilities Water Plc (Ofwat 2007)
Notice of Ofwat's proposed variation to its proposal to impose a penalty on Thames Water Utilities Limited (Ofwat)
Nugroho R, *Dilemma of Jakarta Water Service Post Public Private Partnership (PPP)* (2009)
Nugroho R, *Reasons not to Privatize Water Undertaking* (2010)
OECD, *OECD Principles of Corporate Governance* (2004)
Ofcom (FER0072933) (Information Commissioner's Office)
The Office of Communication (Ofcom) v Information Commissioner and T-Mobile (UK) Limited, EA/2006/0078 (Information Tribunal)
Office of Public Employment, *Code of Conduct for the Victorian public sector* (Government of Victoria 1995)

Ofwat and Defra, 'The development of water industry in England and Wales' <www.ofwat.gov.uk/wp-content/uploads/2015/11/rpt_com_devwatindust270106.pdf> accessed 16 May 2016

Ofwat, 'Overview of the Business Plan Information Requirements for PR09' <http://goo.gl?GPKTu0> accessed 21 May 2016

Ofwat, 'Periodic review 2009: water & sewerage companies' final business plans – one page summaries' <goo.gl/TpKQUI> accessed 21 May 2016

Ofwat, 'Price review 2009 timeline' <http://goo.gl/ XXCLGx> accessed 21 May 2016

Ofwat, 'Price Review 2009' <http://goo.gl/DDpoVL> accessed 21 May 2016

Ofwat, 'Publication of the June return 2009' (2009) <http://webarchive.nationalarchives.gov.uk/20090606091533/ofwat.gov.uk/regulating/junereturn/ltr_rd0809_jr09> accessed 22 May 2016

Ofwat Review Will Consider Future Challenges Facing Industry (Department for Environment Food and Rural Affairs) <www.defra.gov.uk/news/2010/08/26/ofwat-review/> accessed 25 April 2011

Ofwat, 'Regulatory compliance – a proportionate and targeted approach, a consultation' (2011) <http://goo.gl/ezfhI2> accessed 21 May 2016

Ofwat, *Chapters 30 & 31: Transactions with Associated Companies, June return reporting requirements and definitions manual 2011, Issue 1.0 – January 2011* (Ofwat 2011)

Ofwat, *Getting it right for customers: how can we make monopoly water and sewerage companies more accountable?* (2010)

Ofwat, *Ofwat: Meeting the demand for water, Twenty-fourth Report of Session 2006–07* (2007)

Ofwat, *Regulatory compliance – a proportionate and targeted approach, A consultation* (2011)

Ofwat, *Rules of procedure for the Water Services Regulation Authority* (2010) ofwatrecruitmentboard.com, 'Background to the appointments' <www.ofwatboardrecruitment.com/sections/about_the_org/background_to_the_appointments> accessed 12 November 2011

Ofwat Review Will Consider Future Challenges Facing Industry (Department for Environment Food and Rural Affairs) <www.defra.gov.uk/news/2010/08/26/ofwat-review/> accessed 25 April 2011

Ofwat's Final Report on a dispute between Dr Lashley and Anglian Water about entitlement to payment under the Guaranteed Standard Scheme (GSS) (2005)

Olson WP, 'Secrecy and Utility Regulation' 18 The Electricity Journal 48

O'Reilly JT, 'Confidential submissions to utility regulators: reconciling secrets with service' 18 Ohio Northern University Law Review 217

O'Shea P and Rickett C, 'In defence of consumer law: the resolution of consumer disputes' 28 Sydney Law Review 139

PadCo, 'A Review of Reports by Private-Sector-Participation Skeptics, Prepared for Municipal Infrastructure Investment Unit (MIIU), South Africa and The United States Agency for International Development (USAID), Contract No. 674-0312-C-00-8023-0' (February 2002) <www.ircwash.org/sites/default/files/PADCO-2002-Review.pdf> accessed 13 May 2016

Page B and Bakker K, 'Water governance and water users in a privatised water industry: participation in policy-making and in water services provision: a case study of England and Wales' 3 International Journal of Water 38

Palast G, Oppenheim J and MacGregor T, *Democracy and regulation: how the public can govern privatised essential services* (Pluto Press 2002)

PAM Jaya, 'Direksi PAM Jaya' (*PAM Jaya,*) <www.pamjaya.co.id/Direksi.html> 3 accessed March 2011

PAM Jaya's Concessionaire, *Personal Communication with the Private Sector* (11 January 2011)

Paula Bennett, *Re: Ofwat's excision policy for the June Return data* (email correspondence 21 June 2011)

Payen G, Moss J and Waeyenberge TV, *Private water operators contribute to making the Right to Water & Sanitation real, AquaFed's submission, Part 3 Avoiding misconceptions on private water operators in relation to the Right to Water and Sanitation* (AquaFed 2010)

Payen G, *UN Human Rights Council Public Hearing by the Independent Expert on the Right to Water, Introductory remarks by Gerard Payen* (2010)

Pay Up: How the Water Mafia Controls Access (*The Jakarta Globe*, 2009) <http://goo.gl/Axg3RY> accessed 21 May 2016

Pearson DDR, *Managing the Requirements for Disclosing Private Sector Contracts* (Auditor General of Victoria 2010)

Peraturan Badan Regulator Pelayanan Air Minum DKI Jakarta No. 02 Tahun 2007 Tentang Mekanisme Dan Prosedur Transparansi Pelayanan Air Minum Jakarta

Peraturan Daerah Kabupaten Maros No. 4 Tahun 2011 Tentang Perusahaan Daerah Air Minum

Peraturan Daerah Kabupaten Sragen No. 8 Tahun 2004 Tentang Perusahaan Daerah Air Minum Kabupaten Sragen

Peraturan Daerah Kabupaten Takalar No. 15 Tahun 2003 Tentang Perusahaan Daerah Air Minum

Peraturan Daerah Kendal No. 13 Tahun 2011

Peraturan Daerah Khusus Ibukota Jakarta No. 11 Tahun 1993 Tentang Pelayanan Air Minum di Wilayah Daerah Khusus Ibukota Jakarta

Peraturan Daerah Khusus Ibukota Jakarta No. 13 Tahun 1992 Tentang Perusahaan Daerah Air Minum Daerah Khusus Ibukota Jakarta (PAM Jaya)

Peraturan Daerah Kota Bogor No. 4 Tahun 2004 Tentang Perusahaan Daerah Air Minum Tirta Pakuan Kota Bogor

Peraturan Daerah Kota Bogor No. 5 Tahun 2006 Tentang Pelayanan Air Minum Perusahaan Daerah Air Minum Tirta Pakuan Kota Bogor

Peraturan Daerah Provinsi Kalimantan Barat No. 2 Tahun 2006 Tentang Pendirian Perusahaan Daerah Air Minum Provinsi Kalimantan Barat

Peraturan Gubernur DKI Jakarta No. 118 Tahun 2011 Tentang Badan Regulator Pelayanan Air Minum

Peraturan Gubernur No. 54 Tahun 2005 Tentang Badan Regulator Pelayanan Air Minum

Peraturan Menteri Dalam Negeri No. 23 Tahun 2006 Tentang Pedoman Teknis dan Tata Cara Pengaturan Tarif Air Minum Pada Perusahaan Daerah Air Minum

Peraturan Menteri Kesehatan Republik Indonesia No. 492/Menkes/PER/IV/2010 Tahun 2010 Tentang Persyaratan Kualitas Air Minum

Peraturan Pemerintah No. 16 Tahun 2005 Tentang Pengembangan Sistem Penyediaan Air Minum

Peraturan Pemerintah No. 7 Tahun 2010 Tentang Perusahaan Umum (Perum) Jasa Tirta II

Peraturan Presiden No. 54 Tahun 2010 Tentang Pengadaan Barang/Jasa Pemerintah

Performance Report 2010 (Water Industry Commission for Scotland, 2010)

Personal Communication, *Field Interview with Palyja, Jakarta, 10 January 2011*

Personal Communication, *Field Interview with Stakeholders, Jakarta, 11 January 2011*

Porporato M and Robbins PT, 'Privatisation and corporate governance in emerging economies: What went wrong with Aguas Argentinas SA?' 2 International Journal of Economics and Business Research 187

The proposed acquisition of Dwr Cymru Cyfyngedig by Glas Cymru Cyfyngedig, A Consultation Paper by Ofwat (2000)

The proposed takeover of Thames Water plc by RWE AG: A Consultation Paper by the Office of Water Services (Ofwat 2000)

Prosser T, 'Regulatory contracts and stakeholder regulation' 76 Annals of Public and Cooperative Economics 35

Prosser T, *Law and the regulators* (Oxford University Press, USA 1997)

PR09/20: Water Supply and Demand Policy (Ofwat 2008) <http://goo.gl/MZAVA2> accessed 21 May 2016

Psiru, 'Undermining Democracy and the Environment, PSI Briefing, The Hague World Water Forum' <www.psiru.org/reports/2000-03-W-Htrans.doc> accessed 25 December 2011

PT Aetra Air Jakarta, *Financial Statement, December 31, 2010 and 2009* (2010)

PT Aetra Air Jakarta, *Laporan Tahunan PT Aetra Air Jakarta Tahun 2009* (2009)

PT Aetra, <www.aetra.co.id/index.php/id_id/profilPerusahaan/page?id=pemegang-saham> accessed 16 May 2016

PT Aetra, 'Obligasi' (2008) <www.aetra.co.id/index.php/id_id/hubunganInvestor/page?id=penjualan-obligasi> accessed 13 May 2016

PT Jasa Tirta II, 'Latar Belakang Pembentukan PT Jasa Tirta II' <www.jasatirta2.co.id/pjt.php?x=org&y=15ce99f2079b95cf251cb78b9d4a27df> accessed 16 May 2016

PT PAM Lyonnaise Jaya, *2009 Annual Report* (2009)

PT PAM Lyonnaise Jaya, *Laporan Keuangan* (2011)

Public Administration Act (Victoria) 2004 No. 108 of 2004 Version No. 024

Public Appointments Order in Council 2002, Notice: 1006 (Issue: 56648), 30 July 2002

Public-Private Infrastructure Advisory Facility, *Approaches to private participation in water services: a toolkit* (International Bank for Reconstruction and Development and the World Bank 2006)

Public Private Partnership (Government of Victoria) <http://web.archive.org/web/20110225003309/http://www.ourwater.vic.gov.au/programs/desalination/about-us/ppp> accessed 16 May 2016, p.2

Pudyatmoko YS, *Perizinan: Problem dan Upaya Pembenahan* (Grasindo 2009)

Putusan Mahkamah Konstitusi Nomor 85/PUU-XI/2013 Tentang Pengujuan Undang Undang Nomor 7 Tahun 2004 Tentang Sumber Daya Air

Putusan Nomor 527/PDTG/2012/PNJKTPST (Central Jakarta District Court)

Putusan Nomor: 356/IX/KIP-PS-M-A/2011; YP2IP v BP Migas (Komisi Informasi Pusat)

Putusan Pengadilan Negeri Jakarta Selatan No. 450/PdtG/2012/PNJktSel; KIP v BP Migas (Pengadilan Negeri Jakarta Selatan)

Quesada MG, *Water and Sanitation Services in Europe: Do Legal Frameworks provide for 'Good Governance'?* (UNESCO Centre for Water Law Policy and Science at the University of Dundee 2010)

Railways Act 1993, 1993 c.43

Rancangan Peraturan Pemerintah Tentang Sistem Penyediaan Air Minum (versi 29 April)

Re Actors' Equity Association of Australia and Australian Consumers Association and Australian Broadcasting Tribunal and Federation of Australian Commercial Television Stations [1985] AATA 69

Re Alan Sunderland and the Department of Defence [1986] AATA 278 (19 September 1986)

Re Croom and Accident Compensation Commission (1989) 3 VAR 441
Register of Disclosable Interests – Ofcom Board (Ofcom 2011) <www.ofcom.org.uk/about/how-ofcom-is-run/ofcom-board-2/members/register-of-disclosable-interests/> accessed 11 May 2011
Regulatory Enforcement and Sanctions Act 2008, 2008 c.13
Re Howard and the Treasurer of the Commonwealth (1985) 3 AAR 169
Re News Corporation Limited, Mirror Newspapers Limited, Nationwide News Pty Limited and Control Investments Pty Limited and National Companies and Securities Commission [1983] AATA 311; 8 Aclr 316 (14 September 1983) (Administrative Appeals Tribunal)
Re Organon (Australia) Pty Limited and Department of Community Services and Health and Public Interest Advocacy Centre [1987] AATA 396
Re Peter Cockcroft and Attorney-General's Department and Australian Iron and Steel Pty Limited [1985] AATA 224
Reporting Requirements (Ofwat 2011) <www.ofwat.gov.uk/regulated-companies/company-obligations/annual-performance-report/> accessed 15 May 2016
Re Queensland and Department of Aviation [1986] AATA 142
Re Robyn Frances Murtagh and Commissioner of Taxation [1984] AATA 249 (5 July 1984)
Reza M, *Permintaan Dokumen dan Informasi Kontrak Konsesi Layanan Air Minum Jakarta (Freedom of Information Law Request for Documents and Contractual Information Concerning Jakarta's Water Services Concession)*, Letter No.019/KIP/V/2011 dated 31 October 2011 (KRuHA 2011)
Risk Solutions, *Good practice for communicating about drinking water quality; A report for The Drinking Water Inspectorate* (D5173/R1, 2009)
Rizal, *Tanda Terima Pendaftaran Pengajuan Sengketa Informasi No. A26/RSI/P/XII/KIP/2011, KRuHA vs PDAM DKI Jakarta, 07-12-2011* (Komisi Informasi Pusat (KIP) 2011)
Rogers P and Hall A, *Effective water governance (TEC background papers no. 7)* (Global Water Partnership, Stockholm 2003)
Rouse M, *Institutional governance and regulation of water services*, vol. 2 (2007)
Russell EW, Waterman E and Seddon N, *Audit Review of Government Contracts: Contracting, Privatisation, Probity and Disclosure in Victoria 1992–1999, An Independent Report to Government* (State Government of Victoria May 2000)
Saal D and De Witte K, 'Is a little sunshine all we need? On the impact of sunshine regulation on profits, productivity and prices in the Dutch drinking water sector' 20 Journal of Regulatory Economics 61
Safe Drinking Water Act 2003, No. 46 of 2003 (Victoria)
Sands V, 'The right to know and obligation to provide: public private partnerships, public knowledge, public accountability, public disenfranchisement and prisons cases' 29 University of New South Wales Law Journal 334
Sankey v Whitlam [1978] HCA 43; (1978) 142 CLR 1 (9 November 1978) (High Court of Australia)
Sawitri AS, 'Committee questions Acuatico's suitability as tap water operator' *The Jakarta Post* (Jakarta, 30 November 2006) <http://x.crpg.info/1YpdVwj> accessed 13 May 2016
Sawitri AS, 'Regulatory body casts doubt on takeover bid' *The Jakarta Post* (Jakarta, 14 December 2006)
Schneiders B and Millar R, 'Brumby's giant money pit' <www.theage.com.au/victoria/brumbys-giant-money-pit-20100827-13w2n.html> accessed 24 November 2010

Scholten M, 'Independence vs. Accountability: Dilemma or Misperception?' (The Netherlands Institute of Government Annual Work Conference, Maastricht, 26 November 2010)
Section 22A Water Industry Act 1991: Statement of policy with respect to financial penalties (Ofwat)
Security of supply 2006–07 – supporting information (Ofwat)
Seddon N, *Government contracts: federal, state and local* (4th edn, Federation Press 2009)
Setting Price Controls for 2015–20 – Final Methodology and Expectations for Companies' Business Plans <www.ofwat.gov.uk/wp-content/uploads/2015/11/pap_pos201307finalapproach.pdf> accessed 6 December 2015
Setting Price Controls for 2015–20 – Risk and Reward Guidance <www.ofwat.gov.uk/wp-content/uploads/2015/11/gud_tec20140127riskreward.pdf> accessed 6 December 2015
Setting Price Controls for 2015–20 Final Price Control Determination Notice: Company-Specific Appendix – Affinity Water <www.ofwat.gov.uk/wp-content/uploads/2015/10/det_pr20141212afw.pdf> accessed 6 December 2015
Severn Trent Water Limited Report and Financial Statements for the Year Ended 31 March 2015
Shaw S, 'Prisons: who gains from commercial confidentiality?' 13 Public Money & Management 7
Shugart CT, 'Regulation-by-Contract and Municipal Services: The Problem of Contractual Incompleteness' (PhD Thesis Harvard University 1998)
Si L and Callan J, 'A statistical model for scientific readability' (Proceedings of the Tenth International Conference on Information and Knowledge Management)
Simatupang DP, *Jawaban Tentang Konsesi* (email correspondence 2011)
Simpson R, 'Down and dirty: providing water for the world' 14 Consumer Policy Review 146
Skapová H, *Water industry privatisation in the Czech Republic: money down the drain?* (Transparency International – Czech Republic 2009)
Smartsource Drainage & Water Reports Limited v The Information Commissioner, Upper Tribunal Case No. GI/2458/2010 (The Upper Tribunal (Administrative Appeals Chamber))
Smith W, 'Utility regulators: the independence debate' 127 Public Policy for the Private Sector
Snell R, 'Freedom of Information: the experience of the Australian states – an epiphany?' 29 Federal Law Review 343
Standard Requirements for the Publication of Annual Reports (April 2015) Financial Reporting Directive 30B
Standing Committee on Finance and Public Administration, *Inquiry into the business case for water infrastructure (Transcript), Hearing with Chloe Munro, Chairman of AquaSure Pty Ltd, 17 June 2010* (Victoria Parliament 2010)
State Government of Victoria, 'Appointments to Melbourne region water boards' (6 September 2011) <http://goo.gl/3b2eBF> accessed 21 May 2016
State Owned Enterprises Act 1992 (Victoria), No. 90 of 1992, Version No. 036
Statement of Obligations (General) 2012
Stern J, 'The relationship between regulation and contracts in infrastructure industries' CCRP Working Paper No. 1 <www.city.ac.uk/economics/dps/CCRP%20Working%20Papers/newjs2.pdf> accessed 12 February 2011
Stuhmcke A, 'How good is private justice?' 71(1) The Law Institute Journal 6
Sutton and East Surrey Water PLC, *Annual Report to the Water Services Regulatory Authority June 2010, Public Domain Submission*

Swyngedouw E, 'Dispossessing H_2O: the contested terrain of water privatization' 16 Capitalism Nature Socialism 81
Tenders Vic, Victorian Government Tenders System (Government of Victoria 2012) <www.tenders.vic.gov.au> accessed 3 January 2012
Thames Water Utilities Ltd, *June Return 2006: Statement to Accompany the Public Domain Version* (2006)
Thames Water, 'Code of Practice: important helpful information and advice for household customers' <http://goo.gl/q4pUIj> accessed 21 May 2016
Thames Water, 'Our guarantees to you: Customer Guarantee Scheme' <http://goo.gl/gljzxZ> accessed 21 May 2016
Thames Water, *Thames Water Utilities Limited Interim report and financial statements for the six month period ended 30 September 2010* (2010)
Thwaites v Met Ambulance Service (1995/04289) [1994] VICCAT 6 (3 May 1994)
Tortajada C, 'Water management in Singapore' 22 International Journal of Water Resources Development 227
Trade Practices Act 1974, Act No. 51 of 1974 as amended
Turri P, 'Private Sector Participation in Water Services Provision' <www.fes-globalization.org/geneva/documents/Private%20Sector%20Participation%20in%20Water%20Services%20Provision_Turri.pdf>
UNCTAD, *Guidance on Good Practices in Corporate Governance Disclosure* (2006)
Undang Undang No. 17 Tahun 2003 Tentang Keuangan Negara
Undang Undang No. 25 Tahun 2009 Tentang Pelayanan Publik
Undang Undang No. 3 Tahun 1982 Tentang Wajib Daftar Perusahaan
Undang Undang No. 31 Tahun Tahun 2000 Tentang Desain Industri
Undang Undang No. 5 Tahun 1986 Tentang Peradilan Tata Usaha Negara
Undang Undang No. 7 Tahun 2004 Tentang Sumber Daya Air
Undang Undang No. 8 Tahun 1995 Tentang Pasar Modal
Undang Undang No. 10 Tahun 2004 Tentang Pembentukan Peraturan Perundang Undangan
Undang Undang No. 14 Tahun 2008 Tentang Keterbukaan Informasi Publik 2008
Undang Undang No. 40 Tahun 2007 Tentang Perseroan Terbatas
Undang Undang No. 5 Tahun 1962 Tentang Perusahaan Daerah
Undang Undang No. 5 Tahun 1999 Tentang Praktek Monopoli dan Persaingan Usaha Tidak Sehat
Undang Undang No. 23 Tahun 2014 Tentang Pemerintahan Daerah
Undang Undang No. 29 Tahun 2000 Tentang Varietas Tanaman
Undang Undang Pokok Kekuasaan Kehakiman No. 14 Tahun 1970
Undang Undang Pokok Kekuasaan Kehakiman No. 48 Tahun 2009
United Kingdom, *Freedom of Information Act 2000: Designation of additional public authorities, Consultation Paper CP 27/07* (2007)
United Kingdom, *Freedom of Information Act 2000: Designation of additional public authorities, Response to Consultation CP(R) 27/07, 16 July 2009* (2009)
United Kingdom, *Ofwat's Approach to Enforcement* (2009)
United Kingdom, *Providing Best Practice Guidance on the Inclusion of Externalities in the ELL Calculation: MAIN REPORT, Appendix 2 (part 1)*, (2011)
United Kingdom, *Regulatory justice sanctioning in a post-Hampton world: consultation document* (2006)
United Nations, *Subtantive Issues Arising in the Implementation of The International Covenant on Economic, Social and Cultural Rights, General Comment No. 15 (2002)*

The right to water (arts. 11 and 12 of the International Covenant on Economic, Social and Cultural Rights) E/C.12/2002/11, 20 January 2003 (2003)

United Utilities, *June Return 2006: Statement to Accompany the Public Domain Version* (United Utilities 2006)

University of East Anglia (FER0282488) (Information Commissioner's Office)

University of East Anglia (FER0280033) (Information Commissioner's Office)

Utilities Act 2000, 2000 c.27

Victorian Competition and Efficiency Commission, *Water Ways: Inquiry into Reform of the Metropolitan Retail Water Sector, Final Report February 2008* (2008)

Walker A, *The independent review of charging for household water and sewerage services: final report* (Defra 2009)

Waller P, Morris RM and Simpson D, *Understanding the formulation and development of government policy in the context of FOI* (2009)

Watchdog: Why is Water Deal under OSA? – Malaysiakini <www.malaysiakini.com/news/62323> accessed 2 November 2009

Water (Governance) Act 2006 Act No. 85/2006

Water Act 1989 c.15

Water Act 1989 No. 80 of 1989

Water Act 1989 No. 80 of 1989, Version 102

Water Act 2003 c.37

Water Act 2007, Act No. 137 of 2007

Water Act 2014; 2014 c.21 (England)

Water Act, 1945. 8 & 9 GEO. 6. c.42

Water Amendment (Governance and Other Reforms) Act 2012 No. 17 of 2012

Water Charge (Termination Fees) Rules 2009 – F2009L02425

Water Company Licences (Ofwat, no year) <www.ofwat.gov.uk/industrystructure/licences/> accessed 13 January 2016

Water Industry (Charges) (Vulnerable Groups) Regulations 1999 SI 1999/3441 (as amended)

Water Industry (Scotland) Act 2002, 2002 asp 3

Water Industry Act 1991 c.56

Water Industry Act 1991 Section 13(1) Modification of the Conditions of Appointment of United Utilities Water Plc (2005)

Water Industry Act 1991 Section 17 H, Standard Conditions of Water Supply Licences (Defra 2005)

Water Industry Act 1991, Section 13(1) Modification of the Conditions of Appointment of Thames Water Utilities Limited (2007)

Water Industry Act 1991, Section 13(1) Modification of the Conditions of Appointment of Thames Water Utilities Limited (Ofwat 2005)

Water Industry Act 1994 No. 121 of 1994, Version No. 063

Water Industry Act 1994, Statement of Obligation, City West Water Limited (2008)

Water Industry Act 1994, Water Industry Regulatory Order 2003

Water Industry Regulatory Order (WIRO) 2012

The Water Industry (Suppliers' Information) Direction 2009

Water Market Rules 2009 – F2009L02424

Water Resources Act 1991 c.57

Water Services etc. (Scotland) Act 2005, 2005 asp 3

Water and Sewerage Mergers: Guidance on the CMA's Procedure and Assessment <www.gov.uk/government/uploads/system/uploads/attachment_data/file/476839/Water_merger_guidance.pdf> accessed 6 December 2015

Water Supply Licences (Ofwat, no year) <www.ofwat.gov.uk/regulated-companies/licences/> accessed 13 January 2016

Water Supply Licensees' Contact Details (Ofwat, no year) <www.ofwat.gov.uk/competition/wsl/prs_web_wslcontacts> accessed 16 January 2012

The Water Supply Regulations 2010, SI 2010 No. 1991

The Water Supply and Sewerage Services (Customer Service Standards) Regulations 2008, SI 2008 No. 594

The Water White Paper; Second Report of Session 2012–13 <www.publications.parliament.uk/pa/cm201213/cmselect/cmenvfru/374/374.pdf> accessed 30 November 2015

Water Worries: Special Issue (*The Jakarta Globe*, 25 July 2009) <www.thejakartaglobe.com/pages/downloads/Water_Worries.pdf> accessed 4 December 2010

Winpenny J and Camdessus M, *Financing water for all: Report of the world panel on financing water infrastructure* (Global Water Partnership, World Water Council, World Water Forum 2003)

Wood D, 'Bridging the Governance Gap: Civil Society, Democratization and Electricity Sector Reform' (Arusha Conference, 'New Frontiers of Social Policy', 12–15 December 2005)

Wright C, *Memorandum: United Utilities Water Proposed Penalty – Representations of United Utilities Water ('UUW')* (2007)

Yarra Valley Water, *Water Plan 2009/10–2012/13, Yarra Valley Water, November 2008* (2008)

Yorkshire Water, *June Return 2007: Statement to Accompany the Public Domain Version* (Yorkshire Water 2007)

Your right to know: the government's proposals for a Freedom of Information Act (Stationery Office 1997)

Yun G, 'Rethinking China's urban water privatization' (Water Justice) <www.waterjustice.org/?mi=1&res_id=245> accessed 13 May 2016

Zifcak S, 'Complaint resolution in government owned corporations and privatised utilities: some legal and constitutional conundrums' in MJ Whincop (ed.), *From bureaucracy to business enterprise: legal and policy issues in the transformation of government services* (Ashgate 2003)

Zifcak S, 'Contractualism, democracy and ethics' 60 Australian Journal of Public Administration 86

Zinnbauer D and Dobson R (eds), *Global Corruption Report 2008: corruption in the water sector* (Cambridge University Press; Transparency International 2008)

Index

Aarhus Convention 1
access to information 1, 4
accountability 180–1; utilities' corporate governance 15, 123–30, 193–4, 207
accounting method 169
accounting rules 128
accounting standards 136–7
acquisition of information 11, 78–85, 186–8, 206
Aetra 42, 47–8, 116, 122, 136–7, 177, 193; applicability of FOI law 155–8; Cooperation Agreement 42–7, 48–52; corporate restructuring 142–3; corporate structure and board 128–30
affiliation 135–6
Aguas Argentina 14
applicability of FOI laws 17, 144–58, 195–8, 207
AquaFed 200
AquaSure 20, 24, 63, 145–6
Aquatico 46, 47
Aronson, M. 6
Atmosudirdjo, P. 156–7
Attorney-General's Department v Cockcroft 161–2
Auditor General (Victoria) 62, 182
Australia *see* Victoria
Australian Accounting Standards Board (AASB) 130
Australian Competition and Consumer Commission (ACCC) 27

Bakker, K. 99
Bapepam LK Rule 135–6
BHP case 154–5, 169, 174
billing 104
Birkinshaw, P. 148, 162–3
Board of Commissioners 128, 129
boards of directors 15, 123–30, 193–4, 207

Bogor 92, 103, 111–13, 121, 200, 202
BP Migas case 152–3, 169
breach of contract litigation 174–5
Bristol City Council v IC and Portland and Brunswick Squares Association 168
budget/financing, origins of 155–6
business plans 97, 189–90
By-law 11 103, 109
By-law 13 40–1, 126, 127, 142, 193
Byatt, I. 88

Cadbury Report 15
Calland, R. 144
Camdessus Report 1
capital market disclosure rules 137, 193–4
categorisation of information 88
Cave review 36, 38, 167
Coco v A.N. Clark (Engineers) Ltd 172–3
Code of Practice 107
commercial information 161–71, 199–200
commodification of information 2
Companies Act 2006 (CA 2006) (England) 124–5, 131
competition 164–8; unfair 169–71
Competition Appeal Tribunal (CAT) 118–19
Competition Commission 35, 37, 147
Competition and Markets Authority (CMA) 35–6, 37, 118–19
concession contracts 20–1, 156–7; Cooperation Agreement as concession 48–52
confidentiality 6, 7, 60; FOI laws 171–5, 199–200; Jakarta 65–6; Ofwat 88–9
confidentiality clauses 60–1; Jakarta 66, 89–91, 189, 201
conflicts of interest 58, 70–3, 134–6, 183, 205

consent conditions 34
consultation 86
consultation papers 138, 195
Consumer Council for Water (CC Water) 35, 37, 107, 119, 120, 147, 192
contamination 106
Contract Publishing System (CPS) 62, 63
contracts 57–66; annexes to 177–8; concession 20–1, 48–52, 156–7; execution of 60–1; ordinary 49–50; procurement committees 58; publication of 61–6, 181–2, 205; tender processes and expression of interest 58–9
control test 150–1
Cooperation Agreement 42–7, 98–9, 201; as concession 48–52; disclosure of information 89–91; non-compliance 115–16, 192; service levels and customer service 109–11, 112, 191
corporate governance 13–17, 122–43, 193–5, 207
corporate restructuring 16–17, 137–43, 195, 207
corporate structure 15, 123–30, 193–4, 207
Corporations Act 2001 (Victoria) 23, 54, 123, 130
criteria for approving licences 11, 74–5, 184–5, 205
cross subsidisation 13
customer service 11–12, 103–13, 190–1, 206
Customer Service Code (CSC) 104–5, 191, 192
customer services committees (CSCs) 35

decentralisation 55–6
delegation decision 8–9, 53–7, 180, 205
DEFRA (Department for Environment, Food and Rural Affairs) 36–7, 147, 149
desalination plant contract 60–1, 63–4
Determinations 119–20
Director's Report 125
disclosure 5–6, 60, 203; appeals to 7–8; capital market rules 137, 193–4; means of disclosing information 11, 85–92, 188–9, 206; publication of contracts 10, 61–6, 181–2, 205
disincentives 99–100

Drinking Water Inspectorate (DWI) 30, 34–5, 37, 82, 147
drought 96
Dwr Cymru 140–1

Eberhard, A. 3, 7
Energy and Water Ombudsman Victoria (EWOV) 26, 117–18, 145–6, 192
enforcement: law enforcement and investigations 158–61, 198–9; Macrory's enforcement principles 113–15; sanctions 13, 113–17, 191–2, 206
enforcement orders 113, 114
England 17–21, 27–38, 122; applicability of FOI rules 146–51; commercial information 162–8; corporate restructuring 138–41; corporate structure and the board 124–5; exemption clauses 159–60, 162–8, 172–3, 175–6; FOI law 17–18, 146–51, 159–60, 162–8, 172–3, 175–6, 195–200; information flow 82–3, 86–9, 186–9; investment 95–8; licence governance 73–4, 75, 76–7, 77–8, 184–5; memorandums and internal documents 175–6; non-compliance 113–15; obligation of confidence 172–3; Ofwat see Ofwat; privatisation 19, 29–30, 179; redress 118–20; regulator's internal governance 68–9, 71–3, 182–3; regulatory functions 95–8, 101–2, 105–7, 113–15, 118–20, 189–92; related party transactions 131–3; reviews of the water industry 36–8; sectoral rules and regulatory institutions 31–6, 37; service levels and customer service 105–7; tariffs and prices 101–2; transparency 202–3; utilities' corporate governance 124–5, 131–3, 138–41, 193–5
Environment Act 1995 (England) 33
Environment Agency (England) 30, 33–4, 37, 147
Environmental Information Regulation (EIR) 160, 167–8, 176; applicability to water utilities 146–7, 149–51, 196–7
Essential Services Commission (ESC) 20, 25–6, 73, 187; conflict of interest 70–1; disclosure of information 85–6; inquiries 80–1; performance reports 113; selection and removal of regulators 67, 183; tariffs and prices 100–1; Water Plans 93–5, 100, 189

Essential Services Commission Act (ESC Act) 25, 78, 79–81, 85–6, 101, 189
European Court of Justice 149–50
European Union (EU) 148
excisions 62, 63–4
execution of contracts 60–1
exemption clauses 17, 158–78, 198–200, 207
expression of interest 58–9
externalities 14

financial penalties 115, 118
Financial Reporting Directives (FRDs) 61, 64, 123, 124, 182, 195
financial reports 129–30
financing, origins of 155–6
Fish Legal v Information Commissioner 149–50
framework for transparency 8–17, 205–7
France 10, 21; Conseil d'État 21, 51
freedom of information (FOI) laws 17–19, 144–78, 195–200, 207; applicability 17, 144–58, 195–8, 207; England 17–18, 146–51, 159–60, 162–8, 172–3, 175–6, 195–200; exemption clauses 17, 158–78, 198–200, 207; Jakarta 18, 64–5, 109, 151–8, 160–1, 168–71, 173–5, 177–8, 195–200; Victoria 18, 85–6, 144–6, 158–9, 161–2, 171–2, 175, 195–200
Freiberg, A. 4

General Meeting of Shareholders (GMS) 128, 129, 130
Glas Cymru 140, 141
Global Corruption Report 2008 1, 7–8
Global Water Partnership 1
goodwill 162
governance failure 1–4
Government Gazette 77, 101, 113
Governor's Regulation 118 (Pergub-118) 69–70, 73, 91, 152
GR-16 74, 108
Gray review 36, 37–8, 101
Guaranteed Service Levels (GSL) 105
Guaranteed Standard Scheme (GSS) 106–7, 119–20, 190, 191

Habibie government 45
Hadjon, P.M. 49
Hall, D. 3
hardship policy 104–5
Harjojudanto, S. 43, 44

harm test 161–2, 199
Harris report 38
Hendry, S.M. 4
Human Right to Water agenda 9, 179

Independent Expert on the Right to Water 10
Indonesia *see* Jakarta
Indonesian Company Law 134
Indonesian Constitutional Court 56–7
information 203; access to 1, 4; categorisation of 88; commercial 161–71, 199–200; commodification of 2; disclosure *see* disclosure; gathering 5
information asymmetry 5
Information Commissioner's Office (ICO) 149–50, 159
information flow 11, 78–92, 186–9, 206; means of acquiring information 11, 78–85, 186–8, 206; means of disclosure 11, 85–92, 188–9, 206
Information Tribunal 176
inquiries 80–1
institutional capacity 51–2
institutional learning 171
intellectual property rights (IPR) 168–9
Interfaith Center on Corporate Responsibility (ICCR) 2
internal working documents 175–8, 198–9
investigations 158–61, 198–9
investigative power 184–5
investment 12, 93–100, 189–90, 206
Irrigation Law 11 Year 1974 38, 56

Jakarta 8–9, 17–21, 38–52, 122; applicability of FOI rules 151–8; central and local regulations 38–9; commercial information 168–71; Cooperation Agreement *see* Cooperation Agreement; corporate restructuring 141–3; corporate structure and the board 125–30; exemption clauses 160–1, 168–71, 173–5, 177–8; FOI law 18, 64–5, 109, 151–8, 160–1, 168–71, 173–5, 177–8, 195–200; information flow 84–5, 89–92, 186–9; investment 98–100; lack of transparency 200–2; licence governance 74, 184–5; memorandums and internal documents 177–8; non-compliance 115–17; obligation of confidence 173–5; policy in involving

Index

the private sector 20, 42–7, 55–8, 59, 64–6, 179–82; redress 120–1; regulator's internal governance 69–70, 73, 182–3; regulatory functions 98–100, 102–3, 107–13, 115–17, 120–1, 189–92; related party transactions 134–7; service levels and customer service 107–13; tariffs and prices 102–3; utilities' corporate governance 125–30, 134–7, 141–3, 193–5; water businesses 40–8
Jakarta Water Sector Regulatory Body (JWSRB) 46, 201, 202; applicability of FOI law 151–3, 158, 195–6; confidentiality obligation 174; information disclosure 89–92, 189; internal governance 69–70, 183; means of acquiring information 84–5, 187; service levels and customer service 110–11
June Returns 83, 87, 88, 89, 132–3, 188

K factor 33, 101
knowledge transfer, failure of 3
Kothari, M. 10
Kruha v PAM Jaya 152, 153, 177

Lanti, A. 111
Law 7 of Year 2004 39, 56
Law 11 of Year 1974 38, 56
law enforcement 158–61, 198–9
leakage 96–8
licence governance 11, 73–8, 184–5, 205–6; criteria for approving licences 11, 74–5, 184–5, 205; licence conditions 11, 75–7, 184–5, 206; publication of licences 11, 77–8, 185, 206
listed companies 142–3
listing rules 139–41
livelihood 109
lobbying 176
Lobina, E. 3
local regulation 39
London Stock Exchange listing rules 141
LPAW v BHP 154–5, 169, 174

MacRoberts and the City of Edinburgh Council 163–6, 167, 173
Macrory's enforcement principles 113–15
'MALE' (maximum access, limited exemption) principle 174

Marcic v Thames Water Utilities Ltd 95–6
Marin, P. 4
market power 165
market structure 203
memorandums 175–8, 198–9
merger plan 142
Minister for Water (Victoria) 25
Minow, M. 144
monopoly 162; natural 7, 14, 170–1
Mulgan, R. 2–3, 4

National River Authorities (England) 30
National Water Initiative (NWI) (Australia) 22
natural monopoly 7, 14, 170–1
Netherlands, the 21
new appointment and variations (NAV) licences 73, 76, 77–8
non-compliance 13, 113–17, 191–2, 206
Northumbrian Water 133

obligation of confidence 171–5, 199–200
OECD principles of corporate governance 15
Office of Communication (Ofcom) v Information Commissioner and T-Mobile (UK) Ltd 173
Ofwat (Water Services Regulatory Authority) 2, 19, 30, 31–3, 37, 190–1; conflicts of interest 71–3; corporate restructuring 138–41, 195; FOI law 147, 148; internal governance 68–9, 183; law enforcement and investigations 159; leakage 97–8; licence governance 75, 76–7, 77–8, 184–5; means of acquiring information 82–3, 186; means of disclosing information 86–9, 188; non-compliance 114–15; redress 118, 119–20, 192; related party transactions 132–3, 137; review 36, 37–8; risk-based regulation 38, 83, 87–8, 89, 101, 133, 148, 188, 204; tariffs and pricing 32–3, 101–2

PadCo Report 8
Palyja (PT PAM Lyonnaise Jaya) 42, 48, 100, 122, 137, 177; applicability of FOI law 155–8; Cooperation Agreement 42–7, 48–52; corporate restructuring 142–3; corporate structure and board 128–30, 193

PAM Jaya 40–1, 42, 122, 158, 190, 201; and acquisition of TPJ 143; confidentiality obligation 174; Cooperation Agreement 42–7, 48–52; corporate restructuring 142; corporate structure and board 126–8; debt 116–17, 156, 197; internal governance of JWSRB 69, 70; *Kruha v PAM Jaya* 152, 153, 177; means of acquiring information 84–5, 187; means of disclosing information 90, 91; non-compliance 116–17, 192; reporting standards 193; service level and customer service 109, 110
passive disclosure rules 17; *see also* freedom of information (FOI) laws
Payen, G. 3–4
performance reports 113
Pergub-118 69–70, 73, 91, 152
Permen 23 102–3
personal interest 134–5
Perum Jasa Tirta II (PJT II) 40, 42
policy: formulation 175–8, 198–9; in involving the private sector *see* private sector participation (PSP)
political connections 14
poor, the 99–100
Porporato, M. 14
PR-54 58, 59, 64–5
prejudice to commercial interests 162–3, 164
prescribed authorities 144–5
price cap 32–3
prices and tariffs 12–13, 100–3, 189–90, 206
principal–agent problem 5
private sector participation (PSP) 2–4, 8–10, 53–66, 179–82, 205; delegation decision 8–9, 53–7, 180, 205; Jakarta 20, 42–7, 55–7, 57–8, 59, 64–6, 179–82; procurements 8–10, 57–61, 137, 180–1, 205; publication of contracts 10, 61–6, 181–2, 205; Victoria 20, 53–5, 58, 59, 60–4, 179–82
privatisation 3–4, 7; England 19, 29–30, 179
procurement 8–10, 57–61, 137, 180–1, 205
procurement committees 58
production sharing contract (PSC) 152–3
profit and loss account 126, 127
Prosser, T. 3, 6
PSAK (accounting standards) 136–7

PT Aetra *see* Aetra
PT PAM Lyonnaise Jaya *see* Palyja
public bodies 153–5, 156, 157
public interest 6, 169–71, 181
public interest test 160, 164–8
public lawyer approach 5–6
public order 109
public–private partnership (PPP) 3
publication of contracts 10, 61–6, 181–2, 205
publication of licences 11, 77–8, 185, 206

reasoned decision 86
rebates 116
redress 13, 117–21, 192, 207
regional water authorities (RWAs) 29–30
Register of Board Members' Disclosable Interests 72, 183
registers 124–5, 128
regulators' internal governance 10–11, 67–73, 182–3, 205–6; conflicts of interest 70–3, 183, 205; selection and removal of regulators 10–11, 67–70, 182–3, 205
Regulatory Accounting Code (RAC) 131
Regulatory Accounting Guidelines (RAGs) 132
regulatory accounts 16, 186, 194–5
regulatory contracts 3, 7
regulatory functions 11–13, 93–121, 189–92, 206–7; investment 12, 93–100, 189–90, 206; non-compliance 13, 113–17, 191–2, 206; redress 13, 117–21, 192, 207; service levels and customer service 11–12, 103–13, 190–1, 206; tariffs and prices 12–13, 100–3, 189–90, 206
regulatory institutions: England 31–6, 37; Victoria 24–7, 28–9; *see also under individual names*
regulatory style 204
related party transactions 15–16, 130–7, 194–5, 207
relevant market 166, 200
removal of regulators 67–70, 183, 205
reporting duties 186; England 125; Jakarta 126, 127–8, 129–30; Victoria 123–4
re-regulation 36–8
rights, customers' 112–13

Index

risk-based regulation 38, 83, 87–8, 89, 101, 133, 148, 188, 204
Robbins, P.T. 14
Rouse, M. 3
Russell Report 171

Safe Drinking Water Act 2003 (Victoria) 78, 81–2, 105
Salim group 43, 44, 45
sanctions 13, 113–17, 191–2, 206
Sands, V. 4
Scottish Water 148, 163–6, 199–200, 203
sectoral rules: England 31–6, 37; Victoria 24–7, 28–9
Seddon, N. 55
selection of regulators 10–11, 67–70, 182–3, 205
SELL (Sustainable Economic Level of Leakage) 97
service levels 11–12, 103–13, 190–1, 206
sewerage, investment in 95–6
Simatupang, D.P. 49–50
Simpson, R. 7
Smartsource Drainage and Water Reports Ltd v The Information Commissioner 149–50, 167
Soeharto, President 43–4, 45
special powers test 150
special purpose vehicles (SPVs) 143
state-owned enterprises (SOEs): applicability of FOI law to 153–5; Jakarta 40–2; Victoria 19–20, 23–4
State Owned Enterprises Act 1992 (SOE Act) (Victoria) 24
Statements of Obligation (SOOs) 25, 54, 77, 78, 81, 93, 94, 95
stock exchange rules 139–41
Suez 43, 44
suspension of directors 127
Sutton and East Surrey Water plc 149
Swyngedouw, E. 2, 144

tariffs 12–13, 100–3, 189–90, 206
technical targets 98–9, 100
tender processes 58–9
Thames Water 43, 44, 45, 46, 47, 133, 139–40
third parties 187
three-step test 172–3
Thwaites v Met Ambulance Service 171–2
Tortajada, C. 14
TPJ 42, 45, 46, 47, 48, 143; *see also* Aetra

trade secrets 162, 169
transfer pricing 15–16
transparency 1; and economic regulation 5–7; framework for 8–17, 205–7; impact of ownership and regulatory model on 200–4
Transparency International 7–8

UK Upper Tribunal (UKUT) 149–51, 196–7
ultimate ownership 16
UNCTAD guidance on good practices in corporate governance disclosure 15, 16
unfair business competition 169–71
United Kingdom (UK) *see* England
United States (US) 8
United Utilities 141
utilities' corporate governance 13–17, 122–43, 193–5, 207

Victoria 17–21, 22–7, 122, 203; applicability of FOI rules 144–6; commercial information 161–2; corporate restructuring 137–8; corporate structure and the board 123–4; ESC *see* Essential Services Commission; exemption clauses 158–9, 161–2, 171–2, 175; federal regulation 22; FOI law 18, 85–6, 144–6, 158–9, 161–2, 171–2, 175, 195–200; information flow 78–82, 85–6, 186–9; investment 93–5; licence governance 73, 74–5, 75–6, 77, 184–5; National Water Initiative (NWI) 22; non-compliance 113; policy in involving the private sector 20, 53–5, 58, 59, 60–4, 179–82; redress 117–18; regulator's internal governance 67, 70–1, 182–3; regulatory functions 93–5, 100–1, 103–5, 113, 117–18, 189–92; related party transactions 130–1; sectoral rules and regulatory institutions 24–7, 28–9; service levels and customer service 103–5; tariffs and prices 100–1; utilities' corporate governance 123–4, 130–1, 137–8, 193–5; water businesses 23–4
Victoria Government Procurement Board (VGPB) 61, 62, 63, 182

Walker, A. 36
Water Act 1989 (England) 30, 31, 179

Index 233

Water Act 1989 (Victoria) 23, 24
Water Act 2003 (England) 31, 32, 33, 35
Water Act 2014 (England) 32, 37, 38
Water Amendment Act 2012 (Victoria) 54
Water Industry Act 1991 (WIA) (England) 19, 68–9, 82, 86–7, 96–7, 105–6, 189
Water Industry Act 1994 (WIA) (Victoria) 24, 74–5, 78, 79
Water Industry Regulatory Order (WIRO) 26, 54, 104, 188; means of acquiring information 78, 81, 187; regulatory principles 93–4, 94–5, 100
water only companies (WOCs) 30, 31
Water Plans 93–5, 100, 189
Water Resources Act 1991 (WRA) (England) 34
water resources management '6 principles' 56–7
Water Services Regulation Authority *see* Ofwat
water and sewerage companies (WaSCs) 30, 31
water supply licences (WSLs) 73–4, 76, 78
wholesomeness 106
Wonthaggi desalination contract 60–1, 63–4
World Bank 43

Yorkshire Water Services (YWS) 96

Printed in the United States
By Bookmasters